The Discourse Studies Reader

The Discourse Studies Reader

Main currents in theory and analysis

edited by

Johannes Angermuller
University of Warwick /
École des Hautes Études en Sciences Sociales, Paris

Dominique Maingueneau
University of Paris-Sorbonne

Ruth Wodak
Lancaster University

John Benjamins Publishing Company
Amsterdam / Philadelphia

The paper used in this publication meets the minimum requirements of the American National Standard for Information Sciences – Permanence of Paper for Printed Library Materials, ANSI z39.48-1984.

Library of Congress Cataloging-in-Publication Data

The Discourse Studies Reader : Main currents in theory and analysis / Edited by Johannes
         Angermuller, Dominique Maingueneau and Ruth Wodak.
    p. cm.
Includes bibliographical references and index.
1. Discourse analysis. 2. Discourse analysis--Methodology. I. Angermuller, Johannes,
         1973- editor of compilation. II. Maingueneau, Dominique, editor of compilation.
         III. Wodak, Ruth, 1950- editor of compilation.
P302.D565   2014
401'.41--dc23   2014011200
ISBN 978 90 272 1210 8   (Hb ; alk. paper)
ISBN 978 90 272 1211 5   (Pb ; alk. paper)
ISBN 978 90 272 7018 4   (Eb)

John Benjamins Publishing Co. · P.O. Box 36224 · 1020 ME Amsterdam · The Netherlands
John Benjamins North America · P.O. Box 27519 · Philadelphia PA 19118-0519 · USA

Table of contents

VI.　Historical knowledge

VII.　Critical approaches

Preface

We want to thank Walter Allmand, Johannes Beetz, Gerard Hearne, Antonia Mischler, Broder-Cornelius Petersen, who have helped us prepare the manuscript. The Reader would not have been possible without the help of Johannes Beetz to obtain the necessary permissions. We also want to thank Isja Conen and her wonderful colleagues from John Benjamins for their kind help and support.

The Discourse Studies Reader is a product of DiscourseNet (http://www.discourse-analysis.net). Feel free to sign up and receive news in discourse research. The work leading to this publication draws from the DISCONEX project and has received funding from the European Research Council under the European Union's Seventh Framework Programme (*FP7/2007–2013*) / ERC *grant agreement* n° 313172 (DISCONEX).

The Discourse Studies Reader

An introduction

Johannes Angermuller, Dominique Maingueneau, Ruth Wodak

Since the 1960s a new field of research has emerged around the concept of *discourse,* known as Discourse Analysis or – more recently – Discourse Studies. It is not possible to trace the field of Discourse Studies back to one founder, school or field. Discourse studies (abbreviated as DS) is, we believe, the result of the convergence of a number of theoretical and methodological currents originating in various countries (above all in Europe and North America) and in different disciplines of the social sciences and the humanities (linguistics, sociology, philosophy, literary criticism, anthropology, history…). Philosophy, history and the social sciences is said to have seen a 'linguistic turn' since the second half of the 20th century. Likewise, one could speak of a 'discursive turn' which goes hand in hand with cultural, visual and argumentative turns in the social sciences and humanities.

Discourse Studies is an extremely heterogeneous field involving scholars from a range of disciplines. Many contest the idea that it derives from linguistics, even in the larger sense of the term. To this extent, Discourse Studies could be considered as not only a trans-disciplinary or even post-disciplinary project but rather one which runs counter to the division of knowledge into specialized disciplines and sub-disciplines.

In spite of recent developments in electronic modes of communication and the mobility of researchers in our globalized world, the field remains quite heterogeneous for several reasons:

–   *The variety of scientific and intellectual traditions,* which are less and less linked to strictly geographical divisions. In the same country, if not in the same university, one can find researchers working with theoretical and methodological approaches originating from quite different traditions, such as poststructuralist, praxeological, hermeneutic, semiotic approaches and many more.

- *The diversity of disciplinary fields*: Discourse Studies has assumed different forms depending on the field(s) of research to which it pays attention. In the United States, for instance, anthropology, sociolinguistics and sociology, with their focus on oral discursive practices and processes, have played a salient role. In France, by contrast, formal linguistics with a background in Marxism and psychoanalysis has been influential.
- *The diversity of 'schools'* generally associated with the figure of one or several charismatic founders, such as Michel Foucault or Michel Pêcheux, Harvey Sacks or Erving Goffman, Ernesto Laclau or Judith Butler, Norman Fairclough or Teun van Dijk. Some (such as Jürgen Habermas) are public intellectuals known internationally, while others such as Deborah Tannen (1990) and George Lakoff (2004) and Robin Lakoff (1975) have produced best-selling books on discourse-related issues; and some are known for their analytical tools (such as Zellig Harris's distributionalist method) or for a particular large-scale research project.
- *The various types of data, corpora and/or genres* utilised by researchers. Discourse analysts can work with extensive corpora in order to reveal the meaning structures and communication patterns of large discursive communities. Or they may have recourse to small excerpts which they analyse in great detail in order to illustrate some theoretical claims. 'Texts' do not always designate written data; they can comprise written, oral or non-verbal data.
- *Theoretical versus applied research*. While 'discourse' serves as the symbol of a renewed interest in social and cultural theory, poststructuralism in particular lends itself to being a productive source of discourse-theoretical inspiration. At the same time, a great deal of the success of empirically-oriented discourse analytical research deals with the increasing demand for applied research (which is, of course, also theoretically founded).

Discourse Studies as a field

Whether one speaks of 'discourse analysis', 'discourse research' or 'Discourse Studies', the first hurdle one usually encounters is that the discourse that one is supposed to study has no single definition recognized by all researchers. 'Discourse' is used principally in two different ways: (a) in a pragmatic understanding, predominant among linguistic and micro-sociological discourse analysts, which considers discourse as a process or practice of contextualising texts, language in use, the situated production of speech acts or a turn-taking practice (e. g. Gumperz, 1982; Brown and Yule, 1998[1983]); (b) in a socio-historical understanding, preferred by more macrosociological discourse theorists interested in power, for whom 'discourse' refers to an ensemble of verbal and non-verbal practices of large social communities (e.g. Foucault, 1989[1969/1971]; Fairclough, 1992).

The common denominator of the many strands in Discourse Studies is that they consider meaning as a product of social practices. Meaning, in other words, is not to be understood as an inherent property of utterances or texts. Rather, it results from the use that is made of language in specific contexts. In order to have some meaning for somebody, texts need to be contextualized. For discourse analysts, therefore, meaning is a fragile and contested construction of the discourse participants. While discourse may take place between physically present participants of an interaction in an institutional setting, it can also be seen as a product of large communities. Embedded in larger socio-historical configurations and structures, discursive practices can operate with various types of media – oral, written or multimodal – allowing large or small numbers of participants to communicate in face-to-face situations or mediated through written texts (such as newspapers and television) over shorter or longer distances.

As opposed to content analysis or hermeneutic approaches, Discourse Studies does not consider meaning as a given which can be read off the textual surface and reconstructed in spontaneous acts of understanding. Unlike sociolinguists, who usually focus on the language, vernacular and codes used by speakers to signal membership of certain groups, discourse analysts study the way the social order is constructed in discursive practice. They are interested in the practices, rules or mechanisms that can explain how meaning is negotiated between the members of a discourse community.

Discourse Studies, with its many approaches, schools and developments, is now emerging as a new and fully-fledged field in which a number of currents meet – from structuralism to symbolic interactionism, from poststructuralism to problem-oriented strands like Critical Discourse Analysis. Even if Discourse Studies is a field with some autonomy, it nevertheless continues to be heavily indebted to some of the more disciplinary traditions, which provide many productive tools and concepts to assist in meeting both the theoretical and methodological challenges involved in Discourse Studies.

'Discourse' in linguistics

In studying real social and historical objects, Discourse Studies is not so much interested in linguistic phenomena *per se*, such as certain approaches to semantics, syntax, phonology or morphology. Drawing from the pragmatic idea that language is always used in context, linguistic discourse analysts have been critical of 'pure' linguistic theory in the Chomskyan tradition which, with its focus on syntax and grammar, does not analyse or explain phenomena transcending the sentence level. If linguists have turned to discourse to problematize more formalist, grammatical and philological approaches to meaning, 'discourse' is used against the background of various oppositions: *discourse* versus *sentence, discourse* versus *language, discourse* versus *text*.

- If one distinguishes between *discourse* and *sentence*, discourse is considered to be a linguistic unit constituted by a series of sentences. Here, 'discourse' can be synonymous with order on a transphrastic level, such as in Zellig S. Harris (1952), who first introduced the term 'discourse analysis'.

- If one contrasts *discourse* with *language*, discourse typically refers to the uses that can be made of language in a specific context. In this understanding, discourse must not be confounded with language as a system or structure, which is why some linguists, notably those with a discourse pragmatic background, see Saussure (1974[1916]) as antithetical to Discourse Studies.

- One can also oppose *discourse* and *text*, which implies two different understandings of *discourse*: (a) *One discourse corresponds to each text*. From this viewpoint, a text is the product of a discourse, which is perceived as a social activity within a particular context (Adam, 1999; Widdowson, 2007). (b) *Or a group of texts from various genres is associated with one discourse*. Discourse can thus cover a multitude of phenomena: a discipline (psychiatry, astronomy... of whatever epoch); a position in a discursive field ('Communist discourse', 'surrealist discourse'); a type of discourse ('journalistic discourse', 'administrative discourse'); verbal production specific to a category of speakers ('the discourse of nurses', 'the discourse of mothers in a family'); etc.

Most often, then, 'discourse' refers to:

> (...) a cluster of context-dependent practices that are: situated within specific fields of social action; socially constituted and socially constitutive; related to a macro-topic; linked to the argumentation about validity claims such as truth and normative validity, involving several social actors who have different points of view.
>
> (Reisigl and Wodak, 2009: 89)

'Discourse' and the social sciences

Even though linguists have played an important role in making discourse a central concept of the interdisciplinary debate, Discourse Studies is not a sub-discipline of linguistics. Nor is it restricted to linguists who defend the idea of linguistics as a social science. A truly interdisciplinary field at the crossroads of language and society, Discourse Studies also comprises other social scientists and humanists who subscribe to the constructivist view that social and political order is constructed in communication. Discourse Studies have not only been a source of methodological innovation but also crucially inspired the theoretical debate in the social sciences and humanities. A certain gap can sometimes be observed between the more epistemological and political interests of discourse theorists and the methodological focus of discourse analysts, most notably in Europe: on the one hand, discourse theories in the wake of Michel Foucault, Ernesto Laclau or Judith Butler; and on the other, discourse analytical strands in the more empirical, object-oriented sense of large-scale quantitative corpus analysis or more qualitative, micro-sociological studies of situated practices. If the emphasis is sometimes placed more on theory and sometimes more on analysis, Discourse Studies actually only exists as a field where both discourse theory and discourse analysis are integrated in the practice of discourse research.

Discourse studies = discourse theory + discourse analysis

It is an objective of the *Discourse Studies Reader* to close the gap between discourse-theoretical and discourse-analytical strands and to point to the numerous links between the various strands and traditions which have made 'discourse' an object of interdisciplinary interrogation. While discourse theory is sometimes equated with poststructuralism (Torfing, 1999; Howarth, 2000), pragmatics is often considered as the background to more empiricist discourse analyses (e.g. Brown and Yule, 1998[1983]; Gumperz, 1982). Poststructuralist discourse theory, in this sense, covers intellectual and epistemological debates led by Continental European theorists such as Michel Foucault, Jacques Lacan and Louis Althusser, and their North-American commentators such as Judith Butler, Gayatri Spivak (1988) and Edward Said (1978). Better known in Cultural Studies and in the (European) social sciences than in linguistics, discourse theory typically aims to account for the symbolic constitution of society through the circulation of written texts from a more macro-sociological viewpoint; whereas discourse analysis, at least in its pragmatic varieties, has a background in Anglo-American debates on language in use (Leech, 1983; Clark, 1996; Verschueren et al., 1996) and social practices (Mead, 1938; Schatzki, 1996) and analyses oral conversations as situated practices. For some it may appear that the first deals with the great epistemological and political questions of our time while the latter engages in painstaking empirical observations of the minutiae of social life. However, it would be problematic to divide Discourse Studies into discourse theoretical and discourse analytical camps. Discourse theorists have, crucially, relied on discourse analysis and referred to e.g. pragmatics, not only and most notably Habermas (1985[1981]), who makes the case for a communicative turn in Critical Theory, but also Foucault (1989[1969/1971]), whose discourse theory is crucially inspired by enunciative pragmatics. Moreover, some discourse analysts with an ethnomethodological or pragmatic background (McHoul, 1982; Edwards and Potter, 1992; Smith, 2006) have built bridges with poststructuralist discourse theory. It is in this sense that the Reader points out the many productive intersections between various strands within the field of Discourse Studies and makes the plea for an interdisciplinary exchange between discourse theory and discourse analysis.

'Discourse' is one of those polymorphous notions which – despite the efforts of certain individuals to propose a rigorous definition – can mobilise a large number of theoretical options. Theoretically, 'discourse' can be perceived as having amalgamated assumptions borrowed from psychoanalysis, Marxism and poststructuralism, from analytic philosophy, speech act theory and pragmatics, from ethnomethodology and symbolic interactionism. Discourse theory often revolves around the nexus of power, knowledge and subjectivity. Thus, for discourse theorists in the line of Foucauldian governmentality studies, hegemony analysis (Laclau) or psychoanalysis, social relations shape and are shaped by discursive practices. Indeed, society and its actors, social inequality and its agents, symbolic and cultural orders and their subjects are no givens; they are made and unmade in discursive practices. In this sense, discourse does not only represent what people do, think and are in the social world; representing the world can also mean constituting it in a certain way. At the same time, discursive practices testify to the intricate relationship of power and subjectivity. Who is entitled to say what from what position with what effect is discursively regulated: not everybody has the same chance to become visible and exist as a subject, to participate in exchanges with others and thus to shape what counts as reality in a community.

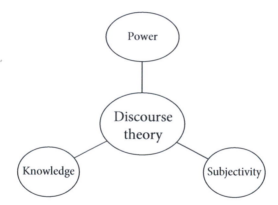

Figure 1. The triangle of discourse theory: power, knowledge, subjectivity

Methodologically, i.e. in terms of discourse *analysis,* the common ground of discourse researchers is that they understand discourse as a complex object that can be studied from various angles. Discourse analysis, therefore, needs to deal with at least three 'components': a language, a practice and a context component. In this view, discourse emerges from the interplay of these three components. In most cases, discourse analytical approaches focus on one point empirically while accounting for the other two theoretically. Enunciative-pragmatic approaches, for example, take their point of departure from utterances (i.e. 'language'), while interactionist approaches may favour turn-taking processes (i.e. 'practices'). Yet in order to be considered as a fully-fledged discourse approach, all three components must be acknowledged and integrated. Many more disciplinary approaches outside Discourse Studies, by contrast, are often characterized by being restricted to only one or two of the aforementioned perspectives/ dimensions: structural linguistics treats language but not practices, and qualitative sociology deals with practices but often neglects language. As opposed to traditional disciplines, which tend to deal with 'pure' objects, Discourse Studies makes the case for cooperative and integrative work going beyond individual disciplines.

The heuristic purpose of the discourse triangle needs to be emphasised: 'Language' designates the semiotic material (formal patterns, conventions, resources) in the broadest sense. It can consist of written and oral texts, but just as easily of audio-visual materials (images, film...), which are needed to construct knowledge about the wider context. 'Practice' refers to specific ways of appropriating and processing language and extends to everything that may take place between the participants in interaction, including the various claims made in the name of expertise and exclusion. 'Context' refers to the setting, situation or knowledge available to the discourse participants contextualizing texts. Such knowledge can be situation-dependent or situation-transcendent, individual or shared by large collectives.

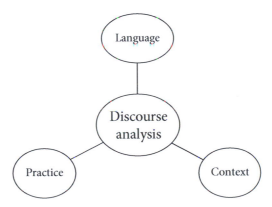

Figure 2. The triangle of discourse analysis: language, practice, context

The development of Discourse Studies

While Discourse Studies has seen ever-increasing institutional success in the last few decades, its antecedents hark back to the origins of modern humanities and social sciences. One can think, for example, of hermeneutic traditions in theology and history, philological and formalist traditions in the literary field as well as pragmatic traditions in philosophy and the early social sciences, especially in psychology and sociology. Building on the insight that meanings are neither divinely given nor an inherent quality of cultural or symbolic artefacts, a large number of specialised research fields have developed in the last 150 years within the disciplines, such as sociolinguistics, semiotics, linguistic anthropology, rhetoric, sociology of language, philosophy of language.... Since the last third of the 20th century, a number of fields have emerged at the crossroads of two or more disciplines, such as Conversation Analysis (between sociology and linguistics), Cultural Studies (between literary criticism and sociology), intellectual history, and so forth. Prolonging trans-disciplinary projects such as Marxism, psychoanalysis, Critical Theory, Discourse Studies brings together the entire range of disciplines in the social sciences and humanities. The fact that, today, Discourse Studies has become established as a field in its own right, in opposition to the usual disciplinary boundaries, can be explained by its preoccupation with an object that was central to the modern social sciences from the very beginning: the social production of meaning through communication and texts of all kinds.

The history of Discourse Studies began in the 1960s, most notably in France, where Discourse Studies has been established as a field under the name *analyse du discours*. Around 1970, Foucault (1989[1969/1971]) and Pêcheux (1982[1975]) proposed discourse theoretical ideas which were to delineate the contours of the new field. While Foucault and Pêcheux raised questions about power and subjectivity, ideology and knowledge, the development of Discourse Studies has also been favoured by some developments in corpus analysis (e.g. Demonet et al., 1975) and text linguistics (Adam, 1999). Joined by colleagues from history (Guilhaumou et al., 1994), sociology, political science and media studies (Charaudeau, 1983), linguists have played a leading role in *analyse du discours*, which has seen a turn to pragmatic models of language in use since the 1970s (Maingueneau, 1999; Angermuller, 2014). Since the 1990s, French Discourse Studies has extended its research agenda beyond the study of political discourse and has also started to integrate qualitative strands from social research.

In the United Kingdom, where Discourse Studies – as in France – nowadays enjoys institutional recognition, a great variety of strands exist. While poststructuralist discourse theories (Laclau and Mouffe, 1985; Hall, 1980; Rose, 1996) dominate in the social sciences, linguistic discourse analysis has followed the line of social semiotics (Halliday, 1978; Kress and van Leeuwen, 1996) or sociolinguistics (Sinclair and Coulthard, 1975; Coulthard, 1977[1977]; Stubbs, 1983). Operating with both oral and with written texts (Brown and Yule, 1998[1983]; Hoey, 2001; Hyland, 2005), Discourse Studies comprise approaches as different as speech act theory (Widdowson, 2007) or corpus analysis (Sinclair, 2004; Baker, 2005). As in France, numerous discourse researchers share a critical interest in power and inequality, particularly as represented by *Critical Discourse Analysis* (CDA) (Fairclough, 1992), which has seen similar developments in Continental Europe (Jäger, 2007[1993]; Wodak and Meyer, 2004; van Dijk, 1985, 2009; Wodak 1989).

In the United States, Discourse Studies is probably less established than in Europe, even though 'discourse' has become an issue since the 1960s, particularly in the ethnography of communication (Gumperz and Hymes, 1986[1972]; Duranti and Goodwin, 1992), sociolinguistics (Labov and Fanshel, 1977; Johnstone, 2008), corpus analysis (Biber et al., 1998) and applied linguistics (Kramsch, 1998). Until recently, *discourse* was still sometimes understood as being synonymous with conversation, i.e. as regulated and situated turn-taking processes, even though the argument between conversation analysts (Schegloff, 1997) and critical discourse analysts (Billig, 1999) has contributed to the perception that 'discourse' refers more to written texts than to conversations. Cognitive strands of discourse linguistics have insisted on the nexus of language and socially shared knowledge (Lakoff and Johnson, 1980).

Although German-language Discourse Studies can be viewed as a relative latecomer vis-à-vis the French and Anglo-American traditions, it testifies to a particularly richness of discourse strands from the entire disciplinary spectrum, especially since the canonization of Foucault in the social sciences and humanities around the year 2000 (Angermüller,[1] 2011; see also the two-volume *Discourse Studies. An interdisciplinary Manual* Angermuller et al. 2014; and the *DiscourseNet Dictionary Interdisciplinary Discourse Studies* Wrana et al. 2014). In the 19th century, the German debate in the social sciences and humanities privileged organic and holistic approaches to Meaning, which have been extended in certain ways by Habermas's deliberative, consensus-based model of discourse (1985) and social phenomenologists such as Berger and Luckmann (1966) and Keller (2005), who place emphasis on the intersubjectively shared character of social knowledge. The numerous poststructuralist developments, by contrast, typically insist on the antagonistic cleavages within discourse (Nonhoff 2006) and critically interrogate humanist theories of the subject (Bröckling et al., 2000; Bublitz et al. 1999; Link 1982). In linguistics, Discourse Studies builds upon pioneering research in text linguistics (Beaugrande and Dressler, 1981) which has explored questions of cohesion and coherence, as well as functional pragmatics (Ehlich and Rehbein, 1986), which has investigated communicative patterns in interaction. Historical semantics (Busse, 1987) has studied the intricate link between knowledge and language in their socio-historical contexts. Until the 1990s the competition between descriptive-analytical approaches (as exemplified by conversation analysis) and normative-critical orientations (such as those of CDA) stood in the way of creating one interdisciplinary field of Discourse Studies.

If Discourse Studies can be considered an international and interdisciplinary field of research today, it has been established through several stages: around 1970, local or national schools developed in France and the USA. After the mid-1970s discourse

---

1.   In 2012, the *umlaut* in the name was eliminated. His publications are today signed by Angermuller.

analysis emerged in the UK, while in Germany Habermas's deliberative discourse theory appeared on the scene. In the 1980s a process of transnational reception of such orientations took shape. While discourse-analytical instruments from qualitative social research in the USA found a widespread audience, discourse theories from Europe have enjoyed huge international recognition, especially Foucault's works on the nexus of knowledge and power. After some intellectual and theoretical figureheads made the traditions of other countries better known, an increasing intellectual hybridization began in the 1990s – e.g. in the project of CDA. At least in Europe a transdisciplinary field has emerged from various sub-disciplinary and national orientations, the most important of which this *Discourse Studies Reader* attempts to represent.

About this Reader

With its 40 selections from key discourse researchers, the *Discourse Studies Reader* aims to represent the main currents in both discourse theory and discourse analysis and to bridge the gap between approaches from North America and Europe. It does not seek to address a particular audience (linguists, sociologists, historians, specialists in education, the mass media etc.), but rather all those who, for the sake of their research or education, are in need of orientation within the immense field of Discourse Studies. Thus, we have divided this book according to the major theoretical orientations and methodological approaches that have developed since the 1960s in various countries of the West. While we, the editors, are based in Europe (albeit in different countries, cities and regions), we do not want to disregard dynamic developments elsewhere, especially in Latin America over the past few decades and more recently in Asia and Africa, which will certainly increase in the course of time. We would have liked to include more contributions to Discourse Studies from these regions as well as from other domains, such as rhetorics, narratology, mass-media communication, multimodality, corpus analysis, argumentation analysis etc., to name but a few. Unfortunately, we had to restrict our choice since we could not get permission for all the contributions which we see as representative of the many strands in Discourse Studies today. For this reason, we have aimed to focus on theoretical and methodological questions rather than to demonstrate the huge variety of objects and problems which Discourse Studies has been and is dealing with. This choice has an advantage: the theoretical presuppositions and claims, as well as methods, are relatively few in number and have remained quite stable over time, whereas the objects of study are extremely diverse and changing constantly.

This Reader is divided into seven sections, each of which corresponds to various viewpoints on discourse research.

The first section ('Theoretical Inspirations: Structuralism versus Pragmatics') brings together texts from authors who are not, strictly speaking, discourse theorists or discourse analysts. As theoretical precursors, however, they have strongly contributed to the development of the field of Discourse Studies. Two of them are linguists (Saussure, Harris); one (Bakhtin) is best known as a literary critic; three are philosophers (Wittgenstein, Austin, Grice); and one (Mead) is a sociologist and psychologist.

The second section ('From Structuralism to Poststructuralism') includes various major authors who are considered to be poststructuralists in the international intellectual debate. They can be divided into two groups: four French thinkers of the 1960/70s, including a psychoanalyst (Lacan) and a Marxist philosopher (Althusser) as well as two theorists of language (Pêcheux, Foucault) whose selected texts appear for the first time in English. Their discourse theoretical contributions have been taken up and developed by poststructuralist discourse theorists in the English-speaking world (Laclau and Butler).

The third section ('Enunciative Pragmatics') presents a major trend in discourse pragmatics. Elaborated mainly by linguists in the French-speaking world, it deals with discourse analytical problems such as deixis (Benveniste, Maingueneau), reported speech (Authier-Revuz) and polyphony/subjectivity (Ducrot, Angermuller).

The fourth section ('Interactionism') is dedicated to interactional discourse analysts, from the Anglo-American world, who come from sociology (Sacks, Goffman, Cicourel), anthropology (Gumperz), education (Gee) and psychology (Potter).

The fifth section is dedicated to an approach that we characterise as 'Sociopragmatics'. Based in linguistics, the authors presented here (Halliday, van Leeuwen, Ehlich, Charaudeau, Swales, Amossy) focus on the constraints imposed by the context of communication. Their work covers a wide variety of orientations; Amossy, for example, positions herself in the field of rhetoric, whereas Halliday is strongly influenced by sociolinguistics.

Discourse Studies does not ignore the fact that meanings are produced under certain historical conditions of production. The section on 'Historical Knowledge' – not surprisingly – is strongly linked to traditions in Germany (Busse/Teubert, Luckmann, Koselleck) and France (Robin).

The book ends with a section entitled 'Critical Approaches', which brings together texts by researchers who refuse to separate discourse analysis from ethical or societal preoccupations. These researchers share an interest in the discursive dimensions of power and injustice, as well as in social and cultural change. The section includes the more theoretical explorations of Habermas and the critical ethnographic explorations of Blommaert/Verschueren, as well as those who, like Fairclough, van Dijk, and Wodak, can be counted as leading proponents of Critical Discourse Analysis (CDA).

References

Adam, Jean-Michel. 1999. *Linguistique textuelle: des genres de discours aux textes*. Paris: Nathan.

Angermuller, Johannes. 2014. *Poststructuralist Discourse Analysis. Subjectivity in Enunciative Pragmatics*. Basingstoke: Palgrave.

Angermüller, Johannes. 2011. 'Heterogeneous Knowledge. Trends in German Discourse Analysis Against an International Background.' *Journal of Multicultural Discourses* 6, no. 2: 121–36. DOI: 10.1080/17447143.2011.582117

Angermuller, Johannes, Martin Nonhoff, Eva Herschinger, Felicitas Macgilchrist, Martin Reisigl, Juliette Wedl, Alexander Ziem (Eds.). 2014. *Diskursforschung. Ein interdisziplinäres Handbuch. 2 vols*. Volume 1: Theorien, Methodologien und Kontroversen. Volume 2: Methoden und Analysepraxis. Bielefeld: transcript.

Baker, Paul. 2005. *Using Corpora in Discourse Analysis*. New York: Continuum.

Beaugrande, Robert-Alain de, and Wolfgang Ulrich Dressler. 1981. *Einführung in die Textlinguistik*. Tübingen: Niemeyer. DOI: 10.1515/9783111349305

Berger, Peter L., and Thomas Luckmann. 1966. *The Social Construction of Reality: A Treatise in the Sociology of Knowledge*. Garden City, New York: Anchor Books.

Biber, Douglas, Susan Conrad, and Randi Reppen. 1998. *Corpus Linguistics. Investigating Language Structure and Use*. Cambridge, New York: Cambridge University Press. DOI: 10.1017/CBO9780511804489

Billig, Michael. 1999. 'Whose terms? Whose ordinariness? Rhetoric and Ideology in Conversation Analysis.' *Discourse and Society* 10, no. 4: 543–58. DOI: 10.1177/0957926599010004005

Bröckling, Ulrich, Susanne Krasmann, Thomas Lemke (Eds.). 2000. *Gouvernementalität der Gegenwart*. Frankfurt am Main: Suhrkamp.

Brown, Gillian, and George Yule. 1998[1983]. *Discourse analysis*. Cambridge: Cambridge University Press.

Bublitz, Hannelore, Andrea B. Bührmann, Christine Hanke, Andrea Seier (Eds.). 1999. *Das Wuchern der Diskurse. Perspektiven der Diskursanalyse Foucaults*. Frankfurt, New York: Campus.

Busse, Dietrich. 1987. *Historische Semantik. Analyse eines Programms*. Stuttgart: Klett-Cotta.

Charaudeau, Patrick. 1983. *Langage et discours. Eléments de sémiolinguistique*. Paris: Hachette.

Clark, Herbert H. 1996. *Using Language*. Cambridge: Cambridge University Press. DOI: 10.1017/CBO9780511620539

Coulthard, Malcolm. 1977[1977]. *An Introduction to Discourse Analysis. New Edition*. London, New York: Longman.

Demonet, Michel, Annie Geffroy, Jean Gouazé, Pierre Lafon, Maurice Mouillaud, and Maurice Tournier. 1975. *Des tracts en mai 68. Mesures de vocabulaire et de contenu*. Paris: Armand Colin.

Duranti, Alessandro, and Charles Goodwin, eds. 1992. *Rethinking context. Language as an interactive phenomenon*. Cambridge: Cambridge University Press.

Edwards, Derek, and Jonathan Potter. 1992. *Discursive Psychology*. London: Sage.

Ehlich, Konrad, and Jochen Rehbein. 1986. *Muster und Institution: Untersuchungen zur schulischen Kommunikation*. Tübingen: G. Narr.

Fairclough, Norman. 1992. *Discourse and Social Change*. Cambridge, Oxford: Polity Press.

Foucault, Michel. 1989[1969/1971]. *The Archaeology of Knowledge & The Discourse on Language*. London: Routledge.

Guilhaumou, Jacques, Denise Maldidier, and Régine Robin. 1994. *Discours et archive. Expérimentations en analyse du discours*. Liège: Mardaga.

Gumperz, John. 1982. *Discourse Strategies*. Cambridge: Cambridge University Press.
DOI: 10.1017/CBO9780511611834

Gumperz, John, and Dell Hymes, eds. 1986[1972]. *Directions in Sociolinguistics. The Ethnography of Communication*. Oxford: Blackwell.

Habermas, Jürgen. 1985[1981]. *The Theory of Communicative Action*. Boston: Beacon Press.

Hall, Stuart. 1980. 'Encoding/Decoding.' In *Culture, Media, Language: Working Papers in Cultural Studies, 1972–79*, edited by Centre for Contemporary Cultural Studies, 128–38. London: Hutchinson.

Halliday, M. A. K. 1978. *Language As Social Semiotic*. London: Edward Arnold.

Harris, Zellig S. 1952. 'Discourse Analysis.' *Language* 28: 1–30. DOI: 10.2307/409987

Hoey, Michael. 2001. *Textual Interaction. An Introduction to Written Discourse Analysis*. London: Routledge.

Howarth, David. 2000. *Discourse*. Buckinghamshire: Open University Press.

Hyland, Ken. 2005. *Metadiscourse. Exploring Interaction in Writing*. London, New York: Continuum.

Jäger, Siegfried. 2007[1993]. *Kritische Diskursanalyse. Eine Einführung*. Münster: Unrast.

Johnstone, Barbara. 2008. *Discourse analysis*. Malden, MA: Blackwell Pub.

Keller, Reiner. 2005. *Wissenssoziologische Diskursanalyse. Grundlegung eines Forschungsprogramms*. Wiesbaden: VS.

Kramsch, Claire. 1998. *Language and culture*. Oxford: Oxford University Press.

Kress, Gunther, and Theo van Leeuwen. 1996. *Reading Images. The Grammar of Visual Design*. London: Routledge.

Labov, William, and David Fanshel. 1977. *Therapeutic discourse. Psychotherapy as conversation*. New York, London: Academic Press.

Laclau, Ernesto, and Chantal Mouffe. 1985. *Hegemony and Socialist Strategy. Towards a Radical Democratic Politics*. London, New York: Verso.

Lakoff, George. 2004. *Don't Think of an Elephant: Know Your Values and Frame the Debate*. New York: Chelsea Green Publishing.

Lakoff, George, and Mark Johnson. 1980. *Metaphors We Live By*. Chicago: University of Chicago Press.

Lakoff, Robin. 1975. *Language and Woman's Place. Text and Commentaries Studies in Language and Gender*. Oxford: Oxford University Press.

Leech, Geoffrey. 1983. *Principles of Pragmatics*. London: Longman.

Link, Jürgen. 1982. Kollektivsymbole und Mediendiskurse. *KultuRRevolution* 1: 6–21.

Maingueneau, Dominique. 1999. 'Analysing self-constituting discourses.' *Discourse Studies* 1, no. 2: 175–99. DOI: 10.1177/1461445699001002003

McHoul, A. W. 1982. *Telling How Texts Talk. Essays on Reading and Ethnomethodology*. London: Routledge.

Mead, George Herbert. 1938. *The Philosophy of the Act*. Chicago, London: The University of Chicago Press.

Nonhoff, Martin. 2006. *Politischer Diskurs und Hegemonie. Das Projekt ‚Soziale Marktwirtschaft'*. Bielefeld: transcript.

Pêcheux, Michel. 1982[1975]. *Language, Semantics and Ideology. Stating the Obvious*. London: Macmillan.

Reisigl, Martin, and Ruth Wodak. 2009. 'The discourse-historical approach (DHA).' In *Methods of Critical Discourse Analysis*, edited by Ruth Wodak and Michael Meyer, 87–121. London: Sage.

Rose, Nikolas. 1996. *Inventing our Selves. Psychology, Power, and Personhood*. Cambridge: Cambridge University Press. DOI: 10.1017/CBO9780511752179

Said, Edward W. 1978. *Orientalism*. London: Penguin.

Saussure, Ferdinand de. 1974[1916]. *Course in General Linguistics*. London: Fontana.

Schatzki, Theodore. 1996. *Social Practices. A Wittgensteinian Approach to Human Activity and the Social*. Cambridge: Cambridge UP. DOI: 10.1017/CBO9780511527470

Schegloff, Emanuel. 1997. 'Whose Text? Whose Context?'. *Discourse & Society* 8, no. 2: 165–87. DOI: 10.1177/0957926597008002002

Sinclair, John. 2004. *Trust the Text. Language, Corpus and Discourse*. London: Routledge.

Sinclair, John McHardy, and Malcolm Coulthard, eds. 1975. *The English Used by Teachers and Pupils*. Oxford: Oxford University Press.

Smith, Dorothy E. 2006. 'Incorporating Texts into Ethnographic Practice.' In *Institutional Ethnography as Practice*, edited by Dorothy E. Smith, 65–88. Lanham, et al.: Rowman & Littlefield.

Spivak, Gayatri Chakravorty. 1988. 'Can the Subaltern Speak?'. In *Marxism and the Interpretation of Culture*, edited by Cary Nelson and Lawrence Grossberg, 271–313. Urbana: University of Illinois Press.

Stubbs, Michael, ed. 1983. *Discourse Analysis: The Sociolinguistic Analysis of Natural Language*. Chicago: Chicago University Press.

Tannen, Deborah. 1990. *You Just Don't Understand. Women and Men in Conversation*. New York: Morrow.

Torfing, Jacob. 1999. *New Theories of Discourse: Laclau, Mouffe and Žižek*. Oxford: Blackwell.

van Dijk, Teun A. 1985. *Prejudice in Discourse*. Amsterdam: Benjamins.

van Dijk, Teun A. 2009. *Society and Discourse. How Social Contexts Influence Text and Talk*. Cambridge: Cambridge University Press. DOI: 10.1017/CBO9780511575273

Verschueren, Jef, Jan-Ola Östman, Jan Blommaert, and Chris Bulcaen, eds. 1996. *Handbook of Pragmatics*. Amsterdam, Philadelphia: John Benjamins Publishing Company.

Widdowson, H. G. 2007. *Discourse Analysis*. Oxford: Oxford University Press.

Wodak, Ruth, ed. 1989. *Language, Power, and Ideology*. Amsterdam: Benjamins.

Wodak, Ruth, and Michael Meyer, eds. 2004. *Methods of Critical Discourse Analysis*. London: Sage.

Wrana, Daniel, Alexander Ziem, Martin Reisigl, Martin Nonhoff, & Johannes Angermuller (Eds.). 2014. *DiskursNetz. Wörterbuch der interdisziplinären Diskursforschung*. Frankfurt am Main: Suhrkamp.

Section I

Theoretical inspirations

Structuralism versus pragmatics

Introduction

Two strands of linguistic theory have turned out to be major inspirations for studying the social production of meaning: a structuralist one, pioneered by the linguist Ferdinand de Saussure (1857–1913, see 1974[1916]), and a pragmatic one, which has received important impulses from the philosophy of the later Ludwig Wittgenstein (1889–1951, see 1997[1953]). Prolonging the grammatical and stylistic traditions in Continental philology, structuralism typically aims at explaining the diversity of meaningful phenomena by a set of grammatical rules. Pragmatics, by contrast, perceives meaning as the product of a linguistic activity in a specific context.

Saussurean structuralism became a major influence in Eastern Europe in the interwar period and in Western Europe after the Second World War. Following the Bolshevik revolution, Russian formalism provided a productive context for the narrative theory of Vladimir Propp (1895–1970) and the circle around Mikhail Bakhtin (1895–1975), whose theory of polyphonic discourse already prefigures a rapprochement with pragmatic ideas of language in use. In linguistics, the Prague School (Nikolai Trubetzkoy, 1890–1938) applied Saussurean insights in phonology and Roman Jakobson (1896–1982) brought structuralism to the Anglo-American world. These theorists typically emphasise the primacy of linguistic form over content. Linguistic and semiotic forms do not express any intrinsic meaning. Rather, their meaning derives from their distinctive value in a system of distinctive elements: no meaning without difference! Saussure's model encouraged a number of tendencies to go beyond the level of the individual sentence and toward a general semiology of social and cultural life. Thus, in line with the holistic 'culturological' tradition in Russia, the Tartu school of semiotics (Uspenskij, 1878–1947; Lotman, 1922–1993) applied Saussure's structural model to cultures as larger semiotic systems.

After the war, Saussure started to have an impact in other parts of the world. Nowhere was the influence of structural linguistics greater than in France. Against the background of Marxist and psychoanalytical theories, it gave rise to the conjuncture of structuralist and poststructuralist theories around 1970 (Angermuller 2014). Against the background of structuralism in decline, discourse analysis consolidated as a field of linguistic research in France. Its name came from a North American linguist, Zellig Harris (1909–1992), who outlined the project of a 'meaning-free' approach to discourse, understood as the regular syntactic distribution of linguistic forms within a text (1952). While Harris's approach informed some of the early more quantifying discourse analyses in France (e.g. Pêcheux 1995), it essentially constituted an early version of text linguistics with little interest in the contexts of discursive activity. In the course of the 1960s, Saussure's structural theory became a general model for the social and human sciences in France elaborated by social scientists like Claude Lévi-Strauss, Roland Barthes, Jean Baudrillard and Pierre Bourdieu. While few linguists still refer to Saussure today, his heritage is still alive in some parts of the social sciences (e.g. in Laclau/Mouffe's theory of hegemony as well as among certain Foucaldian discourse analyses).

There is good reason to consider pragmatic theories of language not only as an alternative to but even as an outright refutation of structuralist orientations. Typically, structuralists have recourse to underlying codes or mechanisms to explain the production of meaning, whereas pragmaticians point out the creative and specific uses that are made of language. Structuralists analyse meaning as an inherent property of the semiotic material, whereas pragmaticians pay attention to the context in which language is used. Structuralism goes beyond the subject's point of view, whereas pragmatics has co-launched the discovery of the actor in the social sciences. Structuralists see order in contingence, whereas pragmaticians see contingence in order.

Pragmatics broadly understood draws on two strands of theorising symbolic action: one from North America, commonly known as pragmatism, the other from Great Britain, where discourse pragmatic theories of language have developed alongside analytical philosophy. North American pragmatism comprises theorists, who have worked on a range of questions – from epistemology (William James, 1842–1910) to public discourse (John Dewey, 1859–1952). Against this background, George Herbert Mead (1863–1931) was the originator of a theory of social action with a decisive impact on interactional micro-sociologists. For Mead, identity emerges in the communicative exchange among actors. Even though we have not included pragmatist theorists in our selections, their intellectual heritage informs the interactional strands of discourse analysis (see the section on 'Interactionism').

In the UK, pragmatics is tied to the emergence of analytical philosophy, both of them going back to Wittgenstein's (1889–1951) seminal work on language. Analytic philosophers, who follow the Viennese circle of logical positivism and the early Wittgenstein's *Tractatus logico-philosophicus* (1961[1921]), ask what utterances can be considered as 'true'. By constructing an ideal language, based on logical structures, their objective is to dissolve philosophical misunderstandings by avoiding the traps of natural language. In the wake of Wittgenstein's later philosophy (1953), however, philosophers turned to the analysis of ordinary language and its language games. No longer asking how language should work but accounting for how it does what it does in a specific context, Wittgenstein delineated the contours of a new theory of language: discourse pragmatics. Discourse pragmatics reflects the performative dimension of language use. Language does not just passively reflect a given state of the world; it involves a situated activity – a 'language game' – which creates and constitutes the object it attempts to describe.

For pragmaticians following Wittgenstein's later philosophy, saying always means doing something. This idea has been developed by the originators of speech-act theory Austin (1962[1955]) and Searle (1992[1969]), who refute the idea that language is a neutral means of representation. When we speak, we always do something with language, such as promising and baptising. And even describing needs to be seen as an activity which constitutes the object it describes. The theory of conversational maxims (Grice 1975), by contrast, asks how those who engage in the communicative exchange infer the implied intentions from each other's utterances. In Grice's perspective, meaning is not produced by reeling off a set of grammatical rules; it mobilises the cognitive resources of those who participate in communication in order to understand the other.

While few of these theoretical strands explicitly deal with 'discourse', they have inspired a number of fields at the crossroads of language and society. North American pragmatism has crucially influenced interactional fields of study such as qualitative micro-sociology, conversation analysis, qualitative sociolinguistics, linguistic anthropology, social psychology and so forth (see the section on 'Interactionism') whereas discourse pragmatics has contributed to the linguistic study of the formal repertoires and markers of 'language in use' (see e.g. deixis, presupposition, polyphony in the section on 'Enunciative Pragmatics', and communicative order, argumentation, stance-taking in the section on 'Sociopragmatics').

Both pragmatic and structural theories of language have spawned a wealth of intellectual developments in the social sciences and humanities. If they are sometimes seen as mutual alternatives, their rather different backgrounds need to be taken note of. Unlike structuralists, whose disciplinary base is in linguistics, the pioneers of pragmatics were based in the UK and the U.S. and initially came from philosophy and sociology. For some observers, they are more concerned with problem-solving on a more local, 'hands-on' level and the achievement of consistency and clarity whereas structuralism, especially in its passage towards poststructuralism, seemed to show affinity for Continental 'grand theory' such as Marxism and psychoanalysis. Today, these intellectual traditions have blended to a degree that these characterisations appear stereotypical and obsolete, especially in a field like discourse analysis which has resulted from the productive encounter of both strands.

A telling case in point is the path the French field of discourse research has taken, where the structural preferences of early developments in discourse research (Foucault 2002[1966]; Pêcheux 1995[1969]) gradually gave way to a critique of structuralism in the light of enunciative and pragmatic models of discourse (Foucault 1972[1969]). Both Saussurean and Wittgensteinian perspectives inform the poststructuralist critique of essentialism (see Butler/Laclau/Žižek 2000). And both Critical Theory (Habermas 1985[1981]) and the many developments in Critical Discourse Analysis rely on structuralist theories of power and pragmatic theories of communication.

This section comprises key passages from some prominent founding fathers of structuralist linguistics, beginning with Saussure, and pragmatic philosophy, starting with Wittgenstein.

References

Angermuller, Johannes. 2014. *The Field of Theory*. London, New York: Continuum.

Austin, John L. 1962[1955]. *How to Do Things with Words. The William James Lectures Delivered at Harvard University in 1955*. Oxford, New York: Oxford University Press.

Butler, Judith, Ernesto Laclau, and Slavoj Žižek. 2000. *Contingency, Hegemony, Universality*. Paris: Verso.

Foucault, Michel. 2002[1966]. *The Order of Things. An Archaeology of the Human Sciences*. London: Routledge.

Foucault, Michel. 1972[1969]. *The Archaeology of Knowledge & The Discourse on Language*. New York: Pantheon.

Grice, H. Paul. 1975. 'Logic and Conversation.' In *Syntax and Semantics. Vol. 3: Speech Act*, edited by Peter Cole and Jerry L. Morgan, 41–58. New York: Academic Press.

Habermas, Jürgen. 1985[1981]. *The Theory of Communicative Action*. Boston: Beacon Press.

Harris, Zellig S. 1952. 'Discourse Analysis.' *Language* 28: 1–30. DOI: 10.2307/409987

Pêcheux, Michel. 1995[1969]. *Automatic Discourse Analysis*. Amsterdam, Atlanta, GA: Rodopi.

Searle, John. 1992[1969]. *Speech Acts. An Essay in the Philosophy of Language*. Cambridge: Cambridge University Press.

Saussure, Ferdinand de. 1974[1916]. *Course in General Linguistics*. London: Fontana.

Wittgenstein, Ludwig. 1997. *Philosophische Untersuchungen / Philosophical Investigations*. Second Edition. Oxford: Blackwell. 1953.

Wittgenstein, Ludwig. 1961[1921]. *Tractatus Logico-Philosophicus*. London: Routledge.

Ferdinand de Saussure

The value of the sign

Saussure (1857–1913) sees language as a grammatical system which allows the speakers to select and combine the smallest distinctive linguistic units and thus to produce an infinite number of correct sentences. Subject to a language system (*langue*), they can realise an infinite number of grammatically correct sentences in speech (*parole*). In this passage, taken from his seminal *Course of General Linguistics* (1916), and compiled from lecture notes from 1906 to 1911 by his followers after his death, Saussure explains the notion of value. For Saussure, every sign has a meaning, to the extent that it has a value in a semiotic system. Meaning, therefore, is perceived as the product of grammatical rules producing sentences. When a speaker produces a sentence, s/he turns the language system (*langue*) into speech (*parole*) and some of the smallest distinctive units are selected from the paradigmatic axis and combined on the syntagmatic axis. Saussure supported the idea that language is an arbitrary system and that linguistic signs are not directly linked with the world. This model has been taken as a model for approaches to discourse which aim at revealing the underlying rules and grammars of social and cultural phenomena.

Ferdinand de Saussure. 1959[1906–1911]. *Course in General Linguistics*,
trans. by Wade Baskin, selected 114–117, 120–122.
New York: Philosophical Library.

Linguistic value from a conceptual viewpoint

When we speak of the value of a word, we generally think first of its property of standing for an idea, and this is in fact one side of linguistic value. But if this is true, how does *value* differ from *signification*? Might the two words be synonyms? I think not, although it is easy to confuse them, since the confusion results not so much from their similarity as from the subtlety of the distinction that they mark.

From a conceptual viewpoint, value is doubtless one element in signification, and it is difficult to see how signification can be dependent upon value and still be distinct from it. But we must clarify the issue or risk reducing language to a simple naming- process (…).

Let us first take signification as it is generally understood (…). As the arrows in the drawing show, it is only the counterpart of the sound-image. Everything that occurs concerns only the sound-image and the concept when we look upon the word as independent and self-contained.

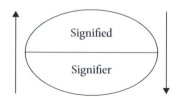

Figure 1

But here is the paradox: on the one hand the concept seems to be the counterpart of the sound-image, and on the other hand the sign itself is in turn the counterpart of other signs of language. Language is a system of interdependent terms in which the value of each term results solely from the simultaneous presence of the others, as in the diagram:

Figure 2

How, then can value be confused with signification, i.e. the counterpart of the sound-image? It seems impossible to liken the relations represented here by horizontal arrows to those represented above by vertical arrows. Putting it another way – and again taking up the example of the sheet of paper that is cut in two – it is clear that the observable relation between the different pieces A, B, C, D, etc. is distinct from the relation between the front and back of the same piece as in A/A′, B/B′, etc.

To resolve the issue, let us observe from the outset that even outside language all values are apparently governed by the same paradoxical principle. They are always composed:

1. of a *dissimilar* thing that can be *exchanged* for the thing of which the value is to be determined.
2. of a *similar* thing that can be *compared* with the thing of which the value is to be determined.

Both factors are necessary for the existence of a value. To determine what a five franc piece is worth one must therefore know: (1) that it can be exchanged for a fixed quantity of a different thing, e.g. bread; and (2) that it can be compared with a similar value of the same system, e.g. a one-franc piece, or with coins of another system (a dollar, etc.). In the same way a word can be exchanged for something dissimilar, an idea; besides, it can be compared with something of the same nature, another word. Its value is therefore not fixed so long as one simply states that it can be 'exchanged' for a given concept, i.e. that it has this or that signification: one must also compare it with similar values, with other words that stand in opposition to it. Its content is really fixed only by the concurrence of everything that exists outside it. Being part of a system, it is endowed not only with a signification but also and especially with a value, and this is something quite different.

A few examples will show clearly that this is true. Modern French *mouton* can have the same signification as English *sheep* but not the same value, and this for several reasons, particularly because in speaking of a piece of meat ready to be served on the table, English uses *mutton* and not *sheep*. The difference in value between *sheep* and *mouton* is due to the fact that *sheep* has beside it a second term while the French word does not.

Within the same language, all words used to express related ideas limit each other reciprocally: synonyms like French *redouter* 'dread', *craindre* 'fear', and *avoir peur* 'be afraid' have value only through their opposition: if *redouter* did not exist, all its content would go to its competitors. Conversely, some words are enriched through contact

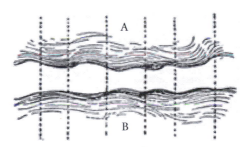

Figure 3

with others: e.g. the new element introduced in *décrépit* (*un vieillard décrépit*) results from the coexistence of *décrépi* (*un mur décrépi*). The value of just any term is accordingly determined by its environment; it is impossible to fix even the value of the word signifying 'sun' without first considering its surroundings: in some languages it is not possible to say 'sit in the sun.'

Everything said about words applies to any term of language, e.g. to grammatical entities. The value of a French plural does not coincide with that of a Sanskrit plural even though their signification is usually identical; Sanskrit has three numbers instead of two (*my eyes, my ears, my arms, my legs,* etc. are dual); it would be wrong to attribute the same value to the plural in Sanskrit and in French; its value clearly depends on what is outside and around it.

If words stood for pre-existing concepts, they would all have exact equivalents in meaning from one language to the next; but this is not true. French uses *louer* (*une maison*) 'let (a house)' indifferently to mean both 'pay for' and 'receive payment for', whereas German uses two words, *mieten* and *vermieten*; there is obviously no exact correspondence of value. The German verbs *schätzen* and *urteilen* share a number of significations, but that correspondence does not hold at several points.

Inflection offers some particularly striking examples. Distinctions of time, which are so familiar to us, are unknown in certain languages. Hebrew does not recognize even the fundamental distinctions between the past, present, and future. Proto-Germanic has no special form for the future; to say that the future is expressed by the present is wrong, for the value of the present is not the same in Germanic as in languages that have a future along with the present. The Slavic languages regularly single out two aspects of the verb: the perfective represents action as a point, complete in its totality: the imperfective represents it as taking place, and on the line of time. The categories are difficult for a Frenchman to understand, for they are unknown in French; if they were predetermined, this would not be true. Instead of pre-existing ideas then, we find in all the foregoing examples *values* emanating from the system. When they are said to correspond to concepts, it is understood that the concepts are purely differential and defined not by their positive content but negatively by their relations with the other terms of the system. Their most precise characteristic is in being what the others are not.

Now the real interpretation of the diagram of the signal becomes apparent. This

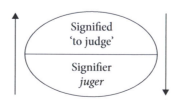

Figure 4

means that in French the concept 'to judge' is linked to the sound-image *juger*; in short, it symbolizes signification. But it is quite clear that initially the concept is nothing, that it is only a value determined by its relations with other similar values, and that without them the signification would not exist. If I state simply that a word signifies something when I have in mind the associating of a sound-image with a concept, I am making a statement that may suggest what actually happens, but by no means am I expressing the linguistic fact in its essence and fullness. (…)

The sign considered in its totality

Everything that has been said up to this point boils down to this: in language there are only differences. Even more important: a difference generally implies positive terms between which the difference is set up; but in language there are only differences *without positive terms*. Whether we take the signified or the signifier, language has neither ideas nor sounds that existed before the linguistic system, but only conceptual and phonic differences that have issued from the system. The idea or phonic substance that a sign contains is of less importance than the other signs that surround it. Proof of this is that the value of a term may be modified without either its meaning or its sound being affected, solely because a neighboring term has been modified (see Figure 2).

But the statement that everything in language is negative is true only if the signified and the signifier are considered separately; when we consider the sign in its totality, we have something that is positive in its own class. A linguistic system is a series of differences of ideas; but the pairing of a certain number of acoustical signs with as many cuts made from the mass of thought engenders a system of values; and this system serves as the effective link between the phonic and psychological elements within each sign. Although both the signified and the signifier are purely differential and negative when considered separately, their combination is a positive fact; it is even the sole type of facts that language has, for maintaining the parallelism between the two classes of differences is the distinctive function of the linguistic institution.

Certain diachronic facts are typical in this respect. Take the countless instances where alternation of the signifier occasions a conceptual change and where it is obvious that the sum of the ideas distinguished corresponds in principle to the sum of the distinctive signs. When two words are confused through phonetic alternation (e.g. French *décrépit* from *dēcrepitus* and *décrépi* from *crispus*), the ideas that they express will also tend to become confused if only they have something in common. Or a word may have different forms (cf. *chaise* 'chair' and *chaire* 'desk'). Any nascent difference will tend invariably to become significant but without always succeeding or being successful on the first trial. Conversely, any conceptual difference perceived by the mind seeks to find expression through a distinct signifier, and two ideas that are no longer distinct in the mind tend to merge into the same signifier. When we compare signs – positive terms – with each other, we can no longer speak of difference; the expression would not be fitting, for it applies only to the comparing of two sound-images, e.g. *father* and *mother*, or two ideas, e.g. the idea 'father' and the idea 'mother'; two signs, each having a signified and signifier, are not different but only distinct. Between them there is only *opposition*. The entire mechanism of language, with which we shall be concerned later, is based on oppositions of this kind and on the phonic and conceptual differences that they imply.

What is true of value is true also of the unit (…). A unit is a segment of the spoken chain that corresponds to a certain concept; both are by nature purely differential.

Applied to units, the principle of differentiation can be stated in this way: *the characteristics of the unit blend with the unit itself.* In language, as in any semiological system, whatever distinguishes one sign from the others constitutes it. Difference makes character just as it makes value and the unit.

Another rather paradoxical consequence of the same principle is this: in the last analysis what is commonly referred to as a 'grammatical fact' fits the definition of the unit, for it always expresses an opposition of terms: it differs only in that the opposition is particularly significant (e.g. the formation of German plurals of the type Nacht: *Nächte*). Each term present in the grammatical fact (the singular without *umlaut* or final *e* in opposition to the plural with umlaut and *-e*) consists of the interplay of a number of oppositions within the system. When isolated, neither *Nacht* nor *Nächte* is anything: thus everything is opposition. Putting this in another way, the *Nacht:Nächte* relation can be expressed by an algebraic formula a/b in which a and b are not simple terms but result from a set of relations. Language, in a manner of speaking, is a type of algebra consisting solely of complex terms. Some of its oppositions are more significant than others; but units and grammatical facts are only different names for designating diverse aspects of the same general fact: the functioning of linguistic oppositions. This statement is so true that we might very well approach the problem of units by starting from grammatical facts. Taking an opposition like *Nacht:Nächte,* we might ask what are the units involved in it. Are they only the two words, the whole series of similar words, a and $ä$, or all singulars and plurals, etc.?

Units and grammatical facts would not be confused if linguistic signs were made up of something besides differences. But language being what it is, we shall find nothing simple in it regardless of our approach; everywhere and always there is the same complex equilibrium of terms that mutually condition each other. Putting it another *way, language is a form and not a substance* (…). This truth could not be overstressed, for all the mistakes in our terminology, all our incorrect ways of naming things that pertain to language, stem from the involuntary supposition that the linguistic phenomenon must have substance.

Mikhail Bakhtin

Polyphonic discourse in the novel

In the first half of the 20th century, Saussurean structuralism proved to be a powerful intellectual influence for many debates both inside and outside linguistics, especially in Eastern Europe. Having followed the literary and aesthetic discussions of Russian formalism in Soviet Russia in its early days, Mikhail Bakhtin (1895–1975) is today known as the originator of a polyphonic or dialogic conception of language and culture. Bakhtin perceives the novel as a diversity of social speech types (sometimes even a diversity of languages) and a diversity of individual voices, artistically organized. Accordingly, discourse never just expresses one single point of view; rather, it is inherently dialogic. While in his critical work on Dostoevsky, Bakhtin (1984a) develops the idea of the literary work as a polyphonic intersection of different languages, registers and discourses, in other works, such as in his book on Rabelais (1984b), Bakhtin explores the carnivalesque cultures of early modern Europe. Bakhtin's work came to the West mainly through literary theory (Kristeva, 1973; Todorov, 1984) which has celebrated Bakhtin as an example of 'subversive' resistance to centralised forms of control, even though Bakhtin's real political stance was probably more ambivalent. Given that the authorship of a number of works, initially attributed to Bakhtin, has been subject to controversy, it cannot but appear as ironic that Bakhtin today counts as the originator of the concept of polyphony in cultural and literary theory.

References

Bakhtin, Mikhail. 1984a[1929]. *Problems of Dostoevsky's Poetics*. Minneapolis: University of Minnesota Press.

Bakhtin, Mikhail. 1984b[1965]. *Rabelais and His World*. Bloomington, London: Indiana University Press.

Kristeva, Julia. 1973. 'The Ruin of a Poetics.' In *Russian Formalism: A Collection of Articles and Texts in Translation*, ed. by Stephen Bann and John E. Bowlt, 102–119. Edinburgh: Scottish University Press.

Todorov, Tzvetan. 1984[1981]. *Mikhail Bakhtin. The Dialogical Principle*. Manchester: Manchester University Press.

Mikhail Bakhtin. 1981[1934–1935]. 'Discourse in the Novel'.
In *The Dialogic Imagination. Four Essays*, 259–422, selected 261–265, 268–275.
Austin: University of Texas Press.

(…) The novel as a whole is a phenomenon multiform in style and variform in speech and voice. In it the investigator is confronted with several heterogeneous stylistic unities, often located on different linguistic levels and subject to different stylistic controls.

We list below the basic types of compositional-stylistic unities into which the novelistic whole usually breaks down:

1. Direct authorial literary-artistic narration (in all its diverse variants);
2. Stylization of the various forms of oral everyday narration *(skaz);*
3. Stylization of the various forms of semi-literary (written) everyday narration (the letter, the diary, etc.);
4. Various forms of literary but extra-artistic authorial speech (moral, philosophical or scientific statements, oratory, ethnographic descriptions, memoranda and so forth);
5. The stylistically individualized speech of characters.

These heterogeneous stylistic unities, upon entering the novel, combine to form a structured artistic system, and are subordinate to the higher stylistic unity of the work as a whole, a unity that cannot be identified by any single one of the unities subordinated to it.

The stylistic uniqueness of the novel as a genre consists precisely in the combination of these subordinated, yet still relatively autonomous, unities (even at times comprised of different languages) into the higher unity of the work as a whole: the style of a novel is the system of its 'languages'. Each separate element of a novel's language is determined first of all by one such subordinated stylistic unity into which it enters directly – be it the stylistically individualized speech of character, the down-to-earth voice of narrator in *skaz*, a letter or whatever. The linguistic and stylistic profile of a given element (lexical, semantic, syntactic) is shaped by the subordinated unity to which it is most immediately proximate. At the same time this element, together with its most immediate unity, figures in the style of the whole, itself supports the accent of the whole and participates in the process whereby the unified meaning of the whole is structured and revealed.

The novel can be defined as a diversity of social speech types (sometimes even a diversity of languages) and a diversity of individual voices, artistically organized. The internal stratification of any single national language into social dialects, characteristic group behaviour, professional jargon, generic languages, the language of generations and age groups, tendentious language, the language of authority, of various circles and of passing fashions, language that serves the specific sociopolitical purposes of the day, even of the hour (each day has its own slogan, its own vocabulary, its own emphases) – this internal stratification present in every language at any given moment of its historical existence is the indispensable prerequisite for the novel as a genre. The novel orchestrates all its themes, the totality of the world of objects and ideas depicted and expressed in it, by means of the social diversity of speech types [*raznorečie*] and by the differing individual voices that flourish under such conditions. Authorial speech, the speech of narrators, inserted genres, the speech of characters are merely those fundamental compositional unities with whose help heteroglossia [*raznorečie*] can enter the novel; each of them permits a multiplicity of social voices and a wide variety of their links and interrelationships (always more or less dialogized). These distinctive links and interrelationships between utterances and language, this movement of the theme through different language and speech types, its dispersion into the rivulets and droplets of social heteroglossia, its dialogization – this is the basic distinguishing feature of the stylistics of the novel.

Such a combining of languages and styles into a higher unity is unknown to traditional stylistics; it has no method for approaching the distinctive social dialogue among languages that is present in the novel. Thus, stylistic analysis is not orientated towards the novel as a whole, but only toward one or other of its subordinated stylistic unities. The traditional scholar bypasses the basic distinctive feature of the novel as a genre; he substitutes for it another object of study, and instead of novelistic style he actually analyzes something completely different. He transposes a symphonic (orchestrated) theme on the piano keyboard.

We notice two such types of substitution: in the first type, an analysis of novelistic style is replaced by a description of the language of a given novelist (or at best of the 'languages' of a given novel); in the second type, one of the subordinated styles is isolated and analyzed as if it were the style of the whole.

In the first type, style is cut off from considerations of genre, and from the work as such, and regarded as a phenomenon of language itself: the unity of style in a given work is transformed either into the unity of an individual language ('individual dialect'), or into the unity of an individual speech (*parole*). It is precisely the individuality of the speaking subject that is recognized as that style-generating factor transforming a phenomenon of language and linguistics and stylistics unity.

We have no need to follow where such an analysis of novelistic style leads, whether to a disclosing of the novelist's individual dialect (that is, vocabulary, his syntax) or to a disclosing of the distinctive features of the work taken as a 'complete speech act', an 'utterance'. Equally, in both cases, style is understood in the spirit of Saussure: as an individualization of the general language (in the sense of a system of general language norms). Stylistics is transformed either into a curious kind of linguistics treating individual languages, or into a linguistics of the utterance.

In accordance with the point of view selected, the unity of style thus presupposes on the one hand a unity of language (in the sense of a system of general normative forms) and on the other the unity of an individual person realizing himself or herself in this language.

Both these conditions are in fact obligatory in the majority of verse-based poetic genres, but even in these genres they far from exhaust or define the style of the work. The most precise and complete description of the individual language and speech of a poet – even if this description does choose to treat the expressiveness of language and speech elements – does not add up to a stylistic analysis of the work, inasmuch as these elements relate to a system of language or a system of speech, that is, to various linguistic unities and not to the system of the artistic work, which is governed by a completely different system of rules than those that govern the linguistic systems of language and of speech.

But – we repeat – in the majority of poetic genres, the unity of the language system and the unity (and uniqueness) of the poet's individuality as reflected in his language and speech, which is directly realized in this unity, are indispensable prerequisites of poetic style. The novel, however, not only does not require these conditions but (as we have said) even makes the internal stratification of language, of its social heteroglossia and the variety of individual voices in it, a prerequisite for authentic novelistic prose.

Thus the substitution of the individualized language of the novelist (to the extent that one can recover this language from the 'speech' and 'language' systems of the novel) for the style of the novel itself is doubly imprecise: it distorts the very essence of the stylistics of a novel. Such substitution inevitably leads to the selection from the novel of only those elements that can be fitted within the frame of a single language system and that express, directly and without mediation, an authorial individuality in language. The whole of the novel and the specific tasks involved in constructing this whole out of heteroglot, multi-voiced, multi-styled and often multi-languaged elements remain outside the boundaries of such a study. (…)

Once rhetorical discourse is brought into the study with all its living diversity, it cannot fail to have a deeply revolutionizing influence on linguistics and on the philosophy of language. It is precisely those aspects of any discourse (the internally dialogic quality of discourse, and the phenomena related to it), not yet sufficiently taken into account and fathomed in all the enormous weight they carry in the life of language, that are revealed with the great external precision in rhetorical forms, provided a correct and unprejudiced approach to those forms is used. Such is the general methodological and heuristic significance of rhetorical forms for linguistics and for the philosophy of language.

The special significance of rhetorical forms for understanding the novel is equally great. The novel, and artistic prose in general, has the closest genetic, family relationship to rhetorical forms. And throughout the entire development of the novel, its intimate interaction (both peaceful and hostile) with living rhetorical genres (journalistic, moral, philosophical and others) has never ceased; this interaction was perhaps no less intense than was the novel's interaction with artistic genres (epic, dramatic, lyric). But in this uninterrupted interrelationship, novelistic discourse preserved its own qualitative uniqueness and was never reducible to rhetorical discourse.

The novel is an artistic genre. Novelistic discourse is poetic discourse, but one that does not fit within the frame provided by the concept of poetic discourse as it now exists. The concept has certain underlying presuppositions that limit it. The very concept – in the course of its historical formulation from Aristotle to the present day – has been oriented toward specific 'official' genres and connected with specific historical tendencies in verbal ideological life. Thus a whole series of phenomena remained beyond its conceptual horizon.

The philosophy of language, linguistics and stylistics [i.e. such as they have come down to us] have all postulated a simple and unmediated relation of the speaker to his unitary and singular 'own' language, and have postulated as well a simple realization of this language in the monologic utterance of the individual. Such disciplines actually know only two poles in the life of language, between which are located all the linguistic and stylistic phenomena they know: on the one hand, the system of a *unitary language*, and on the other the *individual* speaking in this language.

Various schools of thought in the philosophy of language, in linguistics and in stylistics have, in different periods (and always in close connection with the diverse concrete poetic and ideological styles of a given epoch) introduced into such concepts as 'system of language', 'monologic utterance', 'the speaking *individuum*', various differing nuances of meaning, but their basic content remains unchanged. This basic content is conditioned by the specific sociohistorical destinies of European languages and by the destinies of ideological discourse, and by those particular historical tasks that ideological discourse has fulfilled in specific social spheres and at specific stages in its own historical development.

These tasks and destinies of discourse conditioned specific verbal-ideological discourse, and ultimately the specific philosophical concept of discourse itself – in particular, the concept of poetic discourse, which had been at the heart of all concepts of style.

The strength and at the same time the limitations of such basic stylistic categories become apparent when such categories are seen as conditioned by specific historical destinies and by the task that an ideological discourse assumes. These categories arose from and were shaped by the historical *aktuell* forces at work in the verbal-ideological evolution of specific social groups; they comprised the theoretical expression of actualizing forces that were in the process of creating a life for language.

These forces are *the forces that serve to unify and centralize the verbal-ideological world*.

Unitary language constitutes the theoretical expression of the historical processes of linguistic unification and centralization, an expression of the centripetal forces of language. A unitary language is not something given [*dan*] but is always in essence posited [*zadan*] – and at every moment of its linguistic life it is opposed to the realities of heteroglossia. But at the same time it makes its real presence felt as a force for overcoming this heteroglossia, imposing specific limits on it, guaranteeing a certain maximum of mutual understanding and crystallizing into a real, although still relative, unity – the unity of the reigning conversational (everyday) and literary language, 'correct language'.

A common unitary language is a system of linguistic norms. But these norms do not constitute an abstract imperative; they are rather the generative forces of linguistic life, forces that struggle to overcome the heteroglossia of language, forces that unite and centralize verbal-ideological thought, creating within a heteroglot national language the firm, stable linguistic nucleus of an officially recognized literary language, or else defending an already formed language from the pressure of growing heteroglossia.

What we have in mind here is not an abstract linguistic minimum of common language, in the sense of a system of elementary forms (linguistic symbols) guaranteeing a *minimum* level of comprehension in practical communication. We are taking language not as a system of abstract grammatical categories, but rather conceived as ideologically saturated, language as a world view, even as a concrete opinion, ensuring a *maximum* of mutual understanding in all spheres of ideological life. Thus a unitary language gives expression to forces working toward concrete verbal and ideological unification and centralization, which develop in vital connection with the processes of sociopolitical and cultural centralization.

Aristotelian poetics, the poetics of Augustine, the poetics of the mediæval church, of 'the one language of truth', the Cartesian poetics of neoclassicism, the abstract grammatical universalism of Leibniz (the idea of a 'universal grammar'), Humboldt's insistence on the concrete – all these, whatever their differences in nuance, give expression to the same centripetal forces in sociolinguistic and ideological life; they serve one and the same project of centralizing and unifying the European languages. The victory of one reigning language (dialect) over the others, the supplanting of languages, their enslavement, the process illuminating them with the True World, the incorporation of barbarians and lower social strata into a unitary language of culture and truth, the canonization of ideological systems, philology with its methods of studying and teaching dead languages, languages that were by that very fact 'unities', Indo-European linguistics with its focus of attention, directed away from language plurality to a single proto-language – all this determined the content and power of the category 'unitary language' in linguistic and stylistic thought, and determined its creative, style-shaping role in the majority of the poetic genres that coalesced in the channel formed by those same centripetal forces of verbal-ideological life.

But the centripetal forces of the life of language, embodied in a 'unitary language', operate in the midst of heteroglossia. At any given moment of its evolution, language is stratified not only into linguistic dialects in the strict sense of the word (according to formal linguistic markers, especially phonetic), but also – and for us this is the essential point – into languages that are socio-ideological: languages of social groups, 'professional' and 'generic' languages, languages of generations and so forth. From this point of view, literary language itself is only one of these heteroglot languages – and in its turn is also stratified into languages (generic, period-bound and others). And this stratification and heteroglossia, once realized, is not only a static invariant of linguistic life, but also what ensures its dynamics: stratification and heteroglossia widen and deepen as long as language is alive and developing. Alongside the centripetal forces, the centrifugal forces of language carry on their uninterrupted work; alongside verbal-ideological centralization and unification, the uninterrupted processes of decentralization and disunification go forward.

Every concrete utterance of a speaking subject serves as a point where centrifugal as well as centripetal forces are brought to bear. The process of centralization and decentralization, of unification and disunification, intersect in the utterance; the utterance not only answers the requirements of its own language as an individualized embodiment of a speech act, but it answers the requirements of heteroglossia as well; it is in fact an active participant in such speech diversity. And this active participation of every utterance in living heteroglossia determines the linguistic profile and style of the utterance to no less a degree than its inclusion in any normative-centralizing system of a unitary language.

Every utterance participates in the 'unitary language' (in its centripetal forces and tendencies) and at the same time partakes of social and historical heteroglossia (the centrifugal, stratifying forces).

Such is the fleeting language of a day, of an epoch, a social group, a genre, a school and so forth. It is possible to conduct a concrete and detailed analysis of any utterance, once having exposed it as a contradiction-ridden, tension-filled unity of two embattled tendencies in the life of language.

The authentic environment of an utterance, the environment in which it lives and takes shape, is dialogized heteroglossia, anonymous and social as language, but simultaneously concrete, filled with specific content and accented as an individual utterance.

At the same time when major divisions of the poetic genres were developing under the influence of the unifying, centralizing, centripetal forces of verbal-ideological life, the novel – and those artistic-prose genres that gravitate toward it – was being historically shaped by the current of decentralizing, centrifugal forces. At the same time when poetry was accomplishing the task of cultural, national and political centralization of the verbal-ideological world on the higher official socio-ideological levels, on the lower levels, on the stage of local fairs and at buffoon spectacles, the heteroglossia of the clown sounded forth, ridiculing all 'languages' and dialects; there developed the literature of the *fabliaux* and *Schwänke* of street songs, folksayings, anecdotes, where there was no language-centre at all, where there was to be found a lively play with the 'languages' of poets, scholars, monks, knights and others, where all 'languages' were masks and where no language could claim to be an authentic, incontestable face.

Heteroglossia, as organized in these low genres, was not merely heteroglossia vis-à-vis the accepted literary language (in all its generic expressions), that is, vis-à-vis the linguistic centre of the verbal-ideological life of the nation and the epoch, but a heteroglossia consciously opposed to this literary language. It was parodic, and aimed sharply and polemically against the official languages of its given time. It was heteroglossia that had been dialogized.

The linguistics, stylistics and philosophy of language that were born and shaped by the current of centralizing tendencies in the life of language have ignored this dialogized heteroglossia, in which is embodied the centrifugal forces of the life of language. For this very reason they could make no provision for the dialogic nature of language, which was a struggle among sociolinguistic points of view, not an intra-language struggle between individual dialogues (dramatic, rhetorical, cognitive or merely casual); this has hardly been studied linguistically or stylistically up to the present day. One might even say outright that the dialogic aspect of discourse and all the phenomena connected with it have remained to the present moment beyond the ken of linguistics.

Stylistics has likewise been completely deaf to dialogue. A literary work has been conceived by stylistics as if it were a hermetic and self-sufficient whole, one whose elements constitute a closed system presuming nothing beyond themselves, no other utterances. The system comprising an artistic work was thought to be analogous with the system of a language, a system that could not stand in dialogic interrelationship with other languages. From the point of view of stylistics, the artistic work was a whole – whatever that whole might be – a self-sufficient and closed authorial monologue, one that presumeds only passive listeners beyond its own boundaries. Should we imagine the work as a rejoinder in a given dialogue, whose style is determined by its interrelationship with other rejoinders in the same dialogue (in the totality of the conversation) – then traditional stylistics does not offer an adequate means for approaching such a dialogized style. The sharpest and externally most marked manifestations of this stylistic category – the polemical style, the parodic, the ironic – are usually classified as rhetorical and not as poetic phenomena. Stylistics locks every stylistic phenomenon into the monologic context of a given self-sufficient and hermetic utterance, imprisoning it, as it were, in the dungeon of a single context; it is not able to realize its own stylistic implications in a relationship with them; it is obliged to exhaust itself in its own single hermetic context.

Linguistics, stylistics and the philosophy of language – as forces in the service of the great centralizing tendencies of European verbal-ideological life – have sought first and foremost *unity* in diversity. This exclusive 'orientation toward unity' in the present and past life of languages has concentrated the attention of philosophical and linguistic thought on the firmest, most stable, least changeable and most mono-semic aspects of discourse – on the *phonetic* aspects first of all – that are furthest removed from the changing socio-semantic spheres of discourse. Real ideologically saturated 'language consciousness', one that participates in actual heteroglossia and multi-languagedness, has remained outside its field of vision. It is precisely this orientation toward unity that has compelled scholars to ignore all the verbal genres (quotidian, rhetorical, artistic-prose) that were the carriers of the decentralizing tendencies in the life of language, or that were in any case too fundamentally implicated in heteroglossia. The expression of this hetero- as well as polyglot consciousness in the specific forms and phenomena of verbal life remained utterly without determinative influence on linguistics and stylistic thought.

Therefore, proper theoretical recognition and illumination could not be found for the specific feel for language and discourse that one gets in stylizations, in *skaz*, in parodies and in various forms of verbal masquerade, 'not talking straight', and in the more complex artistic forms for the organization of contradiction, forms that orchestrate their themes by means of languages – in all characteristic and profound models and novelistic prose, in Grimmelshausen, Cervantes, Rabelais, Fielding, Smollett, Sterne and others.

The problem of stylistics for the novel inevitably leads to the necessity of engaging with a series of fundamental questions concerning the philosophy of discourse, questions connected with those aspects in the life of discourse that have had no light cast on them by linguistic and stylistic thought – that is, we must deal with the life and behaviour of discourse in a contradictory and multi-languaged world.

Zellig S. Harris

Towards a distributionalist method

If Saussurean structuralism prefigured holistic theories of discourse studying meaning production in large groups and communities, the aim of distributionalism, an early structuralist variety of discourse analysis, is to describe the distribution of linguistic units in discourses, which are still understood as 'texts'. Its major proponent was Zellig Harris (1909–1992), who uses 'analysis' in its Greek sense as 'decomposition'. While Harris extended distributionalism to units beyond sentences ('discourse'), a good paraphrase of his 'discourse analysis' would be: 'the decomposition of transphrastic units'. Harris believed that text regularities could be associated with social phenomena: 'distributional analysis within one discourse at a time yields information about certain correlations of language with other behaviour. The reason is that each connected discourse occurs within a particular situation.' As one can see, Harris still draws on the traditional distinction between 'language' and 'society', like the French literary structuralism of the 1960s, which claimed that the first step of analysis was to study texts as 'structures' and the second was to connect these 'structures' with some social reality, outside of texts. Harris' model especially inspired some of the earlier generations of anti-hermeneutic discourse researchers who, like Pêcheux (1995[1969]), aimed at methodological procedures involving as little subjective interpretation as possible. It is therefore to the credit of Harris' 1952 article on *Discourse Analysis* that it opened up the domain of linguistic scrutiny beyond the level of words and sentences, even though it stops short of investigating the real uses of language in social life.

References

Pêcheux, Michel. (1995[1969]). *Automatic Discourse Analysis*. Amsterdam, Atlanta: Rodopi.

Zellig S. Harris. 1952. *Language*, 28 (1): 1–30, selected 1–3, 29–30.

This paper presents a method for the analysis of connected speech (or writing). The method is formal, depending only on the occurrence of morphemes as distinguishable elements; it does not depend upon the analyst's knowledge of the particular meaning of each morpheme. By the same token, the method does not give us any new information about the individual morphemic meanings that are being communicated in the discourse under investigation. But the fact that such new information is not obtained does not mean that we can discover nothing about the discourse but how the grammar of the language is exemplified within it. For even though we use formal procedures akin to those of descriptive linguistics, we can obtain new information about the particular text we are studying, information that goes beyond descriptive linguistics.

This additional information results from one basic fact: the analysis of the occurrence of elements in the text is applied only in respect to that text alone – that is, in respect to the other elements in the same text, and not in respect to anything else in the language. As a result of this, we discover the particular interrelations of the morphemes of the text as they occur in that one text; and in so doing we discover something of the structure of the text, of what is being done in it. We may not know just WHAT a text is saying, but we can discover HOW it is saying what are the patterns of recurrence of its chief morphemes.

Definite patterns may be discovered for particular texts, or for particular persons, styles or subject-matters. In some cases, formal conclusions can be drawn from the particular pattern of morpheme distribution in a text. And often it is possible to show consistent differences of structure between the discourses of different persons, or in different styles, or about different subject-matters.

PRELIMINARIES

1. The problem

One can approach discourse analysis from two types of problem, which turn out to be related.

The first is the problem of continuing descriptive linguistics beyond the limits of a single sentence at a time. The other is the question of correlating 'culture' and language (i.e. non-linguistic and linguistic behavior). The first problem arises because descriptive linguistics generally stops at sentence boundaries. This is not due to any prior decision. The techniques of linguistics were constructed to study any stretch of speech, of whatever length. But in every language it turns out that almost all the results lie within a relatively short stretch, which we may call a sentence. That is, when we can state a restriction on the occurrence of element A in respect to the occurrence of element B, it will almost always be the case that A and B are regarded as occurring within the same sentence. Of English adjectives, for instance, we can say that they occur before a noun or after certain verbs (in the same sentence): *the dark clouds, the future seems bright*; only rarely can we state restrictions across sentence boundaries, e.g. that if the main verb of one sentence has a given tense-suffix, the main verb of the next sentence will have a particular other tense-suffix. We cannot say that if one sentence has the form NV, the next sentence will have the form N. We can only say that most sentences are NV, some are N, and so on; and that these structures occur in various sequences.

In this way descriptive linguistics, which sets out to describe the occurrence of elements in any stretch of speech, ends up by describing it primarily in respect to other elements of the same sentence. This limitation has not seemed too serious, because it has not precluded the writing of adequate grammars: the grammar states the sentence structure; the speaker makes up a particular sentence in keeping with this structure, and supplies the particular sequence of sentences.

The other problem, that of the connection between behavior (or social situation) and language, has always been considered beyond the scope of linguistics proper. Descriptive linguistics has not dealt with the meanings of morphemes; and though one might try to get around that by speaking not of meanings, but of the social and inter-personal situation in which speech occurs, descriptive linguistics has had no equipment for taking the social situation into account: it has only been able to state the occurrence of one linguistic element in respect to the occurrence of others. Culture-and-language studies have therefore been carried on without benefit of the recent distributional in-vestigations of linguistics. For example, they list the meanings expressed in the language by surveying the vocabulary stock; or they draw conclusions from the fact that in a particular language a particular set of meanings is expressed by the same morpheme; or they discuss the nuances of meaning and usage of one word in comparison with oth-ers (e.g. in stylistics). Culture-and-language studies have also noted such points as that phrases are to be taken in their total meaning rather than as the sum of the meanings of their component morphemes, e.g. that *How are you* is a greeting rather than a question about health – an example that illustrates the correlation of speech with social situation. Similarly, personality characteristics in speech have been studied by correlating an in-dividual's recurrent speech features with recurrent features of his behavior and feeling.[1]

---

1.   Correlations between personality and language are here taken to be not merely related to correla-tions between 'culture' and language, but actually a special case of these. The reason for this view is that most individual textual characteristics (as distinguished from phonetic characteristics) correlate with those personality features which arise out of the individual's experience with socially conditioned interpersonal situations.

2. Distribution within discourse

Distributional or combinatorial analysis within one discourse at a time turns out to be relevant to both of these problems.

On the one hand, it carries us past the sentence limitation of descriptive linguistics. Although we cannot state the distribution of sentences (or, in general, any intersentence relation) when we are given an arbitrary conglomeration of sentences in a language, we can get quite definite results about certain relations across sentence boundaries when we consider just the sentences of a particular connected discourse – that is, the sentences spoken or written in succession by one or more persons in a single situation. This restriction to connected discourse does not detract from the usefulness of the analysis, since all language occurrences are internally connected. Language does not occur in stray words or sentences, but in connected discourse – from a one-word utterance to a ten-volume work, from a monolog to a Union Square argument. Arbitrary conglomerations of sentences are indeed of no interest except as a check on grammatical description; and it is not surprising that we cannot find interdependence among the sentences of such an aggregate. The successive sentences of a connected discourse, however, offer fertile soil for the methods of descriptive linguistics, since these methods study the relative distribution of elements within a connected stretch of speech.

On the other hand, distributional analysis within one discourse at a time yields information about certain correlations of language with other behavior. The reason is that each connected discourse occurs within a particular situation – whether of a person speaking, or of a conversation, or of someone sitting down occasionally over a period of months to write a particular kind of book in a particular literary or scientific tradition. To be sure, this concurrence between situation and discourse does not mean that discourses occurring in similar situations must necessarily have certain formal characteristics in common, while discourses occurring in different situations must have certain formal differences. The concurrence between situation and discourse only makes it understandable, or possible, that such formal correlations should exist.

It remains to be shown as a matter of empirical fact that such formal correlations do indeed exist, that the discourses of a particular person, social group, style, or subject-matter exhibit not only particular meanings (in their selection of morphemes) but also characteristic formal features. The particular selection of morphemes cannot be considered here. But the formal features of the discourses can be studied by distributional methods within the text; and the fact of their correlation with a particular type of situation gives a meaning-status to the occurrence of these formal features. (…)

Summary

Discourse analysis performs the following operations upon any single connected text. It collects those elements (or sequences of elements) which have identical or equivalent environments of other elements within a sentence, and considers these to be equivalent to each other (i.e. members of the same equivalence class). Material which does not belong to any equivalence class is associated with the class member to which it is grammatically most closely tied. The sentences of the text are divided into intervals, each a succession of equivalence classes, in such a way that each resulting interval is maximally similar in its class composition to other intervals of the text. The succession of intervals is then investigated for the distribution of classes which it exhibits, in particular for the patterning of class occurrence.

The operations make no use of any knowledge concerning the meaning of the morphemes or the intent or conditions of the author. They require only a knowledge of morpheme boundaries, including sentence junctures and other morphemic intonations (or punctuation). Application of these operations can be furthered by making use of grammatical equivalences (or individual morpheme occurrence relations) from the language as a whole, or from the linguistic body of which the given text is a part. In that case it is necessary to know the grammatical class of the various morphemes of the text.

Discourse analysis yields considerable information about the structure of a text or a type of text, and about the role that each element plays in such a structure. Descriptive linguistics, on the other hand, tells only the role that each element plays in the structure of its sentence. Discourse analysis tells, in addition, how a discourse can be constructed to meet various specifications, just as descriptive linguistics builds up sophistication about the ways in which linguistic systems can be constructed to meet various specifications. It also yields information about stretches of speech longer than one sentence; thus it turns out that while there are relations among successive sentences, these are not visible in sentence structure (in terms of what is subject and what is predicate, or the like), but in the pattern of occurrence of equivalence classes through successive sentences.

George Herbert Mead

Thought, communication and the significant symbol

If the preceding theorists can be considered as pioneers of structuralism, the following theorists have crucially contributed to pragmatics. A social philosopher and social psychologist who taught at the University of Chicago, George Herbert Mead (1863–1931) was a pioneer of social action theory. Drawing from both North American pragmatism and social behaviourism, Mead theorized the way action, thought and language are interrelated. In a marked contrast to structuralism, he insisted on the meaning-making activity of individuals as they interact with each other. He became famous for his posthumously published books, such as *Mind, Self and Society* (1967[1934]), in which he argues that cognitive categories like self, mind, identity and consciousness are neither given nor inherent to human beings but produced in the interaction between them. He became famous for his distinction of 'Me' (i.e. the social self as a set of expectations and attitudes from others) and 'I' (i.e. the individual's capacity to come up with creative responses to the constraints imposed by others). In order to engage in communication, the actors have recourse to socially significant symbols which allow them to take the perspective of the other. The selected passage is taken from *Mind, Self, and Society*, which discusses how 'self-consciousness and the appearance of the self' emerge from bodily responses to the stimuli produced by others. Over time, the vocal gestures of the actors can turn into symbols which represent certain actions. In this way, language needs to be considered as a symbolic activity embedded in social life. With the focus on the meaning-making activity of actors, Mead is a precursor of the many interactional strands in Discourse Studies and the social sciences more generally (see the section on 'Interactionism').

Reference

Mead, George Herbert. 1967[1934]. *Mind, Self, & Society from the Standpoint of a Social Behaviorist*. Chicago, London: University of Chicago Press.

George Herbert Mead. 1934. *Mind, Self, and Society from the Standpoint of a Social Behaviorist*, edited by Charles W. Morris, selected 68–75. Chicago: University of Chicago.

We have contended that there is no particular faculty of imitation in the sense that the sound or the sight of another's response is itself a stimulus to carry out the same reaction, but rather that if there is already present in the individual an action like the action of another, then there is a situation which makes imitation possible. What is necessary now to carry through that imitation is that the conduct and the gesture of the individual which calls out a response in the other should also tend to call out the same response in himself. In the dog-fight this is not present: the attitude in the one dog does not tend to call out the same attitude in the other. In some respects that actually may occur in the case of two boxers. The man who makes a feint is calling out a certain blow from his opponent, and that act of his own does have that meaning to him, that is, he has in some sense initiated the same act in himself. It does not go clear through, but he has stirred up the centers in his central nervous system which would lead to his making the same blow that his opponent is led to make, so that he calls out in himself, or tends to call out, the same response which he calls out in the other. There you have the basis for so-called imitation. Such is the process which is so widely recognized at present in manners of speech, of dress, and of attitudes.

We are more or less unconsciously seeing ourselves as others see us. We are unconsciously addressing ourselves as others address us; in the same way as the sparrow takes up the note of the canary we pick up the dialects about us. Of course, there must be these particular responses in our own mechanism. We are calling out in the other person something we are calling out in ourselves, so that unconsciously we take over these attitudes. We are unconsciously putting ourselves in the place of others and acting as others act. I want simply to isolate the general mechanism here, because it is of very fundamental importance in the development of what we call self-consciousness and the appearance of the self. We are, especially through the use of the vocal gestures, continually arousing in ourselves those responses which we call out in other persons, so that we are taking the attitudes of the other persons into our own conduct. The critical importance of language in the development of human experience lies in this fact that the stimulus is one that can react upon the speaking individual as it reacts upon the other.

A behaviorist, such as Watson, holds that all of our thinking is vocalization. In thinking we are simply starting to use certain words. That is in a sense true. However, Watson does not take into account all that is involved here, namely, that these stimuli are the essential elements in elaborate social processes and carry with them the value of those social processes. The vocal process as such has this great importance, and it is fair to assume that the vocal process, together with the intelligence and thought that go with it, is not simply a playing of particular vocal elements against each other. Such a view neglects the social context of language.[1]

The importance, then, of the vocal stimulus lies in this fact that the individual can hear what he says and in hearing what he says is tending to respond as the other person responds. When we speak now of this response on the part of the individual to the others we come back to the situation of asking some person to do something. We ordinarily express that by saying that one knows what he is asking you to do. Take the illustration of asking someone to do something, and then doing it one's self. Perhaps the person addressed does not hear you or acts slowly, and then you carry the action out yourself. You find in yourself, in this way, the same tendency which you are asking you that same response which you stirred up in the other individual. How difficult it is to show someone else how to do something which you know how to do yourself! The slowness of the response makes it hard to restrain yourself from doing what you are teaching. You have aroused the same response in yourself as you arouse in the other individual.

In seeking for an explanation of this, we ordinarily assume a certain group of centers in the nervous system which are connected with each other, and which express themselves in the action. If we try to find in a central nervous system something that answers to our word 'chair', what we should find would be presumably simply an organization of a whole group of possible reactions so connected that if one starts in one direction one will carry out one process, if in another direction one will carry out another process. The chair is primarily what one sits down in. It is a physical object at a distance. One may move toward an object at a distance and then enter upon the process of sitting down when one reaches it. There is a stimulus which excites certain paths which cause the individual to go toward that object and to sit down. Those centers are in some degree physical. There is, it is to be noted, an influence of the later act on the earlier act. The later process which is to go on has already been initiated and that later process has its influence on the earlier process (the one that takes place before

---

1.   Gestures, if carried back to the matrix from which they spring, are always found to inhere in or involve a larger social act of which they are phases. In dealing with communication we have first to recognize its earliest origins in the unconscious conversation of gestures. Conscious communication – conscious conversation of gestures – arises when gestures become signs, that is, when they come to carry for the individuals making them and the individuals responding to them, definite meanings or significations in terms of the subsequent behavior of the individuals making them; so that, by serving as prior indications, to the individuals responding to them, of the subsequent behavior of the individuals making them, they make possible the mutual adjustment of the various individual components of the social act to one another, and also, by calling forth in the individuals making them the same responses implicitly that they call forth explicitly in the individuals to whom they are made, they render possible the rise of self-consciousness in connection with this mutual adjustment.

this process, already initiated, can be completed). Now, such an organization of a great group of nervous elements as will lead to conduct with reference to the objects about us is what one would find in the central nervous system answering to what we call an object. The complications are very great, but the central nervous system has an almost infinite number of elements in it, and they can be organized not only in spatial connection with each other, but also from a temporal standpoint. In virtue of this last fact, our conduct is made up of a series of steps which follow each other, and the later steps may be already started and influence the earlier ones. The thing we are going to do is playing back on what we are doing now. That organization in the neural elements in reference to what we call a physical object would be what we call a conceptual object stated in terms of the central nervous system.

In rough fashion it is the initiation of such a set of organized sets of responses that answers to what we call the idea or concept of a thing. If one asked what the idea of a dog is, and tried to find that idea in the central nervous system, one would find a whole group of responses which are more or less connected together by definite paths so that when one uses the term 'dog' he does tend to call out this group of responses. A dog is a possible playmate, a possible enemy, one's own property or somebody else's. There is a whole series of possible responses. There are certain types of these responses which are in all of us, and there are others which vary with the individuals, but there is always an organization of the responses which can be called out by the term 'dog.' So if one is speaking of a dog to another person he is arousing in himself this set of responses which he is arousing in the other individual.

It is, of course, the relationship of this symbol, this vocal gesture, to such a set of responses in the individual himself as well as in the other that makes of that vocal gesture what I call a significant symbol. A symbol does tend to call out in the individual a group of reactions such as it calls out in the other, but there is something further that is involved in its being a significant symbol: this response within one's self to such a word as 'chair,' or 'dog,' is one which is a stimulus to the individual as well as a response. This is what, of course, is involved in what we term the meaning of a thing, or its significance.[2] We often act with reference to objects in what we call an intelligent

---

2.   The inclusion of the matrix or complex of attitudes and responses constituting any given social situation or act, within the experience of any one of the individuals implicated in that situation or act (the inclusion within his experience of his attitudes toward other individuals, of their responses to his attitudes toward them, of their attitudes toward him, and of his responses to these attitudes) is all that an *idea* amounts to; or at any rate is the only basis for its occurrence or existence 'in the mind' of the given individual. In the case of the unconscious conversation of gestures, or in the case of the process of communication carried on by means of it, none of the individuals participating in it is conscious or the meaning of the conversation-that meaning does not appear in the experience of any one of the separate individuals involved in the conversation or carrying it on; whereas, in the case of the conscious conversation of gestures, or in the case of the process of communication

fashion, although we can act without the meaning of the object being present in our experience. One can start to dress for dinner, as they tell of the absent-minded college professor, and find himself in his pajamas in bed. A certain process of undressing was started and carried out mechanically; he did not recognize the meaning of what he was doing. He intended to go to dinner and found he had gone to bed. The meaning involved in his action was not present. The steps in this case were all intelligent steps which controlled his conduct with reference to later action, but he did not think about what he was doing. The later action was not a stimulus to his response, but just carried itself out when it was once started.

When we speak of the meaning of what we are doing we are making the response itself that we are on the point of carrying out a stimulus to our action. It becomes a stimulus to a later stage of action which is to take place from the point of view of this particular response. In the case of the boxer the blow that he is starting to direct toward his opponent is to call out a certain response which will open up the guard of his opponent so that he can strike. The meaning is a stimulus for the preparation of the real blow he expects to deliver. The response which he calls out in himself (the guarding reaction) is the stimulus to him to strike where an opening is given. This action which he has initiated already in himself thus becomes a stimulus for his later response. He knows what his opponent is going to do, since the guarding movement is one which is already aroused, and becomes a stimulus to strike where the opening is given. The meaning would not have been present in his conduct unless it became a stimulus to strike where the favorable opening appears.

Such is the difference between intelligent conduct on the part of animals and what we call a reflective individual. We say the animal does not think. He does not put himself in a position for which he is responsible; he does not put himself in the place of the other person and say, in effect, 'He will act in such a way and I will act in this way.' If the individual can act in this way, and the attitude which he calls out in himself can become a stimulus to him for another act, we have meaningful conduct. Where the response of the other person is called out and becomes a stimulus to control his action, then he has the meaning of the other person's act in his own experience. That is the general mechanism of what we term 'thought,' for in order that thought may exist there must be symbols, vocal gestures generally, which arouse in the individual himself the response which he is calling out in the other, and such that from the point of view of that response he is able to direct his later conduct. It involves not only communication in the sense in which birds and animals communicate with each other, but also an arousal in the individual himself of the response which he is calling out in the other

---

carried on by means of it, each of the individuals participating in it is conscious of the meaning of the conversation, precisely because that meaning does appear in his experience, and because such appearance is what consciousness of that meaning implies.

individual, a taking of the role of the other, a tendency to act as the other person acts. One participates in the same process the other person is carrying out and controls his action with reference to that participation. It is that which constitutes the meaning of an object, namely, the common response in one's self as well as in the other person, which becomes, in turn, a stimulus to one's self.

If you conceive of the mind as just a sort of conscious substance in which there are certain impressions and states, and hold that one of those states is a universal, then a word becomes purely arbitrary – it is just a symbol.[3] You can then take words and pronounce them backwards, as children do; there seems to be absolute freedom of arrangement and language seems to be an entirely mechanical thing that lies outside of the process of intelligence. If you recognize that language is, however, just a part of a cooperative process, that part which does lead to an adjustment to the response of the other so that the whole activity can go on, then language has only a limited range of arbitrariness. If you are talking to another person you are, perhaps, able to scent the change in his attitude by something that would not strike a third person at all. You may know his mannerism, and that becomes a gesture to you, a part of the response of the individual. There is a certain range possible within the gesture as to what is to serve as the symbol. We may say that a whole set of separate symbols with one meaning are acceptable; but they always are gestures, that is, they are always parts of the act of the individual which reveal what he is going to do to the other person so that when the person utilizes the clue he calls out in himself the attitude of the other. Language is not ever arbitrary in the sense of simply denoting a bare state of consciousness by a word. What particular part of one's act will serve to direct cooperative activity is more or less arbitrary. Different phases of the act may do it. What seems unimportant in itself may be highly important in revealing what the attitude is. In that sense one can speak of the gesture itself as unimportant, but it is of great importance as to what the gesture is going to reveal. This is seen in the difference between the purely intellectual

3.   Muller attempts to put the values of thought into language; but this attempt is fallacious, because language has those values only as the most effective mechanism of thought merely because it carries the conscious or significant conversation of gestures to its highest and most perfect development. There must be some sort of an implicit attitude (that is, a response which is initiated without being fully carried out) in the organism making the gesture – an attitude which answers to the overt response to the gesture on the part of another individual, and which corresponds to the attitude called forth or aroused in this other organism by the gesture – if thought is to develop in the organism making the gesture. And it is the central nervous system which provides the mechanism for such implicit attitudes or responses. The identification of language with reason is in one sense an absurdity, but in another sense it is valid. It is valid, namely, in the sense that the process of language brings the total social act into the experience of the given individual as himself involved in the act, and thus makes the process of reason possible. But though the process of reason is and must be carried on in terms of the process of language-in terms, that is, of words – it is not simply constituted by the latter.

character of the symbol and its emotional character. A poet depends upon the latter; for him language is rich and full of values which we, perhaps, utterly ignore. In trying to express a message in something less than ten words, we merely want to convey a certain meaning, while the poet is dealing with what is really living tissue, the emotional throb in the expression itself. There is, then, a great range in our use of language; but whatever phase of this range is used is a part of a social process, and it is always that part by means of which we affect ourselves as we affect others and mediate the social situation through this understanding of what we are saying. That is fundamental for any language; if it is going to be language one has to understand what he is saying, has to affect himself as he affects others.

Ludwig Wittgenstein

Communication as a language game

The work of Ludwig Wittgenstein (1889–1951) is commonly divided into two phases: the early one of *Tractatus Logico-Philosophicus* (1961[1921]), which prolongs the investigation of logicians of the Vienna circle around Carnap. Their objective was to discover a pure logical language devoid of ambivalence and imprecision. The Wittgenstein of the second phase, by contrast, which has become central to discourse research, stands for the opposite idea: that there can be no pure language because we cannot use language without engaging in some sort of action. In the passage selected from his posthumously published *Philosophical Investigations* (1997[1953]), Wittgenstein starts with a critical interrogation of the idea that language describes the world. Opposing the view that words have meaning that refers to something out there, such as a name that is attached to an object, Wittgenstein points out that language in many cases implies that we do something to make sense of words. Therefore, he introduced the term 'language game', which is meant to 'bring into prominence the fact that the speaking of language is part of an activity, or of a form of life' (§23). As a consequence, philosophy can no longer claim privileged access to meaning; the source of meaning is ordinary speech.

References

Wittgenstein, Ludwig. 1961[1921]. *Tractatus Logico-Philosophicus*. London: Routledge.
Wittgenstein, Ludwig. 1997[1953]. *Philosophische Untersuchungen/Philosophical Investigations*. Second Edition. Oxford: Blackwell.

Ludwig Wittgenstein. 1997. *Philosophische Untersuchungen / Philosophical Investigations*,
selected remarks (*Bemerkungen*) 1–6, 10, 11, 23–26, 29, 30, 43.
Oxford: Blackwell.

§1   'When they (my elders) named some object, and accordingly moved towards it, I
saw this and I grasped that the thing was called by the sound they uttered when they
meant to point *it* out. Their intention was shown by their bodily movements, as it were
the natural language of all peoples: the expression of the face, the play of the eyes, the
movement of other parts of the body, and the tone of voice which expresses our state
of mind in seeking, having, rejecting, or avoiding something. Thus, as I heard words
repeatedly used in their proper places in various sentences, I gradually learnt to understand what objects they signified; and after I had trained my mouth to form these
signs, I used them to express my desires.' (Augustine, *Confessions,* I. 8.)

These words, it seems to me, give us a particular picture of the essence of human
language. It is this: the individual words in language name objects; sentences are combinations of such names. In this picture of language, we find the roots of the following
idea: Every word has a meaning. This meaning is correlated with the word. It is the
object for which the word stands.

Augustine does not mention any difference between kinds of word. If you describe
the learning of language in this way you are, I believe, thinking primarily of nouns
like 'table', 'chair', 'bread', and of people's names, and only secondarily of the names of
certain actions and properties; and of the remaining kinds of word as something that
will take care of itself.

Now think of the following use of language: I send someone shopping. I give him a
slip marked 'five red apples'. He takes the slip to the shopkeeper, who opens the drawer
marked 'apples'; then he looks up the word 'red' in a table and finds a colour sample
opposite it; then he says the series of cardinal numbers – I assume that he knows them
by heart – up to the word 'five' and for each number he takes an apple of the same
colour as the sample out of the drawer. It is in this and similar ways that one operates
with words. 'But how does he know where and how he is to look up the word 'red' and
what he is to do with the word 'five'?' Well, I assume that he *acts* as I have described.
Explanations come to an end somewhere. But what is the meaning of the word 'five'?
No such thing was in question here, only how the word 'five' *is* used.

§2   That philosophical concept of meaning has its place in a primitive idea of the
way language functions. But one can also say that it is the idea of a language more
primitive than ours.

Let us imagine a language for which the description given by Augustine is right. The
language is meant to serve for communication between a builder A and an assistant B.

A is building with building-stones: there are blocks, pillars, slabs and beams. B has to pass the stones, and that in the order in which A needs them. For this purpose they use a language consisting of the words 'block', 'pillar', 'slab', 'beam'. A calls them out; B brings the stone which he has learnt to bring at such-and-such a call. Conceive this as a complete primitive language.

§3   Augustine, we might say, does describe a system of communication; only not everything that we call language is this system. And one has to say this in many cases where the question arises 'Will this description do or not?' The answer is: 'Yes, it will, but only for this narrowly circumscribed region, not for the whole of what you were claiming to describe.'

It is as if someone were to say: 'A game consists in moving objects about on a surface according to certain rules...' – and we replied: You seem to be thinking of board games, but there are others. You can make your definition correct by expressly restricting it to those games.

§4   Imagine a script in which the letters were used to stand for sounds, and also as signs of emphasis and punctuation. (A script can be conceived as a language for describing sound-patterns.) Now imagine someone interpreting that script as if there were simply a correspondence of letters to sounds and as if the letters had not also completely different functions. Augustine's conception of language is like such an over-simple conception of the script.

§5   If we look at the example in §1, we may perhaps get an inkling how much this general notion of the meaning of a word surrounds the working of language with a haze which makes clear vision impossible. It disperses the fog to study the phenomena of language in primitive kinds of application in which one can command a clear view of the aim and functioning of the words.

A child uses such primitive forms of language when it learns to talk. Here the teaching of language is not explanation, but training.

§6   We could imagine that the language of §2 was the *whole* language of A and B; even the whole language of a tribe. The children are brought up to perform *these* actions, to use *these* words as they do so, and to react in *this* way to the words of others.

An important part of the training will consist in the teacher's pointing to the objects, directing the child's attention to them, and at the same time uttering a word; for instance, the word 'slab' as he points to that shape. (I do not want to call this 'ostensive definition', because the child cannot as yet *ask* what the name is. I will call it 'ostensive teaching of words'. I say that it will form an important part of the training, because it is so with human beings; not because it could not be imagined otherwise.) This ostensive teaching of words can be said to establish an association between the word and the thing. But what does this mean? Well, it can mean various things; but one very likely thinks first of all that a picture of the object comes before the child's mind when it hears the word. But now, if this does happen is it the purpose of the word? Yes, it *may* be the purpose. I can imagine such a use of words (of series of sounds). (Uttering a word is like striking a note on the keyboard of the imagination.) But in the language of §2 it is *not* the purpose of the words to evoke images. (It may, of course, be discovered that that helps to attain the actual purpose.)

But if the ostensive teaching has this effect, am I to say that it effects an understanding of the word? Don't you understand the call 'slab!' if you act upon it in such-and-such a way? No doubt the ostensive teaching helped to bring this about; but only together with a particular instruction. With a different instruction the same ostensive teaching of numerals would have effected a quite different understanding. (…)

§9 (…) Are 'there' and 'this' also taught ostensively? Imagine how one might perhaps teach their use. One will point to places and things but in this case the pointing occurs in the *use* of the words too and not merely in learning the use. (…)

§10 Now what do the words of this language *signify*? What is supposed to show what they signify, if not the kind of use they have? And we have already described that. So we are asking for the expression 'This word signifies *this*' to be made a part of the description. In other words the description ought to take the form: 'The word … signifies… '.

Well, one can reduce the description of the use of the word 'slab' to the statement that this word signifies this object. This will be done when, for example, it is merely a matter of removing the mistaken idea that the word 'slab' refers to the shape of building-stone that we in fact call a 'block' – but the kind of *'referring'* this is, that is to say the use of these words for the rest, is already known.

Equally one can say that the signs 'a', 'b', etc. signify numbers; when for example this removes the mistaken idea that 'a', 'b', 'c', play the part actually played in language by 'block', 'slab', 'pillar'. And one can also say that 'c' means this number and not that one; when for example this serves to explain that the letters are to be used in the order a, b, c, d, etc. and not in the order a, b, d, c.

But assimilating the descriptions of the uses of words in this way cannot make the uses themselves any more like one another. For, as we see, they are absolutely unlike.

§11 Think of the tools in a toolbox: there is a hammer, pliers, a saw, a screw-driver, a rule, a glue-pot, glue, nails and screws. The functions of words are as diverse as the functions of these objects. (And in both cases there are similarities.)

Of course, what confuses us is the uniform appearance of words when we hear them spoken or meet them written or in print. For their *application* is not presented to us so clearly. Especially when we are doing philosophy! (…)

§23 But how many kinds of sentence are there? Say assertion, question, and command? There are *countless* kinds: countless different kinds of use of what we call 'symbols', 'words', 'sentences'. And this multiplicity is not something fixed, given once for all; but new types of language, new language-games, as we may say, come into existence, and others become obsolete and get forgotten. (We can get a *rough picture* of this from the changes in mathematics.)

Here the term 'language-*game*' is meant to bring into prominence the fact that the *speaking* of language is part of an activity, or of a form of life.

Review the multiplicity of language-games in the following examples, and in others:

Giving orders, and obeying them; describing the appearance of an object, or giving its measurements;
constructing an object from a description (a drawing); reporting an event; speculating about an event;
(…) forming and testing a hypothesis; presenting the results of an experiment in tables and diagrams;
making up a story; and reading it; (…) translating from one language into another; asking, thanking, cursing, greeting, praying.

It is interesting to compare the multiplicity of the tools in language and of the ways they are used, the multiplicity of kinds of word and sentence, with what logicians have said about the structure of language. (Including the author of the *Tractatus Logico-Philosophicus.*)

§24 If you do not keep the multiplicity of language-games in view you will perhaps be inclined to ask questions like: 'What is a question?' Is it the statement that I do not know such-and-such, or the statement that I wish the other person would tell me…? Or is it the description of my mental state of uncertainty? And is the cry 'Help!' such a description?

Think of how many different kinds of thing are called 'description': description of a body's position by means of its co-ordinates; description of a facial expression; description of a sensation of touch; of a mood.

Of course it is possible to substitute the form of statement or description for the usual form of question: 'I want to know whether…' or 'I am in doubt whether…' but this does not bring the different language-games any closer together.
(…)

§25 It is sometimes said that animals do not talk because they lack the mental capacity. And this means: 'they do not think, and that is why they do not talk.' But – they simply do not talk. Or to put it better: they do not use language – if we except the most primitive forms of language. Commanding, questioning, recounting, chatting, are as much a part of our natural history as walking, eating, drinking, playing.

§26 One thinks that learning language consists in giving names to objects, viz. to human beings, to shapes, to colours, to pains, to moods, to numbers. To repeat – naming is something like attaching a name tag to a thing. One can call this a preparation for the use of a word. But *what* is it a preparation *for*?

(…)

§29 Perhaps you say: two can only be ostensively defined in this way: 'This *number* is called 'two'.' For the word 'number' here shows what place in language, in grammar, we assign to the word. But this means that the word 'number' must be explained before the ostensive definition can be understood. The word 'number' in the definition does indeed show this place; does show the post at which we station the word. And we can prevent misunderstandings by saying: 'This *colour* is called so-and-so', 'This *length* is called so-and-so', and so on. That is to say: misunderstandings are sometimes averted in this way. But is there only *one* way of taking the word 'colour' or 'length'? Well, they just need defining. Defining, then, by means of other words! And what about the last definition in this chain? (Do not say: 'There isn't a 'last' definition.' That is just as if you chose to say: 'There isn't a last house in this road; one can always build an additional one.')

Whether the word 'number' is necessary in the ostensive definition depends on whether without it the other person takes the definition otherwise than I wish. And that will depend on the circumstances under which it is given, and on the person I give it to.

And how he 'takes' the definition is seen in the use that he makes of the word defined.

§30 So one might say: the ostensive definition explains the use – the meaning – of the word when the overall role of the word in language is clear. Thus if I know that someone means to explain a colour-word to me the ostensive definition 'That is called 'sepia'' will help me to understand the word. And you can say this, as long as (…) you do not forget that all sorts of problems are tied to the words 'to know' or 'to be clear'.

One has already to know (or be able to do) something in order to be capable of asking a thing's name. But what does one have to know? (…)

§43 For a *large* class of cases – though not for all – in which we employ the word 'meaning' it can be defined thus: the meaning of a word is its use in the language.

And the *meaning* of a name is sometimes explained by pointing to its *bearer.*

John L. Austin

Performing speech

Wittgenstein spawned two major lines of thought: an analytical strand exploring the truth of utterances and a discourse pragmatic strand analysing communicative acts and processes. J. L. Austin (1911–1960), who initiated speech-act theory (1962), is a representative of the latter. Examples such as 'I declare you husband and wife' or 'I promise you to give the book back to you' testify to the fact that utterances are not only produced to describe a certain state of the world but also to perform certain actions such as weddings and promises. In the section below, the theoretical ramifications of this insight are spelt out with respect to the 'meaning of a word'. Austin reveals that words are not like the names given to a referent. Instead, it is a fundamental characteristic of words to have different meanings according to the context in which they are used. This emphasis on the practical dimension of meaning production reminds us of the crucial distinction between texts and discourses: texts (or words) are abstract entities which have no meaning outside of discourse. Austin's speech-act theory has inspired a variety of theoretical strands in pragmatics (Searle 1992) and poststructuralism (Butler 1997).

References

Austin, John L. 1962[1955]. *How to Do Things with Words. The William James Lectures delivered at Harvard University in 1955*. Oxford, New York: Oxford University Press
Butler, Judith. 1997. *Excitable Speech. A Politics of the Performative*. New York, London: Routledge.
Searle, John. 1992. *Speech acts. An Essay in the Philosophy of Language*. Cambridge: Cambridge University Press.

John L. Austin. 1979[1961]. 'The Meaning of a Word'.
In *Philosophical Papers*, 3rd edition, 55–75, selected 56–62, 72–75.
Oxford: Oxford University Press.

I begin with some remarks about 'the meaning of a word'. I think many persons now see all a part of what I shall say: but not all do, and there is the tendency to forget it, or to get it slightly wrong. Insofar as I am merely flogging the converted, I apologize to them.

A preliminary remark. It may justly be urged that, properly speaking, what alone has meaning is a *sentence*. Of course, we can speak quite properly of, for example, 'looking up the meaning of a word' in a dictionary. Nevertheless, it appears that the sense in which a word or a phrase 'has a meaning' is derivative from the sense in which a sentence 'has a meaning': to say a word or a phrase 'has a meaning' is to say that there are sentences in which it occurs which 'have meanings': and to know the meaning which the word or phrase has, is to know the meanings of the sentences in which it occurs. All the dictionary can do when we 'look up the meaning of a word ' is to suggest aids to understanding of sentences in which it occurs. Hence it appears correct to say that what 'has meaning' in the primary sense is the sentence. And older philosophers who discussed the problem of 'the meaning of words' tend to fall into *special* errors, avoided by more recent philosophers, who discuss rather the parallel problem of 'the meaning of sentences'. Nevertheless, if we are on our guard, we perhaps need to fall into these special errors, and I propose to overlook them at present.

There are many sorts of sentence in which the words 'the meaning of the word so-and-so' are found, e.g. 'He does not know, or understand, the meaning of the word *handsaw*': 'I shall have to explain to her the meaning of the word *pikestaff*': and so on. I intend to consider primarily the common question, 'What is the meaning of so-and-so?' or 'What is the meaning of the word so-and-so?'

Suppose that in ordinary life I am asked: 'What is the meaning of the word *racy*?' There are two sorts of thing I may do in response: I may reply in *words*, trying to describe what raciness is and what it is not, to give examples of sentences in which one might use the word *racy*, and of others in which one should not. Let us call the *sort* of thing 'explaining the syntactics' of the word 'racy' in the English language. On the other hand, I might do what we may call 'demonstrating the semantics' of the word, by getting the questioner to *imagine*, or even actually to *experience*, situations which we should describe correctly by means of sentences containing the words 'racy' 'raciness', etc., and again in other situations where we should *not* use these words. This is, of course, a simple case: but perhaps the same two *sorts* of procedure would be gone through in the case of at least most ordinary words. And in the same way, if I wished to find out 'whether he understands the meaning of the word *racy*', I should test him at some length in these two ways (which perhaps could not be entirely divorced from each other).

Having asked in this way, and answered, 'What is the meaning of (the word) 'rat'?', 'What is the meaning of (the word) 'cat'?', 'What is the meaning of (the word) 'mat'?', and so on, we then try, being philosophers, to ask the further *general* question. We do not intend to mean by it a certain question which would be perfectly all right, namely, 'What is the meaning of (the word) 'word'?', *that* would be no more general than is asking the meaning of the word 'rat', and would be answered in a precisely similar way.

No: we want to ask rather, 'What is the meaning of a-word-in-general?' or 'of *any* word' – not meaning 'any' word you like to choose, but rather *no particular* word *at all*, just 'any word'. Now if we pause even for a moment to reflect, this is a perfectly absurd question to be trying to ask. I can only answer a question of the form 'What is the meaning of 'x'?' if 'x' is some *particular* word you are asking about. This supposed *general* question is really just a spurious question of a type which commonly arises in philosophy. We may call it the fallacy of asking about 'Nothing-in-particular' which is a practice decried by the plain man, but [which] the philosopher called 'generalizing' and regarded with some complacency. Many other examples of the fallacy can be found: take, for example, the case of 'reality' – we try to pass from such questions as 'How would you distinguish a real rat from an imaginary rat?' to 'What is a real thing?', a question which merely gives rise to nonsense.

We may expose the error in our present case thus. Instead of asking 'What is the meaning of (the word) 'rat'?' we might clearly have asked 'What is a 'rat'?' and so on. But if our questions have been put in *that* form, it becomes very difficult to formulate any *general* question which could impose on us for a moment. Perhaps 'What is any-thing?'? Few philosophers, if perhaps not none, have been foolhardy enough to pose such a question. In the same way, we should not perhaps be tempted to generalize such a question as 'Does he know the meaning of (the word) 'rat'?' 'Does he know the meaning of a word?' would be silly.

Faced with the nonsense question 'What is the meaning of a word?', and perhaps dimly recognizing it to be nonsense, we are nevertheless not inclined to give it up. Instead, we transform it in a curious and noteworthy manner. Up to now, we had been asking 'What-is-the-meaning-of (the word) 'rat'?', etc.; and ultimately 'What-is-the-meaning-of a word?' But now, being baffled, we change so to speak, the hyphenation, and ask 'What is the-meaning-of-a-word?' or sometimes, 'What is the 'meaning' of a word?': I shall refer, for brevity's sake, only to the other. It is easy to see how very different this question is from the other. At once a crowd of traditional and reassuring answers present themselves: 'a concept', 'an idea', 'an image', 'a class of similar sensa', etc. All of which are equally spurious answers to a pseudo-question. Plunging ahead, however, or rather retracing our steps, we now proceed to ask such questions as 'What is the-meaning-of-the-(the-word) 'rat'?' which is as spurious as 'what-is-the-meaning-of (the word) 'rat'?' was genuine. And again we answer 'the idea of a rat' and so forth.

How quaint this procedure is, may be seen in the following way. Supposing a plain man puzzled, were to ask me 'What is the meaning of (the word) 'muggy'?', and I were to answer, 'The idea or concept of 'mugginess' or 'The class of sense of which it is correct to say 'This is muggy': the man would stare at me as at an imbecile. And this is sufficiently unusual for me to conclude that that was not at all the sort of answer he expected: nor, in plain English, *can* that question *ever* require that sort of answer. (…)

All this must seem very obvious, but I wish to the point out that it is fatally easy to forget it: no doubt I shall do so myself many times in the course of this paper. Even those who see pretty clearly that 'concepts', 'abstract ideas', and so on are fictitious entities, which we owe in part to asking questions about 'the meaning of a word', nevertheless themselves think that there *is something* which is 'the meaning of a word'. Thus Mr. Hampshire attacks to some purpose the theory that there is such a thing as 'the meaning of a word': what *he* thinks is wrong is the belief that there is a *single* thing called *the* meaning: 'concepts' are nonsense, and no single particular 'image' can be *the* meaning of a general word. So, he goes on to say, the meaning of a word must really be 'a *class* of similar particular ideas'. 'If we are asked 'What does this mean?' we point to a class of particular ideas'. But a 'class of particular ideas' is every bit as fictitious an entity as a 'concept' or 'abstract idea'. In the same way Mr. C. W. Morris (in the *Encyclopaedia of Unified Science*) attacks, to some purpose, those who think of 'a meaning' as a definite something which is 'simply located' somewhere: what *he* thinks is wrong is that people think of 'a meaning' as a kind of entity which can be described wholly without reference to the total activity of 'semiosis'. Well and good. Yet he himself makes some of the crudest possible remarks about 'the designatum' of a word: every sign has a designatum, which is not a particular thing but a *kind* of object or *class* of object. Now this is quite as fictitious an entity as any 'Platonic idea': and is due to precisely the same fallacy of looking for 'the meaning (or designatum) of a word'.

Why are we tempted to slip back in this way? Perhaps there are two main reasons. First, there are the curious beliefs that all words are names, i.e. in effect *proper* names, and therefore stand for something or designate it in the way that a proper name does. But this view that general names 'have denotation' in the same way that proper names do, is quite as odd as the view that proper names 'have connotation' in the same way that general names do, which is commonly recognized to lead to error. Secondly, we are afflicted by a more common malady, which is this. When we have given an analysis of a certain sentence, containing a word or a phrase 'x', we often feel inclined to ask, of our analysis, 'What in it, is 'x'?' For example, we give an analysis of 'The State owns this land', in sentences about individual men, their relations and transactions: and then at last we feel inclined to ask: well now, *what*, in all that, *is* the State? And we might answer: the State *is* a collection of individual men united in a certain manner. Or again, when we have analysed the statement 'trees can exist unperceived': hence theories about 'sensibilia' and what not. So in our present case, having given all that is required, viz. an account of 'What-is-the-meaning-of 'What is-the-meaning-of (the word) 'x'?'' we *still* feel tempted, wrongly supposing our original sentence to contain a constituent 'the-meaning-of (the-word)-'x'', to ask 'Well now, as it turns out, what *is* the meaning of the word 'x', after all?' And we answer, 'a class of similar particular ideas' and what not.

Of course, all my account of our motives in this matter may be only a convenient didactic schema: I do not think it is – but I recognize that one should not impute motives, least of all rational motives. Anyhow, what I claim is clear, is that there is *no* simple and handy appendage of a word called 'the meaning of (the word) 'x'. (…)

6.   Another case which often provides puzzles, is that of words like 'youth' and 'love': which sometimes mean the object loved, or the thing which is youthful, sometimes the passion 'love' or the quality 'youth'. These cases are of course easy (rather *like* 'healthy'). But suppose we take the noun 'truth': here is a case where the disagreements between different theorists have largely turned on whether they interpreted this as a name of a substance, of a quality, or of a relation.

7.   Lastly, I want to take a specially interesting sort of case, which is perhaps commoner and at the bottom of more muddles than we are aware of. Take the sense in which I talk of cricket bat and cricket ball and cricket umpire. The reason that all are called by the same name is perhaps that each has its part – its *own special* part – to play in the activity called cricketing: it is no good to say that cricket *simply* means 'used in cricket': for we cannot explain what we mean by 'cricket' *expect* by explaining the special parts played in cricketing by the bat, ball, etc. Aristotle's suggestion was that the word 'good' might be used in such a way: in which case it is obvious how far astray we should go if we look for a 'definition' of the word 'good' in any ordinary simple sense: or look for the way in which 'good' things are 'similar' to each other, in any ordinary sense. If we tried to find out by such methods what 'cricket' meant, we should very likely conclude that it too was a simple unanalyzable supersensible quality.

Another thing that becomes plain from such examples is that the apparently common-sense distinction between 'What is the meaning of the word x' and 'What particular things *are* x and to what degrees?' is not of universal application by any means. The question cannot be distinguished in such cases. Or a similar case would be some word like 'golfing': it is not sense to ask 'What is the meaning of golfing?' 'What things are golfing?' Though it *is* sense to ask what component activities go to constitute golfing, what implements are used in golfing ('golf' clubs, etc.) and in what ways. Aristotle suggests 'happiness' is a word of this kind: in which case it is evident how far astray we shall go if we treat it as though it were a word like 'whiteness'.

These summarily treated examples are enough to show how essential it is to have a thorough knowledge of the different reasons for which we call different things by the same name, before we can embark confidently on an inquiry. If we rush up with a demand for a definition in the simple manner of Plato or many other philosophers, if we use the rigid dichotomy 'same meaning, different meaning', or 'What x means', as distinguished from 'the things which are x', we shall simply make hashes of things. Perhaps some people are now discussing such questions seriously. All that is to be found in traditional logics is the mention that there are, besides univocal and equivocal words, 'also analogous words': which, without further explanation, is used to lump together all cases where a word has not always absolutely the same meaning, nor several absolutely different meanings. All that 'similarity' theorists manage is to say that all things called by some one name are similar to some one pattern, or are all more similar to each other than any of them is to anything else; which is *obviously* untrue. Anyone who wishes to see the complexity of the problem, has only got to look in a (good) dictionary under such a word as 'head': the different meanings of the word 'head' will be related to each other in all sorts of different ways at once.

To summarize the contentions of this paper then. Firstly, the phrase 'the meaning of a word' is a spurious phrase. Secondly and consequently, a re-examination is needed of phrases like the two which I discuss, 'being a part of the meaning of' and 'having the same meaning'. On these matters, dogmatists require prodding: although history indeed suggests that it may sometimes be better to let sleeping dogmatists lie.

H. Paul Grice

Using language to mean something

If pragmaticians such as Wittgenstein and Austin have pointed to the crucial role of context as well as the performative dimension of discourse, H. P. Grice's (1913–1988) work turns on the question of how meaning is inferred from what is said (1989). Discourse, in this view, operates not only with what the utterances explicitly say but also with the cognitive knowledge the participants actively construct to understand the meaning of an utterance. Grice is known for his theory of intentionality which postulates that the activity of those involved in communication aims to construct what others, through their utterances, actions or gestures, intend or mean to get across. The objective of communication, therefore, is to communicate 'intentions' against the background of a communicative pact between the participants who mutually presuppose that the others want to say something. Just like many conversation analysts, Grice points to conversational maxims as timeless laws of discourse, which the communication partners rely on in the process of communication, e.g. the principles of quantity ('make your contribution as informative as is required...') and quality ('do not say what you believe to be false...'), which were collapsed into one principle ('relevance') by Sperber and Wilson (1993[1986]). By pointing out the complex cognitive processes involved in communication, Grice not only contributes to explaining why the same words can mean radically different things when uttered in different contexts, but also paves the way for a cognitive turn in linguistic and discursive theory.

References

Grice, H. Paul. 1989. *Studies in the Way of Words*. Cambridge: Harvard University Press.
Sperber, Dan, and Deirdre Wilson. 1993[1986]. *Relevance: Communication and Cognition*. Oxford, Cambridge: Blackwell.

H. Paul Grice. 1957. 'Meaning.'
Philosophical Review 66: 377–388, presently published by Duke University Press: Durham.

Consider the following sentences:

'Those spots mean (meant) measles.'
'Those spots didn't mean anything to me, but to the doctor they meant measles.'
'The recent budget means that we shall have a hard year.'
(…)

Now contrast the above sentences with the following:

'Those three rings on the bell (of the bus) mean that the 'bus is full.''
'That remark, 'Smith couldn't get on without his trouble and strife,' meant that Smith found his wife indispensable.'
(…)

When the expressions 'means', 'means something', 'means that' are used in the kind of way in which they are used in the first set of sentences, I shall speak of the sense, or senses, in which they are used, as the *natural* sense, or senses, of the expressions in question. When the expressions are used in the kind of way in which they are used in the second set of sentences, I shall speak of the sense, or senses, in which they are used, as the *non-natural* sense, or senses, of the expressions in question. I shall use the abbreviation 'means$_{NN}$' to distinguish the non-natural sense or senses.

I propose, for convenience, also to include under the head of natural senses of 'mean' such senses of 'mean' as may be exemplified in sentences of the pattern '*A* means (meant) *to do* so-and-so (by *x*)', where *A* is a human agent. By contrast, as the previous examples show, I include under the head of non-natural senses of 'mean' any senses of 'mean' found in sentences of the patterns '*A* means (meant) something by *x*' or '*A* means (meant) by *x* that' (This is over-rigid, but it will serve as an indication.)

I do not want to maintain that *all* our uses of 'mean' fall easily, obviously, and tidily into one of the two groups I have distinguished; but I think that in most cases we should be at least fairly strongly inclined to assimilate a use of 'mean' to one group rather than to the other. The question which now arises is this: 'What more can be said about the distinction between the cases where we should say that the word is applied in a natural sense and the cases where we should say that the word is applied in a non-natural sense?' Asking this question will not of course prohibit us from trying to give an explanation of 'meaning$_{NN}$' in terms of one or another natural sense of 'mean'.

This question about the distinction between natural and non-natural meaning is, I think, what people are getting at when they display an interest in a distinction between 'natural' and 'conventional' signs. But I think my formulation is better. For some things which can mean$_{NN}$ something are not signs (e.g. words are not), and some are not conventional in any ordinary sense (e.g. certain gestures); while some things which mean naturally are not signs of what they mean (cf. the recent budget for example).

I want first to consider briefly, and reject, what I might term a causal type of answer to the question 'What is meaning$_{NN}$?' We might try to say, for instance, more or less with C. L. Stevenson (1944, Chapter 3), that for x to mean$_{NN}$ something, x must have (roughly) a tendency to produce in an audience some attitude (cognitive or otherwise) and a tendency, in the case of a speaker, to *be* produced *by* that attitude, these tendencies being dependent on 'an elaborate process of conditioning attending the – use of the sign in communication' (Stevenson, 1944: 57). This clearly will not do.

1.   Let us consider a case where an utterance, if it qualifies at all as meaning$_{NN}$ something, will be of a descriptive or informative kind and the relevant attitude, therefore, will be a cognitive one, for example, a belief. (I use 'utterance' as a neutral word to apply to any candidate for meaning$_{NN}$; it has a convenient act–object ambiguity.) It is no doubt the case that many people have a tendency to put on a tailcoat when they think they are about to go to a dance, and it is no doubt also the case that many people, on seeing someone put on a tailcoat, would conclude that the person in question was about to go to a dance. Does this satisfy us that putting on a tailcoat means$_{NN}$ that one is about to go to a dance (or indeed means$_{NN}$ anything at all)? Obviously not. It is no help to refer to the qualifying phrase 'dependent on an elaborate process of conditioning…'. For if all this means is that the response to the sight of a tailcoat being put on is in some way learned or acquired, it will not exclude the present case from being one of meaning$_{NN}$. But if we have to take seriously the second part of the qualifying phrase ('attending the use of the sign in communication'), then the account of meaning$_{NN}$ is obviously circular. We might just as well say, 'X has meaning$_{NN}$ if it is used in communication', which, though true, is not helpful.

2.   If this is not enough, there is a difficulty – really the same difficulty, I think – which Stevenson recognizes: how we are to avoid saying, for example, that 'Jones is tall' is part of what is meant by 'Jones is an athlete', since to tell someone that Jones is an athlete would tend to make him believe that Jones is tall. Stevenson here resorts to invoking linguistic rules, namely, a permissive rule of language that 'athletes may be non-tall'. This amounts to saying that we are not prohibited by rule from speaking of 'non-tall athletes'. But why are we not prohibited? Not because it is not bad grammar, or is not impolite, and so on, but presumably because it is not meaningless (or, if this is too strong, does not in any way violate the rules of meaning for the expressions concerned). But this seems to involve us in another circle. Moreover, one wants to ask why, if it is legitimate to appeal here to rules to distinguish what is meant from what is suggested, this appeal was not made earlier, in the case of groans, for example, to deal with which Stevenson originally introduced the qualifying phrase about dependence on conditioning.

A further deficiency in a causal theory of the type just expounded seems to be that, even if we accept it as it stands, we are furnished with an analysis only of statements about the *standard* meaning, or the meaning in general, of a 'sign'. No provision is made for dealing with statements about what a particular speaker or writer means by a sign on a particular occasion (which may well diverge from the standard meaning of the sign); nor is it obvious how the theory could be adapted to make such provision. One might even go further in criticism and maintain that the causal theory ignores the fact that the meaning (in general) of a sign needs to be explained in terms of what users of the sign do (or should) mean by it on particular occasions; and so the latter notion, which is unexplained by the causal theory, is in fact the fundamental one. I am sympathetic to this more radical criticism, though I am aware that the point is controversial.

I do not propose to consider any further theories of the 'causal tendency' type. I suspect no such theory could avoid difficulties analogous to those I have outlined without utterly losing its claim to rank as a theory of this type.

I will now try a different and, I hope, more promising line.

If we can elucidate the meaning of

'x meant$_{NN}$ something (on a particular occasion)' and
'x meant$_{NN}$ that so-and-so (on a particular occasion)'

and of

'A meant$_{NN}$ something by x (on a particular occasion)' and
'A meant$_{NN}$ by x that so-and-so (on a particular occasion)',

this might reasonably be expected to help us with

'x means$_{NN}$ (timeless) something (that so-and-so)',

'A means$_{NN}$ (timeless) by x something (that so-and-so)' and with the explication of 'means the same as', 'understands', 'entails' and so on. Let us for the moment pretend that we have to deal only with utterances which might be informative or descriptive.

A first shot would be to suggest that 'x meant$_{NN}$ something' would be true if x was intended by its utterer to induce a belief in some 'audience' and that to say what the belief was would be to say what x meant$_{NN}$'. This will not do. I might leave B's handkerchief near the scene of a murder in order to induce the detective to believe that B was the murderer; but we should not want to say that the handkerchief (or my leaving it there) meant$_{NN}$ anything or that I had meant$_{NN}$ by leaving it that B was the murderer. Clearly we must at least add that, for x to have meant$_{NN}$ anything, not merely must it have been 'uttered' with the intention of inducing a certain belief but also the utterer must have intended an 'audience' to recognize the intention behind the utterance.

This, though perhaps better, is not good enough. Consider the following cases:

1. Herod presents Salome with the head of St. John the Baptist on a charger.
2. Feeling faint, a child lets its mother see how pale it is (hoping that she may draw her own conclusions and help).
3. I leave the china my daughter has broken lying around for my wife to see.

Here we seem to have cases which satisfy the conditions so far given for meaning$_{NN}$. For example, Herod intended to make Salome believe that St. John the Baptist was dead and no doubt also intended Salome to recognize that he intended her to believe that St. John the Baptist was dead. Similarly for the other cases. Yet I certainly do not think that we should want to say that we have here cases of meaning$_{NN}$.

What we want to find is the difference between, for example, 'deliberately and openly letting someone know' and 'telling' and between 'getting someone to think' and 'telling'.

The way out is perhaps as follows. Compare the following two cases:

1. I show Mr. *X* a photograph of Mr. *Y* displaying undue familiarity to Mrs. *X*.
2. I draw a picture of Mr. *Y* behaving in this manner and show it to Mr. *X*.

I find that I want to deny that in (1) the photograph (or my showing it to Mr. *X*) meant$_{NN}$ anything at all; while I want to assert that in (2) the picture (or my drawing and showing it) meant$_{NN}$ something (that Mr. *Y* had been unduly unfamiliar), or at least that I had meant$_{NN}$ by it that Mr. *Y* had been unduly familiar. What is the difference between the two cases? Surely that in case (1) Mr. *X*'s recognition of my intention to make him believe that there is something between Mr. *Y* and Mrs. *X* is (more or less) irrelevant to the production of this effect by the photograph. Mr. *X* would be led by the photograph at least to suspect Mrs. *X* even if instead of showing it to him I had left it in his room by accident; and I (the photograph shower) would not be unaware of this. But it will make a difference to the effect of my picture on Mr. *X* whether or not he takes me to be intending to inform him (make him believe something) about Mrs. *X*, and not to be just doodling or trying to produce a work of art.

But now we seem to be landed in a further difficulty if we accept this account. For consider now, say, frowning. If I frown spontaneously, in the ordinary course of events, someone looking at me may well treat the frown as a natural sign of displeasure. But if I frown deliberately (to convey my displeasure), an onlooker may be expected, provided he recognizes my intention, *still* to conclude that I am displeased. Ought we not then to say, since it could not be expected to make any difference to the onlooker's reaction whether he regards my frown as spontaneous or as intended to be informative, that my frown (deliberate) does *not* mean$_{NN}$ anything? I think this difficulty can be met; for though in general a deliberate frown may have the same effect (as regards inducing belief in my displeasure) as a spontaneous frown, it can be expected to have the same effect only *provided* the audience takes it as intended to convey displeasure. That is, if we take away the recognition of intention, leaving the other circumstances (including the recognition of the frown as deliberate), the belief-producing tendency of the frown must be regarded as being impaired or destroyed.

Perhaps we may sum up what is necessary for A to mean something by x as follows: A must intend to induce by x a belief in an audience, and he must also intend his utterance to be recognized as so intended. But these intentions are not independent; the recognition is intended by A to play its part in inducing the belief, and if it does not do so something will have gone wrong with the fulfilment of A's intentions. Moreover, A's intending that the recognition should play this part implies, I think, that he assumes that there is some chance that it will in fact play this part, that he does not regard it as a foregone conclusion that the belief will be induced in the audience whether or not the intention behind the utterance is recognized. Shortly, perhaps, we may say that 'A meant$_{NN}$ something by x' is roughly equivalent to 'A uttered x with the intention of inducing a belief by means of the recognition of this intention'. (This seems to involve a reflexive paradox, but it does not really do so.)

Now perhaps it is time to drop the pretense that we have to deal only with 'informative' cases. Let us start with some examples of imperatives or quasi-imperatives. I have a very avaricious man in my room, and I want him to go; so I throw a pound note out of the window. Is there here any utterance with a meaning$_{NN}$? No, because in behaving as I did, I did not intend his recognition of my purpose to be in any way effective in getting him to go. This is parallel to the photograph case. If on the other hand I had pointed to the door or given him a little push, then my behaviour might well be held to constitute a meaningful$_{NN}$ utterance, just because the recognition of my intention would be intended by me to be effective in speeding his departure. Another pair of cases would be (1) a policeman who stops a car by standing in its way and (2) a policeman who stops a car by waving.

Or, to turn briefly to another type of case, if as an examiner I fail a man, I may well cause him distress or indignation or humiliation; and if I am vindictive, I may intend this effect and even intend him to recognize my intention. But I should not be inclined to say that my failing him meant$_{NN}$ anything. On the other hand, if I cut someone in the street I do feel inclined to assimilate this to the cases of meaning$_{NN}$ and this inclination seems to me dependent on the fact that I could not reasonably expect him to be distressed (indignant, humiliated) unless he recognized my intention to affect him in this way. (Cf., if my college stopped my salary altogether I should accuse them of ruining me; if they cut it by 2/6^{d} I might accuse them of insulting me; with some intermediate amounts I might not know quite what to say.)

Perhaps then we may make the following generalizations.

1. 'A meant$_{NN}$ something by x' is (roughly) equivalent to 'A intended the utterance of x to produce some effect in an audience by means of the recognition of this intention'; and we may add that to ask what A meant is to ask for a specification of the intended effect (though, of course, it may not always be possible to get a straight answer involving a 'that' clause, for example, 'a belief that …').

2. 'x meant something' is (roughly) equivalent to 'Somebody meant$_{NN}$ something by x.' Here again there will be cases where this will not quite work. I feel inclined to say that (as regards traffic lights) the change to red meant$_{NN}$ that the traffic was to stop; but it would be very unnatural to say, 'Somebody (e.g. the Corporation) meant$_{NN}$ by the red-light change that the traffic was to stop.' Nevertheless, there seems to be *some* sort of reference to somebody's intentions.

3. 'x means$_{NN}$ (timeless) that so-and-so' might as a first shot be equated with some statement or disjunction of statements about what 'people' (vague) intend (with qualifications about 'recognition') to effect by x. I shall have a word to say about this.

Will any kind of intended effect do, or may there be cases where an effect is intended (with the required qualifications) and yet we should not want to talk of meaning$_{NN}$? Suppose I discovered some person so constituted that, when I told him that whenever I grunted in a special way I wanted him to blush or to incur some physical malady, thereafter whenever he recognized the grunt (and with it my intention), he did blush or incur the malady. Should we then want to say that the grunt meant$_{NN}$ something? I do not think so. This points to the fact that for x to have meaning$_{NN}$ the intended effect must be something which in some sense is within the control of the audience, or that in some sense of 'reason' the recognition of the intention behind x is for the audience a reason and not merely a cause. It might look as if there is a sort of pun here ('reason for believing' and 'reason for doing'), but I do not think this is serious. For though no doubt from one point of view questions about reasons for believing are questions about evidence and so quite different from questions about reasons for doing, nevertheless, to recognize an utterer's intention in uttering x (descriptive utterance), to have a reason for believing that so-and-so, is at least quite like 'having a motive for' accepting so-and-so. Decisions 'that' seem to involve decisions 'to' (and this is why we can 'refuse to believe' and also be 'compelled to believe'). (The 'cutting' case needs slightly different treatment, for one cannot in any straightforward sense 'decide' to be offended; but one can refuse to be offended.) It looks then as if the intended effect must be something within the control of the audience, or at least the *sort* of thing which is within its control.

One point before passing to an objection or two. I think it follows that from what I have said about the connection between meaning$_{NN}$ and recognition of intention that (insofar as I am right) only what I may call the primary intention of an utterer is relevant to the meaning$_{NN}$ of an utterance. For if I utter x, intending (with the aid of the recognition of this intention) to induce an effect E, and intend this effect E to lead to a further effect F, then insofar as the occurrence of F is thought to be dependent solely on E, I cannot regard F as in the least dependent on the recognition of my intention to induce E. That is, if (say) I intend to get a man to do something by giving him some information, it cannot be regarded as relevant to the meaning$_{NN}$ of my utterance to describe what I intend him to do.

Now some question may be raised about my use, fairly free, of such words as 'intention' and 'recognition'. I must disclaim any intention of peopling all our talking life with armies of complicated psychological occurrences. I do not hope to solve any philosophical puzzles about intending, but I do want briefly to argue that no special difficulties are raised by my use of the word 'intention' in connection with meaning. First, there will be cases where an utterance is accompanied or preceded by a conscious 'plan' or explicit formulation of intention (e.g. I declare how I am going to use x, or ask myself how to 'get something across'). The presence of such an explicit 'plan' obviously counts fairly heavily in favour of the utterer's intention (meaning) being as 'planned'; though it is not, I think, conclusive; for example, a speaker who has declared an intention to use a familiar expression in an unfamiliar way may slip into the familiar use. Similarly in non-linguistic cases: if we are asking about an agent's intention, a previous expression counts heavily; nevertheless, a man might plan to throw a letter in the dustbin and yet take it to the post; when lifting his hand he might 'come to' and say *either* 'I didn't intend to do this at all' *or* 'I suppose I must have been intending to put it in.'

Explicitly formulated linguistic (or quasi-linguistic) intentions are no doubt comparatively rare. In their absence we would seem to rely on very much the same kinds of criteria as we do in the case of non-linguistic intentions where there is a general usage. An utterer is held to intend to convey what is normally conveyed (or normally intended to be conveyed), and we require a good reason for accepting that a particular use diverges from the general usage (e.g. he never knew or had forgotten the general usage). Similarly in non-linguistic cases: we are presumed to intend the normal consequences of our actions.

Again, in cases where there is doubt, say, about which of two or more things an utterer intends to convey, we tend to refer to the context (linguistic or otherwise) of the utterance and ask which of the alternatives would be relevant to other things he is saying or doing, or which intention in a particular situation would fit in with some purpose he obviously has (e.g. a man who calls for a 'pump' at a fire would not want a bicycle pump). Nonlinguistic parallels are obvious: context is a criterion in settling the question of why a man who has just put a cigarette in his mouth has put his hand in his pocket; relevance to an obvious end is a criterion in settling why a man is running away from a bull.

In certain linguistic cases we ask the utterer afterward about his intention, and in a few of these cases (the very difficult ones, like a philosopher asked to explain the meaning of an unclear passage in one of his works), the answer is not based on what he remembers but is more like a decision, a decision about how what he said is to be taken. I cannot find a non-linguistic parallel here; but the case is so special as not to seem to contribute a vital difference.

All this is very obvious; but surely to show that the criteria for judging linguistic intentions are very like the criteria for judging non-linguistic intentions is to show that linguistic intentions are very like non-linguistic intentions.

References

Stevenson, Charles L. 1944. *Ethics and Language*. New Haven: Yale University Press.

Section II

From structuralism to poststructuralism

Introduction

Saussure – a discourse theorist? Linguists are usually surprised to see that many social scientists, philosophers and historians count Ferdinand de Saussure (1857–1913) as being among the precursors of discourse research. If Saussure aimed to discover the laws of language (*langue*), understood as a code governing the production of grammatically correct sentences (*parole*), discourse linguists point out the specific contexts in which texts are used. In opposition to theories of language as an abstract grammatical system (in particular Noam Chomsky, b. 1928), they hold that meaning is not an inherent quality of signs, utterances and texts. Rather than being determined by a set of abstract rules, meaning is achieved within the interplay of texts and contexts and is thus considered a product of the specific circumstances in which language is used.

Today, few linguists still claim the heritage of Saussure, even in France, where the structural mainstream in linguistics and discourse analysis ended with the enunciative-pragmatic turn of the early 1980s (see the section on 'Enunciative Pragmatics'). Yet the picture is different if we consider the intellectual debate outside linguistics. As a source of intellectual inspiration for the social sciences and humanities, Saussure's model became popular during the controversy over structuralism in the 1960s in France (Angermuller, 2014). Promoted by social, cultural and literary theorists (such as Louis Althusser (1918–1990), Roland Barthes (1915–1980), Jean Baudrillard (1929–2007), Pierre Bourdieu (1930–2002), Jacques Derrida (1930–2004), Michel Foucault (1926–1984), Julia Kristeva (b. 1941), Jacques Lacan (1901–1981), Claude Lévi-Strauss (1908–2009) etc.), Saussure and his epigones in French linguistics, Émile Benveniste (1902–1976) and Algirdas Julien Greimas (1917–1992), attempted to explain the diversity of social and cultural phenomena by the use of a limited number of the smallest distinctive units, selected and combined according to certain rules just as a sentence is formed from words. The structuralists applied Saussure's formal model to non-linguistic objects, such as fashion in Barthes (1983) and furniture in Baudrillard (1996), and even whole social structures (Bourdieu, 1968). Thus, among non-linguists, Saussure has been perceived as a theorist of the general semiology of social life, of which linguistics is only a sub-discipline. It was this vision of a new transdisciplinary and rigorous science that sparked the theoretical imagination of such pioneers as Michel Foucault and Michel Pêcheux (1938–1983), who helped establish discourse analysis as a transdisciplinary field of research in Europe.

Saussure's semiotic model has inspired a number of transdisciplinary developments at the crossroads of language and society, such as psychoanalysis, especially Jacques Lacan's (1901–1981) prolongation of the Freudian project. More than Freud (1856–1939), Lacan insists on the symbolic dimension in the formation of the subject. For Lacan, the subject's discourse does not turn on a non-symbolic essence (such as repressed experiences, biological instincts or other hidden truths). Rather, by entering discourse, it tries to overcome its constitutive lack and represent itself as a unity. Lacanian psychoanalysis is in close affinity with the structural Marxism of Louis Althusser (1918–1990) and his disciples. Their objective was to overcome the determinism of traditional Marxism by pointing to the overdetermination of any one element by all other elements in the social system. Therefore, while Lacan criticises essentialist models of the subject, Althusser calls into question the humanist strands in social theory. For Althusser, subjects are constituted in 'ideology' understood as a practice of interpellation – like a policeman hailing us on the street: 'Hey, you there!', whereupon we inadvertently turn and recognise ourselves in an act of spontaneous self-evidence: 'It's me, of course'!

In light of these explorations, Saussure became a major intellectual reference for many new lines of research associated with the headings of structuralism and poststructuralism. If 'structuralism' was the term commonly preferred in the French field during the intellectual debate of the late 1960s, structuralist thinkers from France, as well as a few other Continental theorists, have been labelled 'poststructuralists' on the international scene since the 1970s. Given their focus on epistemological questions, structuralism and poststructuralism typically share the idea that the subject does not master its discourse. Rather, the 'subject' is an effect of discourse. From this perspective, an individual turns into a subject (with intentions, interests, consciousness, identity etc.) by occupying symbolically predefined subject positions. At the same time, structures are not closed, constituted and self-sufficient entities; they are patchworks articulated around lacks, fissures and gaps.

Structuralism and poststructuralism have made two significant contributions to discourse research. In the French context, these theorists established *discourse analysis* as a subdisciplinary field of linguistics, even though neither Foucault nor Pêcheux were initially linguists. At the outset, French discourse analysis was firmly rooted in text-based practices of formal linguistic analysis. As opposed to interpretive approaches, the representatives of this field make a point of the opaque materiality of (written) texts (see the next section on 'Enunciative Pragmatics'). The international reception of structuralism, by contrast, led to *poststructuralist discourse theory*. At the crossroads of literary, cultural and political investigations, poststructuralist discourse theory cites linguistic models such as Saussure's theory of difference in order to explain the symbolic construction of social, political and cultural order.

Discourse analysis in France. Related to the structuralist debate in France around 1970, French discourse analysis began to take shape in the 1960s. In line with Zellig Harris's (1909–1992) distributionalist method (1952), linguists tried to account for discursive structures beyond words and sentences, notably using quantitative methods from corpus linguistics. However, it was only against the background of the conjuncture of structuralism, Marxism and psychoanalysis, again around 1970, that discourse analysis was established as a field in its own right. Two young intellectuals, Michel Pêcheux and Michel Foucault who had started out as philosophers, crucially helped to delineate the contours of this new field in two works published in 1969: *Automatic Discourse Analysis* (Pêcheux, 1995[1969]) and *Archaeology of Knowledge* (Foucault, 1972[1969]).

While Pêcheux became the head of what is sometimes called the 'French school of discourse analysis' within linguistics, Foucault made discourse popular on the more general intellectual scene, both nationally and internationally. Both were much indebted to the 'anti-humanist' programme of structuralism. However, their contributions to discourse analysis differed in that Pêcheux's discourse theoretical project was consolidated as he moved *into* Saussureanism and called for a 'post-subjectivist approach to subjectivity' (Pêcheux, 1982[1975]), while for Foucault the discovery of the discursive dimension meant moving *away from* Saussureanism and adopting an enunciative-pragmatic approach to discourse which was to inform developments from the 1980s onwards (see the section on 'Enunciative Pragmatics'). Thanks to Pêcheux and his disciples, discourse analysis became an established subfield of French linguistics with a strong focus on the analysis of political discourse. And thanks to Foucault, discourse has become a central theoretical problematic for the entire spectrum of the social sciences and humanities.

Poststructuralist discourse theory. Foucault only published on discourse for a few years around 1970 and never founded any school in France. However, outside France, he became known as the leading representative of poststructuralist discourse theory, associated with such semiotic theorists as Derrida, Barthes and Greimas, who are generally not considered discourse theorists in the French context. Poststructuralist discourse theory originated in U.S. departments of literary criticism, which opened their doors to more intellectual explorations of (French) theory in the mid-1970s. The turn to discourse theory has since been pushed by those imbued in the Continental tradition as an alternative to the indigenous analytical and pragmatic trends in the Anglo-American world. It has attracted activists politicised by the new social movements as well as literary scholars becoming interested the mass media and other non-elite cultural texts.

In this context, poststructuralist discourse theory has sensitised the more philological practices in literary criticism to broader socio-historical contexts in which texts reveal their specific social significance. While the reception of Foucault has revolved around the question of power in its intricate historical interaction with knowledge, for instance in Said's (1935–2003) work on orientalism (1978) or in New Historicism (Greenblatt, 1989), Derrida's approach has been received as a more textualist approach to discourse and as a discursive critique that prolongs the traditions of close literary reading (see the Yale School of deconstruction; Bloom et al., 1979). Pointing to the inherent contradictions of any conceptual edifice, Derridean deconstructivism calls into question the inherent ideologies of 'text'. Therefore, if poststructuralist discourse theory critically interrogates notions of the subject as an intentional source of meaning, two types of anti-essentialist critique can be distinguished. While Foucault's genealogical critique reveals the historical constitution of the present, Derrida's deconstructive critique aims at decentring conceptual systems by pointing out the entanglement of any identity, origin and foundation in the play of semiotic differences.

In North America, these theoretical inputs have been taken up in the literary and cultural field and have crucially contributed to the intellectual popularity of discourse theory. Spivak (b. 1942) (1988), for instance, mobilises deconstructive tools to account for how the postcolonial other is represented in discourse, whereas many Cultural Studies scholars (e.g. Grossberg et al., 1992) cite Foucault's insights into the way knowledge is entangled in power structures. In Europe, Žižek (b. 1949) (1991) made Lacanian psychoanalysis popular by illustrating Lacanian concepts in mass-cultural artefacts like films and novels. Within gender studies, poststructuralist discourse theory has become popular among third-wave feminists who critically interrogate the essentialising notion of biological sex as well as binary oppositions such as man vs woman. These theorists generally adhere to the constructivist idea that, through discursive practices, social structures can be made and unmade.

In Europe, too, poststructuralist discourse theories have been propagated, though more by sociologists and political scientists, e.g. through the Birmingham School of Culture Studies. While the first generation of British Cultural Studies was interested in the everyday culture of the working class, the second generation, led by Stuart Hall (1932–2014) (1980), turned to the mass media and mass culture as early as the 1970s. Just like the first generation, the second generation called into question elite notions of culture. Culture is not a meaningful whole; it does not prescribe set ways of thinking or doing. Rather, it designates a terrain of conflicting practices and rules calling for creative acts of appropriation by the discourse participants. As a result of this turn towards poststructuralism, British Cultural Studies became interested in the question of representation, understood in its multiple sense of symbolic, cultural and aesthetic representation (*Darstellung*), as well as political representation (in the sense of *Vertretung*, Hall, 1997). In this rapprochement with Cultural Studies in North America, discourse is seen to be constitutive of social order. Rather than merely reflecting pre-discursive realities, discourses create social worlds by representing them, e.g. through mass-media texts circulating among large communities. At the same time, special emphasis is placed on the connections of language and power. While discourse participants are not just dupes, they are confronted with certain constraints that can privilege certain perspectives over others (e.g. the 'official' point of view in media coverage).

Another area of discourse theoretical exploration is Governmentality Studies, which emerged from the 1990s onwards in the wake of the posthumous publication of Foucault's lectures on governmentality at *Collège de France* (1977–1978) (Foucault, 2007[1977/78]), where he traced the genealogy of the (neo)liberalisation of contemporary societies. In liberal governmentality, the state no longer prescribes or prohibits; rather, it operates in the mode of 'freedom' and mobilises political, economic and legal resources to make sure that market-oriented production runs smoothly. Moreover, its governmental practices need to be backed up by a great deal of scientific knowledge, especially from the fledgling social sciences, such as demography, political sciences and economics. Discourse is seen as a knowledge-power complex in which legitimate knowledge and administrative power are inextricably linked in a *dispositif* in which subjects are encouraged to rule themselves.

Poststructuralist discourse theories have also received important impulses from post-Marxist approaches to hegemony, notably the discourse theoretical project of Laclau (1935–2014) and Mouffe (b. 1943) (Gramsci 1978; Laclau and Mouffe, 1985). For Laclau/Mouffe, political practice aims at the construction of hegemony, i.e. the articulation of different elements (e.g. feminism, veganism, anti-imperialism, ecologism…) as a hegemonic bloc (e.g. the green hegemony). Laclau/Mouffe's theory of hegemony is based on Saussure's axiom according to which there is no meaning without difference. Political and social phenomena are discursive phenomena since the social order is constructed through political practices following a hegemonic logic of difference and equivalence. In the process of articulating hegemony, more and more elements, never fully determined and with no inherent affinity, are grouped together as equivalent. Different from another hegemonic project, the emerging hegemonic bloc appears as a solid 'naturalised' structure. While Laclau/Mouffe, Butler (b. 1956) and Hall are symptomatic of the linguistic turn in the social sciences, they do not engage in fine-grained linguistic analysis of text and talk. Rather, they make no recourse to linguistic models in order to rethink basic problems in social, cultural and political theory.

The following selections focus on pioneering theoretical contributions which can be seen as relevant to both French discourse analysis and poststructuralist discourse theory. We have not, therefore, included the more semiotic strands of structuralism and poststructuralism which fail to account for the uses of text(s) in context(s). While Lacan and Althusser were important precursors of discourse theory in France, Foucault and Pêcheux were the theoretical founders of the field of discourse analysis in France. Hall, Butler and Laclau are leading representatives of poststructuralist discourse theory, each having contributed to a school or a new field of study.

References

Angermuller, Johannes. 2014. *The Field of Theory*. London, New York: Continuum.

Barthes, Roland. 1983. *The Fashion System*. New York: Hill and Wang.

Baudrillard, Jean. 1996. *The System of Objects*. London: Verso.

Bloom, Harold, Paul de Man, Jacques Derrida, Geoffrey H. Hartman, and J. Hillis Miller, eds. 1979. *Deconstruction and Criticism*. London: Routledge, Kegan Paul.

Bourdieu, Pierre. 1968. 'Structuralism and the Theory of Sociological Knowledge.' *Social Research* 35: 681–706.

Foucault, Michel. 1972[1969]. *The Archaeology of Knowledge & the Discourse on Language*. New York: Pantheon.

Foucault, Michel. 2007[1977/78]. *Security, Territory, Population. Lectures at the College de France*. Basingstoke: Palgrave, Macmillan. DOI: 10.1057/9780230245075

Gramsci, Antonio. 1978. *Selections from the Political Writings*. London: Lawrence and Wishart.

Greenblatt, Stephen. 1989. *Shakespearean Negotiations: The Circulation of Social Energy in Renaissance England*. Berkeley: University of California Press.

Grossberg, Lawrence, Cary Nelson, and Paula Treichler, eds. 1992. *Cultural Studies*. New York, London: Routledge.

Hall, Stuart, ed. 1997. *Representation: cultural representations and signifying practices*. Milton Keynes: Open University Press.

Hall, Stuart, Dorothy Hobson, Andrew Lowe, and Paul Willis, eds. 1980. *Culture, Media, Language*. London: Hutchinson.

Harris, Zellig S. 1952. 'Discourse Analysis.' *Language* 28: 1–30. DOI: 10.2307/409987

Laclau, Ernesto, and Chantal Mouffe. 1985. *Hegemony and Socialist Strategy. Towards a Radical Democratic Politics*. London, New York: Verso.

Pêcheux, Michel. 1995[1969]. *Automatic Discourse Analysis*. Amsterdam; Atlanta, GA Rodopi.

Pêcheux, Michel. 1982[1975]. *Language, semantics and ideology. Stating the obvious*. London: Macmillan.

Said, Edward W. 1978. *Orientalism*. London: Penguin.

Spivak, Gayatri Chakravorty. 1988. 'Can the Subaltern Speak?'. In *Marxism and the Interpretation of Culture*, edited by Cary Nelson and Lawrence Grossberg, 271–313. Urbana: University of Illinois Press.

Žižek, Slavoj. 1991. *Looking Awry. An Introduction to Jacques Lacan through Popular Culture*. Cambridge, MA, London: MIT Press.

Jacques Lacan

The divided subject

Jacques Lacan (1901–1981) was one of the pioneers of psychoanalysis, claiming the return to Freud in France. In his clinical practice and theoretical explorations, Lacan emphasizes the role of language (the 'symbolic') as a medium in which the subject is constituted as an 'illusion of inner unity'. According to Lacan, the subject is split or divided in a fundamental way, and it is through producing a discourse (a 'signifying chain') that it tries to overcome ('suture') its constitutive lack. The subject is not controlled by biological drive ('sex'), nor is it driven by the reality of biographical experience which can be resuscitated by the analyst. Rather, if it keeps hinging on certain gaps and nodal points in the discourse, the objective is to trigger a dynamic of symbolic reconfiguration. Going against academic 'ego-psychology', which postulates the stable interiority of the subject, Lacan argues that it is constituted in the interplay of three registers: the symbolic (language), the imaginary (identifications with the Other) and the real (that which resists representation).

Lacan is a notoriously difficult author, partly due to his non-academic style, which privileges puns, catchy but ambiguous phrases and at times counterintuitive formulae. Given his reputation as an intellectual obscurantist, it cannot be emphasized enough that Lacan's lasting influence relates to his seminars, where he proved his intellectual talent as a theoretical improviser and which were not meant for publication but taken up and popularized by such disciples as Slavoj Žižek (1989; also see Althusser, Laclau, Butler). In this selection, which offers a glimpse of his sometimes wild conceptual style, Lacan comments on the theory of the four discourses, of 'the master, the university, the hysteric and the analyst', which designate universal relations between subject, signifier and the object of desire. While he criticizes the idea of organic intersubjectivity between discourse participants, he explores the idea of a discourse 'being founded from a structure'. Indeed, Lacan has a non-historical understanding of discourse as a universal structure in which the subject is invested through desire.

References

Žižek, Slavoj. 1989. *The Sublime Object of Ideology*. London, New York: Verso.

Jacques Lacan. 1970–1971. *Seminar XVIII. On a discourse that might not be a semblance*, selected 1–8. Online-source, translated by Cormac Gallagher.

Seminar 1: Wednesday 13 January 1971
[Lacan writes on the board]

D'un discours qui ne serait pas du semblant
(On a discourse that might not be a semblance)

A discourse, it is not mine that is at stake. I think I made you sense well enough last year what should be understood by this term *discourse*. I remind you of the discourse of the Master and what we could call its four positions, the displacements of its term with respect to a structure, reduced to being tetrahedral. I left whoever wanted to work on it to specify what motivates … these … slidings (*glissements*) which could have been more diversified, I reduced them to four. If no one has worked on it, I will perhaps this year give an indication in passing about the privileged status of these four.

I only took up these references with respect to what was my end, stated under the title of *The reverse side of psychoanalysis*. The discourse of the Master is not the reverse side of psychoanalysis, it is where there is demonstrated the torsion that is proper, I would say, to the discourse of psychoanalysis, what ensures that this discourse poses the question of a front and a back (*un endroit et un envers*) because you know the importance, the emphasis, that is put in the theory, ever since Freud stated it, the importance and the stress that is put on the notion of double inscription. Now what I wanted you to put your finger on, is the possibility of a double inscription, on the front, on the back, without an edge being crossed. It is the structure well known for a long time, that I only had to use, which is called the Moebius strip.

These places and these elements, where there is outlined that what is properly speaking discourse, can in no way be referred from a subject, even though it determines him. This, no doubt, is the ambiguity of that through which I introduced what I thought I should make understood within psychoanalytic discourse. Remember my terms, at the period that I entitled a certain report as the function and the field of speech and language in psychoanalysis. At the time I wrote *intersubjectivity*, and God knows the number of false tracks that the statement of terms like that can give rise to. I hope I will be excused for having been the first to make these tracks. I was not able to go ahead except through a misunderstanding. *Inter*, certainly, in effect, is the only thing that subsequently allowed me to talk about an inter-significance (*intersignifiance*), subjectivity from its consequences, the signifier being what represents a subject for another signifier where the subject is not. This indeed is how it is, because of the fact that where he is represented he is absent, that nevertheless being represented, he thus finds himself divided. As for discourse, it is not simply that it can henceforth only be judged in the light of its unconscious sources, it is also the fact that it can no longer be stated as anything else than what is articulated from a structure where somewhere he finds himself alienated in an irreducible fashion. Hence my introductory statement: *On a discourse* – I stop – it is not mine. It is from this statement, a discourse not being able, as such, to be a discourse of any particular person, but being founded from a structure, and from the emphasis that is given by the division, the sliding of certain of its terms, it is from this that I am starting this year for what is entitled '*On a discourse that will not be a semblance*'.

For those who were not able last year to follow these statements which were made previously, I indicate that the appearance, which dates already for more than a month, of *Scilicet 2/3*, will give them the written references. *Scilicet 2/3*, because it is a writing, it is an event, if not an advent of discourse. First of all by the fact, that it is the one that I find myself to be the instrument of, without avoiding the fact that it requires the pressure of your numbers, in other words that you should be there and very precisely, under this aspect, a singular aspect of which creates this pressure, undoubtedly with, let us say, the incidences of our history which is something that can be touched, which renews the question of what is involved in discourse in so far as it is the discourse of the Master, this something that can only be made of something that one questions oneself about in naming it. Do not go on too quickly to make use of the word 'revolution'. But it is clear that it is necessary to discern what it is in short that allows me to pursue my statements, with this formula *On a discourse which will not be a semblance*. Two features are to be noted here in this issue of *Scilicet*. I put to the test, after all, more or less, something which is moreover my discourse of last year, in a setting which precisely is characterised by the absence of what I called this pressure of your presence. And to give it its full emphasis, I will say it in these terms, what this presence signifies, I would pinpoint as a pressurised surplus enjoying (*plus-de-jouir pressé*). Because it is precisely from this figure that there can be judged, if it goes beyond a discomfort, as they say, as regards too much semblance in the discourse in which you are inscribed, the University discourse, the one that is easy to denounce for neutrality, for example, that this discourse cannot claim to be sustained by a competitive selection when all that is at stake are signs that are addressed to those who are in the know, in terms of a formation of the subject, when it is something quite different that is at stake. Nothing allows us to go beyond this kind of discomfort of semblances – so that something can be hoped for which allows us to get out of it – than to posit that a certain style, that a certain style that is required in the advancement of a discourse, does not split, in a dominant position in this discourse, what is involved in this triage, these globules of surplus enjoying, in the name of which you find yourselves caught up in the University discourse. It is precisely that someone, starting from the analytic discourse, places himself with respect to you in the position in an analysand. This is not new, I already said it but no one paid any attention to it. This is what constitutes the originality of this teaching. This is what justifies what you contribute to it by your pressure and that is why in speaking on the radio, I put to the test this subtraction precisely of this presence, of this space into which you press yourselves, cancelled out and replaced by the pure It exists (*Il existe*) of this inter-significance that I spoke about earlier in order that the subject can vacillate in it. It is simply a switching of points towards something whose possible import we will learn in the future.

There is another feature of what I called this event, this advent of discourse, it is this printed thing that is called *Scilicet*, it is, as a certain number already know, that people write in it without singing. What does that mean? That each of these names that are put in a column on the last page of these three issues that constitute one year, can be permuted with each of the others, affirming in this way that no discourse can be that of an author. This is a wager. Here, it speaks (*ça parle*). In the other case, it is … here the future will tell if it is the formula that, let us say, in five or six years all the other journals will adopt. I mean the good journals. It is a gamble, we shall see!

I am not trying in what I am saying to escape from what is experienced, sensed in my statements, as accentuating, as sticking to the *artefact* of discourse. This means of course, it is the least that can be said, that doing this rules out my claiming to cover all of it, it cannot be a system and in this regard it is not a philosophy. It is clear for whoever attempts to renew what is involved in discourse, this implies that one moves around, I would say, in a *désunivers*, it is not the same thing as *divers* (diverse). But I would not even reject this diverse and not simply because of what it implies in terms of diversion. It is very clear also that I am not talking about everything. It is even in what I state, it resists anyone saying everything about it. You can put your finger on that every day. Even on the fact that I state that I am not saying everything, that is something different, as I already said, that comes from the fact that the truth is only a half-saying.

This discourse then, which limits itself to acting only in the artefact, is in short only the prolongation of the position of the analyst, in so far as it is defined by putting the weight of its surplus enjoying at a certain place. It is nevertheless the position that here I cannot sustain, very precisely by not being in this position of the analyst. As I said earlier, except for the fact that you lack knowledge about it, it is rather you who will be in it, by the pressure of your numbers. This having been said, what can be the import of what, in this reference, I am stating?

On a discourse which might not be a semblance, that can be stated from my place and in function of what I previously stated. It is a fact in any case that I am stating it. Note that it is a fact also *because* I state it. You may be completely hoodwinked by it, namely, think that there is nothing more than the fact that I am stating it. Only, if

I spoke in connection with discourse about the artefact, it is because for discourse, there is no fact, as I might say, already there, there is only a fact from the fact of saying it, the stated fact is entirely a fact of discourse. This is what I am designating by the term artefact, and of course, this is what has to be reduced. Because if I speak about artefact, it is not to give rise in it to the idea of something that might be different, a nature, that you would be wrong to get engaged in with a view to tackling its obstacles, because you would never get out of it. The question is not set up in terms: is it or is it not discourse, but in the following: it is said or it is not said. I start from what is said, in discourse whose artefact is supposed to be sufficient for you to be there; a cut here, because I am not adding, that you should be here in the state of *pressurised surplus enjoying*. I said a cut because it is questionable whether it is already as pressurised surplus enjoying that my discourse gathers you together. It is not decided, whatever one or other may think, that it is this discourse, the one made up of the series of statements that I present you, that places you where? – in this position from which it can be questioned by the 'not talking' of the discourse which might not be a semblance.

D'un semblant, what does that mean in this statement? A semblance of discourse, for example. You know that this is the position described as logical positivism. The fact is that if starting from a signifier, to be put to the test of something that decides by yes or no, what cannot present itself for this test, this is what is defined as meaning nothing. And with that, people think they have finished with a certain number of questions described as metaphysical. This is certainly not what I hold to. I want to point out to you that the position of logical positivism is untenable, in any case starting from analytic experience in particular.

If analytic experience finds itself implicated by taking its claims to nobility from the Oedipal myth, it is indeed because it preserves the cutting edge of the oracle's enunciation, and I would say more, that in it interpretation always remains at the same level. It is only true by its consequences, like every oracle. Interpretation is not put to the test of a truth that can be settled by a yes or a no, it unleashes truth as such. It is true only in so far as it is truly followed. We will see later that the schemas of implication, I mean of logical implication, in their most classical form, these schemas themselves require the foundation of this truthfulness in so far as it belongs to the word, even if it is properly speaking senseless. The passage from the moment where the truth is settled by its simple unleashing, to that of a logic that is going to try to embody this truth, is precisely the moment when discourse, *qua* representative of representation, is dismissed, disqualified. But if it can be so, it is because some part of it is always there, and this is what is called repression. It is no longer a representation that it represents, it is this continuation of discourse that is characterised as effect of truth.

The effect of truth is not a semblance. The Oedipus complex is there to teach us, if you will allow me, to teach us that it is red blood. Only there you are, red blood does not reject the semblance, it colours it, it makes it re-semble (*re-semblant*), it propagates it. A little bit of sawdust and the circus starts up again. This indeed it is why it is at the level of the artefact of the structure of discourse, that the question can be raised about a discourse that might not be a semblance. In the meantime, there is no semblance of discourse, there is no meta-language to judge it, there is no Other of the Other, there is no true of the true.

I amused myself one day by making the truth speak. I ask where is the paradox, what could be more true than stating 'I am lying'? The classical quibbling that is stated under the term of paradox is only embodied if you put this *I am lying* on paper, as something written. Everyone knows that there is nothing truer that one can say on some occasions than to say: 'I am lying'. It is even very certainly the only truth that in this case is not broken (*brisée*). Everyone knows that in saying: 'I am not lying', one is absolutely not protected from saying something false. What does that mean? The truth that is at stake, when it speaks, the one that I said speaks I, which states itself as an oracle, *who* speaks?

This semblance is the signifier in itself. Who can fail to see that what characterises this signifier that, as far as linguists are concerned, I use in a way that embarrasses them, there were some who wrote these lines designed to clearly warn that undoubtedly Ferdinand de Saussure did not have the slightest idea about it. What do we know about it? Ferdinand de Saussure was like me, he did not say everything; the proof is that people found in his papers, things that were never said in his classes. People think that the signifier is a nice little thing that has been tamed by structuralism, people think that it is the Other, *qua* Other, and the battery of signifiers, and everything that I explain, of course. Naturally it comes down from heaven, because from time to time I am an idealist!

Louis Althusser

The subjectivity effect of discourse

As much as he was influenced by Lacan's theory of the subject, Louis Althusser (1918–1990) represented a rather different type of intellectual: an academic philosopher who taught at the prestigious Ecole Normale Supérieure in Paris and who inspired the minds of some of the brightest philosophy students of the time (such as Jacques Rancière, Etienne Balibar) with his clear didactic style. If Lacan constantly crossed the line between theoretical and clinical practice, Althusser's project cannot be understood without the delicate balancing act performed between philosophy and politics. An expert of Spinoza and Marx and a major protagonist of the structuralist debate, Althusser was also involved in the French Communist Party (as were many of his contemporaries). While his ambition was to refound Marxism as an anti-dialectical and anti-humanist project, he shared with Lacan the idea that the 'subject' was a problem to be explained rather than the solution to a problem (Althusser, 1996). In *Reading Capital* (Althusser and Balibar, 1997[1965]), he and his friends outlined a 'symptomal reading,' which aimed to reveal the lacunae of the unsaid in Marx's discourse. His theory of ideology made a seminal contribution to Marxist theory (Althusser, 1984). In Althusser's famous definition, ideology defines the imaginary relationship the subject entertains with his position in the social. Ideology is universal in that all human beings need to be symbolically placed in the social structure. In our selection, published posthumously and found among his correspondence, he delineates the contours of a theory of discourse whereby the subject is seen as an effect of language use. While Althusser is strongly influenced by Lacan, the crucial difference between both theories needs to be pointed out: For Lacan, the subject is a discourse-producing being, whereas for Althusser discourse determines and creates the subject in discursive acts of interpellation.

References

Althusser, Louis. 1984. *Essays on Ideology*. London: Verso.
Althusser, Louis. 1996. *Writings on Psychoanalysis: Freud and Lacan*. New York: Columbia University Press.
Althusser, Louis, and Etienne Balibar. 1997[1965]. *Reading Capital*. London: Verso.

Louis Althusser. 2003[1966]. 'Three Notes on the Theory of Discourses.'
In *The Humanist Controversy and Other Writings (1966–67)*, 33–84, selected 47–53.
London, New York: Verso.

The character of the unconscious

To determine the nature of the theoretical elements that must be assembled in order to constitute the general theory of psychoanalysis, we have to set out from the characteristics of the object of the regional theory of psychoanalysis: the unconscious.

It is well known that this regional theory has been developed on the basis of observations and experiences provided by the practice of the cure as well as observations provided by other phenomena external to the cure (the effects of the unconscious in 'everyday' life, art, religion, and so on).

We can characterize the unconscious as follows:

a. The unconscious is manifested, that is, *exists* in its *effects,* both normal and pathological: these effects are discernible in dreams, all the various forms of symptoms, and all the different kinds of 'play' (including 'wordplay').

b. This manifestation is not that of an essence whose effects are its phenomena. *That which exists* is the mechanisms of a system that functions by producing these effects. These mechanisms are themselves determinate. It may be said that, in the narrow sense of the word, *that which exists* is the formations of the unconscious – in other words, the determinate systems that function by producing certain determinate effects. 'The unconscious' designates nothing other than the theoretical object which allows us to think the formations of the unconscious, that is, systems functioning in accordance with mechanisms producing effects.

c. The unconscious is a structure (or system) combining determinate elements subject to determinate laws of combination and functioning in accordance with determinate mechanisms.

d. The unconscious is a structure whose elements are *signifiers*.

e. Inasmuch as its elements are *signifiers,* the laws of combination of the unconscious and the mechanisms of its functioning depend on a general theory of the signifier.

f. Inasmuch as these signifiers are the signifiers of the *unconscious,* not of some other system of signifiers (for example language [*la langue*], ideology, art, science, etc.), the unconscious depends on the general theory that allows us to think this specific difference. What this general theory is is a question we shall provisionally leave in abeyance, but it does not seem as if a general theory of the signifier can by itself produce (by deduction) the specific difference that distinguishes the discourse of science from the discourses of ideology, art, and the unconscious. It should make this difference possible through the play of the possible variations inscribed in the theory of discourse – but it cannot construct it.

g. In order to determine which general theory will allow us to specify the difference that produces the characteristic form of the discourse of the unconscious as distinct from other forms of discourse, we must try to bring out this difference by a process of reduction, and then compare it to what the theory of the signifier is capable of producing as the required theoretical effect.

h. If we compare the different existing *forms* of discourse – that is, the forms of unconscious discourse, ideological discourse, aesthetic discourse and scientific discourse – we can demonstrate the existence of *a common effect: every discourse produces a subjectivity-effect.* Every discourse has, as its necessary correlate, a subject, which is one of the effects, if not the major effect, of its functioning. Ideological discourse 'produces' or 'induces' a subject-effect, a subject; so do the discourse of science, the discourse of the unconscious, etc.

i. The theory of the production of the subjectivity-effect falls within the province of the theory of the signifier.

j. If we compare the various subject-effects produced by the different forms of discourse, we observe that (i) the relationship these subjects bear to the discourses in question is not the same; (ii) in other words, the subject position 'produced' or induced by the discourse vis-à-vis that discourse varies. Thus the ideological subject *in person* forms part of ideological discourse, *is present in person* in it, since it is itself a determinate signifier of this discourse. We observe that the subject of scientific discourse, in contrast, is *absent in person* from scientific discourse, for there is no signifier designating it (it is an evanescent subject which is inscribed in a signifier only on condition that it disappear from the [signifying] chain the moment it appears there – otherwise science slides into ideology). The subject of aesthetic discourse may be said to be present in aesthetic discourse *through the mediation of others* [*par personnes interposées*] (always in the plural). The subject of unconscious discourse occupies a position that is different from all those described so far: it is 'represented' in the chain of signifiers by *one* signifier which 'stands in' for it [*qui en tient lieu*], which is its 'lieu-tenant' [*son lieu-tenant*]. Thus it is absent from the discourse of the unconscious by 'delegation' [*par 'lieu-tenance'*]. The theory of the signifier, which must account for the subject-effect of every discourse, must also account for these different *forms of the subject* as so many *possibilities* of variation of the subject-form.

k. The differential nature of the subject-effect, and the place (position) that the subject which it characteristically 'produces' as an effect occupies with respect to a given discourse, must be correlated with assignable *differences of structure* in the structures of that discourse. In other words, the structure of scientific discourse must differ from the structures of ideological discourse, aesthetic discourse, and the discourse of the unconscious. It is this difference of structure which allows us to characterize (and designate) the different discourses differently; in other words, it is this difference which makes it possible to talk about scientific discourse on the one hand and ideological discourse on the other, about aesthetic discourse and the discourse of the unconscious.

For example: ideological discourse, in which the subject-effect is present in person and is thus a signifier of this discourse, the main signifier of this discourse, possesses a structure of *speculary centring*; the subject induced is duplicated by a producing subject (the empirical subject is duplicated by the transcendental subject, the man-subject by God, etc.).

For example: scientific discourse, in which the subject-effect is absent in person and thus is not a signifier of this discourse, possesses a decentred structure [*une structure de décentration*] (that of a *system of abstract relations,* whose elements are concepts, none of which is 'constituent': as soon as a concept becomes 'constituent', we are in the realm of ideological discourse).

For example: aesthetic discourse, in which the subject-effect is present through the mediation of others (by way of a combination of *several* signifiers), possesses an *ambiguous structure of cross-references,* in which each presumable 'centre' is such only by virtue of the presence, that is, the negation of some other 'centre', which stands in the same relation of indecision [*indécision*] with regard to the first. When the work of art possesses a single centre, it lapses from aesthetic discourse into ideological discourse. When it evicts every subject from its domain, it lapses into scientific discourse.

For example: [in] the discourse of the unconscious, in which the subject-effect is absent by 'delegation', we are dealing with a pseudo-centred structure, subtended by a *structure of flight* or 'lack' [*béance*] (a metonymic structure?).

I.   It seems that it is at last possible to establish a pertinent relation between the structures of these different discourses on the one hand, and, on the other, the *nature* of the *signifiers* comprising the characteristic elements of each of these structures.

The signifiers of language [*langue*] are morphemes (material: phonemes).
The signifiers of science are concepts (material: words).
The signifiers of aesthetic discourse are extremely varied (material: words, sounds, colours, etc.).
The signifiers of ideological discourse are also varied (material: gestures, modes of behaviour, feelings, words and, generally speaking, any other element of other practices and other discourses?).
The signifiers of the unconscious are fantasies (material: the imaginary).

m. With the reservations required whenever one employs the concept *function*, it may be suggested that the reason for the structural specificities (and their subject-effects) has basically to do with the specific function of the formations of which these structures provide the concept. This function can be defined only by the place occupied by the signifying structure considered (i) with respect to other signifying structures; (ii) with respect to other, non-signifying structures, and by its *articulation* with these structures (place-articulation).

n. Thus we can distinguish different functions:

   – of knowledge (science)
   – of recognition-misrecognition (ideology)
   – of recognition-perception (art?)
   – of a circulation of signifiers (language?) corresponding to the different structures.

o. We may, very cautiously, risk a suggestion as to which mode of articulation is at work in the case of the structure of the unconscious.

   This mode could well be the following: In every social formation, the base requires the support-*[Träger]* function as a function to be assumed, as a place to be occupied in the technical and social division of labour. This requirement remains abstract: the base defines the *Träger*-functions (the economic base, and the political or ideological superstructure *as well)*, but the question of *who* must assume and carry out this function, and how the assumption of it might come about, is a matter of *perfect indifference* to the structure (base or super- structure) that defines these functions: it 'doesn't want to know anything about it' (as in the army).

   It is ideology which performs the function of *designating* the subject (in general) that is to occupy this function: to that end, it must *interpellate it* as subject, providing it with the reasons-of-a-subject for assuming the function. Ideology interpellates individuals by constituting them as subjects (ideological subjects, and therefore subjects of its discourse) and providing them with the reasons-of-a-subject (interpellated as a subject) for assuring the functions defined by the structure as functions-*of-a-Träger*. These reasons-of-a-subject appear explicitly in its ideological discourse, which is therefore necessarily a discourse that relates to the subject to which it is addressed, and therefore necessarily includes the subject as a signifier of this discourse; that is why the subject must appear in person among the signifiers of ideological discourse. In order for the individual to be constituted as an interpellated subject, it must recognize itself as a subject in ideological discourse, must figure in it: whence a first speculary relation, thanks to which the interpellated subject can see itself in the discourse of interpellation. But ideology is not a commandment (which would still be a form of the 'I don't want to know anything about it'); this recognition is not an act of pure force (there is no such thing as pure force), not a pure and simple injunction, but an enterprise of con-viction-persuasion: accordingly, it must *provide its own guarantees* for the subject it interpellates. The centring structure of ideology is a structure of *guarantee,* but in the form of interpellation, that is, in a form such that it contains the subject it interpellates (and 'produces' as an effect) in its discourse. Hence the *duplication of the subject* within the structure of ideology: God, in His various forms. 'I am that I am', the subject *par excellence,* Who provides the subject the guarantee that He is truly a subject, and that He is the subject Whom the Subject is addressing: 'I have shed this particular drop of blood for you'; 'God trieth the hearts and reins' (compare the speculary relations of the same order [between] the transcendental subject / transcendental logic and the empirical subject/formal logic), and so on.

Ideology is articulated with the economic and political structures in that it enables the '*Träger*'-function to function by transforming it into a *subject-function.*

It would be interesting to examine the case of *Träger*-function *of ideology.* A reduplication function of ideology exists which enables the *Träger* of the ideological as such to be transformed into a subject, that is, an *ideology of the ideologue:* we should try to establish whether Marx did not take this reduplication for ideology itself (with all the illusions that that would involve), and whether this reduplication is not (at least under certain circumstances) one of the elements of the articulation of scientific discourse with the ideological (when an ideologue 'advances' in the direction of scientific discourse through the 'critique' of ideology, which is then conflated with the critique of the ideology *of* the ideologue, of the *Träger*-function of ideology).

I would propose the following idea: that the *subject-function* which is the char-acteristic effect of ideological discourse in turn requires, produces or induces a characteristic effect, the unconscious-effect or the effect *subject-of-the-unconscious,* that is, the peculiar structure which makes the discourse of the unconscious pos-sible. The latter function makes it possible for the subject-function to be guaran-teed amid misrecognition.

Michel Pêcheux

From ideology to discourse

Michel Pêcheux's (1938–1983) career as a discourse researcher began with his *Automatic Discourse Analysis* (Pêcheux, 1995[1969]), a both visionary and technical work, which attempted to operationalize Harris's distributionalist method but found few followers. In subsequent years, Pêcheux turned to more theoretical explorations in line with Althusser's Marxism, which integrated structuralist and psychoanalytical ideas. With a firm rooting in structuralist ideas, Pêcheux placed discourse against the background of a class society in which what is said and thought is inextricably linked to one's social position (Haroche et al., 1971). During the 1970s, while claiming the heritage of Saussure, Marx and Lacan, Pêcheux became the leader of a group of discourse linguists who were especially interested in the question of interdiscourse and heterogeneity: discourse, in this view, is never one with itself. Following Althusser, Pêcheux considered the subject as a discursive effect and pleaded for a strictly anti-hermeneutic procedure: texts are to be taken in their opaque materiality (see Authier in the section on 'Enunciative Pragmatics'). By means of formal deictic markers of enunciation, texts reflect both the interdiscursive and heterogeneous nature of discourse, which is never the expression of one party only but always operates on different discursive levels at the same time (Conein et al., 1981).

References

Conein, Bernard, Jean-Jacques Courtine, Françoise Gadet, Jean-Marie Marandin, and Michel Pêcheux. 1981. *Matérialités discursives, Actes du Colloque des 24–26 avril 1980, Paris X-Nanterre*. Lille: Presses Universitaires de Lille.
Haroche, Claudine, Paul Henry, and Michel Pêcheux. 1971. 'La sémantique et la coupure saussurienne: langue, langage, discours.' *Langages* 24: 93–106. DOI: 10.3406/lgge.1971.2608
Pêcheux, Michel. 1995[1969]. *Automatic Discourse Analysis*. Amsterdam; Atlanta, GA Rodopi.

Michel Pêcheux and Catherine Fuchs. 1975. 'Mises au point et perspectives
à propos de l'analyse automatique du discours.'
Langages 37: 7–80, selected 9–16, 20–22.

Development and perspectives of the automatic analysis of discourse

The point of the first part consists of the relationship between the three areas we previously identified and reflected in the general title of the first part.[1] It should be immediately noted that, under present conditions of academic work, this all combines to
make the theoretical articulation between these areas rather difficult. Besides the fact
that this articulation may appear to some to be of doubtful theoretical taste, the fact
remains that, with the best political and theoretical intentions in the world, it is difficult
to remove organizational and epistemological barriers related to the balkanization of
knowledge and especially to the repressed academic appropriation of historical materialism. The experience teaches us that it is very difficult to avoid spontaneous trans-
lations which lead to historical materialism becoming 'sociology' wherein discourse
theory is limited to the 'social aspect of language', etc. Even for Marxist researchers it
is common that, while they are capable of a lucid critique of their original discipline,
they remain blind to certain idealistic academic aspects of neighbouring disciplines,
to the point that they think that they can directly find there 'instruments' useful for
their own practice, including their critical practice.

The formulation of the articulation proposed here is not of course immune to the
risk that we point out, since this risk is coextensive with the terms of current academic
practice. Returning to the latest status of this formulation (Haroche et al., 1971), we will
say first that the area of historical materialism that we are concerned with here is that
of the ideological superstructure in relation to the mode of production dominating the
social formation in question. Recent Marxist works (see in particular Althusser, 1970)
show that it is not sufficient to consider the ideological superstructure as an expression
of the 'economic base', as if ideology was constituted by the 'sphere of ideas' over the
world of things, economic facts, etc. In other words, the area of ideology must be characterized by a specific materiality articulated to the economic materiality: in particular,
the functioning of the ideological instance should be seen as 'ultimately determined' by
the economic instance to the extent that it appears as one of the (non-economic) conditions of reproduction of the economic base, specifically of the relations of production

---

1. Editor's note: the 'three areas' mentioned earlier (p. 8) are 'historical materialism as a theory of
social formations and their transformations, including the theory of ideologies,' 'linguistics as a theory
of syntactic mechanisms and, at the same time, of processes of enunciation' and 'discourse theory as
a theory of historical determination of the semantic process'.

inherent in the economic base.[2] The particular mode of operation of the ideological instance on the reproduction of relations of production consists of what has been called *the interpellation* or the subjection/subjectivation/subjugation (*assujettissement*) of the subject as an ideological subject so that everyone is *led*, without realizing it, and with a sense of exercising his free will, *to take one's place* in one or other of the two antagonistic social classes of the mode of production (or in the category, layer or section of a class connected to one of them).[3] This continual reproduction of class relations (economic, but also as we have just seen, non-economic) is materially provided by the existence of complex realities that have been designated by Althusser as 'ideological state apparatuses' and characterized by the fact that they involve practices associated with places or relations of places that refer to classes without, however, exactly rendering these classes. At a given historical moment, class relations (class struggle) are characterized by confrontation, even within these apparatuses, of political and ideological positions that are not an individual fact but are organized into formations maintaining among themselves relations of antagonism, alliance or domination. We will speak of *ideological formation* to characterize an item (e.g. an aspect of struggle in the apparatuses) capable of acting as a force facing other forces in the ideological conjuncture characteristic of a social formation in a given time; each ideological formation is thus a complex set of attitudes and representations[4] that are neither 'individual' nor 'universal' but relate more or less directly to *positions of classes* in conflict against each other (Haroche et al., 1971: 102). We are thus led to ask ourselves the question of the relationship between ideology and discourse. Given the above, it is clear that it is impossible to *identify* ideology and discourse (that would be an idealistic conception of ideology as a sphere of ideas and discourse), but we must conceive discourse as material aspects of what

---

2. The relations of production are not frozen in an eternal repetition as claimed by functionalist sociology: in reality, to the extent that the relations of production correspond to class relations, we must speak of a reproduction and the transformation of relations of production. This is not the place to develop further this essential point of historical materialism.

3. Bourgeois ideology, as the most fully developed form, instructs us not only in relation to the functioning of the ideological instance in general, but also to the historical forms which preceded it. However, we should not project the bourgeois forms of interpellation on previous forms: it is not obvious, for example, that the interpellation always consists of referring the subject to its own determination. The autonomy of the subject as 'a representation of the imaginary relationship' is, in fact, closely related to the development and extension of the legal political bourgeois ideology. In the social formations dominated by other modes of production, the subject can represent its own determination being imposed on it as a constraint or an alien will, without the represented relationship ceasing to be imaginary.

4. We are aware of the fact that by using words such as 'attitudes' and 'representations' borrowed from the vocabulary of sociology, we introduce ambiguity; practices in the Marxist sense are not 'social behavior' or 'social representations'.

we called the ideological materiality. In other words, the discursive *species* belongs, in our opinion, to an ideological *genre*, which means that the ideological formations that we have been speaking about 'necessarily include[5] as one of their components one or more interrelated *discursive formations* that determine what can and needs to be said (articulated as a harangue, a sermon, a pamphlet, a statement, a programme, etc.) from a position given in a conjuncture' (Haroche et al., 1971: 102), i.e. in a certain relation of places within an ideological apparatus and placed in a class relation. We say therefore that any discursive formation falls within the specific *conditions of production*[6] identified by what we have just designated.

Thus 'ideology interpellates individuals as subjects': this constituent law of *Ideology* is never applied 'in general', but always through a determined complex of *ideological formations* that, within this set, in each historical phase of the class struggle, plays necessarily an unequal role in the reproduction and transformation of relations of production, and this is because of both their 'regional' characteristics (Law, Morality, Knowledge, God, etc.) and their class characteristics. On both accounts, discourse formations are involved in these ideological formations as components. For example, the religious ideological formation represents, in the feudal mode of production, the form of the dominant ideology. It actualizes 'the interpellation of individuals as subjects' through the 'Ideological Apparatus of the religious State', 'specialized' in the relationship between God and men, subjects of God, in the specific form of ceremonies (offices, baptisms, marriages and funerals, etc.) which, in the guise of religion, in fact, interferes in legal relations and economic production, within the feudal relations of production. In the actualization of these ideological relations of classes, various discursive formations, each time specifically combined forms, are involved as components. For example, and as a historical hypothesis to be verified: on one hand the *rustic preaching*, reproduced by the 'Lower Clergy' within the peasantry, on the other the *Sermon of Upper Clergy for the Greats of the Nobility*, thus two discourse formations, the first

---

5.   This necessity refers to the specific role of language as an inherent feature of human beings as ideological animals.

6.   It should be noted that the term *production* can result in some ambiguity here. To avoid this, we will distinguish the economic sense of the term from its epistemological sense (production of knowledge), from its psycho-linguistic use (production of message), and finally from the meaning that it receives in the expression 'production of an effect'. It is primarily in the latter sense that this term needs to be understood here. We will see further, however, that mechanisms of discourse production by the subject are also involved. Moreover, the use of this term takes in our view, a polemical function regarding the repeated use of the term 'circulation', even 'creation', to describe meaning processes.

Moreover, the verbal materiality (phonic or graphic) is one of the presuppositions of economic production, as both infrastructural conditions of trade (and generally of contract), and as a condition for the implementation of social productive forces (transmission of the 'operating instructions' for means of work and 'education' of the workforce).

is subject to the second, so that it deals both with the same 'things' (poverty, death, submission, etc.) but in different forms (for example, submission of the people to the Greats / submission of the Greats to God) and also different 'things' (for example: work on the land / destiny of the Greats).

Finally, it should be noted that a discursive formation exists historically within given class relations and may provide elements integrating into new discourse formations, constituting itself within new ideological relations involving new ideological formations. For example, it can be argued (this should also be subject to historical verification) that the discursive formations mentioned above, disappeared as such, provided the ingredients that used to be 'turned' in different historical forms of bourgeois atheism and re-appropriated, in the form of new discursive formations (for example, integrating some parliamentary discourses of the Revolution of 1789), into the ideological domination of the bourgeois class.

Here arises a difficulty very familiar to Marxist theorists: the difficulty in characterizing real boundaries of real objects corresponding to introduced concepts (e.g. ideological formation, discursive formation, conditions of production). This 'difficulty' is not the result of an unfortunate accident but the result of the contradiction between the nature of these concepts and a spontaneously rigid and classificatory use which we cannot avoid trying to make play, in the form of seemingly inevitable questions such as 'how many ideological formations are there in a social formation? How many discourse formations can each of them contain? etc.' In fact, precisely in view of the dialectic character of the realities designated here, such a *discretization* is utterly impossible, unless it includes in the same determination of each of these objects the possibility to be transformed into another, that is to say specifically to denounce their discreteness as an illusion.

The relative externality of an ideological formation in relation to a discursive formation is reflected within this very discursive formation: it refers to the necessary effect, in a given discursive formation, of ideological non-discursive elements (representations, images related to practices, etc.). Better yet, it induces inside of a discourse a gap that reflects this externality. This is the gap between one discursive formation and another, the first serving as a kind of representational material for the second, as if the discursivity of this 'raw material' vanished in the eyes of the speaker (see Henry, 1971, Henry, 1974). This is what we will characterize as oblivion 1, inevitably inherent in the subjective practice related to language. But simultaneously, and this is an another form of the same oblivion, the process by which a specific discursive sequence is produced or recognized as having a meaning for a subject fades in the eyes of the subject. We mean that we believe the production of meaning is strictly inseparable from the paraphrase relations[7] between sequences such as the paraphrastic family of these sequences, which

---

7.   Thus we do not presuppose an 'identity of meaning' between paraphrastic family members; we assume instead that it is in this relationship that sense and identity of sense can be defined.

might be called the matrix of meaning. This means that it is from the relationship inherent to this family that the effect of meaning is constituted as well as the relation to a referent involved in this effect.[8] If you are following us, it is therefore understandable that the vivid evidence of a subjective reading according to which text is bi-univocally associated with its meaning (syntactic ambiguities and/or even semantic ones) is a constituent illusion of the subject-effect with respect to language, and contributing in this specific field to produce the effect of subjection/subjectivation/subjugation (*assujettissement*) mentioned above: in fact, we assume that the 'meaning' of a sequence is materially conceivable only since this sequence is conceived of as necessarily belonging to such a discursive formation and/or such other (which explains, by the way, that it can have several meanings).[9] It is this necessity for any kind of sequence to belong to a discursive formation, to be 'endowed with meaning', which is repressed for (or by?) the subject and covered for it with the illusion of being the source of meaning, in the form of grasping a pre-existing universal sense (this explains in particular the eternal binary opposition individuality/universality characteristic of the discursive illusion of the subject). (…)

Language, ideology, discourse

Let us consider what we have designated respectively by the name of 'oblivion 1' and 'oblivion 2'.[10] We see that these two oblivions differ profoundly, one from the other. Indeed, it appears that the subject can *consciously penetrate* into zone 2 and that it actually does it constantly by a return upon itself of its discourse, an anticipation of its effect

---

8. Let us give right away an example of what we mean by 'praphrastic family', from a discursive perspective. Here is a 'semantic domain' that we got from a recent study which has been conducted with the help of AAD [Automatic Analysis of Discourse]:

More equitable			goods
Fairer	} distribution of {	wealth
Better		income

9. We emphasize that this concept is not identical to that of 'plural readings' which suggests the idea of an infinite proliferation of meanings, each subject demonstrating its singularity. It would, we believe, mean losing sight of the materiality of discourse and A. Trognon seems to do this when he writes: 'What the discourse says is what we write about it in the question which we have defined for ourselves' (Trognon, 1972: 28).

10. These two 'oblivions' are characterized just below, in the same paragraph. In the section 2 of the article the authors had defined oblivion 2 as a kind of oblivion to which the speaker can access (s/he can remember what elements s/he had to reject when s/he spoke). [Trans. note]

and by taking into account the gap introduced by the discourse of the other.[11] To the extent that the subject returns to its own speech to make explicit for him – or itself what it says, to deepen 'what it thinks' and to formulate it more adequately, we can say that zone 2, which is that of the *process of enunciation,* is characterized by a preconscious/conscious type of operation. In contrast, oblivion n° 1, whose zone is inaccessible to the subject, appears precisely because of being constitutive of subjectivity in language. Therefore, it can be argued that this repression (including both the discourse process itself and the inter-discourse[12] to which it is articulated by relations of contradiction, subjugation or encroachment) is *unconscious* by nature in the sense that ideology is constitutively unconscious of itself (and not just distracted from itself, constantly escaping itself…, see in particular Haroche and Pêcheux, 1972: 67–83).

This opposition between the two types of oblivion is not unrelated to the aforementioned opposition between the concrete empirical situation in which the subject is situated and which is marked by the character of the imaginary identification where the other is another me ('other' with a small 'o'), and the process of interpellation-subjection of the subject, referring to what J. Lacan metaphorically designates by the 'Other' with a capital 'O'; in this sense, the monologue is a special case of dialogue and of interpellation.

In other words, we assume that the relationship between the two oblivions, n° 1 and n° 2, refers to the relationship between the condition of existence (not subjective) of the subjective illusion on the one hand and subjective forms of its realization on the other.[13]

Using here Freudian terminology that distinguishes the pre-conscious-conscious on the one hand, and the unconscious on the other, we do not claim to address the issue of the relationship between ideology, the unconscious and discursivity; we only want to point out the fact that a discursive formation is constitutively bordered by what is outside of it, thus by *what is strictly unsayable since it determines it,* and at the same time to stress that in no way can the constitutive exteriority be confused with *the subjective space of enunciation,* the imaginary space that provides *the speaking subject's movement within the reformulable,* so that it constantly returns to what is formulated, and recognizes itself in the 'reflexive or preconscious relationship to words which makes them appear to us as the expression of things', according to the formulation of M. Safouan

---

11. This zone 2 is the area of what is sometimes called the 'discourse strategies', including in particular the rhetorical interrogation, tendentious reformulation and manipulative use of ambiguity. On this issue see Haroche (1974).

12. By this we mean the 'specific exterior' of a given discursive process (see Pêcheux, 1969: 111), that is to say, the processes involved in its formation and organization.

13. On this issue, and in particular on the distinction unconscious law / preconscious-conscious rule, cf. T. Herbert (1968); see also the discussion by R. Robin (1973).

in 'On the structure in psychoanalysis' (1968: 282). The term *preconscious* refers, as we know, to the first Freudian theory (topographic theory), and disappears as such in the second.[14] However, it is largely in the context of this second theory that the Lacanian re-elaboration of Freudianism was made and to which we refer here. In another study we will return to this theoretical 'incoherence' to explain it, elaborate it and reduce it.

This 'inequality' between the two oblivions corresponds to the relation of dominance which can be characterized by saying that 'the unasserted precedes and dominates the asserted' (see Culioli et al., 1970).

In addition, we must not forget that the repression that characterizes oblivion 1 ultimately rules the relation between the said and the unsaid in oblivion 2, where the discursive sequence is structured. This must be understood in the sense that for Lacan 'all discourse is an occultation of the unconscious'.

To conclude this overview, we will say that there are two more mistakes to avoid regarding the term 'discourse', as it functions in the term 'discourse theory'. The first is to confuse discourse and speech (as it is defined by Saussure): discourse would be the actualization in verbal acts of subjective freedom 'escaping the system' (of *langue*). Against this interpretation we reaffirm that discourse theory and the procedures it employs cannot be identified with the 'linguistics of *parole*'. The second error is opposed to the first in that it 'twists in the other sense' the meaning of the term discourse, seeing it as a social supplement of the utterance (énoncé), thus a particular element of the language system that 'classical linguistics' would have overlooked. From this perspective, the level of discourse would be integrated into the language system (*langue*), for example, as a particular type of competence whose properties vary according to social position, which would amount to the idea that there are languages (*langues*), by taking *literally* the expression being politically sound but linguistically questionable that 'employers and workers do not speak the same language'.

Faced with these two deformations of reality designated by the term 'discourse', we believe it to be useful to introduce the distinction between (linguistic) base and (discursive) process; developing on this base,[15] the only distinction that we believe can allow us to take into consideration relations of contradiction, antagonism, alliance, absorption... among discursive formations belonging to different ideological formations, without implying the existence of a mythical plurality of 'languages' belonging to these different formations.

---

14. The term 'topographic theory' is used to designate the psychoanalytic theory as proposed by Freud prior to 1923. It divides the mental apparatus into the systems Conscious/Pre-conscious/Unconscious. After 1923 Freud makes a distinction between ego/superego/id. [Trans. note]

15. The processes of enunciation constitute what, within the very linguistic 'base', allows processes to develop in relation to it.

References

Althusser, Louis. 1970. 'Idéologie et appareils idéologiques d'Etat.' *La Pensée* 151: 3–38.

Culioli, Antoine, Catherine Fuchs, and Michel Pêcheux. 1970. *Considérations théoriques à propos du traitement formel du langage. Documents de linguistique quantitative*. Paris: Dunod.

Haroche, Claudine. 1974. *Grammaire, implicite et ambiguïté. A propos des fondements de l'ambiguïté inhérente au discours*.: Laboratoire de psycho-sociale.

Haroche, Claudine, Paul Henry, and Michel Pêcheux. 1971. 'La sémantique et la coupure saussurienne: langue, langage, discours.' *Langages* 24: 93–106. DOI: 10.3406/lgge.1971.2608

Haroche, Claudine, and Michel Pêcheux. 1972. 'Facteurs socio-économiques et résolution de problèmes.' *Bulletin du CERP* 21, no. 2–3: 67–83.

Henry, Paul. 1974. *De l'énoncé au discours. Présupposition et processus discursifs*.: CNRS EPHE.

Henry, Paul. 1971. 'On processing of reference in context.' In *Social contexts of messages*, edited by E. A. Carswell and R. Rommveit. London: Academic Press.

Herbert, Thomas. 1968. 'Remarques pour une théorie générale des idéologies.' *Cahiers pour l'analyse* 9: 74–92.

Pêcheux, Michel. 1969. *Analyse automatique du discours*. Paris: Dunod.

Robin, Régine. 1973. *Histoire et linguistique*. Paris: Colin.

Safouan, Moustapha. 1968. 'De la structure en psychanalyse. Contribution à une théorie du manque.' In *Qu'est-ce que le structuralisme?*, edited by O. Ducrot et al., 239–98. Paris: Le Seuil.

Trognon, Alain. 1972. *Analyse de contenu et théorie de la signification*. University of Paris VII.

Michel Foucault

An archaeology of discourse

There is probably nobody who epitomises the project of discourse theory better than Michel Foucault (1926–1984). Given that he consecrated only one monograph to the problem of discourse analysis – his *Archaeology of Knowledge* (1972[1969]) – his international prominence as a leading discourse theorist is surprising. Translated into English for the first time, the text selected, 'Response to a Question', succinctly recapitulates the ideas on discourse that Foucault developed around 1970. For Foucault, the smallest constitutive units of discourse are utterances (*énoncés*). Produced in historically located speech acts (*énonciations*), utterances are to be taken in their specific modalities and with respect to the circumstances in which they came into existence. With his critique of abstract formalism in classical structuralism, Foucault paved the way for a turn to enunciative discourse pragmatics (see the section on 'Enunciative Pragmatics'): discourses do not realise an underlying set of grammatical rules; instead, Foucault conceives of a discourse as an ensemble of singular utterances dispersed on the sociohistorical terrain. Foucault's *Archaeology* is unique in that it is his only outright theoretical work. Yet it would be a mistake to understand it as a theory for other more historical studies preceding and following it. The *Archaeology* remains a programmatic book, putting discourse theory into practice without ever analysing a discourse. The *Order of Things* (2002[1966]), the preceding work on historical thought systems (*epistemai*), gives an account of the structural evolution in proto-scientific knowledge domains. At no point does it mention 'discourse'. The succeeding works, sometimes labelled his geneaological phase, turn to questions of power, governmentality and subjectivity. Even though the notion of 'discourse' pervades these works, its use is often rather metaphorical, and especially in his later works it designates the circulation of legitimate knowledge. In the selected text, Foucault succinctly summarises the discourse theoretical programme of his *Archaeology*.

References

Foucault, Michel. 1972[1969]. *The Archaeology of Knowledge & the Discourse on Language*. New York: Pantheon.
Foucault, Michel. 2002[1966]. *The Order of Things. An Archeology of the Human Sciences*. London: Routledge.

Michel Foucault. 2001[1968]. 'Réponse à une question.'
In *Dits et écrits, I*, 701–723, selected 702–715.
Paris: Gallimard.

Response to a question

How can I not admit in this undertaking, that you have characterized it with extreme accuracy? And what you have called, at the same time, the point of inevitable discord: 'To introduce the constraint of the system and of the discontinuity in the history of the mind'? Yes, I recognize myself here almost entirely. Yes, I recognize that this is almost unjustifiable talk. Such a fatal relevance: you have succeeded in giving a definition of my work to which I cannot avoid subscribing but that no one would ever reasonably take over. Suddenly, I feel all my strangeness. My strangeness that is so barely legitimate. And this work which was doubtlessly a little lonely, but always patient, without another law but itself, fairly applied, as I thought, in order to defend itself – I realize now how much it deviated from the established norms, how much it was garish. However, two or three details in this very true definition you provide annoy me, preventing me from adhering to it completely.

First, you use the word *system* in the singular. However, I am a pluralist. Here is what I mean. (Please allow me to speak not only of my last book, but also of those which precede it; since together they form a cluster of research whose themes and chronological benchmarks are closely related; also, because each of them constitutes a descriptive experience and so refers to the other two by a number of features.) I am a pluralist: the problem I asked myself is that of the *individualization* of discourses. To individualize discourses, there are criteria that are known and secure (or almost so): the linguistic system to which they belong, the identity of the subject who has articulated them. But other criteria, which are no less familiar, are much more enigmatic. When we talk about psychiatry, or medicine, or grammar, or biology, or economics, what are we talking about? What are these curious units we believe to be recognizable at first glance, but that we would be very embarrassed to define the limits of? Units, some of which seem to date back to the origins of our history (medicine no less than mathematics), while others have appeared recently (economics, psychiatry), and others perhaps have disappeared (casuistry). Units in which the new utterances are indefinitely inscribed, being constantly modified by them (the strange unit of the sociology or of the psychology that since their birth have continued to evolve). Units obstinately remaining after so many mistakes, so many oblivions, so many novelties, so many metamorphoses, but sometimes going through such radical mutations that it would be problematic to see them as identical to themselves (how can we affirm that this is the same economy that we find, uninterrupted, from the physiocrats to Keynes?).

Perhaps there are discourses that can at any moment redefine their own individuality (for example, mathematics can reinterpret its entire history at each point in time), but in none of the cases I have mentioned, can the discourse restitute its entire history in the unity of a formal architecture. Two traditional recourses remain. The historical-transcendental recourse: trying to search, beyond any manifestation and any historical birth, for an original foundation, for the opening of an inexhaustible horizon, for a project that would be a step back from any event, and would maintain throughout the history a sketch always connected to a unit that does not end. The empirical or psychological recourse: to search for the founder, to interpret what he or she meant, to detect the implicit meaning quietly sleeping in his or her discourse, to follow the thread or the fate of his or her meanings, to relate the traditions and the influences, to set the time of awakenings, of omissions, of awareness, of crises, of changes in the mind, the sensitivity or the interests of men. However, it seems to me that the first of these remedies is tautological, the second extrinsic and inessential. It is by identifying and systematizing their own characters that I would try to individualize the large units that mark the universe of our discourses in simultaneity or succession.

I have selected three groups of criteria:

1. The criteria of *formation*. What allows us to individualize a discourse such as the political economy or general grammar is not the unity of an object; it is not a formal structure; neither a coherent conceptual architecture; it is not a fundamental philosophical choice; but rather it is the existence of rules of formation for all objects (whether dispersed or not) for all their operations (which can often be neither superimposed nor enchained), for all their concepts (which may be perfectly incompatible), for all their theoretical options (which often exclude one another). There is an individualized discursive formation whenever we can define a similar set of rules.

2. The criteria of *transformation* or of *threshold*. I would say that natural history or psychopathology are units of discourse if I can define the conditions that had to be combined in a very precise moment of time, for their objects, their operations, their concepts and theoretical options to be formed; if I can define what internal modifications they were susceptible to, if, finally, I can define at what threshold of transformation the new rules were put into play.

3. The criteria of *correlation*. I will say that clinical medicine is an independent discursive formation if I can define all the relationships that define it and situate it among other types of discourse (such as biology, chemistry, political theory or the analysis of society) and in the non-discursive context in which it operates (institutions, social relations, economic and political environment).

These criteria allow us to replace the themes of totalizing history (whether that of 'the progress of reason' or 'the spirit of a century') by differentiated analysis. They allow us to describe, as an *episteme* of a period, not the sum of its knowledge, or the general style of its research, but the gap, the distances, the oppositions, the differences, the relationships of its multiple scientific discourses: the *episteme* is not *a kind of a grand underlying theory*, it is a space of *dispersion*, it is an *open field of relationships, no doubt indefinitely describable*. They also allow us to describe not the great history that would carry forth all the sciences in a single flight, but the types of histories – that is to say those of persistence and of transformation – that characterize the different discourses (the history of mathematics does not follow the same pattern as the history of biology, which no longer obeys that of psychopathology): *the episteme is not a slice of the history* common to all sciences; this is a *simultaneous game of specific persistences*. Finally, they allow us to situate the different thresholds at their respective places: because there is no evidence in advance (and nothing demonstrates it after examination), that their chronology is the same for all types of discourse; the threshold which can be described for the analysis of language in the early nineteenth century has surely no symmetrical episode in the history of mathematics; and – the most paradoxical thing – the threshold of formation of the political economy (marked by Ricardo) does not coincide with the constitution – by Marx – of an analysis of the society and of the history.[1] The *episteme* is not a *general stage of reason*; it is a *complex relationship of successive shifts*.

Nothing, as you can see, is more foreign to me than the search for a constraining form, sovereign and unique. I am not trying to detect, from various signs, the unitary spirit of a time, the general form of its consciousness: something like a *Weltanschauung*. I did not describe either the emergence or the eclipse of a formal structure that would reign for a time over all manifestations of thought: I did not make the history of a syncopated transcendence. Finally, I did not describe further the thoughts or the secular sensibilities emerging, stammering, struggling, dying out as great ghostly souls playing their shadow theatre on the backstage of history. I studied, successively, sets of discourse; I characterized them; I defined the games of rules, transformations, thresholds, persistences; I composed them together, I described relationship clusters. Wherever I deemed it necessary, I made systems proliferate.

*

---

1.   This fact, already identified by Oscar Lange, explains both the limited and perfectly circumscribed space occupied by the concepts of Marx in the epistemological field that goes from Petty to contemporary econometrics, and the founding character of these same concepts for a theory of history. I hope I have time to analyze the problems of historical discourse in a forthcoming book which will be called something like: *The Past and the Present: another archaeology of human sciences*.

A thought, you say, that 'emphasizes the discontinuity'. Actually, the importance of this concept, acknowledged by both historians and linguists, cannot be underestimated. But the use of the singular does not seem to me quite appropriate. Again, I am a pluralist. My problem: replacing the abstract, general and monotonous form of 'change', in which we so readily think of the succession, by the analysis of *different types of transformation*. This implies two things: to put in brackets all the old forms of the soft continuity by which we usually attenuate the wilderness of change (tradition, influence, habits of thought, main mental forms, constraints of the human mind), and, on the contrary, obstinately to bring out all the vivacity of the difference: meticulously to establish the gap. Then, to put in brackets all psychological explanations of change (genius of great inventors, crises of consciousness, appearance of a new form of mind), and to define, very carefully, the transformations that, I do not say caused, but *constituted* the change. Replace, in short, the theme of *becoming* (general form, abstract element, primary cause and universal effect, confused mixture of the identical and of the new) by the analysis of the *transformations* in their specificity.

1. *Inside* a given discursive formation, to detect changes that affect the objects, the operations, the concepts and the theoretical options. Thus, there can be distinguished (I limit myself to the example of *General Grammar*[2]): changes by inference or implication (the theory of verb-copula involved the distinction between a noun root and a verbal inflection); changes by generalization (extension of the theory of word-designation to the verb and therefore disappearance of the theory of the verb-copula); changes by delimitation (the concept of the attribute is specified by the notion of the complement); changes by passage to the complementary (from the project to construct a universal and transparent language derived from the search for secrets hidden in the most primitive language); changes by passing to another term of an alternative (the primacy of vowels or the primacy of consonants in the formation of roots); changes by permutation of dependencies (the theory of the verb can be based on the theory of the noun or vice versa); changes by inclusion or exclusion (the analysis of languages as systems of representative signs makes searching for their family relations fall into disuse – searching, which is reintroduced, however, by the quest for a primitive language).

    All those different types of change constitute a set of characteristic *derivations* of a discursive formation.

---

2. French: *grammaire générale* (17th and 18th centuries). During that period, it was a dominant trend, heavily influenced by Descartes, in the French philosophy of language. Its central thesis is that grammar points to mental processes which are universal. It was named after the title of a book by A. Arnauld and C. Lancelot (1660): *Grammaire générale et raisonnée contenant les fondemens de l'art de parler, expliqués d'une manière claire et naturelle* ('General and Rational Grammar, containing the fundamentals of the art of speaking, explained in a clear and natural manner'). [Trans. note]

2. To detect changes that affect discursive formations *themselves*:

    – displacement of the lines that define the field of possible objects (the subject
      of medicine in the early nineteenth century ceases to be taken on the surface
      of classification; it is identified in the three-dimensional space of the body);
    – new position and *the* new role of the speaking subject in discourse (the subject
      in the discourse of the eighteenth-century naturalists becomes exclusively how
      the subject looks according to a grid and *noticing* according to a code; he ceases
      to be listening, interpreting, decrypting);
    – new functioning of the language in relation to objects (from Tournefort,[3] the
      discourse of naturalists has no role to penetrate into things, to capture in them
      the language which they secretly envelop and to produce it in the light of the
      day; but to reach a surface of transcription where the form, the number, the size
      and the disposition of the elements will possibly be translated unequivocally);
    – new form of location and circulation of discourse in society (clinical discourse
      is not formulated in the same places, it has different methods of recording, it
      does not spread, it does not accumulate, it is neither kept nor contested in the
      same way as the medical discourse of the eighteenth century).

    All these changes of a type superior to the previous ones define the transformations
    that affect the discursive spaces themselves: *mutations*.

3. Finally, the third type of changes – those that simultaneously affect several discur-
    sive formations:

    – inversion in the hierarchy diagram (during the classical period the analysis
      of language had a leading role that it lost in the early years of the nineteenth
      century in favour of biology);
    – alteration in the nature of government (classical grammar as a general theory
      of signs guaranteed the transposition of an instrument of analysis in other
      areas; in the nineteenth century, biology provided the 'metamorphoric' impor-
      tation of a certain number of concepts: organisms → organization; function →
      social function; life → life of words or languages);
    – functional displacements: the theory of the continuity of beings, which was
      within the remit of philosophical discourse in the eighteenth century, was
      covered by scientific discourse during the nineteenth century.

    All these transformations are of a superior type to the other two and characterize
    the changes specific to the *episteme* itself.

---

3. A French botanist (1656–1708). [Trans. note]

This is a small array (about fifteen, perhaps) of various modifications that may be assigned with regard to discourse. You see now why I would prefer to say that I have not stressed *the discontinuity*, but *the discontinuities* (that is to say, the various transformations that can be described regarding the two states of discourse). But the important thing for me now is not to constitute an exhaustive typology of these changes.

1. The important thing is to give a set of specified modifications as content to the monotonous and empty concept of 'change'. The history of 'ideas' or 'sciences' should no longer be a statement of innovations, but the descriptive analysis of various effectuated transformations.[4]

2. What is important for me is not to mix such an analysis with a psychological diagnosis. One (legitimate) thing is to ask whether he was a genius or what were the experiences of his early childhood from which the work bears such a set of modifications. However, another thing is to describe the field of possibilities, the form of operations and the types of transformations that characterize his discursive practice.

3. What is important for me is to show that, on the one hand, there is no inert discourse, which is already more than half dead, and on the other hand, an omnipotent subject who handles it, overturns it and renews it, but that the discoursing subjects form part of the discursive field – they have their place (and their possibilities of displacement), their function (and their possibilities of functional mutation). The discourse is not the place of eruption of pure subjectivity; this is a space of positions and functioning, differentiated for the subjects.

4. What is most important for me is to define, among all these transformations, the game of dependencies:

   - *intradiscursive* dependencies (among objects, operations, concepts of the same formation);
   - *interdiscursive* dependencies (among different discursive formations: such as the correlations that I studied in *The Order of Things* [*Les Mots et les Choses*] (2002[1966]) among natural history, economy, grammar and the theory of representation);
   - *extradiscursive* dependencies (among discursive and other transformations that were produced elsewhere than in the speech: such as the correlations studied in the *Madness and Civilization* [*Histoire de la folie*] (2001[1961]) and *Birth of the Clinic* [*Naissance de la Clinique*] (1973[1963]), between medical discourse and a whole play of economic, political and social changes).

---

4. I follow here the examples of method given several times by Mr. Canguilhem.

I would like to substitute the uniform simplicity of the assignments of causality by all this play of dependencies; and remove the indefinitely extended privilege of the cause to reveal the polymorphic beam of correlations.

As you can see: there is absolutely no question of substituting one category, the 'discontinuous', for the other, no less abstract or general, the 'continuous'. I try instead to show that discontinuity is not a monotonous and unthinkable emptiness between the events that we should rush to fill (with two perfectly symmetrical solutions) with the gloomy plenitude of the cause or with the agile Cartesian devil[5] of the mind; but that it is a game of specified transformations, different from one another (each with its own conditions, rules and level) and linked together according to patterns of dependency. History is the descriptive analysis and the theory of these transformations.

*

I hope that the final point will be shorter. You use the expression 'history of the mind'. In fact, I meant rather the making of the history of the discourse. What is the difference, you would say? 'You do not study the texts that you take as materials according to their grammatical structure; you do not describe the semantic field they cover; it is not the language that is your object. So what? What are you looking for if not to discover the thought that drives them and to reconstruct the representations of which they gave a version that is perhaps durable but undoubtedly unfaithful? What are you looking for, if not to find behind them the intentions of the men who formulated them, the meanings that they have deliberately or unwittingly put in, this imperceptible supplement to the linguistic system and which is something like the opening of the freedom or like the history of the mind?'

Therein lies perhaps the key point. You are right: what I analyze in discourse is not the system of its language nor, in a general way, the formal rules of its construction: because I do not care to know what makes it lawful or affects its intelligibility and what allows it to be used in communication. The question I ask is not one of codes but one of events: the law of the existence of the utterances which made them possible – them and nothing else in their place; the conditions of their singular emergence; their correlation with other events – previous or simultaneous, discursive or not. To this question, however, I try to answer without referring to the consciousness, obscure or explicit, of speaking subjects; without reporting the facts of discourse to the will – perhaps unintended – of their authors; without invoking the intention to say that which is always in excess of wealth compared to what is being said; without trying to capture the incredible lightness of a speech that would have no text.

---

5.   In French *ludion*. The Cartesian devil (or Cartesian diver) is used in a classic science experiment. It is a glass vessel partially filled with water and covered with an airtight membrane; it contains a hollow object, open at the bottom and with just enough air to allow it to float. [Trans. note]

In that way, what I do is neither formalization nor exegesis, but an *archeology*: that is to say, as its name suggests in a far too obvious way, the description of the *archive*. By this word I do not mean the mass of texts which may have been collected in a given epoch or kept from this period through the avatars of deletion. I mean the set of rules which, at a given time and for a given society, define:

- the limits and forms of *sayability*: what is it possible to speak on? What was established as a field of discourse? What type of discursivity was assigned to such and such area (from what do we make the story, from what have we wanted to make a descriptive science, to what have we given a literary formulation, etc.)?
- the limits and forms of *conservation*: what utterances are intended to go away without trace? Which ones are intended, instead, to enter the memory of men (by ritual recitation, pedagogy and education, entertainment or celebration, advertising)? Which ones are noted in order to be reused and for what purpose? Which ones are put into circulation and in which groups? Which ones are repressed and censored?
- the limits and forms of *memory* as it appears in various discursive formations: what are the utterances that each one recognizes as valid or questionable, or definitely disabled? Which ones were left as negligible and which were excluded as foreigners? What types of relationships are established between the system of present utterances and the corpus of passed utterances?
- the limits and forms of *reactivation*: among the discourses of earlier periods or foreign cultures, which ones are those that are retained, valued, imported, which do we try to reconstitute? And what do we do with them, what transformations do we make them experience (comment, exegesis, analysis), what system of assessment do we apply to them, what role do we give them to play?
- the limits and forms of *appropriation*: what individuals, what groups, what classes have access to this type of discourse? How institutionalized is the relationship of the discourse to the one who holds it, to the one who receives it? How is the relationship of the discourse signaled and defined to its author? How do classes, nations, linguistic, cultural or ethnic communities negotiate the struggle for taking charge of discourses?

It is against this background that the analyses that I started stand out, it is toward this that they are directed. What I write is not a history of the mind according to the succession of its forms or according to the thickness of its sedimented significations. I do not question discourses as to what they silently mean, but I question the fact and conditions of their manifest appearance; it is not about the contents they can conceal, but about the transformations they have made; not about the sense that remains as a perpetual origin in them, but about the field where they coexist, remain and disappear. It is a discourse analysis in the dimension of their exteriority. From there, there are three consequences:

– to treat past discourse not as a theme for a *comment* that would revive it but as a *monument*[6] to describe its own disposition;
– to search in discourse not for its laws of construction, as the structural methods do, but for its conditions of existence;[7]
– to refer the discourse not to the thought, the mind or the subject which could give birth to it, but to the practical field in which it opens out.

*

Please forgive me: I have discussed this for quite some time. And all of this for very little: to offer these three slight changes to your definition, and ask you for an agreement to talk about my work as an attempt to introduce 'the diversity of *the systems* and the game of *the discontinuities* in the history of *discourses*'. Do not imagine that I want to rig the game or that I try to avoid the point of your question by discussing its terms ad infinitum. But prior agreement was necessary. Here I am up against the wall. I must respond.

Not, of course, to the question of whether *I* am reactionary nor if my texts *are* (in themselves, inherently, through a certain number of well-coded signs). You are asking me a serious question in another way, the only way, I think, that can be legitimately asked. You ask me about the relationship between what I say and political practice.

It seems to me that we can give two answers to this question. One concerns the critical operations that my discourse makes in its own field (the history of ideas, the sciences, the thought, the knowledge…): did it disregard anything necessary to progressive politics? The other concerns the field of analysis and the domain of objects that my discourse is trying to show: how can they be linked to the effective exercise of progressive politics?

I will summarize as follows the critical operations that I have made:

1. *To establish the limits,* where the history of thought in its traditional form took an undefined space. In particular:

   – to question the general interpretive postulate that the reign of discourse has no assignable borders; the mute things and the silence itself would be populated with words: and where we can no longer hear any word, it is still possible to listen to the deeply buried whisper of meaning; in what people do not say they would continue to speak; a world of sleeping texts would expect us on the white pages of our history. To this theme, I would oppose the assertion that discourses are limited practical areas that have their borders, their rules of formation, their conditions of existence: the historical basis of discourse is not a deeper discourse, both identical and different;

---

6. I take this word from Mr. Canguilhem. He describes better than I did myself what I wanted to do.

7. Is it necessary to specify again that I am not what is called 'structuralist'?

- to question the theme of a sovereign subject who would come from outside to animate the inertia of language codes and who would introduce in discourse the indelible marks of his liberty; to question the theme of a subjectivity which would constitute the meanings and then transcribe them in discourse. To these themes I would like to oppose the identification of the roles and the operations performed by the different 'discoursing' subjects;
- to question the theme of the indefinitely postponed origin and the idea that the role of history, in the domain of thought, is to awaken the omissions, to remove the concealments, to delete – or to bar again – the barrages. I would like to present, in opposition to this theme, the analysis of discursive systems, historically defined, to which we can fix thresholds and assign the conditions of their birth and their disappearance.

In short, establishing these limits, questioning the three themes of the origin, of the subject and of the implicit meaning is undertaking to release the discursive field from the historical-transcendental structure imposed by the philosophy of the nineteenth century – a difficult task, as the extreme resistance demonstrates well.

2. *To delete the spontaneous oppositions.* Here are a few, in order of importance: the opposition between the liveliness of innovations and the heaviness of tradition, inertia of acquired knowledge or old courses of thought; the opposition between medium forms of knowledge (which would represent casual mediocrity) and its deviant forms (which would demonstrate the individuality and loneliness specific to genius); the opposition between periods of stability or universal convergence and the boiling points when consciences come into crisis, when sensitivities are metamorphosed, when all concepts are revised, overturned, revived, or, for an indefinite time, fall into disuse. I would like to substitute all these dichotomies with the analysis of the field of simultaneous differences (which define the possible dispersion of knowledge at a given period) and successive differences (which define all the transformations: their hierarchy, their dependence, their level). Where there was told the history of tradition and invention, of the old and the new, of the dead and alive, of the closed and the open, of the static and the dynamic, I undertake to tell the history of perpetual difference; specifically, to tell the history of ideas as the set of specified descriptive forms of non-identity. And I would like to free it thus from the triple metaphor that has encumbered it for over a century (the evolutionist one, which requires a separation between the regressive and the adaptive; the biological one, which separates the living and the inert; and the dynamic one, which opposes movement and immobility).

3. *To remove the denial* which covered discourse in its own existence (and this is for me the most important of the critical operations I undertake). This denial comprises several aspects:

- never to treat discourse only in terms of indifferent elements without consistency or indigenous law (pure surface of *translation* for mute things; simple places to express thoughts, imagination, knowledge, unconscious themes);
- to identify in discourse only the cuts of the psychological and individualizing models (the work of an author and – why not, indeed? – his early or mature works), the cuts of linguistic or rhetorical models (a genre, a style) and the cuts of semantic models (an idea, a theme);
- to admit that all operations are done before the discourse and outside of it (in the ideality of the thought or in the seriousness of mute practices), that the discourse, therefore, is only this slight supplement which adds an almost impalpable fringe to the things in the mind: a surplus that *goes without saying*, since it does not say anything else beyond what is said.

To this denial I would like to oppose that discourse is not nothing or almost nothing. And what it is – what defines its own consistency, what allows us to make a historical analysis of it – is not what we 'wanted' to say (this dark and heavy burden of intentions that creeps in the shadow of a weight that is much more important than things actually said), it is not what remains mute (these imposing things that do not speak but leave their identifiable marks, their black profile on the light surface of what is said). Discourse is constituted by the difference between what one might correctly say at a given time (according to the rules of grammar and those of logic) and what is actually said. The discursive field is, at any given time, the law of this difference. It thus defines a number of operations that do not have the order of linguistic construction or formal deduction. It deploys a 'neutral' field where speech and writing can cause variations in the system of their opposition and a difference in their functioning. It appears as a set of regulated practices which do not consist simply in giving a visible and external body to the agile interiority of thought, nor to offer to the solidity of the things the surface of appearance which will redouble them. At the bottom of this denial that has weighed on discourse (in favor of the opposition of thought – language, history – truth, speech – writing, words – things), there was a refusal to admit that something in discourse is formed (according to well definable rules); that this something exists, subsists, is transforming, and disappears (according to also definable rules); in short, that besides everything that a society can produce ('besides': that is to say in a relationship assignable to all this), there is also the formation and transformation of 'said things'. It is the history of these 'said things' that I have undertaken.

4. Finally, the last critical task (which summarizes and envelopes all the others): *to liberate from their uncertain status* this set of disciplines called history of ideas, history of science, history of thought, history of knowledge, of concepts or consciousness. This uncertainty manifests itself in several ways:

- difficulty in delineating the areas: where does the history of science end, where do opinions and beliefs begin? How do we separate the history of concepts and the history of notions or themes? Where does the limit pass between the history of knowledge and that of imagination?
- difficulty in defining the nature of the object: do we examine the history of what was known, acquired, forgotten, or the history of mental forms, or the history of their interference? Do we look at the history of the characteristic features that belong collectively to men of a certain epoch or culture? Do we describe a collective mind? Do we analyze the history (teleological or genetic) of reason?
- difficulty in assigning the relationship between these facts of thought or of knowledge and other areas of historical analysis: should we treat them as signs of something else (a social relationship, a political situation, an economic determination), or as their result, or as their refraction through consciousness, or as the symbolic expression of their overall form?

For so much uncertainty I would like to substitute the analysis of discourse itself in its conditions of formation, in the series of its modifications and in the play of its dependencies and its correlations. Thus the discourse would appear in a describable relationship with all the other practices. Instead of dealing with economic history, social history, political history enveloping history of thought (which would be its expression and doublet), instead of dealing with a history of ideas that would be referred (by a play of signs and expressions or by the relations of causality) to extrinsic conditions, we would be dealing with a history of discursive practices in specific relationships that articulate them to other practices. The point is not to write a *global history* –one that would bring together all the elements around a principle or a unique form – but to deploy the field of a *general history* where we could describe the singularity of practices, the play of their relations, the form of their dependencies. And it is in the space of this general history that we could circumscribe the historical analysis of discursive practices as a discipline. (…)

References

Foucault, Michel. 1973[1963]. *The Birth of the Clinic. An Archaeology of Medical Perception*. London: Routledge.

Foucault, Michel. 2001[1961]. *Madness and Civilization: A History of Insanity in the Age of Reason*. London: Routledge.

Foucault, Michel. 2002[1966]. *The Order of Things. An Archeology of the Human Sciences*. London: Routledge.

Stuart Hall

Encoding and decoding the message

Cultural Studies is a field investigating practices of cultural representation while emphasizing the limits of the high versus mass culture divide. While Cultural Studies in the U.S. is based mostly in the literary field and has a long tradition of studying popular mass culture, Cultural Studies in the UK started in the 1960s with sociological studies of workers' everyday cultural practices. Against a background of Marxist theory, the exponents of British Cultural Studies, institutionally centred at Birmingham, made a case for the creative appropriation of cultural forms and standards and their redefinition among consumers in a certain class environment. Under the influence of French poststructuralist theory, the second generation of the Birmingham Centre of Cultural Studies, headed by Stuart Hall, recognised the problem of discourse. While applying semiotic models to mass-media representations of race and class, they kept the characteristic critical emphasis on the relative autonomy of cultural practices. In the selected text, Hall delineates the encoding/decoding model of mass-media communication which criticizes traditional top-down models of the media system (the 'sender') producing and imposing certain messages on the audience (the 'receiver'). It is suggested that the production of media messages passes through various circuits (such as power elites, professionals and viewers or readers), each with codes of their own and certain potential for negotiating a message's meaning. Being against determinist models of ideology production from above, Hall reminds us of the practices of resistance from below.

Stuart Hall. 1980[1973]. 'Encoding, decoding.'
In *Culture, Media, Language. Working Papers in Cultural Studies, 1972–1979*,
ed. by Centre for Contemporary Cultural Studies, 128–138.
London: Routledge.

Traditionally, mass-communications research has conceptualised the process of communication in terms of a circulation circuit or loop. This model has been criticised for its linearity – sender/message/receiver – for its concentration on the level of message exchange and for the absence of a structured conception of the different moments as a complex structure of relations. But it is also possible (and useful) to think of this process in terms of a structure produced and sustained through the articulation of linked but distinctive moments – production, circulation, distribution, consumption, reproduction. This would be to think of the process as a 'complex structure in dominance', sustained through the articulation of connected practices, each of which, however, retains its distinctiveness and has its own specific modality, its own forms and conditions of existence.

The 'object' of these practices is meanings and messages in the form of sign-vehicles of a specific kind organised, like any form of communication or language, through the operation of codes within the syntagmatic chain of a discourse. The apparatuses, relations and practices of production thus issue at a certain moment (the moment of 'production/circulation') in the form of symbolic vehicles constituted within the rules of 'language'. It is in this discursive form that the circulation of the 'product' takes place. The process thus requires, at the production end, its material instruments – its 'means' – as well as its own sets of social (production) relations – the organisation and combination of practices within media apparatuses. But it is in the discursive form that the circulation of the product takes place, as well as its distribution to different audiences. Once accomplished, the discourse must then be translated – transformed, again – into social practices if the circuit is to be both completed and effective. If no 'meaning' is taken, there can be no 'consumption'. If the meaning is not articulated in practice, it has no effect. The value of this approach is that while each of the moments, in articulation, is necessary to the circuit as a whole, no one moment can fully guarantee the next moment with which it is articulated. Since each has its specific modality and conditions of existence, each can constitute its own break or interruption of the 'passage of forms' on whose continuity the flow of effective production (that is, 'reproduction') depends.

Thus while in no way wanting to limit research to 'following only those leads which emerge from content analysis', we must recognise that the discursive form of the message has a privileged position in the communicative exchange (from the viewpoint of circulation), and that the moments of 'encoding' and 'decoding', though only 'relatively autonomous' in relation to the communicative process as a whole, are determinate moments. A 'raw' historical event cannot, in that form, be transmitted by, say, a television newscast. Events can only be signified within the aural-visual forms of the televisual discourse. In the moment when a historical event passes under the sign of discourse, it is subject to all the complex formal 'rules' by which language signifies. To put it paradoxically, the event must become a 'story' before it can become a communicative event. In that moment the formal sub-rules of discourse are 'in dominance', without, of course, subordinating out of existence the historical event so signified, the social relations in which the rules are set to work or the social and political consequences of the event having been signified in this way. The 'message form' is the necessary 'form of appearance' of the event in its passage from source to receiver. Thus the transposition into and out of the 'message form' (or the mode of symbolic exchange) is not a random 'moment', which we can take up or ignore at our convenience. The 'message form' is a determinate moment; though, at another level, it comprises the surface movements of the communications system only and requires, at another stage, to be integrated into the social relations of the communication process as a whole, of which it forms only a part.

From this general perspective, we may crudely characterise the television communicative process as follows. The institutional structures of broadcasting, with their practices and networks of production, their organised relations and technical infrastructures, are required to produce a programme. Production, here, constructs the message. In one sense, then, the circuit begins here. Of course, the production process is not without its 'discursive' aspect: it, too, is framed throughout by meanings and ideas: knowledge-in-use concerning the routines of production, historically defined technical skills, professional ideologies, institutional knowledge, definitions and assumptions, assumptions about the audience and so on frame the constitution of the programme through this production structure. Further, though the production structures of television originate the television discourse, they do not constitute a closed system. They draw topics, treatments, agendas, events, personnel, images of the audience, 'definitions of the situation' from other sources and other discursive formations within the wider socio-cultural and political structure of which they are a differentiated part. Philip Elliott has expressed this point succinctly, within a more traditional framework, in his discussion of the way in which the audience is both the 'source' and the 'receiver' of the television message. Thus – to borrow Marx's terms – circulation and reception are, indeed, 'moments' of the production process in television and are reincorporated, via a number of skewed and structured 'feedbacks', into the production process itself. The consumption or reception of the television message is thus also itself a 'moment' of the production process in its larger sense, though the latter is 'predominant' because it is the 'point of departure for the realisation' of the message. Production and reception of the television message are not, therefore, identical, but they are related: they are differentiated moments within the totality formed by the social relations of the communicative process as a whole.

At a certain point, however, the broadcasting structures must yield encoded messages in the form of a meaningful discourse. The institution-societal relations of production must pass under the discursive rules of language for its product to be 'realised'. This initiates a further differentiated moment, in which the formal rules of discourse and language are in dominance. Before this message can have an 'effect' (however defined), satisfy a 'need' or be put to a 'use', it must first be appropriated as a meaningful discourse and be meaningfully decoded. It is this set of decoded meanings which 'have an effect', influence, entertain, instruct or persuade, with very complex perceptual, cognitive, emotional, ideological or behavioural consequences. In a 'determinate' moment the structure employs a code and yields a 'message': at another determinate moment the 'message', via its decodings, issues into the structure of social practices. We are now fully aware that this re-entry into the practices of audience reception and 'use' cannot be understood in simple behavioural terms. The typical processes identified in positivistic research on isolated elements – effects, uses, 'gratifications' – are themselves framed by structures of understanding, as well as being produced by social and economic relations, which shape their 'realisation' at the reception end of the chain and which permit the meanings signified in the discourse to be transposed into practice or consciousness (to acquire social use value or political effectivity).

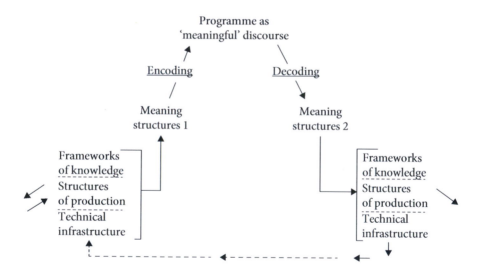

Clearly, what we have labelled in the diagram 'meaning structures 1' and 'meaning structures 2' may not be the same. They do not constitute an 'immediate identity'. The codes of encoding and decoding may not be perfectly symmetrical. The degrees of symmetry – that is, the degrees of 'understanding' and 'misunderstanding' in the communicative exchange – depend on the degrees of symmetry/asymmetry (relations of equivalence) established between the positions of the 'personifications', encoder-producer and decoder-receiver. But this in turn depends on the degrees of identity or non-identity between the codes which perfectly or imperfectly transmit, interrupt or systematically distort what has been transmitted. The lack of fit between the codes has a great deal to do with the structural differences of relation and position between broadcasters and audiences, but it also has something to do with the asymmetry between the codes of 'source' and 'receiver' at the moment of transformation into and out of the discursive form. What are called 'distortions' or 'misunderstandings' arise precisely from the lack of equivalence between the two sides in the communicative exchange. Once again, this defines the 'relative autonomy', but 'determinateness', of the entry and exit of the message in its discursive moments.

The application of this rudimentary paradigm has already begun to transform our understanding of the older term, television 'content'. We are just beginning to see how it might also transform our understanding of audience reception, 'reading', and response as well. Beginnings and endings have been announced in communications research before, so we must be cautious. But there seems to be some ground for thinking that a new and exciting phase in so-called audience research, of a quite new kind, may be opening up. At either end of the communicative chain the use of the semiotic paradigm promises to dispel the lingering behaviourism which has dogged mass-media research for so long, especially in its approach to content. Though we know the television programme is not a behavioural input, like a tap on the kneecap, it seems to have been almost impossible for traditional researchers to conceptualise the communicative process without lapsing into one or other variant of low-flying behaviourism. We know, as Gerbner has remarked, that representations of violence on the television screen 'are not violence but messages about violence': but we have continued to research the question of violence, for example, as if we were unable to comprehend this epistemological distinction.

The televisual sign is a complex one. It is itself constituted by the combination of two types of discourse, visual and aural. Moreover, it is an iconic sign, in Peirce's terminology, because 'it possesses some of the properties of the thing represented'. This is a point which has led to a great deal of confusion and has provided the site of intense controversy in the study of visual language. Since the visual discourse translates a three-dimensional world into two-dimensional planes, it cannot, of course, be the referent or concept it signifies. The dog in the film can bark but it cannot bite! Reality exists outside language, but it is constantly mediated by and through language: and what we can know and say has to be produced in and through discourse. Discursive 'knowledge' is the product not of the transparent representation of the 'real' in language but of the articulation of language on real relations and conditions. Thus there is no intelligible discourse without the operation of a code. Iconic signs are therefore coded signs too – even if the codes here work differently from those of other signs. There is no degree zero in language. Naturalism and 'realism' – the apparent fidelity of the representation to the thing or concept represented – is the result, the effect, of a certain specific articulation of language on the 'real'. It is the result of a discursive practice.

Certain codes may, of course, be so widely distributed in a specific language community or culture, and be learned at so early an age, that they appear not to be constructed – the effect of an articulation between sign and referent – but to be 'naturally' given. Simple visual signs appear to have achieved a 'near-universality' in this sense: though evidence remains that even apparently 'natural' visual codes are culture-specific. However, this does not mean that no codes have intervened: rather, that the codes have been profoundly naturalised. The operation of naturalised codes reveals not the transparency and 'naturalness' of language but the depth, the habituation and the near-universality of the codes in use. They produce apparently 'natural' recognitions. This has the (ideological) effect of concealing the practices of coding which are present. But we must not be fooled by appearances. Actually, what naturalised codes demonstrate is the degree of habituation produced when there is a fundamental alignment and reciprocity – an achieved equivalence – between the encoding and decoding side of an exchange of meanings. The functioning of the codes on the decoding side will frequently assume the status of naturalised perceptions. This leads us to think that the visual sign for 'cow' actually is (rather than represents) the animal, cow. But if we think of the visual representation of a cow in a manual on animal husbandry – and, even more, of the linguistic sign 'cow' – we can see that both, in different degrees, are arbitrary with respect to the concept of the animal they represent. The articulation of an arbitrary sign – whether visual or verbal – with the concept of a referent is the product not of nature but of convention, and the conventionalism of discourses requires the intervention, the support, of codes. Thus Eco has argued that iconic signs 'look like objects in the real world because they reproduce the conditions (that is, the codes) of perception in the viewer'. These 'conditions of perception' are, however, the result of a highly coded, even if virtually unconscious, set of operations – decodings. This is as true of the photographic or televisual image as it is of any other sign. Iconic signs are, however, particularly vulnerable to being 'read' as natural because visual codes of perception are very widely distributed and because this type of sign is less arbitrary than a linguistic sign: the linguistic sign, 'cow', possesses none of the properties of the thing represented, whereas the visual sign appears to possess some of those properties.

This may help us to clarify a confusion in current linguistic theory and to define precisely how some key terms are being used in this article. Linguistic theory frequently employs the distinction 'denotation' and 'connotation'. The term 'denotation' is widely equated with the literal meaning of a sign: because this literal meaning is almost universally recognised, especially when visual discourse is being employed, 'denotation' has often been confused with a literal transcription of 'reality' in language – and thus with a 'natural sign', one produced without the intervention of a code. 'Connotation', on the other hand, is employed simply to refer to less fixed and therefore more conventionalised and changeable, associative meanings, which clearly vary from instance to instance and therefore must depend on the intervention of codes.

We do not use the distinction – denotation/connotation – in this way. From our point of view, the distinction is an analytic one only. It is useful, in analysis, to be able to apply a rough rule of thumb which distinguishes those aspects of a sign which appear to be taken, in any language community at any point in time, as its 'literal' meaning (denotation) from the more associative meanings for the sign which it is possible to generate (connotation). But analytic distinctions must not be confused with distinctions in the real world. There will be very few instances in which signs organised in a discourse signify only their 'literal' (that is, near universally consensualised) meaning. In actual discourse, most signs will combine both the denotative and the connotative aspects (as redefined above). It may, then, be asked why we retain the distinction at all. It is largely a matter of analytic value. It is because signs appear to acquire their full ideological value – appear to be open to articulation with wider ideological discourses and meanings – at the level of their 'associative' meanings (that is, at the connotative level) – for here 'meanings' are not apparently fixed in natural perception (that is, they are not fully naturalised), and their fluidity of meaning and association can be more fully exploited and transformed. So it is at the connotative level of the sign that situational ideologies alter and transform signification. At this level we can see more clearly the active intervention of ideologies in and on discourse: here, the sign is open to new accentuations and, in Voloshinov's terms, enters fully into the struggle over meanings – the class struggle in language. This does not mean that the denotative or 'literal' meaning is outside ideology. Indeed, we could say that its ideological value is strongly fixed – because it has become so fully universal and 'natural'. The terms 'denotation' and 'connotation', then, are merely useful analytic tools for distinguishing, in particular contexts, between not the presence or absence of ideology in language but the different levels at which ideologies and discourses intersect.

The level of connotation of the visual sign, of its contextual reference and positioning in different discursive fields of meaning and association, is the point where already coded signs intersect with the deep semantic codes of a culture and take on additional, more active, ideological dimensions. We might take an example from advertising discourse. Here, too, there is no 'purely denotative', and certainly no 'natural', representation. Every visual sign in advertising connotes a quality, situation, value or inference, which is present as an implication or implied meaning, depending on the connotational positioning. In Barthes's example, the sweater always signifies a 'warm garment' (denotation) and thus the activity or value of 'keeping warm'. But it is also possible, at its more connotative levels, to signify 'the coming of winter' or 'a cold day'. And, in the specialised sub-codes of fashion, the sweater may also connote a fashionable style of haute couture or, alternatively, an informal style of dress. But set against the right visual background and positioned by the romantic sub-code, it may connote 'long autumn walk in the woods'. Codes of this order clearly contract relations for the sign with the wider universe of ideologies in a society. These codes are the means by which power and ideology are made to signify in particular discourses. They refer signs to the 'maps of meaning' into which any culture is classified; and those 'maps of social reality' have the whole range of social meanings, practices, and usages, power and interest 'written in' to them. The connotative levels of signifiers, Barthes remarked, 'have a close communication with culture, knowledge, history, and it is through them, so to speak, that the environmental world invades the linguistic and semantic system. They are, if you like, the fragments of ideology.'

The so-called denotative level of the televisual sign is fixed by certain, very complex (but limited or 'closed') codes. But its connotative level, though also bounded, is more open, subject to more active transformations, which exploit its polysemic values. Any such already constituted sign is potentially transformable into more than one connotative configuration. Polysemy must not, however, be confused with pluralism. Connotative codes are not equal among themselves. Any society or culture tends, with varying degrees of closure, to impose its classifications of the social and cultural and political world. These constitute a dominant cultural order, though it is neither univocal nor uncontested. This question of the 'structure of discourses in dominance' is a crucial point. The different areas of social life appear to be mapped out into discursive domains, hierarchically organised into dominant or preferred meanings. New, problematic or troubling events, which breach our expectancies and run counter to our 'commonsense constructs', to our 'taken-for-granted' knowledge of social structures, must be assigned to their discursive domains before they can be said to 'make sense'. The most common way of 'mapping' them is to assign the new to some domain or other of the existing 'maps of problematic social reality'. We say dominant, not 'determined ', because it is always possible to order, classify, assign and decode an event within more than one 'mapping'. But we say 'dominant' because there exists a pattern of 'preferred readings'; and these both have the institutional political/ideological order imprinted in them and have themselves become institutionalised. The domains of 'preferred meanings' have the whole social order embedded in them as a set of meanings, practices and beliefs: the everyday knowledge of social structures, of 'how things work for all practical purposes in this culture', the rank order of power and interest and the structure of legitimations, limits and sanctions. Thus to clarify a 'misunderstanding' at the connotative level, we must refer, through the codes, to the orders of social life, of economic and political power and of ideology. Further, since these mappings are 'structured in dominance' but not closed, the communicative process consists not in the unproblematic assignment of every visual item to its given position within a set of prearranged codes, but of performative rules – rules of competence and use, of logics-in-use – which seek actively to enforce or prefer one semantic domain over another and rule items into and out of their appropriate meaning-sets. Formal semiology has too often neglected this practice of interpretative work, though this constitutes, in fact, the real relations of broadcast practices in television.

In speaking of dominant meanings, then, we are not talking about a one-sided process which governs how all events will be signified. It consists of the 'work' required to enforce, win plausibility for and command as legitimate a decoding of the event within the limit of dominant definitions in which it has been connotatively signified. (…)

It was argued earlier that since there is no necessary correspondence between encoding and decoding, the former can attempt to 'prefer' but cannot prescribe or guarantee the latter, which has its own conditions of existence. Unless they are wildly aberrant, encoding will have the effect of constructing some of the limits and parameters within which decodings will operate. If there were no limits, audiences could simply read whatever they liked into any message. No doubt some total misunderstandings of this kind do exist. But the vast range must contain some degree of reciprocity between encoding and decoding moments, otherwise we could not speak of an effective communicative exchange at all. Nevertheless, this 'correspondence' is not given but constructed. It is not 'natural' but the product of an articulation between two distinct moments. And the former cannot determine or guarantee, in a simple sense, which decoding codes will be employed. Otherwise communication would be a perfectly equivalent circuit, and every message would be an instance of 'perfectly transparent communication'. We must think, then, of the variant articulations in which encoding and decoding can be combined. To elaborate on this, we offer a hypothetical analysis of some possible decoding positions, in order to reinforce the point of 'no necessary correspondence'.

We identify three hypothetical positions from which decodings of a televisual discourse may be constructed. These need to be empirically tested and refined. But the argument that decodings do not follow inevitably from encodings, that they are not identical, reinforces the argument of 'no necessary correspondence'. It also helps to deconstruct the commonsense meaning of 'misunderstanding' in terms of a theory of 'systematically distorted communication'.

The first hypothetical position is that of the dominant-hegemonic position. When the viewer takes the connoted meaning from, say, a television newscast or current affairs programme full and straight, and decodes the message in terms of the reference code in which it has been encoded, we might say that the viewer is operating inside the dominant code. This is the ideal-typical case of 'perfectly transparent communication' – or as close as we are likely to come to it 'for all practical purposes'. Within this we can distinguish the positions produced by the professional code. This is the position (produced by what we perhaps ought to identify as the operation of a 'metacode') which the professional broadcasters assume when encoding a message which has already been signified in a hegemonic manner. The professional code is 'relatively independent' of the dominant code, in that it applies criteria and transformational operations of its own, especially those of a technico-practical nature. The professional code, however, operates within the 'hegemony' of the dominant code. Indeed, it serves to reproduce the dominant definitions precisely by bracketing their hegemonic quality and operating instead with displaced professional codings which foreground such apparently neutral technical questions as visual quality, news and presentational values, televisual quality, 'professionalism' and so on. The hegemonic interpretations of, say, the politics of Northern Ireland, or the Chilean coup or the Industrial Relations Bill are principally generated by political and military elites: the particular choice of presentational occasions and formats, the selection of personnel, the choice of images, the staging of debates are selected and combined through the operation of the professional code. How the broadcasting professionals are able both to operate with 'relatively autonomous' codes of their own and to act in such a way as to reproduce (not without contradiction) the hegemonic signification of events is a complex matter which cannot be further spelled out here. It must suffice to say that the professionals are linked with the defining elites not only by the institutional position of broadcasting itself as an 'ideological apparatus' but also by the structure of access (that is, the systematic 'over-accessing' of selective elite personnel and their 'definition of the situation' in television). It may even be said that the professional codes serve to reproduce hegemonic definitions specifically by not overtly biasing their operations in a dominant direction: ideological reproduction therefore takes place here inadvertently, unconsciously, 'behind men's backs'. Of course, conflicts, contradictions and even misunderstandings regularly arise between the dominant and the professional significations and their signifying agencies.

The second position we would identify is that of the negotiated code or position. Majority audiences probably understand quite adequately what has been dominantly defined and professionally signified. The dominant definitions, however, are hegemonic precisely because they represent definitions of situations and events which are 'in dominance' (global). Dominant definitions connect events, implicitly or explicitly, to grand totalisations, to the great syntagmatic views-of-the-world: they take 'large views' of issues: they relate events to the 'national interest' or to the level of geopolitics even if they make these connections in truncated, inverted or mystified ways. The definition of a hegemonic viewpoint is, first, that it defines within its terms the mental horizon, the universe, of possible meanings, of a whole sector of relations in a society or culture;

and, second, that it carries with it the stamp of legitimacy – it appears coterminous with what is 'natural', 'inevitable', 'taken for granted' about the social order. Decoding within the negotiated version contains a mixture of adaptive and oppositional elements: it acknowledges the legitimacy of the hegemonic definitions to make the grand significations (abstract), while, at a more restricted, situational (situated) level, it makes its own ground rules – it operates with exceptions to the rule. It accords the privileged position to the dominant definitions of events while reserving the right to make a more negotiated application to 'local conditions', to its own more corporate positions. This negotiated version of the dominant ideology is thus shot through with contradictions, though these are only on certain occasions brought to full visibility. Negotiated codes operate through what we might call particular or situated logics: and these logics are sustained by their differential and unequal relation to the discourses and logics of power. The simplest example of a negotiated code is that which governs the response of a worker to the notion of an Industrial Relations Bill limiting the right to strike or to arguments for a wages freeze. At the level of the 'national interest' economic debate the decoder may adopt the hegemonic definition, agreeing that 'we must all pay ourselves less in order to combat inflation'. This, however, may have little or no relation to his or her willingness to go on strike for better pay and conditions or to oppose the Industrial Relations Bill at the level of shop-floor or union organisation. We suspect that the great majority of so-called 'misunderstandings' arise from the contradictions and disjunctures between hegemonic-dominant encodings and negotiated-corporate decodings.

It is just these mismatches in the levels which most provoke defining elites and professionals to identify a 'failure in communications'.

Finally, it is possible for a viewer perfectly to understand both the literal and the connotative inflection given by a discourse but to decode the message in a globally contrary way. He or she detotalises the message in the preferred code in order to retotalise the message within some alternative framework of reference. This is the case of the viewer who listens to a debate on the need to limit wages but 'reads' every mention of the 'national interest' as 'class interest'. He or she is operating with what we must call an oppositional code. One of the most significant political moments (they also coincide with crisis points within the broadcasting organisations themselves, for obvious reasons) is the point when events which are normally signified an decoded in a negotiated way begin to be given an oppositional reading. Here the 'politics of signification' – the struggle in discourse – is joined.

Ernesto Laclau

The impossibility of society

Ernesto Laclau (1935–2014) was well-known for the theory of hegemony which he developed with Chantal Mouffe (b. 1943) (Laclau and Mouffe, 1985). According to Laclau/Mouffe, political demands are constructed following a logic of difference and equivalence. For them, the social is the product of a political practice, but the question is how to account for the irreducible contingency that characterises the discursive construction of any hegemonic alliance (Laclau, 1990). In the selected text, Laclau spells out the consequences for a discursive theory of the political. For Laclau, the terrain of the social is constructed in the discursive articulations of the political. While his aim is to delineate a general discourse theoretical framework for the way in which the political and the social are interlinked, he leaves it to others to account for how discourse and hegemonies are formed empirically. Just like the Foucauldians, Laclau, Mouffe and their followers usually prefer to study discursive strategies and logics in interpretive ways (Howarth and Glynos, 2007).

References

Howarth, David, and Jason Glynos. 2007. *Logics of Critical Explanation in Social and Political Theory*. London: Routledge.
Laclau, Ernesto. 1990. *New Reflections on the Revolution of Our Time*. London, New York: Verso.
Laclau, Ernesto, and Chantal Mouffe. 1985. *Hegemony and Socialist Strategy. Towards a Radical Democratic Politics*. London, New York: Verso.

Ernesto Laclau. 1990. 'The Impossibility of Society.'
In *New Reflections on the Revolution of Our Time*, 89–92.
London, New York: Verso.

I should like to refer here to several problems which are central to the contemporary Marxist theory of ideology. In discussing these problems, it is evident that we presently live at the centre of a theoretical paradox. The terms of this paradox could be formulated as follows: in no previous period has reflection upon 'ideology' been so much at the centre of Marxist theoretical approaches; at the same time, however, in no other period have the limits and referential identity of the 'ideological' become so blurred and problematic. If the increasing interest in ideology runs parallel to a widening of the historical effectivity attributed to what was traditionally considered as the domain of the 'superstructures' – and this widening is a response to the crisis of an economistic and reductionistic conception of Marxism – then the very crisis puts into question the social totality constituted around the base-superstructure distinction. As a consequence it is no longer possible to identify the object 'ideology' in terms of a topography of the social.

Within the Marxist tradition, we can identify two classical approaches to the problem of ideology. These approaches have often – but not always – been combined. For one of them, 'ideology' is thought to be a *level of the social totality*, for the other, it is identified with *false consciousness*. Today, both approaches appear to have been undermined as a consequence of the crisis of the assumptions on which they were grounded: the validity of the first depended on a conception of society as an intelligible totality, itself conceived as the structure upon which its partial elements and processes are founded. The validity of the second approach presupposed a conception of human agency – a subject having an ultimate essential homogeneity whose misrecognition was postulated as the source of 'ideology'. In this respect, the two approaches were grounded in an *essentialist* conception of both society and social agency. To see clearly the problems which have led the theory of ideology to its present impasse, we need to study the crisis of this essentialist conception in its two variants.

Let me turn, first, to the crisis of the concept of social totality. The ambition of all holistic approaches had been to fix the meaning of any element or social process *outside* itself, that is, in a *system of relations* with other elements. In this respect, the base-superstructure model played an ambiguous role; if it asserted the *relational* character of the identity of both base and superstructure, at the same time it endowed the relational system with a centre. And so, in a very Hegelian fashion, the superstructures ended up taking their revenge by asserting the 'essentiality' of the appearances. More importantly, the structural totality was to present itself as an object having a positivity of its own, which it was possible to describe and to define. In this sense, this totality operated as an underlying principle of intelligibility of the social order. The status of this totality was that of an essence of the social order which had to be *recognized* behind the empirical variations expressed at the surface of social life. (Note that what is at stake here is not the opposition, structuralism, vs. historicism. It does not matter if the totality is synchronic or diachronic; the important point is that in both cases it is a *founding totality* which presents itself as an intelligible object of 'knowledge' [cognitio] conceived as a process or re-cognition.) Against this essentialist vision we tend nowadays to accept the *infinitude of the social,* that is, the fact that any structural system is limited, that it is always surrounded by an 'excess of meaning' which it is unable to master and that, consequently, 'society' as a unitary and intelligible object which grounds its own partial processes is an impossibility. Let us examine the double movement that this recognition involves. The great advance carried out by structuralism was the recognition of the relational character of any social identity; its limit was its transformation of those relations into a system, into an identifiable and intelligible object (i.e. into an essence). But if we maintain the relational character of any identity and if, at the same time, we renounce the *fixation* of those identities in a system, then the social must be identified with the infinite play of differences, that is, with what in the strictest sense of the term we can call *discourse* – on the condition, of course, that we liberate the concept of discourse from its restrictive meaning as speech and writing.

This first movement thus implies the impossibility of fixing meaning. But this cannot be the end of the matter. A discourse in which meaning cannot possibly be fixed is nothing else but the discourse of the psychotic.

The second movement therefore consists in the attempt to effect this ultimately impossible fixation. The social is not only the infinite play of differences. It is also the attempt to limit that play, to domesticate infinitude, to embrace it within the finitude of an order. But this order – or structure – no longer takes the form of an underlying essence of the social; rather, it is an attempt – by definition unstable and precarious – to act over that 'social', to *hegemonize* it. In a way which resembles the one we are pursuing here, Saussure attempted to limit the principle of the arbitrariness of the sign with the assertion of the relative character of that arbitrariness. Thus, the problem of the social totality is posed in new terms; the 'totality' does not establish the limit of 'the social' by transforming the latter into a *determinate* object (i.e. 'society'). Rather, the social always exceeds the limits of the attempts to constitute society. At the same time, however, that 'totality' does not disappear. If the suture it attempts is ultimately impossible, it is nevertheless possible to proceed to a relative fixation of the social through the institution of nodal points. But if this is the case, questions concerning those nodal points and their relative weight cannot be determined *sub species aeternitatis.* Each social formation has its own forms of determination and relative autonomy, which are always instituted through a complex process of overdetermination and therefore cannot be established *a priori*. With this insight, the base-superstructure distinction falls and, along with it, the conception of ideology as a necessary level of every social formation.

If we now pass to the second approach to ideology – ideology as false consciousness – we find a similar situation. The notion of false consciousness only makes sense if the identity of the social agent can be fixed. It is only on the basis of recognizing its true identity that we can assert that the consciousness of the subject is 'false'. And this implies, of course, that that identity must be *positive and non-contradictory*. Within Marxism, a conception of subjectivity of this kind is at the basis of the notion of 'objective class interests'. Here I am not going to discuss in detail the forms of constitution, the implications and the limitations of such a conception of subjectivity. I shall rather just mention the two processes which led to its progressive abandonment. In the first place, the gap between 'actual consciousness' and 'imputed consciousness' grew increasingly wider. The way this gap was filled – through the presence of a Party instituted as the bearer of the objective historical interests of the class – led to the establishment of an 'enlightened' despotism of intellectuals and bureaucrats who spoke in the name of the masses, explained to them their true interests, and imposed upon them increasing totalitarian forms of control. The reaction to this situation inevitably took the form of the assertion of the actual identity of the social agents against the 'historical interests' which burdened them. In the second place, the very identity of the social agents was increasingly questioned when the flux of differences in advanced capitalist societies indicated that the identity and homogeneity of social agents was an illusion, that any social subject is essentially decentred, that his/her identity is nothing but the unstable articulation of constantly changing positionalities. The same excess of meaning, the same precarious character of any structuration that we find in the domain of the social order, is also to be found in the domain of subjectivity. But if any social agent is a decentred subject, if when attempting to determine his/her identity we find nothing else but the kaleidoscopic movement of differences, in what sense can we say that subjects misrecognize themselves? The theoretical ground that made sense of the concept of 'false consciousness' has evidently dissolved.

It would therefore look as if the two conceptual frameworks which formerly made sense of the concept of ideology have broken up, and that the concept should consequently be eliminated. However, I do not think this to be a satisfactory solution. We cannot do without the concept of misrecognition, precisely because the very assertion that the 'identity and homogeneity of social agents is an illusion' cannot be formulated without introducing the category of misrecognition. The critique of the 'naturalization of meaning' and of the 'essentialization of the social' is a critique of the misrecognition of their true character. Without this premise, any deconstruction would be meaningless. So, it looks as if we can maintain the concept of ideology and the category of misrecognition only by inverting their traditional content. The ideological would not consist of the misrecognition of a positive essence, but exactly the opposite: it would consist of the non-recognition of the precarious character of any positivity, of the impossibility of any ultimate suture. The ideological would consist of those discursive forms through which a society tries to institute itself as such on the basis of closure, of the fixation of meaning, of the non-recognition of the infinite play of differences. The ideological would be the will to 'totality' of any totalizing discourse. And insofar as the social is impossible without some fixation of meaning, without the discourse of closure, the ideological must be seen as constitutive of the social. This social only exists as the vain attempt to institute that impossible object: society. Utopia is the essence of any communication and social practice.

Judith Butler

Speaking to the postcolonial Other

Judith Butler (b. 1956) is well-known for her critique of the sex-gender distinction (1990). For Butler, the cultural distinctions of gender are as much constructed in discursive practices as the biological distinctions of sex. Through discursive interpellations, the binary construction of human beings as 'man' or 'woman' is established in what she calls the heterosexual matrix. Identities, however, can also be unmade through practices of subversive iteration. Therefore, discourse is understood in terms of a politics of performance (1997). In her more recent work she has shown interested in ethical and political questions (2000). In the selected text, Butler reflects on the intertextual construction of political identities. Her example is a comment by Sartre on Fanon which illustrates how the subject positions of the European and the postcolonial other are negotiated through written texts.

References

Butler, Judith. 1990. *Gender Trouble. Feminism and the Subversion of Identity*. Routledge: London, New York.

Butler, Judith. 1997. *The Psychic Life of Power*. Stanford: Stanford University Press.

Butler, Judith, Ernesto Laclau, and Slavoj Žižek. 2000. *Contingency, Hegemony, Universality*. Paris: Verso.

Judith Butler. 2008. 'Violence, Nonviolence. Sartre on Fanon.'
In *Race after Sartre,* ed. by Jonathan Judaken, 211–232, selected 211–215.
Albany: SUNY Press.

What is immediately strange about Sartre's controversial preface to Fanon's *The Wretched of the Earth*[1] is its mode of address. To whom is this preface written? Sartre imagines his reader as the colonizer or the French citizen who recoils from the thought of violent acts of resistance on the part of the colonized. Minimally, his imagined reader is one who believes that his own notions of humanism and universalism suffice as norms by which to assess the war for independence in Algeria and similar efforts at decolonization. Sartre's address to his audience is direct and caustic: 'What does Fanon care whether you read his work or not? It is to his brothers that he denounces our old tricks.' At one point, he seems to take his implied readers aside, addressing the preface to them directly:

> 'Europeans, you must open this book and enter into it. After a few steps in the darkness you will see strangers gathered around a fire; come close, and listen, for they are talking of a destiny they will mete out to your trading centers and to the hired soldiers who defend them. They will see you, perhaps, but they will be talking among themselves, without even lowering their voices. This indifference strikes home: their fathers, shadowy creatures, *your* creatures, were but dead souls; you it was who allowed them glimpses of light, to you only did they dare to speak, and you did not bother to reply to such zombies…. Turn and turn about; in these shadows from whence a new dawn will break, it is you who are the zombies (*les zombies, c'est vous!*).'
> (13)

There are many curious aspects of this mode of address. It may well have been presumptuous of Sartre to address those living under conditions of colonization directly, since it would have put him in a position of pedagogical power over them. He has no information to impart *to them*, no advice, no explanation; and certainly no apology for European colonial dominance and, in particular, French colonial rule in Algeria. So he speaks, as it were, to his white brethren, knowing perhaps that his own name on the preface will attract such readers to this text by Fanon. So Sartre or, rather, Sartre's name, is bait for the European reader. But do we understand what 'Europe' is in this context or, for that matter, the European? Sartre himself assumes that the European

---

[1].   Jean-Paul Sartre, *The Wretched of the Earth*, trans. by Constance Farrington (New York: Grove, 1963); Frantz Fanon *Les Damnés de la terre* (Paris, Éditions Maspéro, 1961). The 1991 Gallimard edition omits the Sartrean preface. And the new English version, trans. by Richard Philcox, includes commentary by both Jean-Paul Sartre and Homi Bhabha (Grove, 2004). Citations are to the original Grove Press edition except where explicitly noted. All citations to Homi Bhabha are to the new edition.

is white and a man. And so two separate zones of masculinity are contoured when he imagines Fanon speaking to his brothers, his colonized brothers, in the text, whereas Sartre speaks to his European brothers, collaborators with the powers of colonization in one way or another.

We might ask whether these two racially divided fraternities are being built through the modes of direct address that structure this text. Matters are made more complex by the fact that Fanon speaks to many audiences, and sometimes his lines of address interrupt each other. A European, in Sartre's view, will read this text only as a kind of eavesdropping: 'Europeans, you must open this book and enter into it. After a few steps in the darkness you will see strangers gathered around a fire; come close, and listen (*approchez, écoutez*).' So Fanon's text is a conversation figured as a conversation *among* colonized men, and Sartre's preface is less a conversation *among* the colonizers than an exhortation of one to the other, asking the European to read as one would listen to a conversation that is *not* meant for the one, the 'you' addressed by Sartre. Just as Sartre's preface is not intended for the colonized population (though we might nonetheless consider it as a kind of display of Sartre's politics for them), so Fanon's text is construed as not addressed to a white, European audience. In effect, Sartre writes, 'Come listen to this text that is not meant for you, that is not speaking to you, that cuts you out as its audience, and learn why this text had to be addressed instead to those living in the decolonized state of being, that is, neither fully dead nor fully living. Come and listen to the voices that are no longer petitioning you, no longer seeking inclusion in your world, no longer concerned with whether you hear and understand or not.' Sartre petitions his European brothers, presumptively white, to bear up under this rejection and indifference and to come to understand the reasons why they are not the intended audience of Fanon's book. Of course, it is unclear how they could come to learn this lesson or see this truth without becoming its audience and reading the book. But that is the paradox at stake here. In the course of exhorting them to 'listen in' on this book, Sartre is positioning his white audience at a curious distance where it is made at once to suffer peripheral status. The white audience can no longer presume itself to be the intended audience, equivalent to 'any' reader, anonymous and implicitly universal. The paradox, as I mentioned, is that the white brethren are asked to read on nonetheless and are even exhorted to read on, though their reading on is to be construed as a listening in, instating their outside status at the moment of their comprehension. This seems another way of saying: this book is for you, you would do well to read it. The kind of displaced comprehending that Sartre proposes for the white reader is one that deconstitutes the presumptive privilege of the European reader in the act of taking in this new historical constellation. Decentering and even rejection are absorbed, undergone, and a certain undoing of the *presumption* of racial privilege is enacted between the lines or, rather, in the nonaddress that is, paradoxically, delivered through Sartre's preface to the European. The preface thus functions as a strange mode of delivery, handing the white reader the discourse not intended for him, and so handing him dislocation and rejection as the condition of possibility for his comprehension. Sartre's writing to the European reader is a way of acting upon that reader, positioning him outside the circle, and establishing that peripheral status as an epistemological requirement for understanding the condition of colonization. The European reader undergoes a loss of privilege at the same time that he is asked to submit to an empathetic enactment with the position of the socially excluded and effaced.

So Fanon's text, figured by Sartre as plurivocal and fraternal – that is, as a conversation among a group of men – undoes the notion of Fanon the singular author. Fanon is a budding movement. His writing is the speaking of several men. And when Fanon writes, a conversation takes place; the written page is a meeting, one in which strategy is being planned, and a circle is drawn tight among fellow travelers. Outside of the circle are those who understand that this speaking is indifferent to them. A 'you' is being spoken around the fire, but the European no longer counts as part of that 'you.' He may hear the word 'you' only to recognize that he is not included within its purview. If we ask how this exclusion came about for the European, Sartre claims that it follows dialectically from the way that white men suspended the humanity of the fathers of those who have lived under colonialism. The sons saw their fathers humiliated, treated with indifference, and now that very indifference has been taken up and returned to its sender in new form.

Interestingly, it is the humanity of the fathers subjugated under colonialism that is at issue here, and that implies that the dehumanization of others under colonialism follows from the erosion of paternal authority. It is this offense that mandates exclusion from the conversation that composes Fanon's text. This is a choreography of men, some forming inner circles, some cast to the periphery, and it is their manhood or, rather, the manhood of their fathers, that is at stake in the direct address. Not to be addressed as a 'you' is to be treated as less than a man. And yet, as we will see, the 'you' functions in at least two ways in Fanon: as the direct address that establishes human dignity through masculinization and as the direct address that establishes the question of humanity beyond the framework of masculinization and feminization alike. In either case, though, the 'you' does not merely refer to the one who is addressed, but address itself is the condition of becoming a human, one who is constituted within the scene of address (for a further elaboration of this position, see Butler, 2005).

If the excluded European asks *why* he is not privy to the conversation, then he must consider the implications of being treated with indifference. The problem to consider is not just that colonizers bear bad attitudes toward the colonized. If the colonized are excluded from the conversation in which humans are not only addressed but constituted through the address, the very possibility of being constituted as a human is foreclosed. To be excluded from the conversation is the unmaking of the human as such. The fathers of these men were not treated as men, certainly not addressed, directly or otherwise, as men, and so, failing that address, they were never fully constituted as human. If we seek to understand their ontology, these men who were never addressed as men, we find that no fixed determination is possible. The face-to-face address to a 'you' has the capacity to confer a certain acknowledgment, to include the other in the potentially reciprocal exchange of speech; without that acknowledgment and that possibility for reciprocal address, no human may emerge. In the place of the human a specter takes form, what Sartre refers to as the 'zombie,' the shadow figure who is never quite human and never quite not. So if we are to tell the prehistory of this complex scene of address within Fanon's *The Wretched of the Earth*, or rather the two scenes of address that separate its traditional preface from the text itself, we would begin, according to Sartre, with the view that the colonizers had no 'you' for the colonized, that they could and would not address them directly, and, as a result, withheld a certain ontological determination, one that follows only through recognition as a reciprocal exchange, a mutually constituting set of acts.

The colonizer had no 'you' for the colonized, but once again, in Sartre's preface, the 'you' is paradoxical, and again, *not* deployed for the colonized, but reserved exclusively for the colonizer. Who will speak to the colonized? For Fanon, the colonizer is not the 'you', or so Sartre tells us, but for Sartre, the colonized is not the 'you'. So Sartre continues the very tradition of nonaddress that he seeks to indict. Sartre speaks as a spectral double: in the name of the European who shows how deconstituting his own privilege is apparently done, but also in a prescriptive vein, calling upon other Europeans to do the same. When Sartre effectively says 'you' are not the intended reader of this text, he constitutes the group who ought to undergo the deconstitution of their privilege; in addressing them, however, he does not deconstitute them, but rather constitutes them anew. The problem, of course, is that in addressing them as the privileged, as one privileged speaker to another, he solidifies their privilege as well. And where before, in withholding address from the colonized, the colonizers imperiled an ontological determination for them, now, in Sartre's usage, the 'you' – directed toward his European counterparts – is being asked to assume responsibility for this colonial condition of destitution. Sartre mobilizes the second person, strikes out with his 'you' in order to accuse and demand accountability: 'their fathers, shadowy creatures, *your* creatures, were but dead souls; *you* it was who allowed them glimpses of light, to you only did they dare to speak, and you did not bother to reply to such zombies'.

In the stark scene of colonial subjugation that Sartre lays out, the colonized did not address each other but spoke only to *you,* the colonizer. If they could have addressed one another, they would have started to take shape within a legible social ontology, they would have risked existence through this communicative circuit. They only dared to speak to 'you' – in other words, you were the exclusive audience for any direct address. You [the colonizer] did not bother to reply, for to reply would have meant to confer a certain human status on the one speaking to you. The mode of address, far from being a simple rhetorical technique, enacts the social constitution of ontology. Or let me put it more starkly: The mode of address enacts the social possibility of a livable existence. Correspondingly, refusing to reply to or address another who speaks, or requiring an asymmetrical form of address according to which the one in power is the exclusive audience for the second person – these are all ways of deconstituting ontology and orchestrating a nonlivable life. This is clearly the paradox of dying while alive, a further permutation of what Orlando Patterson, invoking Hegel in the context of describing slavery, called *social death* (Mohamed, 1995). And there, as well as here, this social death touches fathers first, which means it leaves its legacy of shame and rage for the sons. Most importantly, social death is a not a static condition but a perpetually lived contradiction that takes shape as a particularly masculine conundrum. In the context of Algeria and the war for independence, the colonized man is left with a choice that cannot culminate in a livable life: 'If he shows fight, the soldiers fire and he's a dead man; if he gives in, he degrades himself and he is no longer a man at all; shame and fear will split up his character and make his inmost self fall to pieces' (15).

References

Butler, Judith. 2005. *Giving an Account of Oneself*. New York: Fordham University Press.
    DOI: 10.5422/fso/9780823225033.001.0001
Mohamed, Abdul Jan. 1995. *The Death-Bound Subject: Richard Wright's Archaelogy of Death*. Durham, N.C.: Duke University Press.

Section III

Enunciative pragmatics

Introduction

The enunciative-pragmatic approach to discourse has been developed in France and has spread to many countries, particularly Latin America. This approach may be considered a variety of discourse pragmatics but it is above all an analysis of language as a system, deeply concerned with subjectivity, not a theory of communication. Nowadays it can be counted among the most prominent currents in discourse analysis. Like others, e.g. the systemic functional model of Halliday (see the section on 'Sociopragmatics'), this approach highlights the reflexivity of speech activity, which allows the speakers to convert the system of language into discourse.

The contribution of linguists

A great deal of research in pragmatics has been conducted within philosophy or sociology (see section on 'Theoretical Inspirations'). Enunciative theories were originally developed by linguists, especially by 'Continental' linguists, working on deictic expressions, speech acts or implicit meaning. One can mention the Russian linguist Roman Jakobson (1896–1982) and the Swiss Charles Bally (1865–1947), who studied certain facets of enunciative phenomena. Since the 1960s, enunciative pragmatics has been put centre stage in linguistic theories of discourse. The most important author in this area is Émile Benveniste (1902–1976), a French expert of Indo-European languages and general linguistics. He published two collections *Problèmes de linguistique générale* [*Problems of general linguistics*] (1971[1966]) and *Problèmes de linguistique générale II* (1974). In the context of enunciative pragmatics, two other names should also be mentioned: Antoine Culioli (b. 1924), who proposed a linguistic model based on cognitive operations (Culioli, 1991, 1999), and Oswald Ducrot (b. 1930), who associated enunciation with a pragmatic outlook. For Ducrot, the nature of language is basically argumentative (Ducrot, 1972, 1984).

The very term 'enunciation' raises certain problems for translation; in Romance languages a distinction can easily be made between 'enunciation' (*énonciation*), which refers to the activity of language use, and *énoncé* ('*enunciado*' in Spanish or Portuguese, '*enunciato*' in Italian), which refers to the product of this activity. In English the situation is more complicated since 'utterance' can cover both the activity (*énonciation*) and its product (*énoncé*) while the term 'enunciation' usually designates '*pronunciation*', especially a speaker's particular way of articulating his or her discourse.

Another problem is that even in Romance languages *énonciation* can be polysemous. For example, in his *Problems of General Linguistics* I and II [*Problèmes de linguistique générale*], Benveniste uses *énonciation* to indicate various meanings (Ono, 2007): (1) pronunciation; (2) the conversion of language into discourse; (3) an individual, unique act through which the subject affirms itself as the point of reference (for persons, time, space) of discourse activity; (4) a way of influencing the addressee; (5) the actualization of sentences in discourse, by which reference to the world is made possible. But the usual definition of the term *énonciation* is 'putting the language into operation through an individual act of use' (Benveniste 1974: 80). From this viewpoint, *énonciation* is considered as an individual act of language production in a given situational context. While the utterance is the product (*énoncé*), the uttering itself is the *énonciation*. From the smallest semantic unit to sentences and texts, *énonciation* implies the presence of communicating subjects in language.

For linguists putting enunciation at the centre of the linguistic system, the term designates the process through which language and the world are connected. On the one hand, this process allows speakers to represent facts in their utterances; on the other, an utterance is also a fact, an event, which takes place in time and space. So, enunciative categories call into question the very frontier between language and the world. In that respect, the key category is that of 'enunciator', a speaking instance immanent in discourse which exists through the very act of using language. From this viewpoint, the distinction between 'locutor' (in French *locuteur*) and 'enunciator' (or 'voice', 'source', in French *énonciateur*) is most important: the being who is producing an utterance is neither inside the linguistic system nor outside of language. The pronouns *I* or *me* point to the enunciator, who exists only when he or she is enunciating: if nobody speaks there is no enunciator.

Various linguistic phenomena, such as markers or traces (*marques, repères*) of the discursive activity, are usually taken into account by enunciative pragmatics. One can mention in particular:

–   Deictic expressions, whose point of reference is the very act of using language in a certain context: 1st and 2nd person pronouns, tense, various groups of time and space adverbs. Benveniste (1971[1966]) made a distinction between *discourse* and *story* (in French *histoire*), which are considered the two main kinds of *énonciation*: on the one hand there is 'discourse', that is to say utterances in which there are formal traces of the presence of the enunciator (such as deictic expressions and markers of modality); on the other there are utterances, which are presented as independent of the situation of *énonciation* (whose poles are I-NOW-HERE), in particular narrative texts ('stories') in literature or history. Since the term 'story' seemed to be too restrictive, it has been extended to any kind of utterance which is not a deictic expression: proverbs, scientific texts, narratives etc.

- Noun determiners: particularly articles and demonstratives (*a, the, this, that*), which are used to construct reference, particularly in anaphora.
- Modality: words expressing the attitude of the enunciator towards the utterance and the addressee, paraphrases and reformulations, etc.
- The phenomena that are associated with 'dialogism' (M. Bakhtin): polemic negation, reported speech, irony, words between brackets, viewpoint shifts, etc. As an example of a viewpoint shift, one can mention the use of *but*, as in 'p *but* q'. Here the function of *but* is not merely to connect propositions but to block the anticipation of an inference: in 'p *but* q' the propositional content p invites the conclusion 'therefore r'; however, q is presented as having superior force that blocks r.

In discourse analysis

When various strands of discourse analysis appeared in France in the late sixties, enunciative pragmatics was mobilised on two complementary levels:

1. Enunciative pragmatics provides a wide range of tools to analyse the way the linguistic system is used to produce texts.
2. Any *énonciation* of a text implies a genre, a communicative frame in which it develops and that it must also validate (Maingueneau, 2002, 2007).

Therefore, the analysis of *énonciation* involves both the analysis of the constraints underlying linguistic communication and the study of linguistic markers, which are traces of the verbal interaction between an enunciator and an addressee. Culioli has called the addressee 'co-enunciator' in order to emphasize that this instance of the other is always co-constructed with the enunciator.

The recourse to enunciative pragmatics is tightly connected to the work of many French-speaking discourse analysts, whose main purpose is to study the way institutions and discourse shape each other, the complex relationship between text organization and social positions (particularly discourse genres or positionings in a field). The enunciative approach is more appropriate to study discourse than other trends in linguistics (mainly structural or generative trends) whose categories are quite independent of discourse activity. Besides rather than speaking of multiple 'identities', researchers use enunciative concepts and methods in order to avoid using psychological or sociological categories independently of linguistic forms.

The philosophical background of French discourse analysis may be another reason for why enunciative pragmatics from the 1960s onwards has been used in most French-speaking approaches to discourse (see the section on 'From Structuralism to Poststructuralism', Angermuller, 2014). Its most prominent thinkers, who are also the most radical, i.e. Foucault (1989[1969, 1971]) and Pêcheux (1995[1969], 1982[1975]), shared a common interest in subjectivity tied to the concept of 'discursive formation'. Their theoretical differences notwithstanding, both criticize the traditional conception of the subject, considered as a conscious and autonomous individual, as a meaning-producing source of his or her utterances. Both defend the idea that the subject is produced within discourse and subjected to a discourse which constructs subject positions by which they attain meaning and can have effects on the world. As Foucault (1972[1969]: 55) says,

> Discourse is not the majestically unfolding manifestation of a subject who thinks, who knows, and who speaks, but, on the contrary, a set, in which the dispersion of the subject and his [sic] discontinuity with himself may be determined. It is a space of exteriority in which a network of distinct sites is deployed (…) it is neither by recourse to a transcendental subject nor by recourse to a psychological subjectivity that the regulation of its enunciations should be defined.[1]

From the perspective of enunciative pragmatics, the challenge is to find a way between a structuralist stance, which would eliminate the subject, and a conception of discourse, in which subjects are considered as 'actors' endowed with psychological and sociological attributes that allow them to design 'strategies' and pursue 'goals'.

The texts of this section present various aspects of the enunciative approach to discourse.

– An article by Émile Benveniste: it focuses on the key role that enunciation plays in the linguistic system.
– An article by Jacqueline Authier-Revuz who, drawing on the psychoanalysis of Lacan, reflects on the relationship between enunciation and subjectivity.
– An article by Dominique Maingueneau who, from a discourse analytical viewpoint, presents the concept of the scene of enunciation.
– A contribution by Oswald Ducrot, who presents his conception of polyphony, i.e. the various voices that can be staged by the speaker in his or her utterance.
– An excerpt from Johannes Angermuller, who uses polyphony to account for the readers' contextualising activity.

---

1.   We have slightly modified the English translation.

References

Angermuller, Johannes. 2014 [2013]. *Poststructuralist Discourse Analysis. Subjectivity in Enunciative Pragmatics*. Basingstoke: Palgrave.

Benveniste, Émile. 1971[1966]. *Problems in General Linguistics*. Coral Gables, Florida: University of Miami Press.

Benveniste, Émile. 1974. *Problèmes de linguistique générale II*. Paris: Gallimard.

Culioli, Antoine. 1991. *Pour une linguistique de l'énonciation (1) Opérations et représentations*. Paris: Ophrys.

Culioli, Antoine. 1999. *Pour une linguistique de l'énonciation (2) Formalisation et opérations de repérage*. Paris: Ophrys.

Ducrot, Oswald. 1972. *Dire et ne pas dire. Principes de sémantique linguistique*. Paris: Hermann.

Ducrot, Oswald. 1984. *Le Dire et le dit*. Paris: Minuit.

Foucault, Michel. 1972[1969]. *The Archaeology of Knowledge & the Discourse on Language*. London: Routledge.

Maingueneau, Dominique. 2002. 'An academic genre.' *Discourse studies*, 4 (3): 319–342. DOI: 10.1177/14614456020040030401

Maingueneau, Dominique. 2007. *Analyser les textes de communication*. Paris: Armand Colin.

Ono, Aya. 2007. *La notion d'énonciation chez Emile Benveniste*. Limoges: Lambert-Lucas.

Pêcheux, Michel. 1995[1969]. *Automatic Discourse Analysis*. Rodopi: Amsterdam-Atlanta, GA.

Pêcheux, Michel. 1982[1975]. *Language, Semantics and Ideology. Stating the Obvious*. London: Macmillan.

Émile Benveniste

The formal apparatus of enunciation

This short article by Émile Benveniste (1902–1976) was published in 1970, but it summarises texts from the late 1950s and the 1960s. It aims to expose a pragmatic conception of language and is anchored in the study of linguistic markers of subjectivity related to the way in which utterances reflect the presence of language users. Benveniste begins by insisting on the specificity of the enunciation: the main difficulty 'is to capture this large-scale phenomenon, so banal that it seems to be confused with language itself, so necessary that it is out of sight'. In his view, enunciation must be distinguished from 'discourse' and 'speech', namely *parole*, as it was defined in the *Course in General Linguistics* by Ferdinand de Saussure, who opposes *langue*, the abstract system of language, and *parole*, the individual acts of speech. Benveniste defines enunciation as a process of 'appropriation' of the system of language by the very act of producing an utterance. This appropriation is basically a relation to an addressee: the 'figurative framework' of enunciation implies the primacy of a dialogic relation. Then, Benveniste makes an inventory of the main categories of linguistic markers 'whose function is to put the speaker in a constant and necessary relation to his [sic] enunciation'. He distinguishes: (1) deictic markers, which refer to the partners of the enunciation (in particular personal pronouns, some noun determiners), tense, demonstrative forms, and (2) modality.

Émile Benveniste. 1970. 'L'appareil formel de l'énonciation.'
Langages 17 (5): 12–18, selected 12–18.

Our linguistic descriptions often attach importance to the 'use of forms'. What we mean by that is a set of rules establishing the conditions under which *syntactic* forms can or should normally appear, provided that they belong to a paradigm that contains possible choices. These rules of use are articulated to the rules of formation previously indicated, in order to establish some correlation between morphological variations and the combinatorial latitude of signs (agreement, mutual selection, prepositions and regimes of nouns and verbs, place and order, etc.). It seems that since the choices are limited for either side, we thus obtain an inventory of uses as well as forms that could theoretically be exhaustive, and therefore at least an approximate image of the language in use.

We would, however, introduce here a distinction in terms of functioning that is considered only from the perspective of morphological and grammatical nomenclature. The conditions for the use of forms are not, in our opinion, the same as the conditions for the use of language. They are different worlds, and it may be useful to emphasize this difference, which implies another way of seeing the same things, another way to describe and interpret them.

The use of forms, as a necessary part of any description, has led to many models as varied as the linguistic types from which they proceed. The diversity of linguistic structures, as far as we know how to analyze them, cannot be reduced to a small number of models that would always include only the fundamental elements. We do, however, have some representations that are precise enough, built using a proven technique.

A fairly different thing is the use of language, which refers to a total and consistent mechanism that, in one way or another, affects the entire language. The difficulty lies in capturing this large-scale phenomenon, so banal that it seems to be confused with language itself, so necessary that it is out of sight.

The enunciation is the enactment of language through an individual act of use.

It can be asked whether the discourse which is produced every time we speak, this event of enunciation, is not simply 'speech (parole)'.[1] One must be careful about the specific condition of the enunciation: our object is not the text of the utterance but the very act of producing an utterance. This act is the act of the speaker mobilizing the language on his or her behalf. The relation of the speaker to the language determines the linguistic characteristics of the utterance. It must be considered the act of the speaker,

---

1. Here Benveniste refers to the opposition of *langue* versus *parole* from the *Course in General Linguistics* by Saussure: *langue* is the abstract system of language, and *parole* individual acts of speech. [Trans. note]

who takes the language as an instrument, and with reference to the linguistic features which mark this relation.

Various aspects of this extensive process can be studied. We see three major ones. The most immediately perceptible and the most direct – although in general not related to the general phenomenon of enunciation – is the vocal realization of language. The sounds emitted and perceived, whether studied in the context of a particular idiom or their general manifestations, such as the processes of acquisition, dissemination, alteration – these are also branches of phonetics – always proceed from individual acts, which the linguist discovers as much as s/he can in the native production, within the speech. In scientific practice, one tries to eliminate or reduce the individual features of phonic enunciation by using different subjects and multiplying the recordings, in order to get an average image of the sound, distinct or linked. But everyone knows that, for the same subject, the same sounds are never reproduced exactly and that the notion of identity is only approximate, even where the experiment is repeated in detail. These differences reflect the diversity of situations in which the utterance is produced.

The mechanism of this production is another major aspect of the same problem. Enunciation assumes the individual conversion of language into speech. Here, the issue – very difficult and scarcely studied – is to see how the 'meaning' forms in 'words', to what extent we can distinguish between the two concepts and in what terms to describe their interaction. It is the semantization of language that is at the centre of this aspect of enunciation, and it leads to the theory of the sign and to the analysis of significance.[2] Via the same consideration we rubricize the devices by which linguistic forms of enunciation diversify and are engendered. 'Transformational grammar' is intended to codify and formalize them, to extricate a permanent framework. It proposes to ascend from a theory of universal syntax to a theory of mental functioning.

Finally, we can consider another approach, which is to define enunciation in the formal framework of its realization. This is the proper object of these pages. We try to outline, within language, the formal characteristics of enunciation from the individual manifestation that it actualizes. Some of these characteristics are necessary and permanent, whereas others appear to be related to the peculiarity of the chosen language. For convenience, the data used here are taken from common French and from the language of conversation.

In the enunciation, we consider, successively, the very act, the situations where it is realized, the instruments for its achievement.

The individual act by which one uses language first introduces the speaker as a parameter among the necessary conditions for the enunciation. Before the enunciation, the language is only a possibility of language. After the enunciation, the language is

---

2.   We treat it specifically in a study published in the journal *Semiotica*, I, 1969.

effectuated in an instance of discourse that emanates from the speaker, the sound form which reaches the listener and provokes another enunciation in return.

As an individual realization, the enunciation can be defined in relation to language as a process of *appropriation*. The speaker appropriates the formal apparatus of the language and sets out his/her position as speaker by specific indices on one hand, and by incidental methods on the other.

But, immediately, as soon as he declares himself as the speaker and assumes the language, he implants *the other* in front of him, regardless of the degree of presence he attributes to this other. Any enunciation is, explicitly or implicitly, an allocution and it postulates an addressee.

Finally, in the enunciation, the language is used to express a certain relationship to the world. The very condition for this mobilization and this appropriation of language is, for the speaker, the need to refer, via the discourse and for the other, to the possibility of co-referring identically, in a pragmatic consensus that makes every speaker a co-speaker. Reference is an integral part of the enunciation.

These initial conditions will govern the whole reference mechanism in the process of enunciation, creating a most singular situation, of which one is not conscious.

The individual act of appropriation of language introduces somebody who speaks via his or her speech. This is a constituent datum of the enunciation. The presence of the speaker in his or her enunciation makes every instance of discourse constitute a centre of internal reference. This situation is manifested in the play of specific forms whose function is to put the speaker in a constant and necessary relation with his or her enunciation.

This somewhat abstract description applies to a linguistic phenomenon which is commonly used, but whose theoretical analysis is only just beginning. It is primarily the emergence of indices of person (the relation *I-you*) that are produced only in and via the enunciation: the term *I* denotes the individual who utters the enunciation, the term *you* denotes the individual who is present as an addressee.

Similar and related to the same structure of enunciation are many indices of *ostension* (such as *this, here* etc.), terms that imply a gesture indicating an object that is pronounced at the same time as the instance of the term.

Forms traditionally called 'personal pronouns', 'demonstratives' now appear to be a class of 'linguistic individuals', forms that always and only refer to 'individuals', be they people, moments, places, as opposed to nominal terms that refer always and only to concepts. The status of these 'linguistic individuals' is based on the fact that they are born out of an enunciation, that they are produced by this individual event and are, so to say, 'semel-native'.[3] They are generated again each time an enunciation is uttered, and every point of time they designate as the first point of time.

---

3. From Latin *semel*, 'only once'. [Trans. note]

The third set of terms relating to enunciation consists of the whole paradigm – often large and complex – of the temporal forms which are determined in relation to the EGO, the centre of the enunciation. The tenses, whose axial form, the 'present', coincides with the time of enunciation, are part of this necessary apparatus.[4]

This relation to time deserves our attention, to meditate its *necessity*, and to wonder what its base is. One might think that temporality is an innate framework of thought. In reality it is produced in and by enunciation. From enunciation proceeds the category of the present, and from the category of the present is born the category of time. In fact, the present is the source of time. It is this presence in the world that only the act of enunciation makes possible because, upon reflection, man has no other way to experience the 'now' and to make it relevant unless realizing it by insertion of discourse into the world. The central position of the present could be shown by the analysis of temporal systems in various languages. The formal present only makes explicit the present which is inherent in enunciation, which is renewed with each generation of discourse; and from this present continuous, coextensive with our own presence, is printed in the consciousness the sense of continuity that we call 'time', continuity and temporality engendering in the incessant present of the enunciation, which is the present of being itself, and marking out itself, via internal reference, between what will become the present and what it is not anymore.

Thus the enunciation is directly responsible for certain classes of signs that it literally promotes into existence. This is because they could not arise or find employment in the cognitive use of language. We must therefore distinguish entities having, in the language, their full and permanent status, and those which, emanating from the enunciation, only exist in the network of 'individuals' that the enunciation creates in relation to the 'here and now' of the speaker. For example, the 'I', 'that' and 'tomorrow' of grammatical description are only metalinguistic 'names' for *I, that, tomorrow* that are produced within the enunciation.

In addition to the forms it controls, the enunciation provides the necessary conditions for large syntactic functions. As soon as the enunciator uses language to influence in any manner the behaviour of the addressee, he or she makes use, for this purpose, of a device of functions. It is, first, *an interrogation*, which is an enunciation constructed to generate an 'answer' via a linguistic process which is, at the same time, a process of double-entry behaviour. All lexical and syntactic forms of interrogation, particles, pronouns, sequence, intonation etc. fall within this aspect of enunciation.

Similarly, we assign here those terms or forms that we call *intimation*: orders, appeals designed in categories such as the imperative, the vocative, involving a live and

---

4. The details of the facts of language that we embrace here as a synthetic view are presented in several chapters of our *Problèmes de linguistique générale* (Paris, 1966); that frees us from insisting on it here.

immediate relation of the enunciator to the other in a necessary reference to the time of the enunciation.

Less obvious perhaps, but equally certain, is that the *assertion* belongs to the same group. In its syntactic turn, as in its intonation, the assertion aims to communicate a certitude, it is the most common manifestation of the presence of the speaker in the enunciation; it even has its specific instruments to express or involve it, the words *yes* and *no,* asserting positively or negatively a proposition. Negation as a logical operation is independent of enunciation, it has its own form, which is *not.* But the assertive particle *no,* as a substitute for a proposition, ranks as the particle *yes,* with which it shares similar status, in forms stemming from the enunciation.

More broadly, though in a manner less categorical, are ranked here all sorts of formal modalities, the ones belonging to verbs with their 'modes' (optative, subjunctive) of uttering the attitudes of the enunciator towards what it utters (wait, wish, apprehension), others belonging to phraseology ('maybe', 'no doubt', 'probably') and indicating uncertainty, possibility, indecision etc., or a deliberate refusal of assertion.

What is generally characteristic of enunciation is *the accentuation of the discursive relationship to the partner* – real or imagined, individual or collective.

This characteristic sets as a necessity what might be called the *figurative framework* of the enunciation. As a form of discourse, enunciation creates two equally necessary 'figures'; one is the source, the other is the target of the enunciation. This is the structure of *dialogue.* The two figures in a partner position are the alternating protagonists of the enunciation. This framework is necessarily given with the definition of the enunciation.

(…) Many other developments could be studied in the context of enunciation. One could consider the lexical changes that the enunciation determinates, the phraseology that is the frequent, perhaps necessary, hallmark of 'orality'. We should also distinguish the spoken enunciation and the written enunciation. The latter moves on two levels: the writer enunciates himself [sic] by writing and makes individuals enunciate themselves within his writing. Far-reaching perspectives are thus opened up for the analysis of complex forms of discourse via the formal framework outlined here.

Dominique Maingueneau

The scene of enunciation

Dominique Maingueneau (b. 1950) is professor of linguistics at the University of Paris-Sorbonne. He has published many books on discourse analysis; with P. Charaudeau, he co-edited a *Dictionary of Discourse Analysis* in French (2002). His research associates a pragmatic outlook with linguistic enunciation theories and Michel Foucault's archaeology. He is particularly interested in 'self-constituting discourses' (philosophical, religious, scientific, literary…) (Maingueneau 1999). Unlike the other texts presented in this section, this article considers enunciation from the viewpoint of discourse genres, in order to adapt the reflection on linguistic enunciation to the specific constraints of discourse analysis. Drawing on the work of two linguists, Benveniste and Culioli, the article makes a distinction between two levels: the level of the linguistic system, which defines abstract *positions* (first, second, third person), and the level of speech, where these positions can correspond to various *places* occupied by partners in the linguistic activity. Secondly, the author introduces the concept of the 'enunciation scene', that is relevant for research on genre(s). It is no surprise that the metaphor of scene is borrowed from the theatre as e.g. in Goffman. But in Maingueneau's framework the recourse to a theatrical metaphor does not refer to ongoing discourse activity; rather it mainly concerns 'instituted genres' (Maingueneau, 2002). The enunciation scene is divided into three nested sub-scenes which define the frame in which the enunciation activity becomes meaningful: 'enclosing scene', 'generic scene', 'scenography'. This distinction allows Maingueneau to reveal his classification of discourse genres, based on the relationship between generic scene and scenography.

References

Charaudeau, Patrick, and Dominique Maingueneau (eds). 2002. *Dictionnaire d'analyse du discours*. Paris: Seuil.

Maingueneau, Dominique. 1999. 'Analysing self-constituting discourses,' *Discourse studies*, 1 (2): 175–200. DOI: 10.1177/1461445699001002003

Maingueneau, Dominique. 2002. 'An academic genre.' *Discourse studies*, 4 (3): 319–342. DOI: 10.1177/14614456020040030401

Dominique Maingueneau. 2003. 'La situation d'énonciation entre langue et discours'
(The situation of enunciation, between language and discourse).
In *Dix ans de S.D.U.*, edited by the Association des chercheurs en linguistique française,
197–209, selected 198–206.
Craiova: Editura Universitaria Craiova.

1. The level of the utterance

1.1 The situation of enunciation

The concept of 'situation of enunciation' can be easily misunderstood. It does not designate a physical or social environment in which interlocutors are located. Rather, following the linguistic theory of Antoine Culioli,[1] who conceptualized it from the 1960s onwards in the wake of Émile Benveniste,[2] the 'situation of enunciation' is a system of virtual linguistic coordinates by which any utterance (*énoncé*) reflects its own enactment. Here we find the premise, common to the pragmatics of enunciation, of the essential reflexivity of language. From this perspective, the 'situation of enunciation' cannot be a situation of communication, socially describable, but rather the system where the three basic positions of *enunciator, co-enunciator* and *non-person* are defined:

- The position of *enunciator* is the origin of enunciative coordinates, the *reference point*, but also that of its modalities. In French, the autonomous pronoun *Je* [I] is the marker of coincidence between enunciator and syntactic subject.
- Between the enunciator and the *co-enunciator* (whose marker in French is *Tu* [you]) there is a relationship of 'difference', otherness. Indeed, these two poles of the enunciation are both united and opposed on the same level. The term 'co-enunciator' should not be interpreted in terms of a symmetrical relation between two positions.
- The position of *non-person*, a term that comes from Benveniste, is that of entities which are presented as not taking charge of an utterance. Between this position and those of enunciator and co-enunciator, there is a separation: the non-person does not figure on the same plane. This is why Benveniste preferred to speak of a 'non-person' rather than of a 'third person', as the grammatical tradition did. From his perspective, the linguistic differences between enunciator/co-enunciator

---

1. The problematic of Culioli was addressed in a number of articles. The publication of various collections of papers came later (Culioli 1990).

2. The seminal works of Benveniste, about persons and verb tenses, date from the end of the 1950s but gained recognition through the *Problèmes de linguistique générale* (1966).

on the one hand and non-person on the other were widely described; what is most remarkable is the impossibility of anaphoric substitution for markers of the positions of enunciator or co-enunciator: we can only repeat *I* or *you* ('*I* know *I* am late'), while the non-person has a range of anaphoric devices both lexical and pronominal (*he/she/it, that, his/hers…*) […].

1.2   The speech situation

The 'situation of enunciation', as we have seen, constitutes a system of virtual *positions* on which the uttering activity is based. But these positions – as grammarians and rhetoricians noted long ago – do not necessarily coincide with the *places* occupied in the verbal exchange, 'persons' within the meaning of 'roles' in speech. To put it simply, it is not because we find *I* in an utterance that its referent in the verbal exchange must necessarily play the role of a speaker, and it is not because we find *you* that its referent must necessarily play the role of an addressee.

We are thus led to distinguish three positions of the situation of enunciation and three places of what might be called the *speech situation*. The first two places are those of the *interlocutors*, the speaker and the addressee:

- the place of a *speaker* is that of the one who speaks;
- the place of the *addressee* that of the recipient of the utterance;
- a third place must be added to these two, that of the *referent* the interlocutors talk about.

Obviously, the *positions* of the 'situation of enunciation' and the *places* of the 'speech situation' normally tend to harmonize, to correspond term to term: *I*, as a general rule, designates the speaker, and so on. But grammarians continue to point out that this is not always the case, that there are many discrepancies between the two systems. Here are two examples:

(1)   *I* have slept well; *I* will go with my mom (a mother speaking to her baby: its use here is called 'hypocoristic')
(2)   *He* is cute, the doggy (a man speaking to his dog; another hypocoristic use)

The interpretation of such utterances is precisely constructed by taking into account the tension between the enunciative position (the coordinates of the situation of enunciation) as it is indicated by the marker of the person and the place taken in the speech situation, namely that of the addressee. For example, in the hypocoristic (i.e. indicating intimacy) use of *I* in utterance (1), the use of the first person marker can be explained by the fact that the addressee (a baby) is, by nature, unable to answer: as the baby is not a speaking subject, and as the enunciation is doomed to remain unanswered, the locutor deletes the otherness between the two places.

2.   Communication setting and scene of enunciation

So far we have considered the case of elementary utterances, decontextualized sentences. But it is not necessary to be a linguist to see that in fact these basic utterances are not the only units for which the terms 'situation of enunciation' or 'communication setting' are relevant from a certain point of view. The basic utterances themselves are actually constituents of *texts*, which belong to genres of discourse (= devices of verbal communication socio-historically defined).

Where texts are concerned, it seems preferable to speak of a 'communication setting' rather than 'a situation of enunciation'. In fact, four terms are in competition here to describe this: context, situation of discourse, communication setting, scene of enunciation.

The notion of 'context' is intuitive and convenient. It covers the linguistic context – often called 'co-text' to avoid ambiguity – as well as the physical environment of the enunciation, and knowledge shared by the participants in a verbal interaction. This notion of 'context' also plays a key role in semantic theories inspired by pragmatics, dominant today, which assume that the addressee constructs the interpretation of a basic utterance or text through instructions extracted from various planes of context. But we must recognize that such a polyvalent concept can hardly be used restrictively.

When we tackle verbal productions from the perspective of the study of texts, the concepts of communication setting and scene of enunciation prove more appropriate. Here I will use them in a slightly unusual way by saying that they allow us to consider the situation of discourse from two complementary approaches.

2.1   Communication setting

When one speaks of *communication setting*, one somehow considers, 'from the outside', the situation from which any text – as much as it refers to a genre – is inseparable. Various models have been proposed since the famous acronym SPEAKING from Dell Hymes in the 1960s and 1970s (Hymes 1972). In general, these models involve a number of parameters:

- *The purpose*: any genre of discourse aims to modify the situation. The correct determination of this purpose is essential for the addressee who wants to respond appropriately with regard to the genre of the discourse at stake.
- *The status of the partners*: the speech in a genre of discourse does not go from anyone to anyone, but from a person occupying a certain social status to another one. A university course is usually given by a professor who is expected to have a certain kind of knowledge and to have a position in a higher education institution; s/he addresses an audience of students devoid of this knowledge. A commercial transaction connects a buyer and a seller, etc. These statuses come with certain rights and

duties as well as certain types of knowledge: a reader of a scientific journal is not supposed to hold the same information as a viewer of a medical show on public television.

– *Appropriate circumstances*: any genre of discourse implies a certain type of place and a moment appropriate to its success. This constraint does not come from 'outside' but is constitutive. In fact, the notions of 'moment' or 'place', as required by a genre of discourse, must be seen according to different genres of discourse.

– *The mode of inscription into temporality*:

  – *Periodicity*: a course, a mass, a TV news programme are held at regular intervals; however, a statement by a head of state or a tract are not subject to periodicity.

  – *Duration*: the generic competence of the speakers of some community approximately indicates how long the speech activity will last.

  – *Continuity*: a funny story must be told in full, while a novel can be read in an indefinite number of sessions.

  – *Period of expiration*: a weekly magazine is designed to be valid for a week, a daily newspaper for a day, but a fundamental religious text (the Bible, the Koran) claims to be eternal.

– *Medium*: what is called a 'text' is not content that happens to be fixed in a particular medium. It is one with its own material mode of existence: mode of support/ transport and storage, thus memorization. A text can only be passed by sound waves (in the immediate oral interaction) which can be treated and restored by a decoder (radio, telephone); or it can be handwritten, constitute a book, be printed as a single copy by an individual printer, be included in a computer's memory, on an external disk, etc. A significant modification of its material mode of existence radically changes the characteristics of a genre of discourse: a televised political debate is a different kind of discourse than a debate in a room with the present public as the only audience.

– *A text organization*: a genre of discourse is associated with a certain organization, one of the key areas of text linguistics. To control a genre of discourse is to have awareness, more or less clearly, of the modes in which its components are linked at different levels. Some modes of organization can be taught: the essay, the summary note. There are genres whose organization is rigid (such as legal acts), there are others whose 'framework' is flexible and co-managed by the partners in the exchange.

– *Specific linguistic resources*: every speaker, a priori, is faced with a vast repertoire of linguistic varieties: diversity of languages in the world, diversity within a language: language registers, geographical varieties (patois, dialects), professional varieties (legal discourse, administrative, scientific, journalistic), etc. With every genre of discourse certain standards are associated a priori.

2.2   Scene of enunciation

To consider a situation of discourse as a scene of enunciation means to consider it 'from the inside', through the situation which the speech claims to define, the framework which it shows (as this term is defined in pragmatics), in the movement where it is deployed. Text is indeed the trace of a discourse where speech is *staged*.

The concept of scene of enunciation, the usefulness of which I have been trying to show for a number of years (Maingueneau 1993, 1998), is not simple. To comprehend it we have to distinguish three scenes operating on complementary levels: *enclosing scene*, *generic scene* and *scenography*.

– *Enclosing scene and generic scene*
The enclosing scene is one that corresponds to the *type* of discourse. When you receive a flyer in the street, you should be able to determine whether it belongs to an advertising, religious or political type of discourse – in other words, in what enclosing scene it must be situated to be interpreted, in what terms it involves its reader. A political enunciation, for example, involves a 'citizen' addressing 'citizens'.

To say that the scene of enunciation of a political utterance is the enclosing scene of political discourse, that the one of a philosophical utterance is the enclosing scene of philosophical discourse, and so on, is not enough to specify verbal activities, since we are dealing with specific *genres of discourse*: a political discourse, for example, may include a press conference by a head of state, a leaflet from a militant newspaper, etc. As we have seen, these genres can be analyzed via their various components: here we can speak of a *generic scene*. These two scenes, 'enclosing' and 'generic', define what might be called the *scenic framework* of the text.

– *Scenography*
Enclosing scene and generic scene are not sufficient to describe the scene of enunciation. The addressee is involved in a third scene, a 'scenography', which is chosen by the speaker, according to his or her goals. For example, a computer's manual which, instead of proceeding in the way of the usual genre of manual, might present an adventure story where a hero goes to explore an unknown world and faces different enemies. In this case, the place assigned to the reader is located in a narrative scene constructed by the text, a 'scenography', which has the effect of pushing the scenic framework into the background; so the reader is caught in a kind of trap, since he or she receives the text first as an adventure story, not as a manual. For many genres of discourse, especially those that are in competition to capture audiences, taking the floor is, to varying degrees, risky. This is particularly evident when we consider advertising or political texts which, in order to carry the support of reticent addressees, mobilize innovative scenographies.

The scenography is not just a framework or decor, as if the discourse occurred within a space already constructed, independent of this discourse; in its own development, the enunciation attempts gradually to install its own speech setting. Discourse, by its own deployment, claims to convince by establishing the scene of enunciation which legitimates itself. In our example, the scenography of the adventure novel is somehow imposed from the beginning, but on the other hand, it is through the enunciation of this story that the scenography thus imposed can be legitimized, by making the reader accept the role which is assigned to him in this scenography – the one of reader of an adventure novel.

Therefore, a scenography involves a loop. As soon as it emerges, the enunciation of the text requires a certain scene, which in fact it is validating gradually through its very enunciation. The scenography thus appears as both what generates the discourse and what is generated by this discourse; it legitimizes an utterance which, in turn, should legitimize it: it must establish that this scenography from which the speech comes is precisely the scenography required to speak appropriately of politics, philosophy, science etc., or to promote some merchandise. The more the text advances, the more the addressee must be convinced that the adventure story is the best way to access the computer, that computer science should be regarded as an exciting world to be discovered. What the text says is meant to validate the scene through which the content arises.

However, there are many genres of discourse without an original scenography, whose scenes of enunciation are somehow frozen, e.g. the telephone directory or expert reports which conform strictly to their routine generic scenes. Other genres of discourse are more likely to elicit scenographies that deviate from a standard template. Thus, in the example of a manual, mentioned above, presented as an adventure novel: instead of being satisfied with the usual scenography of a didactic type, the authors used a more seductive scenography.

We can allocate the genres of discourse on a scale between two extreme poles. On the one hand, there are genres which are not likely to allow original scenographies (prescriptions, telephone directories etc.). On the other hand, there are genres which inherently require innovative scenographies, such as in the case of advertising genres. Some advertisements present conversational scenographies, others scientific scenographies, and so on. This is also the case with many texts relating to journalistic, philosophical or literary discourses. For example, there is a variety of scenographies that allow the narrator of a novel to construct the corresponding figure of the reader. Political discourse is also likely to elicit innovative scenographies: this candidate may speak to his or her electorate as a young manager, or as a technocrat, a labourer, a man or woman of experience etc., and confer the corresponding roles on the respective audiences.

Between these two extremes most texts stick to the routine imposed by the generic scene (e.g. manuals). This variation is tightly related to the purpose of the genres of discourse. The phone book, which does not produce innovative scenographies, is a purely utilitarian genre. On the other hand, advertising discourses or political discourses mobilize innovative scenographies to influence their addressees.

2.3   Example

These three planes of the scene of enunciation can be seen in action e.g. in the electoral programme of the French president, François Mitterrand, who in 1988 ran for election for a second term. This programme was presented in the form of a 'Letter to all the French', which was published in the press and sent by post to a number of voters. The political content of this text is inseparable from the way it is staged, i.e. as private correspondence: the President thus tries to campaign as an individual above the parties, as the father of a family, not as the head of a party.

> My dear compatriots,
>
> You will understand this. I want, through this letter, to talk to you about France. Thanks to your trust, I've been holding the highest office in the Republic for seven years. At the end of this mandate, I would not have conceived the project to resubmit to your votes again if I had not been convinced that we have much to do together to ensure that our country plays the role expected of it in the world and to protect the unity of the Nation.
>
> But I also want to talk to you about you, your worries, your hopes and your legitimate interests.
>
> I choose this way – to write to you to express myself on all major issues which are worthy of being treated and discussed among the French, a kind of thinking together, as usually happens in the evening around the table, in your family (…).

The *enclosing scene* here is political discourse. The *generic scene* is the electoral platform; and the *scenography* is one of private correspondence, connecting two individuals who have a personal, even familial relationship. This scenography invokes, in the third paragraph of the excerpt, the guarantee of another scene of speech: 'a kind of thinking together, as usually happens in the evening around the table, in your family'. So, it is not only a letter which is supposed to be read by the voter: s/he must participate, with her/his imagination, in the family conversation around the table, where the President implicitly takes the role of the father and delegates, to voters, the role of children. This example illustrates a very common method: the scenography happens to be based on scenes of speech which we can call '*validated*', that is to say already established in the collective memory, whether as an accepted or rejected model. The repertoire of available validated scenes varies depending on the discourse target group: a strongly committed community (a religious sect, a school of philosophy) has its own memory but, in general, with all types of audiences, even large and heterogeneous, we can associate a stock of presumably shared scenes. The validated scene is not a scenography but an autonomized and decontextualized stereotype, available for reinvestment in other texts. These could be genres of discourse (the postcard, the conference) or historical events (see the Appeal by General de Gaulle of June 18, 1940 who asked us to resist the Germans instead of collaborating with them).

References

Benveniste, Émile. 1966. *Problèmes de linguistique générale*. Paris: Gallimard.

Culioli, Antoine. 1990. *Pour une linguistique de l'énonciation*. Paris: Ophrys.

Hymes, Dell Hathaway.1972. 'Models of Interaction of Language and Social Life'. In *Directions in Sociolinguistics. The Ethnography of Communication*, edited by John J. Gumperz and Dell H. Hymes, 35–71. New York: Holt, Rinehart & Winston.

Maingueneau, Dominique. 1993. *Le Contexte de l'œuvre littéraire*. Paris: Dunod.

Maingueneau, Dominique. 1998. *Analyser les textes de communication*. Paris: Dunod.

Jacqueline Authier-Revuz

Enunciative heterogeneity

This text, written by the French linguist Jacqueline Authier-Revuz (b. 1940), was published in 1984. It is quite typical of the trend sometimes called 'The French School of Discourse analysis', whose main initiator and leading figure was Michel Pêcheux (see the section on 'From Structuralism to Poststructuralism'), who associated linguistics with the Marxist philosophy of Althusser and psychoanalysis. One of the key ideas of such Pêcheux's theory of discourse is the postulate that the sovereignty of the subject is an illusion. For Authier-Revuz, the subject cannot 'appropriate' language either. Since discourse analysts can only deal with split subjects, they must analyse the marks of 'heterogeneity' as symptoms of the subject's inability to master his or her speech. As Authier-Revuz says in her article, 'the presence of the Other emerges, indeed, in the discourse, at points where its insistence disrupts the continuity, the homogeneity, and destabilizes the mastery of the subject'. This point is emphasized at the beginning of the text: speakers believe that their discourse is controlled by their intentions, but in reality it is dominated by 'interdiscourse'. Here, 'interdiscourse' has a close affinity with the concepts of ideology or hegemony (Antonio Gramsci, Ernesto Laclau). It is what can be said in light of the relations between discursive formations that are constitutive of discursive entities.

Jacqueline Authier-Revuz. 1984. 'Hétérogénéité(s) énonciative(s).'
(Enunciative heterogeneities)
Langages 73:98–111, selected 99–107.

1.

(…) Faced with the claim – spontaneous or referred to a theoretical level – of the subject to be an independent source of a meaning that s/he communicates via language, various theoretical approaches have revealed that any speech is *determined outside* the control of a subject, and that it 'is spoken rather than speaking'.

This 'outside' is not what a sense-bearing subject would inevitably encounter and according to which it would determine the concrete forms of its existence and those of its discourse; it is from *the outside in the subject*, in the discourse, as a constitutive condition of the existence.

The issue here is not to present, even schematically, each of these approaches in their coherence – even less to claim to 'articulate' them. I just evoke, fragmentarily, the points which specifically refer to what I call the constitutive heterogeneity of the subject and its discourse.

1.1 The 'dialogism' of the Bakhtin circle, as we know, does not feature, as a nucleus, the conversational face to face of the dialogue, but constitutes, through multiform reflections, semiotic as well as literary, a theory of *internal dialogization of the discourse*. The words are always, inevitably, 'the words of others': this intuition passes through the analysis of multilingualism and the boundary games constituent of 'social dialects', linguistic and discursive forms of hybridization, bivocality, which allow discursive representation of the discourse of the other, literary genres showing a 'Galilean consciousness of language', carnival laughter, the polyphonic novel.[1]

'Only the mythical Adam approaching with his first speech a world not yet put in question' (Bakhtine, 1975: 100, 102, 114) would have been able to produce a discourse subtracted from what has already been said in the speech of others. No word is 'neutral', each is inevitably 'loaded', 'occupied', 'inhabited', 'crossed' with discourses in which 'it has lived his socially underpinned existence'. What Bakhtin means by 'saturation of language' constitutes a theory of production of meaning and of discourse: it raises the 'context' of other discourses not as an environment likely to generate connotative halos around a nucleus of sense, but as a *constitutive outside*, that of the already said, of which the very tissue of discourse is inevitably made.

---

[1]. On these points see, in the same vein, Authier-Revuz (1982: 101–23), and for an overall presentation Todorov (1981).

The status of the subject of the discourse as it appears through the notion of 'intention' or 'orientation of a discourse to an object' does not occupy a central place and remains problematic:[2] it is one of the points which impede, despite undeniable encounters, an overly systematic approximation of dialogical and 'structuralist' perspectives in the approach to discourse.

1.2   Thus I refer to the theory of *discourse as a product of interdiscourse,* as it was developed in a series of studies devoted to discourse and discourse analysis.[3] Supported by the ideas of Foucault and Althusser, this theory postulates a regulated functioning which, from outside the interdiscourse, explains the production of the discourse and the structural machinery ignored by the subject who, in the illusion, thinks of it as the source of its discourse while it is only its support and effect.

The specificity of any discursive formation is to hide in the transparency of the formed meaning the contradictory material objectivity of the interdiscourse determining this discursive formation as such, the material objectivity that resides in the fact that '*that speaks*' always '*before, elsewhere and independently*'.[4]

The notion of *preconstruct*, the trace of the interdiscourse in the intradiscourse – that is to say, identifiable in the thread of the discourse – is, for example, characteristic of this question in its opposition to presupposition as an act of language.

The revelation of the real processes which determine the meaning and the discourse is, indeed, inseparable from the theory of the subjective illusion of speech[5] and from calling into question the linguistic theories of enunciation to the extent that they may reflect the 'necessary constitutive illusion of the subject' by 'just' reproducing, on the theoretical level, this illusion of the subject through the idea of an uttering subject – bearer of choice, intentions, decisions' (Pêcheux and Fuchs, 1975: 19).

1.3   From another perspective – that of the theory of its proper object, the unconscious – psychoanalysis, as made explicit via the theory of Saussure in the Lacanian reading of Freud,[6] conceives of speech as *basically heterogeneous* and of the subject as *divided*.[7]

---

2.   See Kristeva (1970), 'The work of Bakhtin puts us on the edge of the theory of the meaning that would need a theory of the subject.'

3.   E.g. Pêcheux (1975), Pêcheux, and Fuchs (1975), Henry (1977), Marandin (1979), Courtine (1981), Conein *et alii* (1981).

4.   Pêcheux (1975: 147) – my emphasis.

5.   That of 'the interpellation' of individuals as speaking subjects, the sources of their discourse.

6.   The reference that is not absent, of course, in many works on the discourse mentioned above, see especially Henry (1977), Conein et al. (1981).

7.   For last-minute editorial reasons the initially written development is replaced by the following summary. For a more detailed presentation in the same vein, see Authier-Revuz (1982).

Always under the words 'other words' are said: it is the material structure of the language that allows, in the linearity of the chain, for the unintentional polyphony of any discourse to be heard, through which analysis can try to identify the traces of the 'punctuation of the unconscious'.

This conception of discourse crossed by the unconscious is articulated as that of a subject which is not a homogeneous entity external to language but the result of a complex structure, the effect of language: the *decentred* subject, divided, split, blocked… the word does not matter, on condition that, far from the duplication of the subject[8] or from the division as an effect which meeting with the outside world has on the subject, a division which one might tend to remove by a work of restoration of the unity of the person, the *structural, constitutive character of the cleavage* of the subject is maintained.

That is where the character of a 'narcissistic wound' resides, that which Freud recognized by the discovery of the unconscious in a subject who 'is no longer the master in his house', and this is what is thereby always about to be covered. Thus, we can consider that it is through opposing political inscriptions, the anti-psychiatry of Laing for example, where the alienating nature of the social environment is denounced, *causing* the 'Divided Self' (Laing, 1960) and adaptive ego-psychology trying to construct an autonomous 'strong Me', which would 'dislodge the id',[9] that they join together[10] as brothers-enemies in the ignorance of the Freudian unconscious, and of the decentred subject that it structures.

What Freud actually points out is that *there is no centre* of the subject beyond illusion and fantasy, rather it is the function of this *instance of the subject that is me* to be the bearer of this necessary illusion.

It is to this position – that of the *function of the ignorance of the Ego* which, in the imaginary of the divided subject, reconstructs the image of the autonomous subject, deleting the division (obviously irreconcilable with all variations of the conceptions of the subject which reduce it to me or centre it on me) – that refers the view according to which 'the centre is a 'setup' for the subject of which the human sciences [and in our field the theories of enunciation, JAR] make their object, ignoring that it is imaginary' (Roudinesco, 1977: 42).

---

8. See the pre-Freudian descriptions (Janet, Breuer) of a second personality related to 'weakness of the psychological synthesis' (See, for example, 'Clivage du moi' and 'Subconscient' in Laplanche and Pontalis, 1968).

9. See Anna Freud, and especially H. Hartmann. See Clément (1972).

10. This is beyond the difference in their explicit relation to Freud, since Laing, rejecting psychoanalysis, draws from existential philosophies where theories of the autonomous me are presented as the 'underpinnings' of Freudian concepts.

1.4   Breaking with the Ego, the basis of classic subjectivity, conceived as an interior face of the exteriority of the world, the basis of the subject is here moved, dislodged, 'into a multiple place, fundamentally heteronomous, where the externality is inside the subject' (Clément, 1972). These conceptions of discourse, of ideology, of the unconscious, which the theories of enunciation cannot avoid without risk in linguistics, are joined in the assertion that, *constitutively*, in the subject, in its discourse, there is *the Other*.

2.

Quite different is the linguistic point of view on how to describe the forms of heterogeneity shown in discourse, those through which the apparent uniqueness of the *thread of discourse* alters, because they inscribe the other in it (according to different modalities, with or without unequivocal marks of identification).

2.1   For all of the *marked* forms, which I am concerned with here, it is significant that a fragment in the thread of discourse has another status, which falls within autonymy.[11]

In simple autonymy[12], the heterogeneity which constitutes a *mentioned* fragment, among the linguistic elements which one uses,[13] is accompanied by a syntactic break. The fragment mentioned in the framework of a direct or reported discourse,[14] or introduced by a metalinguistic term (the word, the term, the expression, the phrase 'X'), clearly delimited in the thread of discourse, is shown as an object; it is extracted from the normal enunciative thread and referred to elsewhere: that of another enunciative act (*Z said*: 'X', *the expression of Z*, 'X'...) or, in a strictly metalinguistic gesture, that of language (*the word, the term* 'X').[15]

In the case on which I focus here, in particular the autonymic connotation, the fragment mentioned is at the same time a fragment which is used: it is the case of an

---

11. I refer to Rey-Debove (1978) for the implementation of these concepts which I used to describe the forms of the reported speech and the quoted 'speech held at a distance' (Authier, 1978, Authier, 1981).

12. French: *autonymie* (self-reference of language, especially in quotations in direct speech) [Trans. Note]

13. I refer here to the classical opposition between *mention* and *use* in the logical tradition; the instrumental control of the subject of the language supposed by those terms and going against the views developed in 1. is to be moved to the level of the representation that the subject gives of his uttering activity.

14. As opposed to indirect speech which is a homogenizing mode of restitution of another act of enunciation.

15. Between the two poles, the reference of the fragment to an act of individual enunciation versus the reference to the language (*the words of de Gaulle*, '*l'intendance suivra*', *went down in history* versus *the word* '*cheval*' *which has two syllables*) there is in fact a continuum which falls within the order of discourse.

item enclosed in quotation marks, put in italics or (sometimes and) paraphrased in parentheses.[16] Unlike the previous case, a fragment which is designated as other is integrated into the discourse, without a syntactic break: with complex status the item mentioned is integrated *in* the syntactic continuity of the discourse while, via the marks, which are not redundant in this case, it is referred to as *outside* of it.

A double designation is thus made by the forms of the manifest heterogeneity: that of a *place* for a fragment of another status in the linearity of the chain, that of an *otherness* to which the fragment refers.

2.2   The nature of this otherness is or is not specified in the context of the fragment mentioned. In the forms of autonymy mentioned above, the otherness is explicitly specified and refers either to another act of enunciation or to language being outside of the discourse while it is uttered.[17]

In contrast, it is implicit in non-paraphrased quotes and italics, that is to say that any understanding, interpretation of these marks passes through a specification of the otherness to which it refers, according to its discursive environment: for example, another language or language variety, another different or enemy discourse etc.[18]

With regard to that, the special interest that I see in the same structure of autonymic connotation, in innumerable forms – literally infinite number of expressions – paraphrases, edits, comments on a fragment of the chain (pointed out or not by a quote or in italics[19]) – is that they specify the parameters, the angles, the perspectives, with respect to which a discourse explicitly raises an otherness in relation to itself.

Designated as 'elsewhere' in relation to discourse and interfering with the course of it as a point of heterogeneity:

– *another language*,[20]
– *another discursive register*, familiar, pedantic, young, rude etc.,[21]

---

16. (1) the 'sit-in' of the students was extended. (2) the *sit-in* of the students… (3) the 'sit-in' of the students, as they say now… (4) the sit-in of the students, as they say now… [the English word *sit-in* is used in these French examples (Trans. note)]. The incision can paraphrase a mention already marked elsewhere (3), or confer by itself the status 'mentioned' to a fragment (4), in which case, the possible problems of syntactic-semantic implications of the incision present problems of delimitation of the mentioned fragments.

17. There are of course also autonomous forms without explanation via a metalinguistic term ('cheval' has two syllables); they can create ambiguities in the oral speech (tell me 'why' / tell me why).

18. See the study of the values of words in brackets in Authier (1981).

19. On these types of paraphrases, cf. Authier-Revuz (1982:92–96).

20. E.g. al dente as the Italians say.

21. E.g. to use an expression of the younger generation, some bosses 'whoop'.

– *another discourse*, technical, feminist, Marxist, Jacobin, fundamentalist etc.,[22] that can only be characterized as the discourse of others, the common discourse if you will, of certain others, of another individual,[23]

– *another modality of making sense* of a word, referring explicitly to the elsewhere of another specified discourse,[24] or of that of language as a place of polysemy, homonymy, metaphor etc., dismissed or, on the contrary, deemed to be the meaning of the word.[25] In both cases, rather than being taken for granted, the meaning constituted for a word is made by reference to one or other sense produced outside of interdiscourse, or to that of language,

– *another word*, potential or explicit in the expressions of reserve (*X, finally X, if you want; X if you will, somehow, say...*), of hesitation and rectification (*X or rather Y; X, I should have said Y; X, nay; X, I was going to say Y*), of confirmation (*X, in the case of say; X, it is X I mean*), a variant, inverse, of the previous,

– *another person, the interlocutor*, different from the speaker and as such likely not to understand, or not to admit (*if you see what I mean, if you will excuse the expression, forgive me the term, if you want...*); these operations are implicitly accepted as self-evident, also in the discourse, from an interlocutor – a cog in 'normal' communication.

2.4.1   The double designation of another fragment, and of the otherness to which it refers, constitutes, *by difference*, a *double assertion of the one*.

On the level of the thread of discourse, locating a point of heterogeneity means circumscribing it, that is to say, identifying it, by difference, in relation to the rest of the chain of homogeneity or uniqueness of the language, discourse, meaning, etc.; the delimited foreign body, the marked fragment receives clearly through the glosses of

---

22. E.g. existing socialism, as the Communist Party persists in saying. Or: the language (natural as logicians feel the need to say).

23. E.g. so-called 'human sciences'. Or: doesn't this mean in some way (as we say today)... Or: you have to, I apologize for this expression which may seem like a stereotype, work a concept. Or: to flirt, like my grandmother said.

24. E.g a contradiction, in the materialistic sense of the word. Or: the destiny within the meaning of the Greeks. Or: 'romantic places' in the sense that it was heard then. The specification by another discourse, 'materialist', 'Greek' ... seems to anticipate the risk of attraction of the word in the force field of interdiscourse, by another 'other-discourse' here, a logical discourse of contradiction, a Christian discourse of destiny.

25. See all the 'X in the proper sense', 'X metaphorically' etc. E.g. language plays, as they say of an assembly. Or: full of duplicity, in both senses of the word; or: girls locked up – without metaphor – by the bosses of silk; or: Tonight we celebrate an event, a happy event if you allow me this formula: the publication this year of a series of works.

correction, reserve, hesitation etc. the character of an accidental particularity, of a local fault. At the same time, the reference to elsewhere, to an outside explicitly specified or given to specify, automatically *determines* by difference the *inside*, that of discourse; that is to say that the designation of a specific outside is through each mark of distance, an operation of establishing the identity of discourse. Also, the area of 'contact' between the outside(s) and the inside that the markers of distance delineate in a discourse is profoundly revealing, firstly, by the points where it explicitly chooses to put the borders, the edges, the boundaries – that is to say from what other it has to distinguish itself, to what other it has to address itself in order to constitute itself – on the other hand, by the type of relation to such other that is at play, relation again, either explicit by the glosses, or interpretable according to context: there are distinctions which fall within the complicit *marivaudage*[26] of a discourse with its (their) outside(s), the effort of a discourse, e.g. theoretical, 'to tear itself away' from the pre-existing tissue of the discourse in which it is found and where it is made, the marking of a 'position' in a controversy, or even a 'struggle for life', when what is at play in the area of contact is not in the order of the discussion, however violent it may be, but with the right to existence for only one of the two, an extreme case of the solidarity constitutive of a discourse with its other.[27]

Overall, the distinctions made by the marked forms of manifest heterogeneity fall within a relationship of *one* to *another*, inscribed in the comparable, in the commensurable, in *plurality*.

2.4.2   At the same time they install an outside with respect to which the discourse constitutes, these forms postulate *another exteriority*: *that of the enunciator* able to be placed at any time at a distance from his or her language, his or her discourse, i.e. occupying in relation to them, and taken locally as an object, an exterior position of an observer. Any marked form of distance refers to this figure of the enunciator, the user and the master of his or her thought, but this figure is particularly present in the glosses of rectification, reserve etc. which specify him or her as the judge, the commentator etc. of his or her own speech.

---

26. Light-hearted gallantries; this phrase refers to the plays of the French writer Marivaux (1688–1763) [note of the translator].

27. Faurisson's speech (see 'Mémoire en défense', La Vieille Taupe, studied by J. Authier-Revuz, and L. Romeu, article forthcoming in Mots, No. 8, 1984) is entirely based on a denunciation of the 'mythical' discourse (my quotes) on the 'gas chambers' (quotes by Faurisson) is a case in point. In the space of this article I cannot analyze the texts with these types of relation to another, cf. schematic elements in Authier (1981). [R. Faurisson (born in 1929) is a French academic who denies the Holocaust (trans. note)].

3.

3.1   The inherent heterogeneity of discourse and the heterogeneity shown in discourse are two different orders of reality: that of the actual processes of constitution of a discourse and the processes, not less real, of representation in a discourse, of its constitution.

The issue is not assimilating one to the other, nor imagining a simple linking, an image, a translation, a projection of one into the other; this direct mapping is prohibited – apart from the fact that it would require transparency of what is said to its real conditions of existence – by the apparent irreducibility of the two heterogeneities.

To a radical heterogeneity, in an internal *exteriority* to both the subject and the discourse, such as *non-localizable* and *non-representable* in a discourse that it constitutes, that of *the Other of the discourse* – in which the inter-discourse and the unconscious play – are opposed the *representation* in the discourse, the differentiations, the disjunction, the borders inside/outside through which *one* – subject, discourse – *is delimited in the plurality of others*, and at the same time affirms the figure of an enunciator outside of his or her discourse.

Faced with the 'that speaks' of constitutive heterogeneity answers, through the 'as the other says' and the 'if I may say' of manifest heterogeneity, an 'I know what I say', that is to say, I know *who* is speaking, I or another, and I know *how* I speak, how I use the words.

If any simple linking of these two planes inevitably involves a reductive assimilation of one to the other,[28] we should not, however, on the basis of their irreducibility, admit locking ourselves into the description of *one* of the two levels, with the constant risk of making from it, explicitly or not, *the* enunciative reality, denying citizenship to the next plane, or, more cautiously, assuming the independence, the autonomy of the two planes, that is to say the irrelevance of one in consideration of the other – approaches that seem to be, very broadly, those of pragmatics on the one hand, and on the other theoretical approaches to the constitutive heterogeneity of the discourse. It

---

28. I think that is what E. Fouquier (1981) does in his study of the forms of the distance, when he arises a relationship of 'homology' between the 'discursive behavior' of distancing and the division of the subject. Despite the references to Freud and Lacan, this mapping is incompatible with the psychoanalytic conception of a decentred subject, because of the language; however, it can, in fact, be consistent with the concepts – opposed – of the subject reduced to the Ego (see 1 above), split, alienated, taken in games of bad faith and theater, of Laing, Sartre, Goffman, using the language in the context of its relations with others. Also, this relationship meets by a roundabout way, the 'full' speaker of the pragmatics and the psychology of enunciation which is deaf to the constitutive heterogeneity of the unconscious and of the order of discourse.

is essential, I believe, to recognize that these two orders of reality are irreducible but joinable, and even necessarily joined together.[29]

3.2.1   According to the paradox of 'constitutive heterogeneity', what the subject, the discourse is made of threatens to defeat it any time; what it is constituted of is also what, being heterogeneous, escapes it.

For the divided subject, the indispensable role of Ego is that of an instance which, in the imagination, is occupied with reconstructing the image of an autonomous subject, cancelling, in ignorance, the real decentring.

The forms marked by manifest heterogeneity are negotiations with the centrifugal forces of disintegration, of constitutive heterogeneity: they construct, in ignorance of it, a representation of enunciation which, though illusory, is a necessary protection for a discourse to occur.[30]

This representation of enunciation is also 'constitutive' in another sense: beyond the 'I' that arises as a subject of his or her discourse, 'by this individual act of appropriation, which introduces the speaker in his speech' (Benveniste, 1970), the marked forms of manifest heterogeneity reinforce, confirm, guarantee that 'I' by a specification of identity, *giving substance to the discourse* – by the form, the contour, the edges, the limits that they draw for it – and *giving figure to the subject enunciator* – by the position and the metalinguistic activity that they stage.

---

29. We note, on the level of the vocabulary used to reflect one plane or another, meetings of relevant words in their delusion: the *division* of the psychoanalytical subject versus the *division* of the speaking subject in figures of the enunciator, speaker…; the heterogeneity which *constitutes* a discourse in the sense that the tissue is made from it versus the shown heterogeneity which *constitutes* a discourse in the sense that, in regard to the outside, it assigns to it a specific form; the *polyphony* of any discourse that cannot 'not align with the number of planes of a partition' versus the 'effects' of *polyphony* that allow certain forms of the shown heterogeneity. If it is essential not to confuse them, this not fortuitous relationship can be understood as a sign of solidarity which does exist between the two planes as a relation of the asymmetric determination.

30. It should be noted that if these forms of representation lend themselves easily to the tricks, the calculations, the devious strategies of the interactional comedy, this mask game with respect to the other should not obscure the fact that, basically, the lure, the trompe-l'œil, is first *in the subject,* in the protective strategy for him or her and his or her discourse, dealing with the intimate and unavoidable threat of the constitutive heterogeneity.

References

Authier, Jacqueline. 1978. 'Les formes du discours rapporté. Remarques syntaxiques et sémantiques à partir des traitements proposés.' *DRLAV* 17: 1–87.

Authier, Jacqueline. 1981. 'Paroles tenues à distance.' In *Matérialités discursives, Actes du Colloque des 24–26 avril 1980, Paris X-Nanterre*, edited by Bernard Conein, Jean-Jacques Courtine, Françoise Gadet, Jean-Marie Marandin and Michel Pêcheux, 127–42. Lille: Presses Universitaires de Lille.

Authier-Revuz, Jacqueline. 1982. 'Hétérogénéité montrée et hétérogénéité constitutive : éléments pour une approche de l'autre dans le discours.' *DRLAV* 26: 91–151.

Bakhtine, Mikhaïl. 1975. *Questions de littérature et d'esthétique*. Moscow.

Benveniste, Émile. 1970. 'L'appareil formel de l'énonciation.' *Langages* 17: 12–18. DOI: 10.3406/lgge.1970.2572

Clément, Catherine. 1972. 'Le Moi et la déconstruction du sujet'. In *Encyclopedia Universalis*, 172–75.

Conein, Bernard, Jean-Jacques Courtine, Françoise Gadet, Jean-Marie Marandin, and Michel Pêcheux, eds. 1981. *Matérialités discursives, Actes du Colloque des 24–26 avril 1980, Paris X-Nanterre*. Lille: Presses Universitaires de Lille.

Courtine, Jean-Jacques. 1981. 'Analyse du discours politique.' *Langages* 62: 9–128.

Fouquier, Eric. 1981. *Approche de la distance*. Paris: Ecole des Hautes Etudes en Sciences Sociales.

Henry, Paul. 1977. *Le Mauvais outil*. Paris: Klincksieck.

Kristeva, Julia. 1970. 'Une poétique ruinée.' In M. Bakhtine: *La poétique de Dostoïevski*, 5–21. Paris: Le Seuil.

Laing, Ronald David. 1960. *The divided self*. London: Tayistock Publications.

Laplanche, Jean, and Jean-Bertrand Pontalis. 1968. *Vocabulaire de la psychanalyse*. Paris: PUF.

Marandin, Jean-Marie. 1979. 'Problèmes d'analyse du discours. Essai de description du discours français sur la Chine.' *Langages* 55: 17–88. DOI: 10.3406/lgge.1979.1823

Pêcheux, Michel. 1975. *Les Vérités de La Palice*. Paris: Maspéro.

Pêcheux, Michel, and Catherine Fuchs. 1975. 'Mises au point et perspectives à propos de l'analyse automatique du discours.' *Langages* 37: 7–80. DOI: 10.3406/lgge.1975.2612

Rey-Debove, Josette. 1978. *Le Métalangage*. Paris: Le Robert.

Roudinesco, Elisabeth. 1977. *Pour une politique de la psychanalyse*. Paris: Maspéro.

Todorov, Tzvetan. 1981. *Mikhaïl Bakhtine, le principe dialogique, suivi des écrits du Cercle de Bakhtine*. Paris: Le Seuil.

Oswald Ducrot

Enunciative polyphony

Oswald Ducrot (b. 1930) is both a linguist and a philosopher of language working in the field of semantics from a pragmatic perspective. Ducrot has developed a theory of 'the argumentation within language' (Ducrot, and Anscombre, 1983), which claims that the linguistic system itself is structured in order for the locutor to exert influence over the addressee, by 'trapping' him or her in the net of language. Ducrot has mainly studied presupposition, implicatures (Ducrot, 1972) and discourse markers (Ducrot et al., 1980). Ducrot's text is taken from a book published in 1984 (*The saying and the said* [*Le Dire et le dit*], chapter VIII), which deals with the question of enunciative polyphony. From an enunciative-polyphonic point of view, an utterance operates with a variety of discursive beings, notably with the locutor as the being responsible for the utterance and the enunciators representing certain points of view. Resembling Goffman's theory of 'footing' (1981), the notion of polyphony refers to the work of Bakhtin. However, unlike Bakhtin, who explores the intertextual organisation of whole texts (his example being Dostoyesky's novels), Ducrot's focus is on enunciative polyphony, i.e. the polyphonic organisation of utterances. In the selected text, Ducrot proceeds in two steps, which correspond to two levels of polyphony. (1) He considers cases of 'double enunciation', in which the usual thesis of the uniqueness of the speaker is called into question. (2) Then, he considers a more radical kind of polyphony, whereby the locutor mobilises various 'enunciators' in his or her utterance. In his or her speech, the locutor, who takes responsibility for the utterance, uses various 'voices' referring to 'enunciators' with which the locutor agrees or disagrees. This is a new definition of *enunciator*. The enunciator is no longer a being at the centre of the enunciation activity, but a 'point of view'. Through 'point of view', Ducrot designates a kind of framing of the explicit or implicit propositional content. Every part of the content is necessarily attributed to a particular point of view, be it the locutor or somebody else in the discourse of the locutor.

References

Bakhtin, Mikhail. 1981[1930s]. *The Dialogic Imagination: Four Essays*. Ed. by Michael Holquist. Austin, London: University of Texas Press.
Ducrot, Oswald. 1972. *Dire et ne pas dire. Principes de sémantique linguistique*. Paris: Hermann.
Ducrot, Oswald, et al. 1980. *Les Mots du discours*. Paris: Minuit.
Ducrot, Oswald, and Jean-Claude Anscombre. 1983. *L'Argumentation dans la langue*. Liège: Mardaga.
Goffman, Erving. 1981. *Forms of talk*. Philadelphia: University of Pennsylvania Press.

Oswald Ducrot. 1984. *Le Dire et le dit*, selected 171, 189–192, 203–210.
Paris: Minuit.

Outline of a polyphonic theory of enunciation

I. The purpose of this chapter is to contest – and, if possible, to replace – a postulate which seems to me a prejudice (usually an implicit one) to all that is now called 'modern linguistics', a term which covers comparativism, structuralism and generative grammar. This prejudice is the uniqueness of the speaking subject. It seems to me that research on language, over at least the past two centuries, has taken for granted the fact that every utterance has one and only one author – an idea that has seemed so obvious that it has not been overtly formulated.

A similar belief has reigned in literary theory for a long time and has only been explicitly questioned during the last fifty years, especially since Bakhtin developed the concept of polyphony. For Bakhtin, there is a whole category of texts, and in particular literary texts, for which we must recognise that many voices are speaking at once, without any of them being dominant or judging the others: this is what he calls popular or carnival literature, also sometimes called masquerade, meaning that the author puts on a series of different masks, as opposed to dogmatic or classical literature. But the theory of Bakhtin, to my knowledge, has only been applied to texts, that is to say, to sequences of utterances, and never to utterances in which these texts are constituted. So it has not led to questioning the postulate that an isolated utterance allows the audibility of only one single voice. (...)

IX. I have indicated the main features of a general framework; once this is established, I can get to the proper theme of this chapter which is, I reiterate, to criticise and to replace the theory of the uniqueness of the subject of enunciation. This is the 'one utterance – one subject' theory which permits the usage of the term 'the subject', taking for granted that there is a unique individual who is the author of the utterance and who is responsible for what is said in the utterance. So if we use this term with neither scruple nor reluctance, it implies that we do not even think of questioning the uniqueness of the origin of the utterance.

What are the properties of this subject? First, s/he is responsible for all the psycho-physiological activity necessary for the production of the utterance. So, to say that a certain X is the subject of the utterance 'The weather is nice' pronounced at a certain place and time is to assign to X the muscle work which made the words *The weather is nice* audible, and also to attribute the underlying intellectual activity to him – the formation of a judgement, the choice of words, the implementation of grammatical rules. The second attribute of the subject is that of being the author, the origin of illocutionary acts performed in production of the utterance (the acts of order, demand, assertion etc.). The subject is the one who orders, demands, asserts etc. Returning to the previous example, we shall say that the same X that produced the words *The weather is nice* is also the one who affirmed the nice weather. To the extent that one person is the producer of the utterance, we must therefore admit that there is only one person at the origin of illocutionary acts performed by him. Often, we can go far in this direction and claim – or rather take as evident – that each utterance accomplishes a single illocutionary act (hence the kind of scandal raised by the existence of indirect acts). Such an assumption is certainly not necessary in order to admit that there is only one origin of the illocutionary activity accomplished by an utterance, but it is in any case sufficient to justify this thesis.

In parentheses, the belief in the uniqueness of the illocutionary act is one of the reasons why many philosophers of language reject, as frankly eccentric, the concept of presupposition developed in *To say and not to say* [Dire et ne pas dire] (Ducrot, 1972). I speak of an illocutionary act of presupposition. However, this raises an immediate objection to 'Who has come?', because when you ask 'Who has come?', your utterance includes the presupposition that someone has come. You therefore think that it is used to perform an act of presupposition, but this is impossible, because everyone knows that the utterance 'Who has come?' is used to perform an act of interrogation. If the performed act is interrogation, it cannot be presupposition. We see immediately that the objection is based on the principle that the utterance must be characterised by a single illocutionary act. Of course, I now have certain reservations about the notion of the act of the presupposition, or at least, as you will see, I present it in a different way than I did at the time of *Dire et ne pas dire*, but in this retraction I am guided certainly not by the fear of having to admit, in case there was an illocutionary act of presupposition, the existence of several acts attached to a single utterance. Instead, I differentiate even more than before the illocutionary activity in a plurality of disjointed pragmatic elements.

In addition to the physical production of an utterance and the performance of illocutionary acts, it is usual to attribute a third property to the speaking subject, which is designated in an utterance by markers of the first person – when they designate an extra-linguistic individual: in this case he is the support of the process expressed by a verb the subject of which is I, the owner of the objects qualified as mine, one who is located in a place called here. And we take for granted that this individual designated by I is also the one who produces the utterance and also the one whose utterance expresses promises, orders, assertions etc. Of course, we are faced with the anti-example of reported speech in direct style, where the pronoun I often does not refer to the person who utters it. However, to eliminate the anti-example, it is sufficient to use the notion of direct reported speech (criticised here in §XI), according to which the occurrences that appear in quotation marks do not refer to an extra-linguistic individual but constitute the simple mention of words of the language. Thus, *I* in *Peter said 'I'm coming'* denotes a grammatical entity, the first person pronoun, and the overall utterance merely means that Peter has used this pronoun, followed by the word coming.

Let us accept, for the time being, this conception of direct reported speech. Is it so obvious that the three properties I have mentioned are attributed to a unique individual in other types of discourse? If it could be so in the case of simple utterances, produced in simple contexts, I would not try to discuss it (I do not think you can blame me for using here, without defining it, a notion as unclear as the one of simplicity: in fact, I do not use it to establish my own thesis but to make a concession to my opponents – which could be expressed, using the terminology that I am going to introduce, by saying that the enunciator of what I say here cannot be attributed to the speaker as such). As an example of a simple utterance in a simple context, let us consider the replica 'Last week I was in Lyon', used to answer the question 'Where were you last week?' There is no difficulty in attributing to the same person the three constitutive properties of the speaking subject. If we denote by 'L' the individual to whom the question is addressed and who articulates the answer, it is L who is designated by *I* (it is about L that it is said that he was in Lyon) and L is still taking responsibility for the act of assertion conveyed by the utterance.

But once you place an utterance, even a simple one, in a slightly more complex dialogue, the thesis of uniqueness begins to encounter difficulty, e.g. when there is resumption (in the broadest sense of the term, which does not involve literal repetition or paraphrase). L, who is accused of having made a mistake, retorts: 'Oh, I am an idiot, well, wait a minute!' L is still the producer of the words and he is also the one who is designated by I. But concerning the act of assertion made in the first utterance it is certainly not L who takes the responsibility – precisely because L has the immodesty of contesting it: on the contrary, L attributes it to his interlocutor, A (although I did not actually talk about stupidity, but only made a complaint which, according to L, logically implies for A a belief in the idiocy of L).

Thus, whenever there is some form of resumption (and nothing is more frequent than a resumption in the conversation), the allocation of the three aforementioned properties to a single speaking subject becomes problematic, even in the case when an utterance is syntactically simple. The proof is even easier with complex utterances, e.g. with utterances constituted by the conjunction *but*. Every mountaineer has, at one time or another, heard the following kind of dialogue on waking: someone unwisely says he or she has not slept all night, and his or her friend kindly responds, 'Maybe you have not slept, but in any case, you have damn well snored.' The author of this utterance, in the physical sense, cannot be held responsible for both of the two affirmations that are made successively. If it seems reasonable to assign to him the second, we cannot do the same for the first, which is corrected by the 'but…'. (…)

XIII.   I have already indicated the first form of polyphony, when I reported the existence of two separate locutors in the case of a 'double enunciation' – a phenomenon made possible by the fact that the locutor is a discursive being, participating in this image of the enunciation provided by the utterance. The notion of enunciator will allow me to describe the second form of polyphony, which is much more frequent. In the example of an echo considered earlier, someone uttered the words *I have pain* and the second person repeated them as: *I have pain. Do not believe that you'll soften me by that,* using in his discourse a duplication of the locutor (whose index is the change of referent of the pronoun I). But it is even more frequent that we hear in discourse the voice of someone who has no properties that I have admitted as being those of the locutor. In Scene 1 of Act I of Britannicus,[1] Agrippina is ironic about her confidante Albina's words, when she attributes to virtue the independent behaviour of Nero.

> Agrippina:
> And this same Nero, whom virtue guides,
> Procures Junia's abduction in the dead of night.
> [Et ce même Néron, que la vertu conduit,
> Fait enlever Junie au milieu de la nuit.]

It is clear that this utterance, and particularly the relative, is meant to express not the point of view of Agrippina, but that of Albina, which is presented as ridiculous. Also, it is apparent that all the markers of the first person in the tirade of Agrippina designate her herself and then force me to identify her as a locutor (if, in the verses I have cited, we introduced a marker of the first person, such as 'without telling me', the *me* would also refer to Agrippina). This suggests the idea that the meaning of the utterance, in the representation it gives of the enunciation, can reveal voices that are not those of only one locutor. I call 'enunciators' those beings who are supposed to express themselves through the utterance, without so far having been assigned specific words; if they 'speak' it is only in the sense that the enunciation is seen as expressing their view, their position, their attitude, but not their words in the material sense of the term.

To define the notion of enunciator, I have sometimes said (see Ducrot et al., 1980, Chapter I) that they are the subjects of elementary illocutionary acts, meaning that few very general acts are marked in the structure of a sentence (affirmation, denial, interrogation, incitation, wish, exclamation). This definition is unfortunately difficult to introduce into the theory of enunciation that I have to provide. In fact, for someone, or me, to perform an illocutionary act generally means 'to present his or her enunciation as requiring…' – and, in this paper, I reserve for the locutor the performance of illocutionary acts: by choosing an utterance, she or he 'presents his or her enunciation as requiring…'. To the extent that the existence of an enunciator belongs to the image of

---

1.   A tragedy by Jean Racine (1669). [Trans. note]

the enunciation provided by the utterance, to assign illocutionary acts to the enunciator we should say 'the utterance attributes to the enunciation the property to be presented by an enunciator as (1) his or her own, (2) requiring…'. But this formula is barely intelligible. It is unclear how such an enunciation could be attributed to an enunciator while the latter, unlike the locutor, is not defined in relation to the occurrence of the word (s/he is not assigned by any word in the material sense of the term). Unable so far to overcome these difficulties in the context of a theoretical construction, I will content myself with comparisons with the theatre first, then with the novel.

I would say that the enunciator is to the locutor as the character is to the author. The author stages characters who perform, in what I called in §3 and according to Anne Reboul, a 'first speech', performing linguistic and extralinguistic actions, the action that the author him/herself is not in charge of. In a 'second speech', the latter can address the public through the characters: s/he either assimilates to one of whom s/he seems to make his representative (when the theatre is directly didactic) or gives significance to the fact that the characters speak and behave in a certain way. In a similar way, the locutor responsible for the utterance confirms through it the existence of enunciators whose views and attitudes it organises. And its own position can be manifested either because it is assimilated to one or another of the enunciators by taking him or her as a representative (the enunciator is then actualised), or simply because it chooses to make them appear and their appearance remains significant, although it does not assimilate to them (the discursive existence which is given to them, the fact that someone takes a certain position, gives some weight to this position, even for one who does not take it on his or her account: is there also another possible weight for linguistic content related to the words whose intrinsic value is impossible to fix or to identify?). We could push the parallel even further: as the enunciator is not responsible for the linguistic material used and imputed to the locutor, so the character in a play cannot be imputed for the materiality of the text written by the author or said by the actors. For example, in *Les femmes savantes*, if Molière and the actors express themselves in verse, it is clear that the represented characters usually speak in prose. And at a time when the character Trissotin recites verses this should be indicated by a particular actor's diction and, from the author, by a particular form of versification.

I want to emphasise that the approximation of the couple locutor-enunciator and of the couple author + actor-character only concerns the role played by the two couples in modes of communication such as theatrical language and non-theatrical language: in my opinion, they have the same semiological function. Let us now assume that we leave aside the semiological point of view and describe what is happening on stage not as a specific mode of communication but as one of many uses of ordinary language, along with conversation or political speech. This makes it necessary to consider the characters since they are the referents of the I pronounced on the stage as locutors – the author and the actors appear this time as speaking subjects. In ordinary language, the same distinction between locutor and speaking subject enables theatre to put it to a particular use: a characteristic of theatre compared to pure narrative – that is to say a story without dialogue related in a direct style – is that the semiological function of the enunciator is performed here by a person, a character, who, with respect to the use made of ordinary language, is a locutor – so that a speaking subject, comedian by trade, pronounces *I* referring to Don Diego,[2] Spanish seigneur. Moreover, the possibility of double enunciation (cf. §11), related to the distinction between the speaking subject and the locutor, explains that the same person on stage can sometimes speak both as a character and as a representative of the character, e.g. when making comments about his or her role: in the parody of *The Cid*, the representative of Don Diego can complain within the play that his comrade had a heavy hand when he knocked him. We can therefore distinguish:

1. actor X, speaking subject;
2. a first locutor, for whom I reserve the term 'actor', defined by the fact that he holds such a specific role, and who can say *I* as the holder of that role;
3. a second locutor, the character played by the actor, the character who also designates himself or herself by *I*.

XIV.   The narrative theory presented in Genette (1972) offers me a second comparison to try to explain my distinction between locutor and enunciator. In fact, this theory shows two types of narrative instances in the story, corresponding in many respects to what I have labelled 'locutor' and 'enunciator' in the study of ordinary language. The correspondent of the locutor is the narrator that Genette puts in opposition to the author, in the same way that I put the locutor in opposition to the empirical speaking subject, that is to say to the actual producer of the utterance. The author of a story (writer or novelist) highlights, according to Genette, a narrator who is in charge of the story and who has features quite different from those which the history of literature or the psychology of fictional creation must attribute to the author. I report three features, among which only the first is developed by Genette.

The first feature, which I tackle quickly, concerns the attitude of the narrator to the related events. While the author imagines or invents these events, the narrator reports them, meaning, for example, that he reproduces the (supposed) memories – in the case of a narrative in the past – or that he provides a linguistic form for what s/he is supposed to live or find – in some narratives in the present.

I will speak more on the second difference between narrator and author, which is related to the first one. This is their relation to time. In his study of grammatical tenses,

---

2.   A character from the play by P. Corneille *Le Cid* (1636). [Trans. note]

Weinrich (1964), notes that futuristic novels are always written in the past tense – what is important for me is that this can be so. If I were writing a novel about the year 2000 today, nothing prevents me from starting: 'At that time France was an empty lot that was a cause of dispute....'. We can see something strange or paradoxical on the grounds that the author, while writing in the past, does not seek to dissimulate that he talks about his future. But the paradox disappears as soon as we have differentiated between author and narrator, since the tense used may very well not take as the point of reference the moment when the author writes, but the one when the narrator relates, and an author living in 1985 can imagine a narrator living in the year 3000 who relates what happened in 2000.

This distinction between narrator (the literary equivalent of my 'locutor') and author (corresponding to what I call the 'actual producer', and external to the story as the producer is external to the meaning of the utterance) even allows – and it is the third difference that I point out – the performing of the act of narration by someone about whom it is said that s/he does not exist or does not exist anymore. If to write you must exist, it is not necessary to narrate. Hence, stories exist in the first person which relate the death of the character designated by the first person, as in Wilder's film, *Sunset Boulevard*, which is narrated by a character who dies before the end. Empirical existence – the necessary predicate of the author – may be denied to the narrator, to the extent that the latter is a fictitious being inside the work, his role is close to the one that I attributed to the locutor – who for me is a discourse being belonging to the meaning of the utterance and falling within this description which the utterance provides for its enunciation.

I can also match the enunciator to one of the roles proposed by Genette. I will put it in parallel with what Genette sometimes calls the 'centre of perspective' (the 'subject of consciousness' of American authors), that is to say the person from whose perspective the events are presented. To distinguish him or her from the narrator, Genette says that the narrator is the one 'who speaks', while the centre of perspective is the one 'who sees'. He also cites many examples where the two roles cannot be attributed to a unique individual. Thus, in *In Search of Lost Time* [*A la recherche du temps perdu*], sometimes the narrator gives a vision of the events he relates that cannot be his own at the moment when he tells the story, nor of the individual designated by I, that is to say, the person he was when he lived the history: the vision reported by the narrator is thus sometimes the one of Swann or of Charles,[3] despite the fact that the narrator himself is identified, using the first person, with another character of the story. This situation seems to me close to the one I tried to describe at the level of the utterance by saying that the locutor presents an enunciation – for which it declares itself responsible – as

---

3.   Two characters from Proust's novel. [Trans. note]

expressing the attitudes for which s/he may refute responsibility. The locutor speaks in the sense that the narrator relates, that is to say that it is given as the source of a discourse. But the attitudes expressed in this discourse can be attributed to enunciators from whom it distances himself – as the points of view manifested in the story may be those of conscious subjects foreign to the narrator.

To illustrate the relationship between enunciator and centre of perspective, I will comment on the first lines of Flaubert's *A Sentimental Education* [*L'Education sentimentale*] (Flaubert, 2000), dedicated to the departure of the boat that goes up the Seine from Paris, taking aboard Frederic Moreau: '*Le 11 septembre 1840, vers six heures du matin, la Ville-de-Montereau, près de partir, fumait à gros tourbillons devant le quai Saint-Bernard.*'[4] It is followed by a description of the quay which is intended to be entirely 'objective' and indicates, in a jumble of isolated notations, the rush and general animation before the departure. The description is interrupted by the utterance that I will comment on in detail: '*Enfin le navire partit ; et les deux berges, peuplées de magasins, de chantiers et d'usines, filèrent comme deux larges rubans que l'on déroule.*'[5]

I find in this utterance at least two markers that reveal the presence of a character who is not the narrator (for convenience, I will assume here that there is a narrator – which is far from obvious). The first is *finally* [*enfin*], which not only serves to point out that a certain event is at the end of a chronological development (as would be found in *Pierre est arrivé, puis Jean et enfin Paul*[6]). It also has an exclamatory value: it is the interjection of someone who sees a too-long-awaited ending: it allows us to hear the sigh of an enunciator from whom, to repeat what I said about the exclamation and expressiveness, it is triggered spontaneously by the situation. But this enunciator, who must attend the described scene, who must live it, is clearly distinct from the narrator who has no reason to get impatient and to exclaim.

The second index of a subjectivity that is not that of the narrator is the metaphor that closes the utterance '*les deux berges (…) filèrent comme deux larges rubans que l'on déroule*'.[7] To see the banks '*unwind*', they should be looked at from a special place – the aft deck of the boat. In fact, it is only from this place that, on the one hand, we can see the two quays at once and, on the other, the view downstream blocked by the Ile Saint-Louis and the Ile de la Cité; the quays 'stretch' as the boat moves away from the islands. Since just after the passage I analysed the way the narrator presents Frederic

---

4. 'On the morning of 15 September 1840 the *Ville de Montereau* was lying alongside the quay Saint-Bernard belching clouds of smoke, all ready to sail.'

5. 'Finally the vessel cast off and the two banks of the river, packed with warehouses, yards and factories, began to unwind like two broad lengths of ribbon.'

6. *Peter arrived / then John and finally Paul.* [Trans. note]

7. 'the two banks (…) began to unwind like two broad lengths of ribbon.'

Moreau looking at Paris from the stern of the boat, it is almost automatic to attribute to him, in retrospective reading, a vision of the banks that began to unwind and, going a little further in the text, the impatience of the word *finally*. We can see, I hope, in this example, how close the concept of enunciator and that of the centre of perspective are: they serve to reveal in the utterance a subject distinct not only from the one who speaks [the writer / the speaking subject] but also from the one who is said to speak [the narrator / the locutor].

References

Ducrot, Oswald. 1972. *Dire et ne pas dire. Principes de sémantique linguistique*. Paris: Hermann.

Ducrot, Oswald, and et al. 1980. *Les Mots du discours*. Paris: Minuit.

Flaubert, Gustave. 2000. *A Sentimental Education: The Story of a Young Man*. Translated by Douglas Parmée. Oxford: Oxford University Press.

Genette, Gérard. 1972. *Figures III*. Paris: Seuil.

Weinrich, Harald. 1964. *Tempus. Besprochene und erzählte Welt*. Stuttgart: Kohlhammer Verlag.

Johannes Angermuller

Subject positions in polyphonic discourse

Discourse as an interdiscursive multitude of intersecting voices, sources and perspectives – this is the view that Johannes Angermuller (b. 1973) takes at the crossroads of linguistics and sociology. Angermuller is a linguist and sociologist from Germany obtained his PhD in France. He is now a professor in discourse at the Centre for Applied Linguistics at Warwick University, UK and leads research on academic discourse at EHESS in Paris, France. The selected passage represents an example of Angermuller's approach to discourse as a positioning practice (Angermuller 2013) which in the selected text he applies to canonical texts from French poststructuralism. Angermuller studies how discursive subject positions are constructed through the textual markers of polyphony. In this view, utterances are the smallest communicative units of discourse. An utterance is the textual realization of a speech act which not only refers to its locutor as the originating instance (the 'author'), but also mobilises many other explicit as well as implicit speakers. It is through the text's markers of polyphony that the many speaking beings in discourse are orchestrated and their relationships defined. Drawing on the 'French' tradition of studying written texts, the 'Anglo-American' tradition of studying processes and practices as well as the 'German' tradition of studying knowledge, Angermuller's polyphonic approach is especially suited to the analysis of the subtle interplay of implicit and explicit demarcations, stances and subjectivities of speakers in written academic discourse. It has also been applied to slogans and textual snippets from political discourse (Angermuller, 2011, 2012).

References

Angermuller, Johannes. 2011. 'From the many voices to the subject positions in anti-globalization discourse. Enunciative pragmatics and the polyphonic organization of subjectivity.' *Journal of Pragmatics* 43: 2992–3000. DOI: 10.1016/j.pragma.2011.05.013

Angermuller, Johannes. 2012. 'Fixing meaning. The many voices of the post-liberal hegemony in Russia.' *Journal of Language and Politics* 11, no. 2: 115–34. DOI: 10.1075/jlp.11.1.06ang

Angermuller, Johannes. 2013. 'How to become an academic philosopher. Academic discourse as a multileveled positioning practice.' In *Sociología histórica*, 3, 263–289.

Johannes Angermuller. 2014. *Poststructuralist Discourse Analysis.*
Subjectivity in Enunciative Pragmatics.
Houndmills, Basingstoke: Palgrave.

Discourse emerges whenever texts are linked with their contexts in acts of reading. In this sense, the enquiry will consider how a theoretical text demands that the reader answer the following question: 'By whom, for whom, where, when, under which circumstances and with which purposes etc. am I uttered?' This is a question which the text cannot answer itself. It needs a cognitive agent to solve its interpretive problems: the reader. Rather than resuscitating an originally intended meaning, the reader has to determine the meaning of the text in each act of reading, with the help of the formal markers, traces and instructions scattered throughout the text. When the reader recognizes the symbolic forms with which the text operates, he or she will begin to look for the enunciative context without which the text would remain devoid of meaning.

As an opaque symbolic materiality, a text is posed between the individual and the world. At the same time, the individual's knowledge about the world is always symbolically mediated. His or her knowledge needs to be inscribed into the symbolic material. In order to gain access to the social world, to the producers of the text and to other individuals in the field, the individual thus has to enter the discourse, use language and produce texts. By having the individual search for an answer to her/his question, the text enables the reader to construct knowledge about a social world where other individuals act and position themselves in relation to each other. Therefore, the task of discourse analysis is to analyze 'the enunciative *dispositif* which connects a textual structure and a social location' (Maingueneau, 1996: 8).

Texts are not repositories for pure ideas, content or messages to be read directly from the symbolic material. They need a reader who completes it with the missing context by associating the many anonymous sources and voices of discourse with definite individuals occupying positions in the social. Thus, to understand a text's social relevance, the reader has to look for the guarantors, references and authorities the locutor quotes implicitly or explicitly in order to legitimate the content for which he or she does not claim responsibility. The reader also has to enquire into the individuals and producers whose discourse is rejected by the locutor. Various analyses have underscored the many ways in which the text confronts the reader with the question: who is speaking? The social efficiency of texts seems to lie precisely in the fact that they allow the reader a certain degree of freedom to determine the sources of enunciation and associate them with actors in the social world.

(…) If we consider discourse to be a decentred space of voices, texts draw from a plurality of sources which are not always easy to identify. Theoretical texts are no exception – even those that seem to correspond perfectly to the norms of academic writing (i.e. texts with citations, bibliographies – see Fløttum, 2005). However, as texts are always contextually underspecified, they demand active readers who will search for the contexts in which they 'make sense'. In order to manage the many anonymous voices, open gaps and undetermined sources that need to be processed in the act of reading, readers tend to have recourse to interpretive hypotheses. 'Structuralism' is one such hypothesis that allows the reader to frame theoretical texts in a certain way. Thus, against a 'structuralist' background, the producers of the following textual fragments will be seen to relate to each other and to form a movement at a certain time and place. The label 'structuralism' presupposes a group of producers, a movement or school (i.e. 'structuralists' such as Lacan, Foucault, Althusser, Derrida and Sollers) who/which can be distinguished from other groups with differing theoretical orientations (e.g. 'humanists'). Such a frame can help the reader solve the interpretive tasks posed by the text. By framing the text as a product of the structuralist movement or conjuncture, the reader can reduce the multitude of discursive voices s/he encounters when reading a limited set of relevant subject positions (such as a conflict between 'structuralists' vs 'humanists'). Texts from different producers can then be seen as dealing with a common topic, theme or problem (i.e. 'the structural model in the human sciences') and thus as contributing to a discourse. (…)

The following analyses draw from Ducrot's model of polyphonic utterances, which has been elaborated by Henning Nølke, Kjersti Fløttum and Coco Norén in the 'Scandinavian theory of linguistic polyphony' or ScaPoLine (*Théorie scandinave de la polyphonie linguistique*, 2004). According to Nølke et al., an utterance is composed of at least four components: the locutor, the points of view (Ducrot's 'voices'), the discursive beings (Ducrot's 'enunciators' or 'speakers') and enunciative connections. The locutor, L, is the 'puppetmaster', the agent responsible for the utterance who orchestrates the different points of view 'pov'. Points of view are 'semantic unities whose source supports the point of view'. The discursive beings (the 'speakers' or 'discursive figures') 'saturate the sources' or fill the enunciative positions of the enunciation, whereas enunciative connections 'tie the discursive beings to the points of view' (2004: 30). Although never appearing himself, the locutor marks its presence in the utterance by constructing 'images' of it vis-à-vis the allocutor, A, and a third party who exists individually as a 'non-person' or collectively (as 'ONE/WE' (*ON*) or as 'LAW' (*LOI*)). There are two 'images' of the locutor, L: the 'responsible' speaker, l_0, of the utterance as well as the textual locutor which is formally realized as pronouns, names etc. Accordingly, the two images from the allocutor are a_0 and its textual realizations. While l_0 and a_0 refer to the locutor and his allocutor, both speaking in the enunciation of the utterance, the textual realizations refer, in contrast, to the formally marked locutor and its counterpart. Nølke et al. do not divide the third persons (*tiers*) in order to avoid complicating the model, but they distinguish between two collective thirds: a heterogeneous ONE/WE (as a background of opinions, postures and knowledge in their manifold existence) and a homogeneous LAW (whose normative presence calls for recognition). (…)

While the reader can read a text in many different ways, the text is not contextualized in a pell-mell fashion. In order to comprehend its meaning, the reader is effectively subject to certain linguistic constraints. In written discourse, there can be no immediate access to the enunciation itself, to the act of speaking, writing or reading. What is accessible to the analyst as well as to any other reader are the formal traces of the enunciation, the enunciative markers instructing the reader about how the discourse is uttered (or 'enunciated'). For it is thanks to these formal markers of enunciation – *I*, *not* or quotation marks – that the text defines the interpretive limits within which the reader may engage in the search for who it is that is speaking in discourse. (…)

By means of the instruments of enunciative analysis, we will analyze the selected theoretical texts as an antagonism between between two voices: of one speaker, a_1, who represents the cause of 'man', the 'subject', the 'author', 'humanism', 'a living presence' … and one speaker, l_0, who rejects a_1. In its formal guise, the theoretical figure of anti-humanism implies at least these two basic points of view:

pov_1: [a_1] (TRUE (p: 'Man is alive'))
pov_2: [l_0] (NO (pov_1))

This is the polyphonic structure of anti-humanist discourse which confronts the reader with an antagonism between the locutor, l_0, and the allocutor, a_1, who represents the cause of 'man'. By setting an intellectual 'now', T_0, which distinguishes 'new' from 'old' tendencies, the speakers become historical vectors of a discourse in which both producers and products are exposed to ongoing processes of obsolescence. The text then offers the reader the interpretive instruction: *Scan the social context for possible protagonists, for the speakers l_0 and a_1, and determine which age group and generation they belong to!* If readers are confronted again and again with interdiscursive antagonisms between l_0 and a_1 and an intellectual 'now' T_0, their knowledge about the field can solidify into a *topos* ('the anti-humanism of the 60s and 70s') which certain slogans ('death of man/subject') can easily reactivate. (…) I will now attempt to demonstrate how they stage a polyphonic spectacle between the antagonistic figures of the (structuralist) 'avant-garde' and the (humanist) 'tradition'.

Michel Foucault. The end of the age of 'Man'

(1) One thing in any case is certain: (2) man is neither the oldest nor the most constant problem that has been posed to human knowledge. (3) Taking a relatively short chronological sample within a restricted geographical area – European culture since the sixteenth century – one can be certain that man is a recent invention within it. (4) It is not around him and his secrets that knowledge prowled for so long in the darkness. (5) In fact, among all the mutations that have affected the knowledge of things and their order, the knowledge of identities, differences, characters, equivalences, words – in short, in the midst of all the episodes of that profound history of the *Same* – only one, that which began a century and half ago and is now perhaps drawing to a close, has made it possible for the figure of man to appear. (6) And that appearance was not the liberation of an old anxiety, the transition into luminous consciousness of an age-old concern, the entry into objectivity of something that had long remained trapped within beliefs and philosophies: (7) it was the effect of a change in the fundamental arrangement of knowledge. (8) As the archaeology of our thought easily shows, man is an invention of recent date. And one perhaps nearing its end. (9) If those arrangements were to disappear as they appeared, if some event of which we can at the moment do no more than sense the possibility – without knowing either what its form will be or what it promises – were to cause them to crumble, as the ground of Classical thought did, at the end of the eighteenth century, then one can certainly wager that man would be erased, like a face in the sand at the edge of the sea.

> Michel Foucault. 1966. *Les Mots et les choses. Une archéologie des sciences humaines.* Paris: Gallimard, 398. Trans. as *The Order of Things: An Archaeology of the Human Sciences*, London and New York: Routledge, 2004[1970], pp. 421–422, trans. adapted.

This passage closes with Michel Foucault's *Les Mots et les choses* [*The Order of Things*], a historical survey of early modern knowledge in Europe with which the author achieved his breakthrough in the French intellectual scene. The public success of this book is surprising, given that its 400 pages are based on mostly forgotten texts from over four centuries which the author compiled from dusty library archives. The book's main concern is a presentation of historical material that utterances (3) refer to. The short conclusion of (3) serves to position Foucault theoretically, as one who discusses the relationship of historical knowledge to the problem of *l'homme* [*man*] (2, 3, 4, 5, 8, 9). The concept word *man* serves a double function: on the one hand, it refers to conceptual content which sums up what had been said in previous sections about the knowledge of the nineteenth century. On the other hand, it moves the problem of 'man' into the middle of a polemic argument in which the locutor positions himself in a specific way. (…)

Many of Foucault's utterances present a simple polyphonic structure:

$$pov_1(x): [a_1] (TRUE (p_x))$$
$$pov_2(x): [l_2] (NO (pov_1(x)))$$

While x stands for the utterance's number, p_x represents the respective content: p_2: 'Man is the oldest and the most constant problem that has been posed for human knowledge' (2); p_4: 'It is around man and his secrets that knowledge prowled for so long in the darkness' (4); p_6: 'And that appearance was the liberation of an old anxiety, the transition into luminous consciousness of an age-old concern, the entry into objectivity of something that had long remained trapped within beliefs and philosophies' (6). Against this background, the polyphonic organization of an utterance's contents can be 'tested' by dividing both points of view into those of two persons engaged in a (fictitious) dialogue. Those individuals would be a questioner, A, and a responder, L, who always says 'no' to A's questions:

A: 'p_2?'
L: 'No.'
A: 'p_4?'
L: 'No.'
A: 'p_6?'
L: 'No.'

This dialogue between a humanist, A, and an anti-humanist, L, which can be taken up by real individuals – let's think of Sartre's 'answer' to Foucault (1966) – can now be supplemented with the propositional content of (3, 5, 7) which give argumentative support and additional content to L's monotonous rejection of A's position:

A: 'p_2?'
L: 'No, because p_3.'
A: 'p_4?'
L: 'No, because p_5.'
A: 'p_6?'
L: 'No, because p_7.'

This question-answer game ends in (8), where L concludes what has been said by programmatically recapitulating the results. This polyphonic way of organizing conceptual content is typical of Foucault's sumptuously baroque style, as it allows the manifold historical knowledge of the producer to join the conceptual fray with his intellectual opponents.

Now, the question is what position the locutor of (8) takes regarding this dialogue between the humanist, A, and his anti-humanist counterpart, L. Does he simply continue to give L further argumentative support? Or does it act as an autonomous judge over A and L, one who ends the testimonies of A and L by reaching a verdict at p_8? At this point, the locutor of (8) seems to be clearly taking sides. If in (8) L is to appear as a neutral judge, then the reader has every reason to doubt its impartiality, for the locutor of (8) is too close to the locutors of (2, 3, 4, 5, 6, 7). In the argument over 'man', the locutor's verdict clearly favours the anti-humanist camp. Or does the locutor, associated with Foucault, perhaps not leave a small back door open, to provide an escape route for the verdict to be examined at a later appeal? At first glance, the concluding utterance of (9) appears simply to confirm what is said in (8). But if the outcome of the trial is already fixed, why is the sentence so bloated with conditions, reservations and supplementary remarks that the reader can hardly glean the locutor's position at a glance?

If (9) is meant to repeat only what is said in (8), it would seem rather odd that (9) relies so heavily on the markers of polyphony. Thus, the argumentative operators *si* [*if*], *ne ... ni ... ni* [*neither ... nor ... nor*] and *mais* [*but*] conjure up a number of speakers who assist, as it were, the judge-locutor in formulating his verdict. It is as if the locutor cannot render his verdict without drawing upon a battalion of witnesses, assistants and counsellors. Thus, the many points of view of this utterance can be articulated in the following formal description:

$\text{pov}_1(9)$: [x_1] (TRUE (p: 'The arrangements were to disappear...')), where it is unknown if the speaker is accepted or rejected by L.

$\text{pov}_2(9)$: [x_2] (TRUE (q: 'Some [event] were to cause these arrangements to crumble')), where the parenthesized element in q relates to the pronoun *dont* [*of which*] which connects to a number of syntactically subordinate points of view:

$\text{pov}_1(\text{pov}_2(9))$: [$l_1$] (TRUE (r: 'We can at the moment sense the possibility of [the event]');

$\text{pov}_2(\text{pov}_2(9))$: [$a_2$] (TRUE (s: 'We know the form and the promise [of the event]'));

$\text{pov}_3(\text{pov}_2(9))$: [$l_3$] (NO ($\text{pov}_2(\text{pov}_2(9))$));

$\text{pov}_4(\text{pov}_2(9))$: [$a_4$] (TRUE (P from ($\text{pov}_1(\text{pov}_2(9))$ BUT ($\text{pov}_3(\text{pov}_2(9))$)), where P indicates what is presupposed by $\text{pov}_1(\text{pov}_2(9))$))) (P would possibly be: 'The possibility of predicting an event implies a knowledge about what it means.'), allocated to the other speaker a_4.

$\text{pov}_3(9)$: [x_3] (TRUE (t: 'Man is erased like...')).

$\text{pov}_4(9)$: [x_4] (PERF ($\text{pov}_3(9)$), where PERF designates a performative speech act ('wager'): 'One wagers on...'.

$\text{pov}_5(9)$: [l_5] (MOD ($\text{pov}_4(9)$), where MOD represents the modal verb 'can'.

$\text{pov}_6(9)$: [l_0] (TRUE ($\text{pov}_5(9)$), IF $x_1=l_1$ and $x_2=l_2$), where IF represents the transition to the conditional mode $\text{pov}_1(9)$ and $\text{pov}_2(9)$ thanks to *si*.

This formal representation of the points of view involved in utterance (9) demands some concentration on the part of the reader. Yet we can immediately identify the position of the locutor vis-à-vis the various speakers carrying the content of the utterances. We see the locutor's four adjutants (x_1, x_2, x_3, x_4), whereby x_1 and x_2 are his 'assessors,' on whose verdicts he will finally make his own independent decision. Assessor x_2 even has at his disposal a 'team' of speakers, each with an individual opinion. Of these, x_2 finally accepts l_1 and l_3 while rejecting a_2 and a_4. In contrast, x_3 might play the role of a judge who has already ruled on a precedent case and whose verdict can now be adopted by L. The role of a juridical observer, however, would devolve upon x_4. The speaker x_4 bets on the judge-locutor referring to the verdict of the other judge. What the locutor then says is that he deems 'possible' the result expected from the mouth of the legal observer x_4, although only if both assessors are not mistaken in their judgments.

While in the largely monophonic utterance (8), the locutor-judge l_0 declares his verdict p ('Man is an invention of recent date') without relying on other speakers, he deploys an entire apparatus of speakers in (9). These speakers prepare, write and submit the verdict to the judge for his final approval. Yet what does the judge do in the end? Instead of declaring the expected victory of the anti-humanist party, he still withholds his signature from the verdict prepared by his adjutants. Finally, he announces only the possibility of his signing soon. The case thus remains in limbo.

Even though it is not wholeheartedly accepted by the locutor in the end, the verdict p ('Man is an invention of recent date') is available from the very beginning: (2), (3) and (5) already contain p. However, it appears as though the locutor-judge always looks for an excuse to postpone his definitive signature under p. Thus, the locutor of (2) does not qualify p as true, but rather as what is called 'certain' in (1). Instead of reaching a final verdict and simply saying p (as could be the case in a monophonic utterance such as: $pov_1(2)$: $[l_0]$ (TRUE (p)), the locutor l_0 prefers to let another speaker ($pov_1(2)$) express what he has asserted:

> $pov_1(2)$: $[l_1]$ (TRUE (p))
> $pov_2(2)$: $[l_0]$ (TRUE ($pov_1(2)$)), where TRUE means that (2) is enunciated in the mode of 'Il est certain que…' ('It is certain that').

Just as in (9): *on peut bien parier que* p [*one can wager that* p], the locutor leaves it to his images, l_1, to say p. In this way, l_0 supports l_1's claim to truth in the form of 'It is certain that p.' If both images of L qualify p to be 'true', this does not mean that p is therefore doubly true. Quite the contrary, saying that p is true reduces p to a mere claim. For if the truth of p did not cause any problem for the locutor, why would he then not simply say: 'Man is an invention'? An analogous observation applies to (3): *on peut être sûr que* p [*one can be certain that* p]. Yet here, the locutor's assent is also limited by the modal verb *can* and relativized by another 'adjutant' (*en*-gerund). Finally, we must note the adverb *peut-être* [*maybe*] (5) which qualifies the entire utterance as well as part of (8). Since the locutor is ultimately responsible only for *maybe* and not for p itself (which would read in Polyphonese: $pov_1(2)$: $[l_1]$ (TRUE (p)); $pov_2(2)$: $[l_0]$ (MAYBE ($pov_1(2)$))), it once again avoids committing himself to p.

Yet I want to emphasize that if, in his written texts (which differ from his oral statements), Foucault seldom takes sides for a certain position as clearly as he does in this fragment, this text, too, follows suit with the strategy, typical of Foucault, of masking or erasing the locutor. Foucault's locutor never decides in the final analysis. Each of the trials staged by an utterance can be appealed again in the next utterance. Thanks to this strategy, Foucault (who shortly after the publication of *Les Mots et les choses* will distance himself from structuralism) enjoys a great deal of flexibility when positioning himself in intellectual discourse. In April 1967, he still half-ironically describes himself in an interview as a 'choir boy of structuralism' (Foucault, 1994: 581). And between September 1967 and 1969 (Foucault, 1994[1967/1969]: 603[187]), he begins to distance himself from this intellectual movement before marking, in his *Archéologie du savoir* (1989[1969/1971]), his staunch opposition to the movement of which he had been widely seen as the leader since *Les Mots et les choses* [Order of Things]. Foucault's dexterity lies in his ability – despite all the theoretical reshufflings and realignments of a field in perpetual ferment – to take such changes into account in his own writings and yet to avoid jeopardizing his own credibility through open contradictions, to ensure the basic coherence of his work and thus to secure the ongoing quotability of his name. A position repudiated once and for all (such as the rejection of 'humanism' in the texts of around 1966) can hardly be revised later without incurring a serious loss of intellectual coherence and credibility. For this reason, at the end of the 1970s, he will turn back to the problem of the subject by framing it as an elaboration and radicalization of earlier positions.

If Foucault partakes in the intellectual polemics of the time, yet avoids at all costs siding too much with one or other party, this strategy bears witness to his caution vis-à-vis all forms of appropriation in an intellectual field where the singularity of the producer and his project must be constantly defended. In fact, each final commitment runs the risk of becoming vulnerable to the ageing process of a discourse in which constant breaks with the past are among the few binding certainties of the time. Yet Foucault is not always successful in his balancing act between masking and profiling himself. In retrospect, his academic career certainly appears to be a brilliant success; but in the academic field, with its more pedagogical relations geared toward reproduction, the strategy of continuously switching positions and always leaving a back door open sometimes encounters obstacles. The dilemma of this strategy, often running contrary to the need for planning, predictability and longevity on the part of academic institutions, is attested to by the fact that Foucault needed two attempts to make it into the Ecole Normale Supérieure; that especially in the more conceptual disciplines (such as philosophy) he could not always and immediately convince his teachers (Pestaña, 2006: 49f.); that he did not found an intellectual school in France; that his books entered only gradually into the university curriculum. Surely, one can recognize in his work an ever critical and challenging spirit following an *éthique de la déprise*, an ethics of 'leaving behind', in which every new book must cast doubt on the one preceding it. However, along with Pestaña (2006: 56), one can also see Foucault's work as the product of the creative tension of a spirit whose multiple interests do not always unite in a coherent and systematic whole. Yet, however one may evaluate Foucault's intellectual versatility, the fact remains that, in a discourse which constantly offers new ideas and remains open to new ideas, such a strategy will grant the producer attention well beyond specialized academic fields and well beyond the period marked with the structuralist label. (…)

In conclusion, discourse can be described as having several 'floors' which the reader must traverse from the bottom to the top if s/he wants to know who says what and to learn who takes what position in the intellectual field. On the first floor, the reader encounters a great number of voices, speakers, 'enunciators' who populate the utterances of discourse. Orchestrated by a text's markers of enunciation, every voice says something. Yet as there is always an excess of voices, the reader will need to reduce the text's polyphonic complexity. Therefore, on the second floor, the reader will discover that behind the multitude of voices of the floor below there is a limited number of discursive subject positions such as 'author' (locutor), Other (allocutor) and other instances to which the voices can be attributed. Here the reader realizes that the hive of voices on the floor below is not without a certain logic. These voices have been orchestrated by the locutor in its role as stage director of the discursive spectacle. It is by means of enunciative markers that the locutor signals which speakers s/he accepts and which ones s/he rejects in the discourse. However, if, still on the second floor, the reader discovers that the numerous speakers of discourse are staged in certain ways by the locutor, the reader's mission has not yet ended. He or she must climb further, to the third floor, where the task is to associate the locutor and the allocutor with the various social actors, to attribute them with names and to give them an institutional address in the discursive space, which thus finally allows him or her to match what is being said to historical beings with interests, motivations and intentions that occupy a certain place in the social.

Third floor: naming the subject positions in a sociohistorical context
L = 'Foucault', professor of philosophy at Vincennes etc.; A = 'Sartre'
↑
Second floor: attributing the voices to the locutor and other instances
$L = l_2, l_3, l_5; A = a_1, a_4$
↑
First floor: a multitude of subpersonal voices
x_1, x_2, x_3, x_4, x_5

References

Fløttum, Kjersti. 2005. 'Moi et autrui dans le discours scientifique: l'exemple de la négation ne…pas.' In *Dialogisme et polyphonie*, edited by Jacques Bres, Patrick Pierre Haillet, Sylvie Mellet, Henning Nølke and Laurende Rosier, 323–37. Bruxelles: De Boeck & Duculot.

Foucault, Michel. 1989[1969/1971]. *The Archaeology of Knowledge & The Discourse on Language*. London: Routledge.

Foucault, Michel. 1994. 'La Philosophie structuraliste permet de diagnostiquer ce qu'est aujourd'hui.' In *Dits et Ecrits, tome 1. 1954–1969*, 580–85. Paris: Gallimard.

Foucault, Michel. 1994[1967/1969]. 'Qui êtes-vous, professeur Foucault?' In *Dits et Ecrits, tome 1. 1954–1969*, 601–20. Paris: Gallimard.

Maingueneau, Dominique. 1996. 'L'analyse du discours en France aujourd'hui.' In *Le Discours: Enjeux et perspectives. Numéro spécial Le Français dans le monde*. Ed. by Sophie Moirand, 8–15. Paris: Hachette.

Nølke, Henning, Kjersti Fløttum, and Coco Norén. 2004. *ScaPoLine. La théorie scandinave de la polyphonie linguistique*. Paris: Kimé.

Pestaña, José Luis. 2006. *En devenant Foucault. Sociogenèse d'un grand philosophe*. Broissieux: Editions du Croquant.

Sartre, Jean-Paul. 1966. 'Jean-Paul Sartre répond.' *L'Arc* 30: 87–96.

Section IV

Interactionism

Introduction

There are countless everyday situations in which we face possibly banal but actually quite difficult tasks of dealing with others, such as making an appointment. In order to contact the person we want to see, we can proceed in ways which may be appropriate under certain circumstances, but not in others. We might be perceived as a bit distant, even impolite, if we use an e-mail or a formal letter, especially with close friends. If we decide to use the telephone, we might appear to be intrusive, such as calling a colleague on her private landline after hours. And when we formulate our wish or proposal, we cannot utter it without possibly putting the relationship at risk. If we are too direct, we might compel the other, who is not yet ready to respond, to refuse or even reject our proposal (think of a man addressing an unknown woman in a metro station). If we do not act fast enough, the other might not understand what we are up to (such as a client who wants to see his or her busy lawyer). Therefore, when we try to relate to others, we have to do more than simply apply a given rule. At every step, we have to perform a delicate balancing act in which we need to prove our practical creativity in order to do things 'appropriately' with others, in context-dependent ways.

From a symbolic interactionist point of view, gestures, verbal and written language are used in order to define the situation, i.e. who the participants are, how they relate to each other, how they come to mean something specific. In that sense, discursive practices designate the symbolically mediated activity of continuously constructing the social order, which is never fully defined in advance. Thus, the social emerges as a product of discursive practices which cannot be reduced to any given code, structure or grammar.

Nowadays, 'symbolic interactionism' is often equated with a strand of qualitative social research inspired by micro-sociologists from North America. The label 'symbolic interactionism' was only created after the Second World War, by Herbert G. Blumer (1900–1987, Blumer, 1986[1969]), an American sociologist who was a promoter of George Herbert Mead's (1863–1931) work. From a symbolic interactionist point of view, social reality is created in an ongoing negotiation between the participants in a social situation in a given material setting. The question is how they deal with the double contingency characteristic of any encounter between persons A and B, who both need to react to each other's acts, knowing that the respective other knows that everything they do and say cannot *not* relate to one another somehow. In interactive processes, in other words, the participants can never fully rely on a given recipe or established norms; they need to demonstrate their practical know-how and creativity in dealing with situations which are never fully defined in advance. That is why symbolic interactionists typically take the actors' point of view, preferring naturalistic data from real situations and advocating qualitative methods such as participant observation.

The antecedents of symbolic interactionism hark back to the beginning of the century, when pragmatism (Charles Sanders Peirce [1839–1914], William James [1842–1910], John Dewey [1859–1952]) entered the philosophical scene and into ethnographic research via the urban sociologists of the Chicago School in the first half of the 20th century. If these philosophers placed concepts such as 'truth' into the practical context of those who use them, they simultaneously paved the way for pragmatic theories of the social and political order.

With their rich empirical studies of inner-city life, the ethnographers and sociologists of the Chicago School, by contrast, made a case for the view from below as a legitimate source of sociological expertise. It was George Herbert Mead (1967[1934]), with his theory of social identity, who made pragmatist philosophical ideas relevant to sociologists, notably to Chicago's ethnographers. For Mead, the self is not given by nature; it emerges from interaction with others in the world. Signs and symbols play a central role in the formation of one's identity, which Mead conceptualises in terms of both the attributions to and expectations of others ('Me'), as a reaction to which the individual builds up its individual capacity of action ('I'). It is real human beings who create the reality of society, which is summed up by the so-called Thomas theorem: 'If men define situations as real, they are real in their consequences' (Thomas and Thomas, 1928:572). Therefore, the point is no longer to investigate large and abstract macro-totalities ('Truth' or 'Society'). Rather, attention is directed towards the creative and reflexive logic of human practice as the ultimate origin of relationships with others.

As a counter-movement to the structuralist and positivistic strands in the social sciences, symbolic interactionism flourished in American sociology in the 1960s and 1970s, when sociologists became increasingly critical of positivist research methods (Cicourel, 1964; Glaser and Strauss, 1967; Garfinkel, 1994[1969]). New orientations in ethnography (Goffman, 1981; Geertz, 1973; Gumperz and Hymes, 1986[1972]) crucially contributed to establishing the field of qualitative social research. During the 1970s, the term 'discourse' became popular among researchers working on symbolically mediated talk in interactional sociolinguistics (see Labov, 1972), linguistic anthropology (Gumperz, 1982; Duranti, 1997) and some strands of conversation analysis (Sacks et al., 1974; Cicourel, 1973). Throughout the 1980s and 1990s, a certain cleavage could be observed between mainstream representatives of the qualitative field, usually from North America, and more macro-oriented discourse analysts and theorists from Europe. Thus, conversation analysts, in line with ethnomethodology (Schegloff, 1997), came into conflict with critical discourse analysts over the way 'context' enters the analysis

(Billig, 1999). While conversation analysts insist on the methodological principle of considering the context only when it is made relevant and explicit by the participants in the text, critical discourse researchers typically emphasise the role of several context layers (situative, structural and so forth), as well as aspects of power and inequality in the production of discourse in society. Nowadays, we can distinguish between more rigid forms of CA (as practised by Schegloff in Sack's tradition) and 'softer' versions as established by James Gee, Lorenza Mondada, John Heritage and others, all of which started to integrate some form of Discourse Studies with CA and to focus on sense- and meaning-making in interaction, apart from the strictly rule-governed organization of talk. In this way, much criticism exists of CA; for example, as Helga Kotthoff (2010: 321) illustrates, Goffman (1981: 14–15) referred to conversation analysts as 'communication engineers', because he saw them as only capturing 'the sheer physical constraints of any communication system'. Against this background, European strands in discourse analysis such as Critical Discourse Analysis and poststructuralism have sometimes been pitted against to the micro-sociological orientation of conversation analysis.

These quarrels notwithstanding, one should not forget the fundamental contribution made by interactionism to the critique of grammatical models of the language system and the turn to language in use. To the degree that interactionists consider discourse a situated turn-taking activity, practically achieved by the participants using symbols and language, they point to the role of context as a dynamic framework or background for the interpretation of utterances. Texts need to be placed in contexts, which is precisely the practical task that the participants need to solve with varying degrees of ingenuity. Discourse, therefore, is a practice which needs to deal with the problem that the meaning of utterances depends on the specific circumstances in which they are used in practice. While these practices are never fully determined in advance, these theorists reject the idea of free and autonomous actors in control of what they do and think. For interactionists, the participants do not follow a plan or theory that they try to realise in discourse; they do not start from a recipe as a given set of rules defining how things are done; they are subject to communicative processes in interaction whose emerging constraints and logic need to be processed in real time.

If the focus of the more 'humanist' strands of interactionism is on face-to-face interactions between two or more persons, more recent developments have broadened the theoretical scope. Thus, against an interactionist background, James Paul Gee (1999) has extended the notion of discourse to things people do with language in large social communities. For Gee language can be used to deal with political questions and to help distribute certain coveted 'goods' among the members of a community. Starting from poststructuralist and sociological reflections of the reading and writing practices that make scientific knowledge 'true' (Ashmore et al., 1995), Jonathan Potter and his colleagues at Loughborough have become known as the originators of discursive psychology (Edwards and Potter, 1992), which is critical of cognitive approaches. In its fine-grained dissection of linguistic material, discursive psychology has more recently come to resemble conversation analysis. While discursive psychology typically deals with oral as well as written texts, it places much emphasis on the decentring of traditional psychological categories such as 'identity', 'consciousness' and 'cognition'.

Following the dialogical model of the self in Mead (1967[1934]), or Goffman's polyphonic speaker model (1981), interactionist theorists have always rejected the notion of the actor as a centred, conscious and isolated entity. Ethnomethodologists, in the tradition of Garfinkel (1994[1969]) in particular, have always argued for the primacy of practices over actors and voiced the radical idea that knowledge, even the most abstract theoretical knowledge of social scientists, is always indexical and thus bound to a context. Against this background, the praxeological turn, which has been taking place in the social sciences since the 1970s, has called into question the micro-macro divisions in discourse research (Schatzki et al., 2001; Reckwitz, 2002). From a praxeological perspective, discursive practices constitute social realities in performative acts. Through the medium of discourse, they can reach beyond the here and now and link people and objects in and across many different contexts. Operating with material objects in a physical setting, they deal with human as well as non-human elements (or 'actants'), as has been argued in Actor-Network-Theory (Latour, 2005). And discursive practices also perform and articulate relations of power and inequality as has been argued by authors as diverse as Butler (1997) and Bourdieu (1977).

These developments remind us of the important contribution made by interactionist and praxeological theorists to discourse research as the study of situated talk, but also more generally as the investigation of communicative processes in larger communities. Preferring the empirical observation of oral discourse through qualitative methods, they have inspired a great deal of research at the crossroads of language and society, such as studies of politeness and face (Brown and Levinson, 1987), of communicative genres (see Luckmann's contribution in the section on 'Historical Knowledge') as well as of materiality and mediality. As the boundaries between different traditions are becoming increasingly blurred, linguistic and sociological approaches necessarily feed into and off each other.

References

Ashmore, Malcolm, Greg Myers, and Jonathan Potter. 1995. 'Discourse, Rhetoric, Reflexivity. Seven Days in a Library.' In *Handbook of Science and Technology Studies*, edited by S. Jasanoff, G. Markle, T. Pinch and J. Petersen, 321–42. London: Sage. DOI: 10.4135/9781412990127.n15

Billig, Michael. 1999. 'Whose terms? Whose ordinariness? Rhetoric and Ideology in Conversation Analysis.' *Discourse and Society* 10, no. 4: 543–58. DOI: 10.1177/0957926599010004005

Blumer, Herbert. 1986[1969]. *Symbolic interactionism. Perspective and method.* Berkeley: University of California Press.

Bourdieu, Pierre. 1977. *Outline of a Theory of Practice.* Cambridge, New York: Cambridge University Press. DOI: 10.1017/CBO9780511812507

Brown, Penelope, and Stephen Levinson. 1987. *Politeness: Some universals in language usage.* Cambridge: Cambridge University Press.

Butler, Judith. 1997. *Excitable Speech. A Politics of the Performative.* New York, London: Routledge.

Cicourel, Aaron V. 1973. *Cognitive Sociology: Language and Meaning in Social Interaction.* Harmondsworth: Penguin.

Cicourel, Aaron V. 1964. *Method and measurement in sociology.* New York: Free Press.

Duranti, Alessandro. 1997. *Linguistic Anthropology.* Cambridge: Cambridge University Press. DOI: 10.1017/CBO9780511810190

Edwards, Derek, and Jonathan Potter. 1992. *Discursive Psychology.* London: Sage.

Garfinkel, Harold. 1994[1969]. *Studies in Ethnomethodology.* Cambridge: Polity.

Gee, James Paul. 1999. *An Introduction to Discourse Analysis. Theory and Method.* London and New York: Routledge.

Geertz, Clifford. 1973. *The Interpretation of Cultures: Selected Essays.* New York: Basic Books.

Glaser, Barney G., and Anselm L. Strauss. 1967. *The Discovery of Grounded Theory. Strategies for Qualitative Research.* Chicago: Aldine.

Goffman, Erving. 1981. *Forms of Talk.* Philadelphia: University of Pennsylvania Press.

Gumperz, John. 1982. *Discourse Strategies.* Cambridge: Cambridge University Press. DOI: 10.1017/CBO9780511611834

Gumperz, John, and Dell Hymes, eds. 1986[1972]. *Directions in Sociolinguistics. The Ethnography of Communication.* Oxford: Blackwell.

Kotthoff, Helga. 2010. 'Sociolinguistic Potentials of Face-to-Face Interaction.' In *The Sage Handbook of Sociolinguistics,* edited by Ruth Wodak, Barbara Johnstone and Paul Kerswill, 315–30. London: Sage.

Labov, William. 1972. *Sociolinguistic Patterns.* Philadelphia: University of Pennsylvania Press.

Latour, Bruno. 2005. *Reassembling the Social. An Introduction to Actor-Network-Theory.* Oxford: Oxford University Press.

Mead, George Herbert. 1967[1934]. *Mind, Self, and Society from the Standpoint of a Social Behaviorist.* Chicago, London: University of Chicago Press.

Reckwitz, Andreas. 2002. 'Toward a Theory of Social Practices. A Development in Culturalist Theorizing.' *European Journal of Social Theory* 5, no. 2: 243–63. DOI: 10.1177/13684310222225432

Sacks, Harvey, Emanuel Schegloff, and Gail Jefferson. 1974. 'A Simplest Systematics for the Organization for Turn-Taking in Conversation.' *Language* 50, no. 4: 696–735. DOI: 10.2307/412243

Schatzki, Theodore R., Karin Knorr Cetina, and Eike von Savigny, eds. 2001. *The Practice Turn in Contemporary Theory.* London, New York: Routledge.

Schegloff, Emanuel. 1997. 'Whose Text? Whose Context?.' *Discourse & Society* 8, no. 2: 165–87. DOI: 10.1177/0957926597008002002

Thomas, William I., and Dorothy Thomas. 1928. *The Child in America.* New York: Alfred Knopf.

Harvey Sacks

Turn-taking in conversations

Influenced by Harold Garfinkel (1994[1969]) and ethnomethodology as well as by his teacher Aaron Cicourel, the American sociologist Harvey Sacks (1935–1975) devised an approach to the study of conversations and interactions which is today known as Conversation Analysis (CA). Together with Emanuel Schegloff and Gail Jefferson, he developed a taxonomy of verbal interaction, focusing first on telephone calls and other routinized and clearly defined, brief genres of interaction. Through the careful and detailed transcription and analysis of sometimes small text extracts, intricate systems of interruptions, turn-taking, repairs, question-answer sequences and so forth could be established which characterize all conversations to a certain degree. CA became most influential when studying relevant social interaction in hospitals, with traffic controllers, and in broadcast and TV interviews and debates. As a methodological principle, conversation analysts typically insist on taking the context into account only if it is made relevant by the discourse participants, which excludes contextual information not directly available to them. Such an approach to context has led to much controversy, for example the debate about text and context between Schegloff (1997) and Billig (1999) in *Discourse & Society*. CA has also adopted some concepts from Goffman, such as the notion of a 'participant framework' which denotes patterns of interaction determined by the positioning of various interactants in a conversation who negotiate and co-construct specific 'frames' together. Below, we reproduce parts of Lecture 1 of Sack's seminal *Lectures on Conversation*, which serves as an excellent introduction to the detailed analysis of the rule-governed organisation of our daily interactions.

References

Billig, Michael. 1999. 'Whose terms? Whose ordinariness? Rhetoric and Ideology in Conversation Analysis.' *Discourse and Society* 10, no. 4: 543–58. DOI: 10.1177/0957926599010004005

Garfinkel, Harold. 1994[1969]. *Studies in Ethnomethodology*. Cambridge: Polity.

Schegloff, Emanuel. 1997. 'Whose Text? Whose Context?'. *Discourse & Society* 8, no. 2: 165–87. DOI: 10.1177/0957926597008002002

Harvey Sacks. 1992[1964]. 'Lecture 1. Rules of Conversational Sequence.'
In *Lectures on Conversation*. Vol. I, 3–11.
Oxford, Cambridge, MA: Blackwell.

I'll start off by giving some quotations.

(1) A: Hello.
     B: Hello.

(2) A: This is Mr Smith, may I help you?
     B: Yes, this is Mr Brown.

(3) A: This is Mr Smith, may I help you?
     B: I can't hear you.
     A: This is Mr Smith.
     B: Smith.

These are some first exchanges in telephone conversations collected at an emergency psychiatric hospital. They are occurring between persons who haven't talked to each other before. One of them, A, is a staff member of this psychiatric hospital. B can be either somebody calling about themselves, that is to say in trouble in one way or another, or somebody calling about somebody else.

I have a large collection of these conversations, and I got started looking at these first exchanges as follows. A series of persons who called this place would not give their names. The hospital's concern was, can anything be done about it? One question I wanted to address was, where in the course of the conversation could you tell that somebody would not give their name? So I began to look at the materials. It was in fact on the basis of that question that I began to try to deal in detail with conversations.

I found something that struck me as fairly interesting quite early. And that was that if the staff member used 'This is Mr Smith may I help you?' as their opening line, then overwhelmingly, any answer other than 'Yes, this is Mr Brown' (for example, 'I can't hear you,' 'I don't know,' 'How do you spell your name?') meant that you would have serious trouble getting the caller's name, if you got the name at all.

I'm going to show some of the ways that I've been developing to analyze stuff like this. There will be a series of ways fitted to each other, as though one were constructing a multi-dimensional jigsaw puzzle. One or another piece can be isolated and studied, and also the various pieces can be studied as to how they fit together. I'll be focusing on a variety of things, starting off with what I'll call 'rules of conversational sequence'.

Looking at the first exchange compared to the second, we are struck by two things. First of all, there seems to be a fit between what the first person who speaks uses as their greeting, and what the person who is given that greeting returns. So that if A says, 'Hello,' then B tends to say, 'Hello.' If A says, 'This is Mr Smith may I help you?' B tends to say, 'Yes, this is Mr Brown.' We can say there's a procedural rule there, that a person who speaks first in a telephone conversation can choose their form of address, and in choosing their form of address they can thereby choose the form of address the other uses.

By 'form' I mean in part that the exchanges occur as 'units'. That is, 'Hello' 'Hello' is a unit, and 'This is Mr Smith may I help you?' 'Yes, this is Mr Brown' is a unit. They come in pairs. Saying, 'This is Mr Smith may I help you?' thereby provides a 'slot' to the other wherein they properly would answer, 'Yes, this is Mr Brown.' The procedural rule would describe the occurrences in the first two exchanges. It won't describe the third exchange, but we'll come to see what is involved in such materials.

Secondly, if it is so that there is a rule that the person who goes first can choose their form of address and thereby choose the other's, then for the unit, 'This is Mr Smith may I help you?' 'Yes, this is Mr Brown,' if a person uses 'This is Mr Smith...' they have a way of asking for the other's name – without, however, asking the question, 'What is your name?' And there is a difference between saying 'This is Mr Smith may I help you?' – thereby providing a slot to the other wherein they properly would answer 'Yes, this is Mr Brown' – and asking the question, 'What is your name?' at some point in the conversation. They are very different phenomena.

For one, in almost all of the cases where the person doesn't give their name originally, then at some point in the conversation they're asked for their name. One way of asking is just the question, 'Would you give me your name?' To that, there are alternative returns, including 'No' and 'Why?' If a caller says 'Why?' the staff member may say something like, 'I want to have something to call you' or 'It's just for our records.' If a caller says 'No,' then the staff member says 'Why?' and may get something like 'I'm not ready to do that' or 'I'm ashamed.'

Now, I'll consider many times the use of 'Why?' What I want to say about it, just to begin with, is that what one does with 'Why?' is to propose some action that it is an 'accountable action'. That is to say, 'Why?' is a way of asking for an account. Accounts are most extraordinary. And the use of accounts and the use of requests for accounts are *very* highly regulated phenomena. We can begin to cut into these regularities by looking at what happens when 'May I have your name?' is followed by 'Why?' Then you get an account; for example, 'I need something to call you.' The other might then say, 'I don't mind.' Or you might get an account, 'It's just for our records.' To which the other might say, 'Well I'm not sure I want to do anything with you, I just want to find out what you do' – so that the records are not relevant.

What we can see is that there are ways that accounts seem to be dealable with. If a person offers an account, which they take it provides for the action in question being done – for example, the caller's name being given – then if the other can show that the interest of that account can be satisfied without the name being given, the name doesn't have to be given. That is, if the account is to control the action, then if you can find a way that the account controls the alternative action than it proposed to control, you can use it in that way.

It seems to be quite important, then, who it is that offers the account. Because the task of the person who is offered the account can then be to, in some way, counter it. Where, alternatively, persons who offer an account seem to feel that they're somehow committed to it, and if it turns out to be, for example, inadequate, then they have to stand by it.

The fact that you could use questions – like 'Why?' – to generate accounts, and then use accounts to control activities, can be marked down as, I think, one of the greatest discoveries in Western civilization. It may well be that that is what Socrates discovered. With his dialectic he found a set of procedures by which this thing, which was not used systematically, could become a systematic device. Socrates will constantly ask 'Why?', there will be an answer, and he'll go on to show that that can't be the answer. And that persons were terribly pained to go through this whole business is clear enough from the Dialogues. And it's also clear in our own experiences. And in the materials I'll present.

We see, then, one clear difference between providing a slot for a name, and asking for a name. Asking for a name tends to generate accounts and counters. By providing a slot for a name, those activities do not arise.

We can also notice that, as a way of asking for the other's name, 'This is Mr Smith…' is, in the first place, not an accountable action. By that I mean to say, it's not required that staff members use it and they don't always use it, but when they do, the caller doesn't ask why. 'This is Mr Smith…' gets its character as a non-accountable action simply by virtue of the fact that this is a place where, routinely, two persons speak who haven't met. In such places the person who speaks first can use that object. And we could say about that kind of item that the matters discriminated by its proper use are very restricted. That is to say, a call is made; the only issue is that two persons are speaking who presumably haven't met, and this object can be used.

Furthermore, the matters are discriminated in different terms than those which the agency is constructed for. That is, they are discriminated in terms of 'two people who haven't met' rather than, for example, that an agency staff member is speaking to someone calling the agency for help. And where one has some organization of activities which sets out to do some task – and in this case it's important for the agency to get names – then if you find a device which discriminates in such a restricted fashion, you can use that device to do tasks for you.

Now, given the fact that such a greeting as 'This is Mr Smith…' provides for the other giving his own name as an answer, one can see what the advantage of 'Hello' is for someone who doesn't want to give their name. And I found in the first instance that while sometimes the staff members use 'Hello' as their opening line, if it ever occurred that the persons calling the agency spoke first, they always said 'Hello.'

Persons calling could come to speak first because, at this agency, caller and staff member are connected by an operator. The operator says, 'Go ahead please,' and now the two parties are on an open line, and one can start talking or the other can start talking. This stands in contrast to, for example, calling someone's home. There, the rights are clearly assigned; the person who answers the phone speaks first. If they speak first, they have the right to choose their form. If they have the right to choose their form, they have the right thereby to choose the other's. Here, where the rights are not clearly assigned, the caller could move to speak first and thereby choose the form. And when callers to this agency speak first, the form they choose is the unit 'Hello' 'Hello.' Since such a unit involves no exchange of names, they can speak without giving their name and be going about things in a perfectly appropriate way.

Now, there are variant returns to 'This is Mr Smith may I help you?', one of which is in our set of three exchanges: 'I can't hear you'. I want to talk of that as an 'occasionally usable' device. That is to say, there doesn't have to be a particular sort of thing preceding it; it can come at any place in a conversation. Here is one from the middle of a conversation, from a different bunch of materials.

> A: Hey you got a cigarette Axum. I ain't got, I ain't got a good cigarette, and I can't roll one right now. Think you can afford it maybe?
> B: I am not here to support your habits.
> A: Huh? My helplessness?
> B: I am not responsible for supporting your habits (   )
> A: My habits ((laughing))

Our third exchange from the psychiatric hospital has the device used at the beginning of the conversation.

> A: This is Mr Smith may I help you?
> B: I can't hear you.
> A: This is Mr Smith.
> B: Smith.

What kind of a device is it? What you can see is this: When you say 'I can't hear you', you provide that the other person can repeat what they said. Now what does that repetition do for you? Imagine you're in a game. One of the questions relevant to the game would be, is there a way in that game of skipping a move? It seems that something like 'I can't hear you' can do such a job. If you introduce it you provide for the other to do some version of a repeat, following which you yourself can repeat. And then it's the other's turn to talk again. What we find is that the slot where the return would go – your name in return to 'This is Mr Smith…' – never occurs.

It is not simply that the caller ignores what they properly ought to do, but something rather more exquisite. That is, they have ways of providing that the place where the return name fits is never opened. So that their name is not absent. Their name would be absent if they just went ahead and talked. But that very rarely occurs. The rules of etiquette – if you want to call them that, though we take etiquette to be something very light and uninteresting and to be breached as you please – seem to be quite strong. Persons will use ways to not ignore what they properly ought to do by providing that the place for them to do it is never opened.

I hope it can also be seen that a device like 'I can't hear you' – the repeat device, providing for a repetition of the thing that was first said, which is then repeated by the person who said 'I can't hear you' – is not necessarily designed for skipping a move. It is not specific to providing a way of keeping in the conversation and behaving properly while not giving one's name. It can be used for other purposes and do other tasks, and it can be used with other items. That's why I talk about it as an 'occasional device'. But where that is what one is trying to do, it's a rather neat device. Let me turn now to a consideration which deals with a variant return to 'May I help you?' That is, not 'Yes...' but 'I don't know'. I'll show a rather elaborate exchange in which the staff member opens with a version of 'This is Mr Smith may I help you?' but the combination gets split. The name is dealt with, and when the 'can I help you' is offered, it occurs in such a way that it can be answered independent of the name.[1]

Op: Go ahead please
A: This is Mr Smith (*B:* Hello) of the Emergency Psychiatric Center can I help you?
B: Hello?
A: Hello.
B: I can't hear you.
A: I see. Can you hear me now?
B: Barely. Where are you, in the womb?
A: Where are you calling from?
B: Hollywood.
A: Hollywood.
B: I can hear you a little better.
A: Okay. Uh I was saying my name is Smith and I'm with the Emergency Psychiatric Center.
B: Your name is what?
A: Smith.

---

1.   The fragment of data is reproduced pretty much as Sacks transcribed it, preserving his attempts to deal with simultaneous talk (i.e., *A:* This is Mr Smith (*B:* Hello) of the Emergency Psychiatric Center) and silence (e.g., *B:* I uh Now that you're here…).

> *B:*   Smith?
> *A:*   Yes.
> *A:*   Can I help you?
> *B:*   I don't know hhheh   I hope you can.
> *A:*   Uh hah   Tell me about your problems.
> *B:*   I uh   Now that you're here I'm embarrassed to talk about it. I don't want you telling me I'm emotionally immature 'cause I know I am.

I was very puzzled by 'I don't know' in return to 'May I help you'. I couldn't figure out what they were doing with it. And the reason I was puzzled was that having listened to so many of these things and having been through the scene so many times, I heard 'May I help you?' as something like an idiom. I'm going to call these idiom-like things 'composites'. That means you hear the whole thing as a form, a single unit. And as a single unit, it has a proper return. As a composite, 'May I help you?' is a piece of etiquette, a way of introducing oneself as someone who is in the business of helping somebody, the answer to which is 'Yes' and then some statement of what it is one wants. We can consider this item in terms of what I'll call the 'base environment' of its use.

By 'base environment' I mean, if you go into a department store, somebody is liable to come up to you and say 'May I help you?' And in business-type phone calls this item is routinely used. And if you come into a place and you don't know what it's like, and somebody comes up to you and uses such an item, that's one way of informing you what kind of a place it is. So, if a new institution is being set up, then there are available in the society whole sets of ways that persons go about beginning conversations, and one could, for example, adopt one or another of a series of them as the ones that are going to be used in this place.

Now the thing about at least some composites is that they can be heard not only as composites, but as ordinary sentences, which we could call 'constructives', which are understood by taking the pieces and adding them up in some way. As a composite, 'May I help you?' is a piece of etiquette, a signal for stating your request – what you want to be helped with. Alternatively, as a constructive, 'May I help you?' is a question. If one hears it as a question, the piece of etiquette and its work hasn't come up, and 'I don't know' is a perfectly proper answer.

Further, 'I don't know' may be locating a problem which 'May I help you?' is designed, in the first place, to avoid. In its base environment, for example a department store, it's pretty much the case that for a customer, the question of whether some person 'can help' is a matter of the department store having made them the person who does that. That is to say, lots of things, like telling you whether you can find lingerie in a certain size, is something anybody can do, and as long as the department store says this person is going to do it, that's enough. But we're dealing with a psychiatric hospital. In a department store, being selected to do a job and having credentials to do it are essentially the same thing. In a psychiatric hospital and lots of other places, however, they are very different things. That is, whether somebody can help you if you have a mental disorder is not solved or is not even presumptively solved by the fact that they've been selected by somebody to do that job. The way it's solved in this society is by reference to such things as having been trained in a particular fashion, having gotten degrees, having passed board examinations, etc.

Now, in the base environment of the use of 'May I help you?' there is, as I say, no difference essentially between having credentials and being selected. If one can formulate the matter in a psychiatric hospital such that those things come on as being the same, then one needn't start off by producing one's credentials at the beginning of the conversation. And in my materials, again and again, when 'May I help you?' is used the person calling says 'Yes' and begins to state their troubles.

As a general matter, then, one can begin to look for kinds of objects that have a base environment that, when they get used in that environment, perform a rather simple task, but that can be used in quite different environments to do quite other tasks. So, a matter like 'credentials' can be handled by this 'May I help you?' device. There will be lots of other devices which have a base environment, which do some other task in some other environment.

Before moving away from 'May I help you?' I want to mention one other thing about it. If the base environment is something like a department store, then, when it's used in other places – for example, a psychiatric hospital – one of the pieces of information it seems to convey is that whatever it is you propose to do, you do routinely. To whomsoever that calls. That is, it's heard as a standardized utterance. How is that relevant? It can be relevant in alternative ways. First of all, it can be a very reassuring thing to hear. Some persons feel that they have troubles, and they don't know if anybody else has those troubles; or, if others do have those troubles, whether anybody knows about them. If someone knows about them, then there may be a known solution to them. Also, and relatedly, a lot of troubles – like mental diseases – are things that persons feel very ambivalent about. That is, they're not sure whether it's some defect of their character, or something else. That, in part, is why they're hesitant to talk about it. And it seems that one of the ways one begins to tell people that they can talk, that you know what they have and that you routinely deal with such matters, is to use manifestly organizational talk.

'May I help you?', then, can be a reassuring way to begin. It can alternatively be something else. Consider the exchange I just showed, in which such standardized utterances as 'May I help you?' and 'Tell me about your problems' are used.

A: Can I help you?
B: I don't know hhheh I hope you can
A: Uh hah   Tell me about your problems
B: I uh   Now that you're here I'm embarrassed to talk about it. I don't want you
       telling me I'm emotionally immature 'cause I know I am.

That is, the use of standardized, manifestly organizational talk can provide for the person calling that they're going to get routine treatment. But 'routine', for them, may not be such a happy thing. Because, for example, they've been through it before. But they may have gone through it, as psychiatrists would say, part way. For example, they were in analysis for three years and ran out of money, or the psychiatrist wouldn't keep them on, or they didn't want to stay. Part way, they may have come to some point in the analysis where they 'knew what was wrong with them'. That is, they knew the diagnostic term. But that diagnostic term may have had a lay affiliate. By that I mean, if a psychiatrist says you're regressed, it's a technical term. But 'regressed' is also a lay term, and as a lay term it doesn't have a great deal of attractiveness. If one finds oneself living with a lay understanding of such a term, where the term is not a very nice thing to have in its lay sense, then when you hear someone using such an item as 'May I help you?', you can hear that some procedure will be gone through, the upshot of which will be the discovery of what you 'already know' – the knowing of which doesn't do you any good.

Related to that are such things as some people seem to feel very much disturbed about the fact that their relationship to a psychiatrist or to other doctors is monetary. What they want, they say, is a personal solution. Ask them what they want, 'Well, that you don't have to pay for it.' When they hear 'May I help you?', they hear 'a professional'. But they feel that the way you get cured is by getting an affiliation to somebody which is like the affiliations that they failed to get in their lives. That is, they may already have come to learn from some other psychiatrist that the failure of love by their parents is the cause of their troubles. Then, what they come to see is that they need the love of somebody else. And they can't get that from a therapist. Because as soon as they don't pay, that's the end of the relationship.

Now let me just make a few general points. Clearly enough, things like 'This is Mr Smith', 'May I help you?' and 'I can't hear you' are social objects. And if you begin to look at what they do, you can see that they, and things like them, provide the makings of activities. You assemble activities by using these things. And now when you, or I, or sociologists, watching people do things, engage in trying to find out what they do and how they do it, one fix which can be used is: Of the enormous range of activities that people do, all of them are done with something. Someone says 'This is Mr Smith' and the other supplies his own name. Someone says 'May I help you?' and the other states his business. Someone says 'Huh?' or 'What did you say?' or 'I can't hear you,' and then the thing said before gets repeated. What we want then to find out is, can we first of all construct the objects that get used to make up ranges of activities, and then see how it is those objects do get used.

Some of these objects can be used for whole ranges of activities, where for different ones a variety of the properties of those objects will get employed. And we begin to see alternative properties of those objects. That's one way we can go about beginning to collect the alternative methods that persons use in going about doing whatever they have to do. And we can see that these methods will be reproducible descriptions in the sense that any scientific description might be, such that the natural occurrences that we're describing can yield abstract or general phenomena which need not rely on statistical observability for their abstractness or generality.

There was a very classical argument that it would not be that way, that singular events were singular events, given a historian's sort of argument, that they just happen and they get more or less accidentally thrown together. But if we could find that there are analytically hard ways of describing these things – where, that is, we're talking about objects that can be found elsewhere, that get placed, that have ways of being used, that are abstract objects which get used on singular occasions and describe singular courses of activity – then that's something which is exceedingly non-trivial too know.

One final note. When people start to analyze social phenomena, if it looks like things occur with the sort of immediacy we find in some of these exchanges, then, if you have to make an elaborate analysis of it – that is to say, show that they did something as involved as some of the things I have proposed – then you figure that they couldn't have thought that fast. I want to suggest that you have to forget that completely. Don't worry about how fast they're thinking. First of all, don't worry about whether they're 'thinking'. Just try to come to terms with how it is that the thing comes off. Because you'll find that they can do these things. Just take any other area of natural science and see, for example, how fast molecules do things. And they don't have very good brains. So just let the materials fall as they may. Look to see how it is that persons go about producing what they do produce.

Erving Goffman

Tacit knowledge in interaction

Erving Goffman (1922–1982) was a Canadian-born sociologist who moved to the USA in the 1940s. From 1958 he worked in the sociology department at the University of Berkeley. His greatest contribution to linguistics is his study of interaction in the form of dramaturgical analysis. It started with his book *The Presentation of Self in Everyday Life* (1959). In social interaction, he makes a distinction between a front stage where individuals, like actors, are on stage, and a back stage, i.e. private places, where individuals can put aside the roles they play in public. Social interactions, he argues, make the world an ordered, predictable place. He considers interactions as rituals; from this viewpoint, when we disrupt the norms of interaction, we thus actually disrupt society. An individual who comes into contact with other individuals tries to control the impression that they might make of him. In particular, he must avoid embarrassing others or being embarrassed. Goffman also studied 'total institutions', such as prisons and psychiatric hospitals (*Asylums: Essays on the Social Situation of Mental Patients and Other Inmates*, 1961), and 'stigmas', i.e. socially constructed aspects of deviance and marginalisation (*Stigma: Notes on the Management of Spoiled Identity*, 1963).

In this text, Goffman deals with presupposition, defined as a 'state of affairs that we take for granted' when we come into contact with somebody. Actually, he only deals with presuppositions involving speech. But, unlike most linguists, who focus on the logical aspects of presupposition, he is interested in 'whatever is relevantly presupposed in the broadly understood, standard meaning of words and clauses on the occasion of uttering them in particular contexts': a pronoun, for example, 'presupposes its antecedent'. When we speak, we are submitted to 'one central obligation: to render our behaviour understandably relevant to what the other can come to perceive is going on'.

Erving Goffman. 1983. 'Felicity's Condition.'
American Journal of Sociology 89 (1): 1–53, selected 1–9, 48–51.

I

A presupposition (or assumption, or implication, or background expectation) can be defined very broadly as a state of affairs we take for granted in pursuing a course of action. We can perform these acts of faith without 'doing' anything. And even appreciation figures variably. We may never come to be aware of something our action presupposes; having once been aware, we may no longer be; having not been aware, we may come to be; being aware, we may try to conceal this fact from others or to allude to it indirectly. Yet, according to one reading of the term, if we explicitly attest to a condition of our action we cease to *presuppose* it, although this ceasing does not lessen our dependency on it.

By this broad definition, in planning at night to leave at dawn, we would be presupposing the sun will come up. We do and it will. So what? We also presuppose that an earthquake will not occur before morning and drop us forever through a fault, and there is an infinitude of other possibilities. Clearly, almost all of what we presuppose is footless to any but those who discuss presuppositions and want to make the point that there are presuppositions of concern to no one. So it behoves the student not merely to uncover presuppositions but also to present reasons for doing so, and not merely for the reason just cited. Opportunity abounds. An imaginative analyst ought to be able to show the significance of presuppositions that no one else had ever thought they would signify,[1] and certainly every quirk and crisis in social life generates sudden insight in this connection, spreading appreciation that what had been unthinkingly taken for granted should have been given thought. For indeed, we are as unthinking about many of the political and economic conditions of our lives as we are about the sun coming up.

Plainly there are unstated grounds for our action that particular others do not require for their understanding of it and their further response (if any) to it. The contrast is with 'social presuppositions', these incorporating a double theme, namely, our tacitly taking something for granted (whether aware of having done so or not), and also unabashedly, even unthinkingly, counting on others involved in the action doing likewise, at least enough so they can easily interpret and understand our action accordingly.[2]

---

1. A wonderfully hilarious (and sound) example is provided by Jacques Derrida's 92-page analysis of the presuppositions employed by John Searle in the latter's 10-page reply to Derrida's 25-page critique of speech act theory (Derrida, 1977).

2. In this simplified pragmatic view I follow Stalnaker (1973).

Of social presuppositions I propose to deal with only one sort, those involving language use. After all, more perhaps than any other class of actions, writing or saying makes sense only if the actor intends a meeting of minds – if only enough to inform self-interestedly. Indeed, almost always in using language we take for granted that what we want to get across will get across (along with the message – true or not – that this is the avowed and controlling purpose of our action). Further, if we could not rely on our listeners grasping the point without extended elaboration, we could hardly afford the time to say anything; similarly, if they could not depend on our taking into consideration what they already know, they could hardly afford the time to listen.

The purpose of this paper, then, will be to consider social presuppositions in language use, particularly speech, not writing. Surely a classical sociological theme. And just as surely I must presuppose, as every student of presuppositions has done and does, the rule that accounts for how I decide which social presuppositions are worth discovering. For as with background expectations in general, there are countless social presuppositions in speech that do not have even academic interest. And the presuppositions that ought to be of interest do themselves involve embarrassment; after all, it should be apparent that spoken (and written) discourse, in context, has the capacity to presuppose anything in the world (including bits of the universe beyond), the sorting of which might well seem to be a hapless, immodest undertaking.

So there are problems. One can take encouragement from the fact that a wide range of social presuppositions in discourse appear to be systematically represented through the ways in which we select, order and prosodically time and intone our words, thus providing a record that is engagingly objective and sensitive – a workable tracing (indeed, machine-preservable) of practices that could otherwise be rendered only by impressionistic analysis. So one can try to work backward from the verbal consequences of presuppositions to what is presupposed, allowing the direction of analysis to constrain what one examines.

II

There is a philosophical view of presuppositions, variously called semantic, existential or logical. This view, which is given much weight in linguistics, purports to be concerned only with the truth value of statements (or propositions), not with whatever might be presupposed in the act of making a particular statement in a particular setting – a constraint on concern with language behaviour also proposed by the Boy Scouts of America. Accordingly, 'entailment' is defined as that relation between two statements such that the entailed one is true if the entailing one is. And (in contrast) one statement can be said to presuppose another if, and only if, the presupposed statement must be true if the presupposing statement is to be true or false in a meaningful way.[3] Take the statement,

> Marsha regretted that John saw the movie last night.

This semantically presupposes (it is felt) that there was a movie last night and that John, who exists, saw it, 'regretted' there being a 'factive' verb. (It is similarly presupposed that a series of nights have occurred, the last one prior to the temporal point of speaking, but matters are not usually carried that far.) It is suggested that presuppositions of this kind hold even when the polarity of the embedding statement is reversed (as when Marsha does *not* regret that John saw the movie last night), something that cannot be said of entailments.

It may seem that here linguists have become overly enamoured of philosophy, but in fact they have reason for their interest in statements of fact, in spite of the questionable status of such avowals as guides to what exists in the real world. For as Kiparsky and Kiparsky have shown in a critical article (1970), it seems '...that whether the speaker presupposes the truth of a complement contributes in several important ways to determining the syntactic form in which the complement can appear in the surface structure' (p. 143). If, then, one has interest in the tacit understandings which make social intercourse possible, and if one sees that constraints on sentence structure imposed by the grammar of a language qualify perfectly in this regard, then 'semantic' presuppositions will have to figure – sociologically no less than linguistically.

Although many students of language strongly support this perspective on presuppositions (here 'implications' might be a better word) – thereby, it seems, tempering any interest in the term apart from their own others argue that no line can ultimately be drawn between what statements semantically presuppose and what people pragmatically do in stating (see, e.g., Sherzer, 1973). Thus, one can widen the semantic approach somewhat to include whatever is relevantly presupposed in the broadly understood, standard meaning of words and clauses on the occasion of uttering them in particular contexts.

Which raises a relevant issue. John, chatting with Marsha, says,

> What did you think of the movie last night?[4]

---

3. The consideration of this sense of presupposition is a minor industry in philosophy and linguistics, beginning with Frege and Russell, moving on through Strawson, Black and Sellars, pausing with Karttunen and the Kiparskys, and now everywhere in full production.

4. An example also employed independently, earlier, and with better effect in a suggestive conference paper given in 1978 by Clark and Marshall (1981).

presupposing with these words that Marsha went to one and to only one film the night before, and so, incidentally, will be able to identify what he is referring to. But Marsha in fact need not actually hold the beliefs about the world (in this particular matter) that John apparently possesses, knowing full well, for example, that she did not actually get out to go to the movie house or, having got to the theatre, found it shut. John, informed about his wrong construing of what took place, can feel that Marsha will nonetheless take it that his error was 'perfectly understandable', in effect that she can easily follow discourse based on this presupposition. So the import is that Marsha and John do not have to share the same presupposition to allow for smooth discourse; they need merely share an understanding of the presuppositions it would be reasonable to have in the circumstances – a matter not of personal belief but other-oriented assessment.

III

If one shifts from an interest in the truth value of sentences to slightly less rarified concerns, an easier beginning for the study of presuppositions in speech is possible. Let John say to Marsha,

> I went to the movie last night but I didn't like it.

Apart from the fact that the conjunction 'but' implies somewhat semantically that John expects to be entertained by the movies he sees, one has the 'it' to consider. As Bloomfield tells us in an elegant chapter (1933, Chapter 15) now considered optimistic, 'it' is a substitute here for something mentioned in the immediately prior text, namely, 'movie'; it is an anaphoric expression, an 'anaphor' that presumably makes for efficiency in communication, introducing a short, familiar term for one that might be less so. This simple possibility – apparently found in some form or other in all languages – can serve as a start. In English we have the use of pronouns, articles and demonstratives with noun phrases and proverbs, the adjectival replacement of nouns, the modification of word order, and even 'gapping' and full ellipsis ('zero anaphora').

Substitution terms are a clear-cut example of the fact that what is actually said need not in itself specify what is meant. This leads us to see that lurking behind the notion of substitution is the notion of what it is that is substituted for, i.e. a word or phrase that is presumably fully explicit and readily understandable on its own. To wit: the *antecedent,* the something that comes before to which the anaphoric expression refers and from which it acquires its relevant sense. Without the antecedent expression the anaphoric one would not be fully meaningful, would not adequately identify what the speaker was talking about. In sum, one can say (although linguists might not) that an anaphoric expression *presupposes* its antecedent, in that without an antecedent insufficient specificity would result. Perhaps one can also say that the coupling of an anaphoric expression with an antecedent brings coherence and connectedness across adjacent statements of a turn at talk.

The task before us now is to expand on these two sides of the reference equation – substitution terms, on the one hand, and antecedents, on the other.

1. First note that the formulation of anaphora I have suggested is crude, and that each little qualification that is necessary points to another little way in which we can rely on our hearers seeking out what we have in mind, and hearers can take it that we assume that they are doing so. For example, in some circumstances, the speaker can presuppose that the hearer will accept a pronoun on faith and wait a moment for the 'antecedent' that will provide its reference – what has been called 'cataphora' or 'backward anaphora', as in,

> It was simply lousy that movie I saw.

(Indeed, odd constructions of the 'right-dislocation' type are merely an extreme in this connection; it seems that every uttering of more than a word or two presupposes that hearers will dutifully exercise a modicum of cognitive patience and wait for a moment to discover the sense they are to make out of what they are now hearing.) Further, as Keith Stenning has argued (1978), every antecedent can be categorized in many different ways, each of which can provide a frame of reference for an anaphor. In truth, the notion of an anaphor 'substituting' for its antecedent confuses one possibility with a whole function; for what the antecedent does is to allow the hearer to pick out and identify what it is the speaker is making reference to, and what an antecedent provides is a guide to this determination, not necessarily the identification itself. In consequence, agreement, for example, in number, can be grammatically evaded:

> It was a long movie; I hate ones like that.

2. It should be apparent that there is no reason why the connection between the substitute expression and the antecedent should not be made across the adjacent talk of two different speakers, not merely adjacent statements within a single speaker's single turn at talk, the difference being that now the 'tying' function of the substitution practice is more pronounced.

When, then, John says,

> What did you think of the movie last night?

Marsha is set up to illustrate the central thrust of a dialogic discourse analysis. For Marsha can construct answers that draw on a variety of practices involving substitution and 'deletion':

> I thought it was bad.
>
> It was bad.
>
> I thought bad.
>
> Thought it was bad.
>
> Bad, I thought.
>
> Bad.

It is a commonplace of discourse analysis (but nonetheless true) to say that examples in the response set depend for their meaning on the immediately prior turn's talk, and indeed often would not make much sense without it. Prior turn's talk in effect provides a frame of reference for the current turn's talk whose very surface structure will reflect this permissible dependency. Prior turn's talk – as information to have in mind in understanding the current turn – is *presupposed,* at least in the broad sense of that term. John's statement (as Sacks's students, among others, have insistently told us) can establish a conditional relevance on any next act by Marsha, leading both John and Marsha to inspect such a next act for what it might imply concerning her feelings about John and his question. Here, in short, one has the sequence implication: the orientation of the current turn's talk to the prior's, or of the next to the current, or (shorter still) 'contingency'. The terms 'coherence' and 'cohesion' have also figured here, an extension of their initial reference as to how the text of a single speaker or writer hangs together.[5]

Current sociolinguistics provides us with various directions along which this global notion of contingency can be specified, e.g. the child's acquisition of conversational competence as exhibited in its tendency to provide temporally sequenced responses at an earlier age than topically relevant ones (Shugar, 1978).[6]

Let me add that this argument about conditional relevance and contingency must be handled carefully. When indeed the immediately prior talk of one speaker is responsively followed by a current statement of another speaker, there remains the issue of whether the interchange projected by the first speaker does in fact materialize, or instead (to extend Stenning) reference is made to some other aspect of the circumstances of speaker and hearer which can now be seen to have some relevance. Thus when John says,

> What did you think of the movie last night?

there will be circumstances in which Marsha can *coherently* reply in a way that John might find thematically disappointing.[7] To wit,

---

5.   See esp. Halliday and Hasan (1976). Substitution practices are not, of course, the only means by which utterances across turns can be tied; repetition of a key word is another.

6.   For other relevant work see Garvey (1975), Snow (1977), and McTear (1977).

7.   A wide and useful review of disjunctive answers to questions can be found in Weiser (1975). See also Lakoff (1973) and McTear (1977).

> I decided not to go.

Or

> The children were fidgeting so I couldn't concentrate.

Or

> John, can't you stop nattering for a moment?

Or

> I thought you weren't talking to me.

Or

> Stop avoiding the topic.

3.   A point is to be made here about the notion of discrete anaphoric terms and discrete antecedents. Reconsider Marsha's first-mentioned set of responses to John's question. Plainly one deals here with something that passes beyond discrete words; one deals with statements taken as a whole. Even in the case of a one-word or one-phrase reply, one could expand each to display the grammatical properties of a canonical sentence – if one wanted to employ that method of asserting traditional linguistic analysis – in which case it remains that the meaning of whole statements is involved, not merely that of isolated words or phrases. Similarly it can be said that the surface structure of a current statement can presuppose the informational content of the whole of an immediately prior turn's talk. Deep structure ambiguity provides the extreme example.

> Are the chickens ready to eat?

thus depends acutely for its meaning on whether the preceding turn's talk had this kind of structure:

> The asparagus is done.

Or this:

> The cows have been fed.

IV

The notion of the surface structure of statements as an objective record of the consequences of presuppositions must now be refined a little.

1.   By the term *sentential utterance* (or utterance for short) I will refer to what could be claimed as an elementary unit of talk, what might also be called a 'tone group', a 'phonemic clause' or a clause spoken without marked pause, or a sentence fragment, this last referring to what editing rules regarding ellipsis and error can expand or contract certain (usually short) strings of words into. An encoding unit for thought seems to be involved, a message unit, the minimal package of propositional-like meaning. A *turn's talk – also* considered by some to be an elementary unit of spoken discourse – must contain at least one sentential utterance but may contain more. Utterances neatly nest in turns, the beginning and ending of a turn's talk coinciding with the beginning and ending of an utterance, albeit not necessarily the same utterance. Finally, there is the *move* – some verbal or physical action that is neither an utterance nor a turn at talk, but a strategic position that can be taken up through one or more of either.

2. In recent years, stimulated by the work of Jackendoff, Bolinger, Halliday, Crystal and others, students have recommended that the prosodic features of an (English) utterance, not merely its syntactic and lexical ones, must be seen to be involved with presuppositions. Typically an utterance, an English one at least, has one point of primary stress or one 'tonic nucleus'; typically, this occurs late in the utterance and, whatever else, the stress helps to distinguish decisive or pivotal facts, as the speaker sees them, from ones she assumes are not critical, this serving to help the hearer organize what he is hearing.

XI

I close with a call to arms. To utter something and not disconfirm that we are sane requires that our saying be heard to draw appropriately on one array of presuppositions – that sustained by our hearers – and avoid being heard to make others – those which are not, although they may be by persons not present. Responding to another's words, we must find a phrasing that answers not merely to the other's words but to the other's mind – so the other can draw both from the local scene and from the distal, wider worlds of her or his experience. Sociologists recently have not been very helpful here: they reiterate the proposition and provide illustrations. But there is no *analysis* of the 'taken for granted'. No framework. Not even a simpleminded classification. The consequence of presuppositions for the surface form and prosody of utterances, on the other hand, has been considerably illuminated by linguists, along with the textinterpretive practices and the repertoire of keyings. The bearing of acquaintanceship and close ties, of the generation and intentional construction of joint biography, of being or not being in a state of talk, of the various locaters we employ to provide a framework for the statements we want to be in a position to utter succinctly – all these critical matters have been little studied. Behind all this, and linking these themes together, is the socially prescribed place of what is taken to be the operation of the mind. A question of who can say what to whom, in what circumstances, with what preamble, in what surface form, and, given available readings, will not be thought mindless in doing so. A question of what we can say and still satisfy Felicity's Condition.

No doubt the most closely examined case is that of 'conversation'. Anaphora and topical continuity are two examples of what has been considered in the literature. More generally, there is the matter of dialogic or sequence constraints. Given a turn at talk, a next turn will be required and will be examined for how it displays relevance to the now prior one. All kinds of discontinuities will be possible because all kinds of excuses will be available that establish respect for relevance even while failing to provide it substantively. Even one's failure to excuse a failure of uptake will be caught in the interpretive net, being read, for example, as a pointed comment on what has not otherwise been responded to.

But if Felicity's Condition is now best documented within conversations, this should not lead us to worship particularistic structures. To be sure, when John directs an assertion or question to Marsha, and Marsha responds by remaining silent, or changing the topic, or turning from John to direct her own opener to Mary, Marsha's act can be perceived by all three as a behavioural comment, a reply in effect. But analytically speaking, to say that in context no answer is an answer is simplistic. Information derived from Marsha's failure to address John's utterance verbally, i.e. canonically, is information given off, not given; it is (on the face of it) expression, not language. As such, this move figures in a special way in regard to what Marsha can be held responsible for having communicated. Whatever John says she meant by her apparent failure of uptake, Marsha has reserved the right to claim otherwise. For she has not *said* anything; she has merely placed participants in a position to draw varieties of conclusion. Should Marsha provide an explicit reply to John's utterance, she can still decline to accept particular readings of its hinted, tacit elements, for these, too, will be expression, not language.

It is true that the prior turn is very likely to provide some of the context in terms of which the current utterance will be interpreted, of which condition the current speakers must demonstrate that they are cognizant. But on the same grounds, the prior turn can never be the only such condition the current speaker will be required (and allowed) to employ as a frame of reference. In speech act terms, respondents must address themselves to the illocutionary force of what is said to them, and to appreciate this force they will have to have access to a vast array of biographical and cultural understandings – these alone allowing them to make sense out of cryptic allusions. Moreover, matters not even alluded to in the prior turn may be available for address by respondents, for in the last analysis it is the situation and circumstances of the prior speaker, as these interact with the situation and circumstances of the respondents that the latter must address, the former's speaking merely providing the occasion for doing so.

Further, a conversation is only a conversation after the fact, this being the point when a student can be assured that a continuous stretch of examples can be culled of current turns being followed by contingent next ones. Occasions of one person's talk that lead to no other person's talk perforce fail to end up in the collection. The frequent necessity for speakers to continue beyond a first 'transition relevance place' and take in their own washing for want of any volunteer is perhaps not given enough weight. Stops and starts and fitfulness generally are underplayed, as are long stretches of easy silence punctuated by unanswered remarks.[8] And the dynamics of participation are neglected, namely, the formation of subordinated communication (whether in the form of collusion, innuendo or open by plays), the occurrence of dual or pivotal participation, the movement of participants from one adjacent conversation to another, and the subdividing and recoalescence of encounters (Goffman, 1981: 133 ff.). Most important of all, the sense in which the current utterance is conditioned by the immediately prior turn's talk – when, indeed, there is such talk – does not speak to the many elements of the same current utterance that are not determined in any way by the prior turn (or prior utterance in the same turn), yet are nonetheless determined in ways that satisfy Felicity's Condition. In any case, an account of second utterances in terms of their contingency on a first leaves unexplained how there could be any firsts; after all, from where could they draw their design? Conversation could never begin. Or, once begun, it would be one utterance away from the end. Tails would know how to wag, but there would be no dogs.

It is true that utterances must display that their makers are appropriately alive to the circumstances *in* which they make the utterance (as well as, of course, to the world *about* which they make an utterance), and must do so at their makers' peril, demonstrating that the minds of the latter are informed by exactly the required presuppositions. And it is true, too, that speakers can use these constraints as a resource (indeed, are obliged to), allowing them to employ efficient references with the understanding that what they must be mindful of is exactly what their listeners will be mindful of, too. But this informs us about the circumstances in which words are spoken, and these turn out to be very much broader than the circumstances in which conversations are maintained. This is neatly evident, for example, when two individuals are jointly engaged in a physical task and one is directing the other. 'Now loosen the other one the same amount' is a deictic utterance whose required context is an immediately prior movement of a wrench, not a larynx, the resulting sequence melding turns at loosening and turns at talk.[9] There occurs an interchange of acts which are sequentially

---

8. It should be noted that this bias is not a necessary result of the Sacks-Schegloff-Jefferson turn-taking model (1974), for the initial formulation leaves ample room for lapses in talk.

9. A useful analysis of reference and task activity is provided in Grosz (1974a, 1974b).

contingent and satisfy Felicity's Condition, but in a fundamental way the interchange is not conversational. A mutually ratified joint focus of attention is here sustained on and through a physical task, a contributory resource for which is an open state of talk.

Nor (it should now be plain) was it right to define Felicity's Condition restrictively in terms of verbal acts. Speech need not figure even in a reduced way for Felicity's Condition to apply: the general constraint that an utterance must satisfy, namely, that it connect acceptably with what the recipient has in, or can bring to, mind, applies in a manner to nonlinguistic acts in wordless contexts.[10] These acts, too, insofar as they can be perceived by individuals in the vicinity, will have to be styled so as to provide evidence that their doer is engaged in something that perceivers find understandable, even if they are not favoured thereby. This paper has dealt only with utterances, but some of what it has dealt with about utterances could almost as well be dealt with about entirely non-linguistic doings.

In sum, then, whenever we come into contact with another through the mail, over the telephone, in face-to-face talk, or even merely through immediate co-presence, we find ourselves with one central obligation: to render our behaviour understandably relevant to what the other can come to perceive is going on. Whatever else, our activity must be addressed to the other's mind, i.e. to the other's capacity to read our words and actions for evidence of our feelings, thoughts and intent. This confines what we say and do, but it also allows us to bring to bear all of the world to which the other can catch allusions.

References

Bloomfield, Leonard. 1933. 'Substitution.' In *Language*, edited by Leonard Bloomfield, 247–263. New York: Holt.

Clark, Herbert H., and Catherine Marshall. 1981. 'Definite Reference and Mutual Knowledge.' In *Elements of Discourse Understanding*, edited by Aravind K. Joshi, Bonnie Webber, and Ivan Sag, 10–63. Cambridge: Cambridge University Press.

Derrida, Jacques. 1977. 'Limited Inc. abc…. ' *Glyph* 2: 162–254.

Garvey, Catherine. 1975. 'Requests and Responses in Children's Speech.' *Journal of Child Language* 2: 41–63.

Goffman, Erving. 1981. *Forms of Talk*. Philadelphia: University of Pennsylvania Press.

Grice, H. Paul. 1975. 'Logic and Conversation.' In *Syntax and Semantics*, ed. by Peter Cole, and Jerry L. Morgan, Vol. 3, *Speech Acts*, 41–58. New York: Academic Press.

Grosz, Barbara J. 1974a. '*The Representation and Use of Focus in Dialogue Understanding*.' Stanford Research Institute Project 1526 90. Menlo Park, Calif.: Technical Note.

Grosz, Barbara J. 1974b. '*The Structure of Task Oriented Dialogues*.' Stanford Research Institute Project 1526 90. Menlo Park, Calif.: Technical Note.

---

10. A point that Grice (1975: 48) himself makes.

Halliday, Michael Alexander Kirkwood, and Ruqaiya Hasan. 1976. *Cohesion in English*. London: Longmans.

Kiparsky, Paul, and Carol Kiparsky. 1970. 'Fact.' In *Progress in Linguistics*, edited by Manfred Bierwisch, and Karl Erick Heidolph, 143–173. Paris: Mouton.

Lakoff, Robin, et al., 1973. 'Questionable Answers and Answerable Questions.' In *Issues in Linguistics*, edited by Braj B. Bachru, 453–467. Urbana: University of Illinois Press.

McTear, Michael F. 1977. '*Starting to Talk: How Pre-School Children Initiate Conversational Exchanges.*' Belfast Working Papers in Language and Linguistics no. 2. Belfast: Northern Ireland Polytechnic.

Sacks, Harvey, Emanuel A. Schegloff, and Gail Jefferson. 1974. 'A Simplest Systematics for the Organization of Turn-Taking for Conversation.' *Language* 50: 696–735. DOI: 10.2307/412243

Sherzer, Joel. 1973. 'On Linguistic Semantics and Linguistic Subdisciplines: A Review Article.' *Language in Society* 2: 269–289. DOI: 10.1017/S0047404500000750

Shugar, Grace. 1978. 'A Discourse Analysis System Applied to Talk of Children at Age Three to Five.' *Paper presented at the Discourse Symposium, Fifth International Congress of Applied Linguistics*, Montreal, August, 21–26.

Snow, Catherine E. 1977. 'The Development of Conversation between Mothers and Babies.' *Journal of Child Language* 4: 1–22. DOI: 10.1017/S0305000900000453

Stalnaker, Robert. 1973. 'Presuppositions.' *Journal of Philosophical Logic* 2: 447–457.

Stenning, Keith. 1978. 'Anaphora as an Approach to Pragmatics.' In *Linguistic Theory and Psychological Reality*, edited by Joan Bresnan, Morris Halle, and George A. Miller, 162–200. Cambridge, Mass.: MIT Press.

Weiser, Ann. 1975. 'How Not to Answer a Question: Purposive Devices in Conversational Strategy.' *Chicago Linguistic Society* 11: 649–660.

John Gumperz

Intercultural encounters

The American linguist John Joseph Gumperz (1922–2013) was born in Germany but fled to the USA in 1939. He spent most of his career as a professor at the University of Berkeley. His research, which focused on cultural practices of using language, was at the crossroads of sociolinguistics, linguistic anthropology and discourse analysis. In the 1960s, with Dell Hymes, he contributed to founding the *ethnography of communication* (Gumperz, and Hymes, 1972), which sought to be an alternative to the dominant Chomskyan approach to language as an abstract and universal grammar: their belief being that linguistic activity cannot be isolated from the complex of meaning-making practices in which it is embedded. One of its basic assumptions is that societies differ in the communicative resources available to their members. Gumperz is also known as the most prominent representative of 'interactional sociolinguistics' (Gumperz, 1982). In modern urbanized societies, social boundaries are fuzzy and people are always in contact with speakers from different backgrounds. Gumperz studied how linguistic knowledge and social factors interact in the interpretation of discourse, how the context and the cultural background of the interlocutors affect their conversational inferences and their interpretation of non-verbal signs ('contextualization cues'). People from different cultures who speak the 'same' language contextualize what is said differently.

In this text, Gumperz specifies the purpose of his research: he aims to integrate 'what we know about grammar, culture and interactive conventions into a single overall framework of concepts and analytical procedures'. He focuses 'on the participants' ongoing process of interpretation in conversation'. This presentation is illuminated by the study of a short interaction between two American office workers.

References

Gumperz, John, and Dell Hymes (eds). 1972. *Directions in sociolinguistics: The ethnography of communication*. New York: Holt, Rinehart and Winston.
Gumperz, John. 1982. *Discourse Strategies. Studies in Interactional Sociolinguistics*. Cambridge: Cambridge University Press.

John Gumperz. 1982. *Discourse Strategies*, selected 1–7.
Cambridge: Cambridge UP.

Communication is a social activity requiring the coordinated efforts of two or more individuals. More talk to produce sentences, no matter how well formed or elegant the outcome, does not by itself constitute communication. Only when a move has elicited a response can we say communication is taking place. To participate in such verbal exchanges, i.e. to create and sustain conversational involvement, we require knowledge and abilities which go considerably beyond the grammatical competence we need to decode short isolated messages. We do not and cannot automatically respond to everything we hear. In the course of our daily activities we are exposed to a multitude of signals, many more than we could possibly have time to react to. Before even deciding to take part in an interaction, we need to be able to infer, if only in the most general terms, what the interaction is about and what is expected of us. For example, we must be able to agree on whether we are just chatting to pass the time, exchanging anecdotes or experiences, or whether the intent is to explore the details of particular issues. Once involved in a conversation, both speaker and hearer must actively respond to what transpires by signalling involvement, either directly through words or indirectly through gestures or similar non-verbal signals. The response, moreover, should relate to what we think the speaker intends, rather than to the literal meanings of the words used.

Consider the following conversation, recorded in a small office:

(1) A: Are you gonna be here for ten minutes?
     B: Go ahead and take your break. Take longer if you want to.
     A: I'll just be outside on the porch.
         Call me if you need me.
     B: O.K., don't worry.

The exchange is typical of the many brief interactive routines that fill our day and which for the most part pass without special notice. Speakers' moves and addressees' responses follow one another automatically. They tend to be produced without much conscious reflection and alternate with rhythmic synchronization to avoid awkward pauses. Yet if we ask what it is about the passage that leads us to perceive it as a normal everyday occurrence, we soon discover that the episode as a whole consists of more than just a collection of utterances. In other words, neither the grammatical form nor the meaning of individual words or sentences taken in isolation give any indication that they belong together or show how they continue to fit into a single theme.

Speaker A begins with a question which, as our knowledge of English tells us, requires a yes or no answer. Yet B's reply takes the form of a suggestion which does not overtly acknowledge A's question. The relationship between the two utterances becomes evident only if we assume that B implicitly or indirectly signals assent by the way in which she formulates her suggestion. But this raises further problems as to the nature of the knowledge involved in A's and B's ability to see beyond surface content and to understand such indirect messages. Since there are no overt linguistic cues, it seems reasonable to assume that both A and B rely on a shared understanding that the interaction takes place in an office and on their expectations of what normally goes on in offices. That is, it is taken for granted that both participants are office workers, that it is customary to take brief breaks in the course of a working day, and that staff members should cooperate in seeing that someone is present at all times. Such background assumptions then enable B to hypothesize that A is most probably asking her question because she wants to take her break and is checking to make sure that her absence will not inconvenience B. A's reply in the third utterance which implies that she does indeed intend to go out for a while, confirms this interpretation. B's final 'O.K., don't worry' can then be understood as a reassurance that A's absence will not cause any problem. Conversationalists thus rely on indirect inferences which build on background assumptions about context, interactive goals and interpersonal relations to derive frames in terms of which they can interpret what is going on.

For reasons that will become clear below, I believe that understanding presupposes conversational involvement.

A general theory of discourse strategies must therefore begin by specifying the linguistic and sociocultural knowledge that needs to be shared if conversational involvement is to be maintained, and then go on to deal with what it is about the nature of conversational inference that makes for cultural, subcultural and situational specificity of interpretation.

Conversational analysis is a growing field of enquiry which, during the last decade, has been enriched by contributions from a number of disciplinary perspectives. For many years now linguists and other social scientists, mindful of the limitations of positivist-empiricist approaches to the study of human behaviour, have been aware of the need for a deeper understanding of the functioning of verbal signs in human cooperative processes. Linguists, whose grammatical formalisms continue to have some success in clarifying the cognitive processes involved in word and sentence decoding, are nevertheless aware of the limitations of existing grammatical theories and have begun to look for new approaches to the study of conversational processes. Sociologists and psychologists have become centrally concerned with the analysis of communicative processes involved in human learning, social cooperation and underlying social evolution.

Research stimulated by such concerns provides new data and new analytical perspectives which must ultimately be incorporated into a general theory of pragmatics. To cite just a few examples, linguistic anthropologists, employing ethnographic methods to survey what they call rules of speaking as they apply to speech events, have shown that language usage, norms for what counts as appropriate speech behaviour, as well as the very definitions of such events vary from culture to culture and context to context. Their findings are supported by micro-studies of non-verbal communication which examine the interplay of verbal and nonverbal signs in signalling context and constraining interpretive preferences. Among linguistic semanticists there are many who argue that the established grammarians' practice of concentrating on the referential meaning or truth value of isolated propositions is subject to serious theoretical objections. Semantic analysis, they contend, should properly concentrate on the study of speech acts, seen as units of human action. Other linguists have begun to focus on grammatical and semantic signals of textual cohesion and on the role of interpretive frames, scripts or schemata in understanding discourse (Fillmore, 1976; Schank, and Abelson, 1977; Spiro, Bruce, and Brewer, 1980). Perhaps most directly relevant is the work of sociologists who, building on the critical writings of Harold Garfinkel (1967), are creating a new tradition of conversational analysis which concentrates directly on verbal strategies of speaker/listener coordination as revealed in turn-taking and other practices of conversational management.

Yet, important as these contributions are, we are still far from a general theory of verbal communication which integrates what we know about grammar, culture and interactive conventions into a single overall framework of concepts and analytical procedures.

Each of the traditions cited tends to concentrate on certain parts of the total signalling process, while tacitly relying on findings and concepts reflecting other disciplinary perspectives when dealing with different facets of communicative signs. Thus, linguists build on the macro-sociologists' notion of group, status, role and social function in their discussions of social norms of language usage. Sociologists, on the other hand, employ the theoretical linguists' sentence level categories of referential semantics and syntax in their discussions of interactive strategy.

The main objects of study in most existing forms of conversational analysis are communicative signs as such and their patterning in texts, i.e. either in written prose passages or in transcripts of spoken dialogue. Almost all conversational data derive from verbal interaction in socially and linguistically homogeneous groups. There is a tendency to take for granted that conversational involvement exists, that interlocutors are cooperating, and that interpretive conventions are shared. The experience of modern industrial society with its history of communication breakdowns, of increasingly intricate constitutional and legal disputes and its record of educational failure, suggests that such assumptions may not fit the facts of modern urban life. We know that understanding presupposes the ability to attract and sustain others' attention. Yet so far we have no empirical methods for analyzing what is required in the way of shared linguistic and cultural knowledge to create and sustain conversational involvement.

This book attempts to deal with such issues by concentrating on the participants' ongoing process of interpretation in conversation and on what it is that enables them to perceive and interpret particular constellations of cues in reacting to others and pursuing their communicative ends. There is no question that the effective employment of communicative strategies presupposes grammatical competence and knowledge of the culture. But this does not mean that we can rely solely on existing grammars and ethnographies to explain how interlocutors make situated interpretations.

Returning for a moment to our conversational example, we could argue that the background assumptions we list in our discussion are part of the givens of American culture. But not all Americans are familiar with office behaviour, and existing cultural analyses do not cover the details of office routine. Even if we did have exhaustive descriptions and the relevant knowledge were shared, we still need to ask what it is about the situation at hand that enables participants to retrieve relevant items of information. Moreover, the actual words A uses and the way she stresses them are of crucial importance in evoking the office routine frame. Had she used expressions such as 'Do you intend to stay here?' or 'Do you plan to go out?' or had she stressed the initial word 'are' rather than 'be here', the response might have been different and the course of the interaction would have been changed greatly. Such matters of idiom and sentence stress are, as we will show in our discussion, not ordinarily incorporated in grammatical descriptions. The study of conversational inference thus requires assumptions and procedures which are different from those used in either ethnography or grammatical analysis.

Seen from the perspective of the individual disciplines, analyzing inferential processes presents what must seem like almost insuperable problems. Yet conversational exchanges do have certain dialogic properties, which differentiate them from sentences or written texts and which enable us to avoid, or at least bypass, some of the difficulties involved in the study of isolated messages. Two such properties which are illustrated in our example are: (a) that interpretations are jointly negotiated by speaker and hearer and judgements either confirmed or changed by the reactions they evoke – they need not be inferred from a single utterance; and (b) that conversations in themselves often contain internal evidence of what the outcome is, i.e. of whether or not participants share interpretive conventions or succeed in achieving their communicative ends.

If episodes are selected to contain such information, therefore, a single passage can be subjected to multiple forms of analysis. Examination of participants' success in establishing common themes, maintaining thematic continuity or negotiating topic change at the level of content yields empirical evidence about what is achieved. The timing of speakership moves and listenership responses can be examined through rhythmic or nonverbal cues to check for evidence of breakdowns in conversational coordination. Once outcomes are known, linguistic analysis can be employed along with direct interviews of participants and comparative data from other similar episodes to reconstruct what it is about the signalling cues employed and participants' underlying knowledge that led to the achieved effect.

Because it makes no assumptions about the sharedness of rules or evaluative norms, the interpretive approach to conversation is particularly revealing in modern urbanized societies where social boundaries are diffuse, where intensive communication with speakers of differing backgrounds is the rule rather than the exception, and signalling conventions may vary from situation to situation. Much of the work reported on in this book concentrates on encounters involving participants who, while speaking the same language, nevertheless show significant differences in background knowledge and must overcome or take account of the communicative symbols which signal these differences to maintain conversational engagement. In addition, encounters involving style or code-switching are analyzed to demonstrate how known differences in social values and grammar and lexicon are exploited to convey new information.

This interest in linguistic and cultural diversity is in part the result of my earlier fieldwork on social and regional dialects and on bilingualism and small rural communities in India, Norway, Austria and the United States (Gumperz, 1971a). It was a concern with universals of intergroup contact that first led me to turn to interethnic encounters in urban settings. But the more I learned about the nature and functioning of conversational strategies, the more I became convinced that sociocultural differences and their linguistic reflections are more than just causes of misunderstanding or grounds for pejorative stereotyping and conscious discrimination. Language differences play an important, positive role in signalling information as well as in creating and maintaining the subtle boundaries of power, status, role and occupational specialization that make up the fabric of our social life. Assumptions about value differences associated with these boundaries in fact form the very basis for the indirect communicative strategies employed in key gatekeeping encounters, such as employment interviews, counselling sessions, labour negotiations and committee meetings, which have come to be crucial in determining the quality of an individual's life in urban society.

With the disappearance of small, egalitarian face-to-face societies, the diversity of background and communicative conventions comes to take on important signalling functions in everyday interaction. Any sociolinguistic theory that attempts to deal with problems of mobility, power and social control cannot assume uniformity of signalling devices as a precondition for successful communication. Simple dichotomous comparisons between supposedly homogeneous and supposedly diverse groups therefore do not do justice to the complexities of communication in situations of constant social change such as those we live in. We need to be able to deal with degrees of differentiation and, through intensive case studies of key encounters, learn to explore how such differentiation affects individuals' ability to sustain social interaction and have their goals and motives understood. It is in this area of urban affairs that sociolinguistic analysis can yield new insights into the workings of social process. By careful examination of the signalling mechanisms that conversationalists react to, one can isolate cues and symbolic conventions through which distance is maintained or frames of interpretation are created. One can show how these conventions relate to individual or group background. To the extent that it achieves this goal, research on conversational inference can make important contributions not only to sociolinguistic theory as such but also to general theories of social interaction and social evolution.

References

Fillmore, Charles J. 1976. 'Frame semantics and the nature of language.' *Annals of the New York Academy of Sciences: Conference on the Origin and Development of Language and Speech*. 280: 20–32. DOI: 10.1111/j.1749-6632.1976.tb25467.x

Garfinkel, Harold. 1967. *Studies in Ethnomethodology*. Englewood Cliffs, NJ: Prentice-Hall.

Gumperz, John. 1971. *Language in Social Groups*. Stanford: Stanford University Press.

Spiro, Rand J., Bruce, Bertram C., and Brewer, William F. 1980. *Theoretical Issues in Reading Comprehension: Perspectives from Cognitive Psychology, Linguistics, Artificial Intelligence and Education*. Hillsdale, NJ: Erlbaum.

Schank, Roger C., and Abelson, Robert P. (1977). *Scripts, Plans, Goals, and Understanding*. New York: John Wiley & Sons.

Aaron V. Cicourel

Maintaining one's self

The American sociologist Aaron Victor Cicourel (b. 1928) first became famous when opposing mainstream quantitative sociology. In his ground-breaking book *Methods and Measurement in Sociology* (1964), he made the case for an ethnographic qualitative approach to social phenomena, based on a more hermeneutic and intuitive form of text analysis, on extensive participant observation, and on new approaches to interview techniques (e.g. 1968). He remained a critical and sceptical scholar, opposing complex social science taxonomies and stating that many concepts might be useful as metaphors (e.g. 'class' or 'habitus') but had no significance for empirical research. In this way, he aligned with some ethnomethodologists such as Harold Garfinkel and with linguistic anthropologists (e.g. John Gumperz and Dell Hymes).

Most importantly, Cicourel developed approaches to studying context in much detail and distinguished between broad and narrow contexts when analysing texts and discourse. Because of his emphasis on context, he distanced himself from some of his most famous students, such as Harvey Sacks, and the school of Conversation Analysis. For Cicourel, language plays an active role in creating and sustaining social interaction and social reality. In his more recent work he proposed an approach labelled '*ecological sociolinguistics*', i.e. an approach to text in context which considers many layers of context in a more dialectical way. With Karin Knorr-Cetina, he carried out investigations in organisations and became interested in the recontextualisation of oral interviews into formalised written records (by the police as well as in hospitals) which neglected the richness of personal narratives and personal experience.

The entry in this Reader provides an example of Cicourel's more recent work, together with psychologists, neurologists and experts in cognition in the area of child development and childcare.

References

Cicourel, Aaron V. 1964. *Method and Measurement in Sociology*. New York: Free Press.
Cicourel, Aaron V. 1968. *The Social Organization of Juvenile Justice*. New York: Wiley.

Aaron V. Cicourel. 2011. 'The effect of neurodegenerative disease
on representations of self in discourse.'
Neurocase: The Neural Basis of Cognition 17 (3): 251–259,
selected 251–253, 254, 255–256, 257–259.

Introduction

The emergence and loss of self are embedded in the social interaction of individuals with their family members or caregivers. Developmental aspects of self are guided by caregivers; similarly, it is caregivers who sustain loss of self among the aged, with reports of memory lapses, uncountable changes in daily routines, and declines in everyday problem-solving. Clinical specialists begin with family reports, but confirmation relies on probes of the patient's mental status, and neuropsychological testing.

Attributing a social self to infants, young children, adolescents and adults assumes that 'self-awareness' and awareness of others are only possible and sustainable through interaction with caregivers. A paradoxical frame of reference comes into existence: a biological human 'self' can be acknowledged only by other intact human brains. Uncovering how the neurobiology of the brain establishes a 'self', much less its role in making possible sophisticated, sociocultural communities, remains daunting.

This report provides support for the idea that caregivers implement the essential 'scaffolding' practices needed for an emerging 'social self' in infants and parallel practices required to simulate the existence of 'self' in the deteriorating, ageing brain. The socialization of the young into adulthood, and the socialization of adults through to death require evolutionary human neurobiological systems together with locally emerging cognitive, emotional and sociocultural development that are unavoidably nurtured by caregivers' 'scaffolding' activities and practices. 'Motherese' (adult speech to infants and young children) creates scaffolding activities. These local practices are inherent in adult-infant discourse, and equally essential as caregiver discourse to patients. Both types of caregiver utilize repetitive adult scaffolding practices to sustain their own sense of self while supplying the young with necessary developmental knowledge, or providing adult patients with a simulated sense of 'appropriate' discourse.

Newport (1977: 177) underscores the relevance of the linguistic environment and the use of a special language 'register' when speaking to children. Limited complexity in speech has been proposed to facilitate the acquisition of language during infant development, and caregivers are presumed to be sensitive to the child's limitations, including their short-term memory. Adults become selective in their use of 'appropriate' speech acts, which are less complex lexically and structurally simplified when addressing children. Newport underscores that such modification is conserved across groups with socioeconomic, cultural and language differences. I suggest that we can expect the same kinds of speech patterns among caregivers addressing patients with Alzheimer's disease (AD) and fronto-temporal lobar degeneration (FTLD).

In order to illustrate both appropriate discourse and the use of scaffolding practices, the present highly condensed report draws upon evidence from 10 minutes of discourse between each of six couples: two 'control' cases, two cases in which one spouse has been diagnosed with FTLD, and two cases in which one spouse has been diagnosed with AD. The analysis of these exchanges focuses on the caregiver's reliance on scaffolding practices to sustain a semblance of 'appropriate' or 'expected' social interaction. A number of analogical discourse sequences were taken into account in assessing the degree of dependence on scaffolding practices, including:

1. The extent to which each spouse could initiate and pursue a topic.
2. The ability of the subjects to use conceptual blends like metaphors, metonyms and related semantic constructions typical of everyday discourse.
3. The extent to which one spouse dominated the discourse and provided leading questions and tag statements to sustain the speech event.
4. The ability of each subject to sustain a reciprocity of perspectives or an accurate theory of mind (Gopnick, and Meltzoff, 1997; Mead, 1934; Schütz,1962; Tomasello, 1999).
5. The capacity of the subject to remember and conceptualize a future event and plan an activity.

Subjects

Subjects were referred to the Memory and Aging Center at UCSF for psychological testing and clinical examination. Subsequent testing occurred at the Psychophysiology Laboratory at UC, Berkeley. The diagnosis of each case was not known to the author.

One 'control case'

Conflict appears to be self-evident and convincing in the 'control' cases. For example, both spouses initiate detailed observations of past family relationships, social activities and work experiences during the 10-minute sessions.

'Control' Case 7142

Excerpt 1 – Case 7142

1   L.A. (Lab Assistant): Please begin your conversation.
2   H: I was just going to say that the um that we used to go off about is the –
3   you contend that I put my mom first and um I contend I don't.

4	W:	I'm not sure that's the case anymore and my frustration is that you –
5		you tend not to see some of your mother's manipulative tactics
6		and you bought into the whole story about, you know,
7		she wanted you to believe over the years
8		and yet your sister and brother have seen it very clearly.
9		I just think possibly being the oldest child and having been doted on the
10		most. I think you just feel like you would be betraying your mother
11		if you admitted that you saw those things.
12		That's the part that frustrates me.

The couple recreate their 'conflict' about a domineering mother/mother-in-law from the perspective of the wife. Later in the conversation, the husband acknowledges his submissive behaviour but also seeks to justify his mother's behaviour by reference to her ageing years (not shown). Notice the metaphoric-like way in which the husband and wife characterize the 'conflict'. The husband contextualizes the 'conflict' by first alluding to prior occasions ('we used to go off about'), then he summarizes the actual source of the conflict, '…that I put my mom first and um I contend I don't' (lines 2–3).

The wife (line 4) initially retracts her earlier claim by stating 'I'm not sure that's the case anymore…'. Her remarks in lines 4–12 demonstrate her ability to articulate a long-standing 'conflict' by referencing her 'frustration' in lines 4 and 12.

The language used by each party remains articulate and substantively convincing throughout the session. Each spouse appears to engage in animated social interaction with no sign of apathy, as well as displaying a strong command of English syntax, phonology, semantics, paralinguistic skills and task-oriented cognitive reasoning. The case is consistent with research by Gottman and Levenson (1992) on social interaction in 'normal' long-term marriages. (…)

FTD Case 5692

The opening moments of this case reveal the husband's face as expressionless.

Excerpt 7 – Case 5692

1	LA:	We want the two of you to talk about anything you want and then
2	W:	[to Husband] do you have any idea of where we disagree?
3	H:	No. [Wife smiles, Husband begins to 'smile', not clear]
4	LA:	Pick something you'd like to talk about, something you can agree?
5	W:	[fairly animated] Oh, I know. We have differences of opinion on
6		how we're going to be buried.
7	H:	[smiles and seems to 'chuckle']
8	W:	[Wife smiles 'broadly'] but we resolved that.
9		Did you think of something you could talk about?

10		You don't want to talk about that?
11	H:	Nope.
12	W:	We already decided on that. Ah uhm, about this weekend.
13	H:	wh oh (?) ['flat' affect]
14	W:	What we're doing.
15	H:	We're going to play some tennis.

Here, the wife's 'scaffolding' creates a simulated 'stable speech zone' or sociocultural context that enables the patient to access limited, immediate and past memories of events, but does not exceed them. The husband's face consistently lacks expressive features, while the wife seems to be animated at the onset, including during the silent period. The husband shows little evidence of motivation to engage in the discussion. To give the appearance of a speech event, the wife must create the necessary scaffolding, initiating and sustaining of a dialogue that address future events involving one or both spouses. The husband expresses only truncated views about activities proposed by his wife. This pattern of discourse remains consistent throughout the session. In subsequent exchanges, the wife asks leading questions to sustain the conversation. The husband seldom initiates discourse, nor does he attempt to expand on a given topic; his responses lack emotional lexical items and phrases.

(…)

AD Case 5733

Excerpt 24 – Case 5733

p1	H:	We can talk, let's just talk, we'll talk about that.
p2	Lab. Assistant (LA):	about the 'clutter?'
p3	H:	Yah, 'cause then she'll talk a lot. (both husband and wife smile)

Early on, it seems the husband is informing the lab. assistant of the appropriate topic for discussion. The wife's animation appears appropriate when she does speak, yet her facial expressions appear subdued.

Excerpt 25 – Case 5733

1	LA:	You can begin your conversation.
2	W:	About what? (laughs, as does husband) I don't think we have
3		I think we have (animated and smiling) a lot of clutter.
4	H:	Mmm
5	W:	But I don't know what to do in terms of getting the stuff
6		OUT of the house. You know, *I* can't manage to pick up all the,
7		all the stuff. I'd like to take the, the band stuff to the storage space,
8		(H: Mm) but you don't want to do that.
9	H:	I haven't?/

10	W:	/And I can't drive.
11	H:	I know (laughs) I, I, um, I have … you know what?
12		that's the first time you mentioned about the band stuff
13		going in the storage space, but, yeah, we can take it to the storage space.
14	W:	And I think we could have the,
15		I really think that we don't need the one storage space, whatever.
16		I mean we have three storage spaces and one of them is hardly full.
17	H:	I know. Actually, I think I want to try to, well I want to
18		get a hold of (first male name) and see if I can get some of the stuff
19		out of there. (W: Mm)
20	H:	Sooner the better.

In lines 11–13, the husband appears surprised by the wife's remark about 'the band stuff', noting it was 'the first time you mentioned about the band stuff going to the storage space'. At this juncture, the dialogue appears appropriate. Both spouses introduce topics: the wife on moving the 'band stuff' to a storage space, and the husband suggesting he will call someone (name), presumably to help him move the 'stuff'. Also, note the wife's relevant remark about having more storage space than is needed. The husband's expressions of planning actual activities to facilitate the movement of 'clutter' could be considered indicative of his role in creating scaffolding for a wife who periodically appears competent. Though the pattern of discourse is not entirely clear-cut, the next excerpt seems to support the view of the husband being the competent spouse:

Excerpt 26 – Case 5733

21	W:	Okay, so when do you think we should be able to,
22		to get in touch with him?
23		Have we tried?
24	H:	No.
25	W:	So?
26	H:	I'll email him tonight.
27	W:	Okay. And I'll be happy to do any manual lifting you want.
28	H:	Okay. On, on the dining room table
29		I think I need (second male name) to help me carry that.
30	H:	So, I'll have to wait till he gets back.
31	W:	Okay.

In lines 21–22, the wife asks a pertinent question, using two appropriate deictic pronouns ('we', 'him') while remembering earlier discourse. Her next question (line 23) is also appropriate. However, the cognitive skills required for the husband's remarks about using e-mail, and his memory of the second male friend being away, suggest the wife is the AD patient.

(…)

The role of others in neurobiological aspects of 'self'

Unlike the scaffolding that sustains an infant's emerging self, such practices applied to interactions with ageing sufferers of neurodegenerative disease are unlikely to improve patients' cognitive, linguistic or sociocultural skills. Rather, these scaffolding activities make it possible for caregivers to simulate a sense of 'normal cultural stability', which may be important for their own sense of 'stability'. The extent to which caregivers differentially maintain elements of denial vis-à-vis their scaffolding activities is an empirical issue.

Social communication (verbal and non-verbal) is a universal medium for the emergence of self-expression and plays a key role in sustaining, observing and comprehending the acquisition and loss of self. Conspecifics provide the scaffolding for the emergence of self. The role of the ubiquitous 'other' or parent, friend, peer or 'caregiver' (Dunn, 1988) is undeniable; evidence abounds for the interdependence of neurobiological, cognitive, emotional and sociocultural structures and processes.

The 'self' has been associated with specific neurobiological areas of the brain (Seeley, and Sturm, 2007: 317) – the anterior insula cortex (AIC) and anterior cingulate cortex (ACC), among other areas. To complement neurobiological conceptions of 'self', 'others' must embody communal, normative and tacit sociocultural perspectives to motivate a sociocultural, behavioural 'self'. How this feat is achieved at a neurobiological level remains largely unknown, though interaction between different neural networks is thought to be key.

A paper by A. D. Craig (2009: 60) refers to evidence from functional magnetic resonance imaging (fMRI) research strongly suggesting the AIC as a neural substrate of a wide range of subjective human experiences, including sociocultural mental states. The AIC's neurobiological existence and capabilities are necessary *but not sufficient* conditions for human life, which also requires the simultaneous emergence and evolution of parallel cognitive, emotional and sociocultural systems activated by human interaction with other conspecifics.

The complex neurobiological discussions in the Craig and Seeley and Sturm papers, on the emergence of a neurobiological self, unequivocally presuppose and refer to essential socioculturally-based, emotional, cognitive and linguistic competences which remain unexamined in the wider literature.

Seeley and Sturm (2007) highlight developmental milestones when infants first imitate facial expressions of caregivers, and later produce the social smile, indicating an awareness of the effects their own actions have on others. Self-awareness also allows infants to equate their own expressions with particular feelings, and consequently to be able to interpret the expressions of others. What 'normatively appropriate' sociocultural responses or 'scaffolding' must others provide to ensure 'normal' development?

Discussion

Parallel 'scaffolding' exists in adult speech to young children, four-year-olds' speech to two-year-olds (Gelman, and Shatz, 1976; Shatz, 1975), and caregiver speech to aged patients with cognitive, emotional and sociocultural deficits.

Newport (1977: 178) offers a succinct review of this special 'speech register', suggests that the child limits its language environment by repeating (parsing) utterances that go beyond speech production capabilities (Shipley, Smith, and Gleitman, 1969) and ignores language perceived to be too difficult or unfamiliar. As noted by Newport, the nature of the selectivity of utterances suggests the child does not rely on innate preprogramming abilities and is probably incapable of processing complex speech.

Newport underscores the caregiver's perception of the 'needs of the language learner' and the nature of the response or lack of response from the child. She concludes her review by describing an hypothesis by Gelman and Shatz that speakers select utterances perceived for particular contexts by assessing appropriate conversation meaning.

According to Gelman and Shatz, conversational interaction itself must be simple even if the syntax is complex, but the reverse does not hold. The perception that the listener requires a restricted input for understanding the exchange assumes an adult-like sense of 'self' for the speaker while simultaneously attributing a sense of self to the infant. It seems likely that caregivers of aged individuals with deficits make the same distinctions about the listener.

Vygotsky (1978: 81) notes that learning and development occur simultaneously; they each influence the other. Neurobiological maturation and learning are both developmental processes. A key notion of his work (p.85) is that 'what children can do with the assistance of others might be in some sense even more indicative of their mental development than what they can do alone'.

Developmental psycholinguistic reports of mothers' speech to young infants appear to be homologous to the 10-minute exchanges examined in this report. The 'conflicts' resemble representational re/descriptive (Karmiloff-Smith, 1992) stories. Such 'stories' also are a ubiquitous resource for child language and cultural self-development (Miller, 1994) for children as young as two and a half years old.

I propose that the reverse process holds for adults with deficits; caregiver scaffolding can simulate appropriate discourse, but also mask and seemingly deny deterioration.

Concluding remarks: the value of discourse in the diagnosis of FTLD and AD

The above brief analysis of discourse assumes that patients with fairly advanced AD and FTLD encounter difficulties when planning activities. They require continuous scaffolding by others to access and sustain past experiences. Short-term memory is compromised. Spontaneous storytelling is rare, and patients have difficulty integrating themselves into the 'here and now' of local, group social interaction. Yet the two AD patients were able to present 'appropriate' spates of variable, meaningful narratives within the confines of 10 minutes of discourse. This intermittent appearance of competence reveals the limitations of using ethnographically absent, short periods of 'staged' social interaction to make diagnostic inferences on patients with early onset dementia. Both patients (5733, 5268) were early onset AD patients, aged 60 and 59, respectively.

Contrary to the initial assumption that caregivers' scaffolding practices were necessary to sustain a semblance of 'appropriate' social interaction for these patients, the two early onset AD patients, especially case 5268, appeared to initiate and pursue a topic, and to use metaphors and meaningful semantic constructions typical of everyday discourse. By contrast, the necessary, substantial caregiver scaffolding provided by the competent spouse alone was apparent in the 10-minute sessions of the FTLD cases. Control cases were similarly easy to identify.

Identifying early onset FTLD and AD is difficult and input from family members and work colleagues is often necessary. Limited discourse in a staged environment does not fully substitute for observation of routine interaction between spouses in the setting of daily life, and this is one possible basis for my earlier difficulties in the analysis of AD case 5268. This idea is supported by the cases of two patients with early onset dementia whom I have recently videotaped in a domestic setting: In one case (FTLD), the spouse first noticed a problem, while in the second case (AD), colleagues at work reported a problem to the spouse; in each case, the initial medical assessment failed to find anything untoward about the patient's mental status. Only at the insistence of the spouse was further evaluation undertaken and a diagnosis reached, finally confirming what was beginning to become evident in the everyday interactions of the patient.

The take-home message of this report is that the value of ethnographically-based discourse relies on the ubiquitous fact that speaking 'appropriately' is not an art form used by native speakers; rather, it requires normative and local dialectical speech patterns which cannot be tampered with because they are essential elements of sociocultural cognition and communicative practices without which no stable human social order can exist and survive. Scaffolding practices form part of a caregiver speech register which maintains this social order in the setting of cognitive decline due to neurodegenerative disease.

References

Craig, A. D. 2009. 'How do you feel–now? The anterior insula and human awareness.' *Nature Reviews Neuroscience*, 10: 59–70. DOI: 10.1038/nrn2555

Dunn, Judy. 1988. *The beginnings of social understanding*. Cambridge, MA: Harvard University Press. DOI: 10.4159/harvard.9780674330610

Gelman, Rochel, and Shatz, Marilyn. 1976. 'Appropriate speech adjustments: The operation of conversational constraints on talk to two-year-olds.' In *Communication and language: The origins of behavior*, ed. by M. Lewis, and L. Rosenblum, Vol. 5, 27–61. New York: Wiley.

Gopnick, Alison, Andrew N. Meltzoff. 1997. *Words, Thoughts, and Theories*. Cambridge, MA: MIT Press.

Gottman, John M., and Robert W. Levenson. 1992. 'Marital processes predictive of later dissolution: Behavior, physiology, and health.' *Journal of Personal & Social Psychology* 63 (2): 221–233. DOI: 10.1037/0022-3514.63.2.221

Karmiloff-Smith, Annette. 1992. *Beyond modularity: A developmental perspective on cognitive science*. Cambridge, MA: MIT Press.

Mead, George Herbert. 1934. *Mind, self, and society*. Chicago: University of Chicago Press.

Miller, Peggy J. 1994. 'Narrative practices: Their role in socialization and self-construction.' In *The remembering self: Construction and activity in the self-narrative*, ed. by Ulric Neisser, and Robyn Fivush, 158–179. New York: Cambridge University Press. DOI: 10.1017/CBO9780511752858.010

Newport, Elissa. 1977. 'Motherese: The speech of mothers to young children.' In *Cognitive theory*, ed. by N. John Castellan, David B. Pisoni, and George R. Potts, Vol. 2, 177–217. Hillsdale, NJ: Erlbaum.

Shatz, Marilyn. 1975. 'How young children respond to language: Procedures for answering.' *Papers and Reports on Child Language Development*, 10: 97–110.

Schütz, Alfred. 1962. *Collected papers, I: The problem of social reality*, ed. by Maurice Natanson. The Hague: Nijhoff.

Seeley, William W., and Virginia E. Sturm. 2007. 'Self-representation and the frontal lobes.' In *The human frontal lobes: Functions and disorders*, ed. by B. L. Miller, and J. L. Cummings, 2nd edn, 317–334. New York: The Guilford Press.

Shatz, Marilyn. 1975. 'The development of communication skills: Modifications in the speech of young children as a function of the listener.' *SRCD [Society for Research in Child Development] Monographs* 5 (38): 152.

Shipley, Elizabeth S., Carlota S. Smith, and Lila R. Gleitman. 1969. 'A study in the acquisition of language: Free responses to commands.' *Language*, 45: 322–342. DOI: 10.2307/411663

Tomasello, Michael. 1999. *The cultural origins of human cognition*. Cambridge: Harvard University Press.

Vygotsky, Lev S. 1978. *Mind in society: The development of higher psychological processes*, ed. by Michael Cole, Vera John-Steiner, Sylvia Scribner, and Ellen Souberman. Cambridge: Harvard University Press.

James Paul Gee

Language as saying, doing and being

James Paul Gee (b. 1948) situates himself in the field of 'social linguistics' (1990), at the crossroads of psycholinguistics, discourse analysis, sociolinguistics and anthropology. He is particularly interested in the application of his research to literacy and education. For him, literacies (written language, sounds, gestures, images and symbols) must be connected to social practices. So, writing and reading are not just mental activities, inside people's minds. From the 2000s onwards, he has been working particularly on video games, including how they can be applied to the classroom (Gee, 2003), and on the implications of digital media for communication and learning. In his main contribution to discourse studies, *An Introduction to Discourse Analysis: Theory and Method* (1999), he claims that language-in-use is always 'political': 'By 'politics,' I mean how *social goods* are thought about, argued over, and distributed in society. 'Social goods' are anything that a group of people believes to be a source of power, status, value, or worth' (2005: 2). Gee opposes the concept of *Discourse* (with a 'big D') to the concept of *discourse* (with a 'little d'). The latter refers to language in use, whereas the former refers to the combination of language with behaviour, ways of thinking, values, habitus and dress within a specific community. Individuals may belong to many Discourse communities: as a 'good student', a 'mainstream politician', 'a street-gang member' and so on.

In this excerpt from *An Introduction to Discourse Analysis*, Gee presents his conception of discourse and discourse analysis. Language allows us to give information (saying), engage in activities (doing) and take on socially significant identities (being). So, the study of meaning must integrate ways of saying, doing and being. He makes a comparison to a game of cards to show that language gets its meaning from the practices within which it is used. As in a game, there are always winners and losers: language is 'political, social goods are always at stake when we speak'. From this viewpoint, discourse analysis is basically 'critical'.

References

Gee, James P. 1990. *Social Linguistics and Literacies: Ideology in Discourses. Critical Perspectives on Literacy and Education*. London: Falmer Press.
Gee, James P. 2005[1999]. *An Introduction to Discourse Analysis. Theory and Method*. London and New York: Routledge.
Gee, James P. 2003. *What Video Games Have to Teach Us About Learning and Literacy*. New York: Palgrave Macmillan.

James Paul Gee. 2010. *An Introduction to Discourse Analysis. Theory and Method.*
3rd edition, selected 2–10.
New York, London: Routledge.

What is language for? Many people think language exists so that we can 'say things' in the sense of communicating information. However, language serves a great many functions in our lives. Giving and getting information is by no means the only one. Language does, of course, allow us to inform each other. But it also allows us to do things and to be things, as well. In fact, saying things in language never goes without also doing things and being things.

Language allows us to do things. It allows us to engage in actions and activities. We promise people things, we open committee meetings, we propose to our lovers, we argue over politics and we 'talk to God' (pray). These are among the myriad things we do with language beyond giving and getting information.

Language allows us to be things. It allows us to take on different socially significant identities. We can speak as experts – as doctors, lawyers, anime aficionados or carpenters – or as 'everyday people'. To take on any identity at a given time and place we have to 'talk the talk', not just 'walk the walk'. When they are being gang members, street-gang members talk a different talk than do honour students when they are being students. Furthermore, one and the same person could be both things at different times and places.

In language, there are important connections between saying (informing), doing (action) and being (identity). If I say anything to you, you cannot really understand it fully if you do not know what I am trying to do and whom I am trying to be by saying it. To understand anything fully you need to know *who* is saying it and *what* the person saying it is trying to do.

Let's take a simple example. Imagine a stranger on the street walks up to you and says, 'Hi, how are you?' The stranger has said something, but you do not know what to make of it. Who is this person? What is the stranger doing?

Imagine you find out that the person is taking part in a game where strangers ask other people how they are in order to see what sorts of reactions they get. Or imagine that the person is a friend of your twin and thinks you are your sibling (I have a twin and this sort of thing has often happened to me). Or imagine the person is someone you met long ago and have long forgotten, but who, unbeknownst to you, thinks of you as a friend. In one case, a gamer is playing; in another case, a friend of your sibling's is mistakenly being friendly; and, in yet another case, someone who mistakenly thinks he is a friend of yours is also being friendly. Once you sort things out, everything becomes clear (but not necessarily comfortable).

My doctor, who also happens to be a friend, tells me, as she greets me in her office: 'You look tired.' Is she speaking to me as a friend (*who*) making small talk (*what*) or is she speaking to me as a doctor (*who*) making a professional judgement (*what*) about my health? It makes quite a big difference whether a friend (*who*) is playfully insulting (*what*) his friend in a bar or a hard-core biker (*who*) is threatening (*what*) a stranger. The words can be the same, but they will mean very different things. Who we are and what we are doing when we say things matters.

This book is concerned with a theory of how we use language to say things, do things and be things. It is concerned, as well, with a method of how to study saying, doing and being in language. When I talk about 'being things', I will use the word 'identity' in a special way. I do not mean your core sense of self, whom you take yourself 'essentially' to be. I mean different ways of being in the world at different times and places for different purposes, e.g. ways of being a 'good student', an 'avid bird-watcher', a 'mainstream politician', a 'tough cop', a video-game 'gamer', a 'Native American' and so on and so forth, through a nearly endless list.

Language and practices

One of the best ways to see something that we have come to take too much for granted (like language) is to look at an example of it that makes it seem strange again. So consider *Yu-Gi-Oh!*, a popular-culture activity, but one whose use of language will seem strange to many.

Here are some facts about *Yu-Gi-Oh!*: *Yu-Gi-Oh!* is a card game that can be played face to face or in video games. There are also *Yu-Gi-Oh!* television shows, movies and books (in all of which characters act out moves in the card game). There are thousands of *Yu-Gi-Oh!* cards. Players choose a deck of 40 cards and 'duel' each other. The moves in the game represent battles between the monsters on their cards. Each card has instructions about what moves can be made in the game when that card is used. *Yu-Gi-Oh!* is a form of Japanese 'anime', i.e. animated ('cartoon') characters and their stories shown in 'mangas' (comic books), television shows and movies. Japanese anime is now a worldwide phenomenon. If all this seems strange to you, that is all to the good.

Below I print part of the text on one card:

> When this card is Normal Summoned, Flip Summoned or Special Summoned successfully, select and activate one of the following effects: Select one equipped Equip Spell Card and destroy it. Select one equipped Equip Spell Card and equip it to this card.

What does this mean? Notice, first of all, that you, as a speaker of English, recognize each word in this text. But that does you very little good. You still do not really know what it means if you do not understand *Yu-Gi-Oh!*

So how would you find out what the text really means? Since we are all influenced a great deal by how school taught us to think about language, we are liable to think that the answer to this question is this: Look up what the words mean in some sort of dictionary or guide. But this does not help anywhere as much as you might think. There are websites where you can look up what the words and phrases on *Yu-Gi-Oh!* cards mean, and this is the sort of thing you see if you go to such websites:

> **Equip Spell Cards** are Spell Cards that *usually* change the ATK and/or DEF of a Monster Card on the field, and/or grant that Monster Card special ability(ies). They are universally referred to as **Equip Cards**, since Equip Cards can either be Equip Spell Cards or Trap Cards that are treated as Equip Cards after activation. When you activate an Equip Spell Card, you choose a face-up monster on the field to equip the card to, and that Equip Spell Card's effect applies to that monster until the card is destroyed or otherwise removed from the field. When the equipped monster is removed from the field or flipped face down, all the Equip Spell Cards equipped to that monster are destroyed. A fair few Equip Spell Cards are representations of weapons or armour. (http://yugioh.wikia.com/wiki/Equip_Spell_Cards)

Does this really help? If you do not understand the card, you do not understand this much better. And think how much more of this I would have to give you to explicate the whole text on the *Yu-Gi-Oh!* card, short though it is.

Why does it not help? Because, in general, if you do not understand some words, getting yet more of the same sorts of words does not help you to know what the original words mean. In fact, it is hard to understand words just by getting definitions (other words) or other sorts of verbal explanations. Even if we understand a definition, it only tells us the range of meanings a word has, it does not really tell us how to use the word appropriately in real contexts of use.

So if you had to learn what 'Yu-Gi-Oh! language' actually meant, how would you go about it? You probably would not choose to read lots of texts like the one above from the website. Even if you did, I assure you that you would still be lost if you actually had to play *Yu-Gi-Oh!*

The way you could best learn what the language on the card meant would be to learn to play the game of *Yu-Gi-Oh!*, not just read more text. How would you do this? You would watch and play games, let other players mentor you, play *Yu-Gi-Oh!* video games which coach you on how to play the game, watch *Yu-Gi-Oh!* television shows and movies which act out the game, and then, too, read things.

Why is this the best way to learn what the card means? Because, in this case, it is pretty clear that the language on the card gets its meaning from the game, from its rules and the ways players play the game. Language is used – together with other actions (remember language itself is a form of action) – to play (enact) the game as an activity or practice in the world.

The language on *Yu-Gi-Oh!* cards does not get its meaning first and foremost from definitions or verbal explanations, i.e. from other words. It gets its meaning from what it is used to do, in this case, play a game. This is language as doing.

However, *Yu-Gi-Oh!* is an activity – a way of doing things (in this case, playing a game) – because certain sorts of people take on certain sorts of identities, in this case identities as gamers and enthusiasts of certain sorts (here, fans of anime and anime card games, such as *Pokémon* and *Yu-Gi-Oh!* and others). This is language as being.

If there were no anime gamers/fans (being), then there would be no anime games and gaming (doing). If there were no anime gamers/fans and no anime games and gaming, then the words on the cards would be meaningless, there would be no saying (information). Saying follows, in language, from doing and being.

Is this *Yu-Gi-Oh!* example just strange and untypical? In this book I want to argue that it is actually typical of how language works. Its very strangeness allows us to see what we take for granted in examples of language with which we are much more famil-iar and where we have forgotten the roles of doing and being in language and remember only the roles of saying and communicating.

In the case of the language on the *Yu-Gi-Oh!* card, we said that the language on the card got its meaning, not from dictionaries or other words, but from a game and its rules and the things players do. In a sense, all language gets its meaning from a game, though we do not typically use the word 'game'. We use the more arcane word 'practice'.

A game is composed of a set of rules that determine winners and losers. Other activities, such as taking part in a committee meeting, a lecture, a political debate or 'small talk' among neighbours, are not games, but they are conducted according to certain 'rules' or conventions. These 'rules' or conventions do not determine winners and losers (usually), but they do determine who has acted 'appropriately' or 'normally' or not, and this in society can, indeed, be a type of winning and losing.

These sorts of activities – things like committee meetings, lectures, political debates and 'small talk' – are often called 'rules practices', though we could just as well use the word 'games' in an extended sense. This book will argue that all language – like *Yu-Gi-Oh!* Language – gets its meaning from the games or practices within which it is used. These games or practices are always ways of saying, doing and being.

Language and 'politics'

If you break the rules of *Yu-Gi-Oh!*, either you are playing the game incorrectly or you are attempting to change the rules. This can get you into trouble with other players. If you follow the rules, you are playing appropriately and others will accept you as a *Yu-Gi-Oh!* player, though not necessarily as a good one. If you follow the rules – and use them well to your advantage – you may win the game often and others will consider you a good player.

If you care about *Yu-Gi-Oh!* and want to be considered a player or even a good player, then having others judge you as a player or a good player is what I will call a 'social good'. Social goods are anything some people in a society want and value. Being considered a *Yu-Gi-Oh!* player or a good *Yu-Gi-Oh!* player is a social good for some people. In that case, how they play the game and how others accept their game play is important and consequential for them.

Above, I said that just as *Yu-Gi-Oh!* language is used to enact the game of *Yu-Gi-Oh!*, so too other forms of language are used to enact other 'games' or practices. Consider, for example, the practice ('game') of being a 'good student' in elementary school. In different classrooms and schools this game is played somewhat differently. And this game changes over time. What made someone a 'good student' in the seventeenth century in the United States – how 'good students' talked and behaved – is different than what makes someone a 'good student' today.

However, in each case, there are conventions (rules) about how 'good students' talk and behave ('good students' here being the ones teachers and school personnel say are 'good students', that is why the phrase is in quotes). Many children want to be accepted in this identity, just as some people want to be accepted as good *Yu-Gi-Oh!* players. Many parents want their children to be accepted as 'good students' as well. So being accepted as a 'good student' is, for these people, a social good.

In this sense, even though practices like being a 'good student' are not really games – their 'rules' or conventions are usually much less formal – there are still, in these practices, in a sense, 'winners' and 'losers'. The winners are people who want to be accepted as a 'good student' and gain such acceptance. The 'losers' are people who want such acceptance, but do not get it.

There are, as we have said, different practices – different 'games' – concerning how good students talk and act in different classrooms and schools. There are also people, like in the case of *Yu-Gi-Oh!*, who want to interpret the 'rules' differently or change them altogether. For example, should it be a 'rule' that 'good students' always closely follow the teacher's instructions or should 'good students' sometimes innovate and even challenge teachers? Is a student who asks a teacher how she knows something she has claimed to know being a 'good student' or a 'problem student'?

You may not want to be accepted as a *Yu-Gi-Oh!* player and perhaps you resisted being a 'good student' in school. Then these are not social goods for you. But some things are social goods for you. Perhaps, being accepted as an 'acceptable' ('normal', 'good', 'adequate') citizen, man or woman, worker, friend, activist, football fan, educated person, Native American, religious person, Christian, Jewish person or Islamic person, or what have you, is a social good for you.

The 'games' or practices where you want to 'win' (be accepted within them as 'acceptable' or 'good') are cases where social goods are at stake for you. In these cases, how you use language (and more generally how you say, do and be) and how people respond to you are deeply consequential to you and for you. If you get accepted – 'win' the game – you gain a social good. If you do not get fully accepted – 'lose' the game – you lose a social good.

People fight over the rules of *Yu-Gi-Oh!* in terms of what they really mean and how exactly they should be applied. People sometimes try to change the rules or agree to play by somewhat different rules. So, too, with practices in society. People fight over what the 'rules' for being a 'good student' ought to be. They sometimes seek to change them or to agree a new set of 'rules'. They fight over these things because important social goods are at stake.

Let's take a dramatic case to make the point clear. Marriage is a practice. There are formal and informal laws and conventions (rules) about how married people talk and act and how others talk and act with regard to marriage as an institution. Today, people fight over whether it is appropriate to talk about gay people being married to each other, whether they can rightly say they are married, and whether such marriages should be recognized in law or by the church.

For many gay people, a failure to use the language of marriage for their union with each other is to deny them a social good. They fight to interpret the rules – or change the rules – of marriage in ways that will allow them this social good. For many gay people, a different term, such as 'legal union', even if it gives all the same legal protections as marriage, is still unacceptable.

All forms of language – like *Yu-Gi-Oh!* language or the language we use in the practice of marriage – get their meaning from the games or practices they are used to enact. These games or practices determine who is 'acceptable' or 'good' – who is a 'winner' or 'loser' – in the game or practice. 'Winning' in these practices is often, for many people, a social good. Thus, in using language, social goods are always at stake, at least for some people. If no one cared about a game or practice anymore – no one saw being accepted as 'acceptable' or 'good' in the game or practice as important anymore – the game or practice would no longer have any social goods to offer and would cease to exist.

Thus, in using language, social goods are always at stake. When we speak or write, we always risk being seen as a 'winner' or 'loser' in a given game or practice. Furthermore, we can speak or write so as to accept others as 'winners' or 'losers' in the game or practice in which we are engaged. In speaking and writing then, we can both gain or lose and give or deny social goods. Gay people who say they are married to their partner are bidding for a social good. How we act out the 'game' of marriage practice in our society can give or deny them this social good. And how people talk about marriage or anything else is never just a decision about saying (informing), it is a decision about doing and being, as well.

Social goods are the stuff of politics. Politics is not just about contending political parties. At a much deeper level it is about how to distribute social goods in a society: who gets what in terms of money, status, power and acceptance on a variety of different terms, all social goods. Since, when we use language, social goods and their distribution are always at stake, language is always 'political' in a deep sense.

Two forms of discourse analysis: descriptive and 'critical'

Discourse analysis is the study of language in use. There are many different approaches to discourse analysis. Some of them look only at the 'content' of the language being used, the themes or issues being discussed in a conversation or a newspaper article, for example. Other approaches pay more attention to the structure of language ('grammar') and how this structure functions to make meaning in specific contexts. These approaches are rooted in the discipline of linguistics. This book is about one such approach.

Different linguistic approaches to discourse analysis use different theories of grammar and take different views about how to talk about meaning. The approach in this book looks at meaning as an integration of ways of saying (informing), doing (action) and being (identity), and grammar as a set of tools to bring about this integration. To take an example, consider the two sentences below:

(1) Hornworms sure vary a lot in how well they grow.
(2) Hornworm growth exhibits a significant amount of variation.

Sentence 1 is in a style of language (called the 'vernacular') we use when we want to talk as an 'everyday person', not as a specialist of any kind. This is the identity (being) it expresses. It is a way to express an opinion based on one's own observations (of hornworms in this case). This is an action (doing). The sentence can be used to do other actions as well, such as show surprise or entice someone to grow hornworms. The sentence is about hornworms, which are cute green caterpillars with little yellow horns. This is a part of what the sentence says (informing).

Sentence 2 is in a specialist style of language, one we would associate with biology and biologists. It expresses one's identity (being) as such a specialist. It is not just expressing an opinion based on one's observations of hornworms, it is making a claim based on statistical tests of 'significance' that are 'owned' and 'operated' by the discipline of biology, not any one person, including the speaker or writer. This is an action (doing). The sentence is not about hornworms, but 'hornworm growth', an abstract trait of hornworms (much less cute than hornworms). This is part of what the sentence says (informing).

The grammar (structure) of the two sentences is very different. In sentence 1, the subject of the sentence – which names the 'topic' of the sentence – is the noun 'hornworms'. But in sentence 2, the subject is the noun phrase 'hornworm growth'. 'Hornworm growth' is a noun phrase that expresses a whole sentence's worth of information ('hornworms grow') and is a much more complex structure than the simple noun 'hornworms'. It is a way to talk about an abstract trait of hornworms, and not the hornworms themselves. It is also part of what makes this language 'specialist' and not 'everyday'.

The phrase 'significant amount of variation' in sentence 2 uses an abstract noun ('variation') rather than the verb 'vary' in sentence 1 and combines this noun with 'significant amount'. So a process (varying) has been tuned into an abstract thing ('variation') that can be quantified using statistics ('significant amount'). This too, is, again, part of what makes this language 'specialist' and ties it to tools (such as statistical texts of significance) in a discipline and not just to an individual's observations of the world.

So the grammar of the two sentences offers us different ways to say things that amount to different ways of doing (actions) and being (identity). Looking closely at the structure of language as it is being used can help us uncover different ways of saying things, doing things and being things in the world.

But why would we want to do this? Some approaches to discourse analysis, which we can call 'descriptive', answer this question by saying that their goal is to describe how language works in order to understand it, just as the goal of the physicist is to describe how the physical world works in order to understand it. In both cases – the discourse analyst and the physicist – their hope may also be to offer deep explanations of how language or the world works and why they work in that way. Though their work may have practical applications in the world, these discourse analysts and physicists are not motivated by those applications.

Some other approaches to discourse analysis, which we can call 'critical' as in 'critical discourse analysis', answer this question differently. Their goal is not just to describe how language works or even to offer deep explanations, though they do want to do this. They also want to speak to and, perhaps, intervene in, social or political issues, problems and controversies in the world. They want to apply their work to the world in some fashion.

People who take a descriptive approach often think that a critical approach is 'unscientific' because the critical discourse analyst is swayed by his or her interest or passion for intervening in some problem in the world. People who take a critical approach often think that a purely descriptive approach is an evasion of social and political responsibility.

My view […] is that all discourse analysis needs to be critical, not because discourse analysts are or need to be political, but because language itself is, as we have discussed above, political. I have argued that any use of language gains its meaning from the 'game' or practice of which it is a part and which it is enacting. I have argued, as well, that such 'games' or practices inherently involve potential social goods and the distribution of social goods, which I have defined as central to the realm of 'politics'. Thus, any full description of any use of language will have to deal with 'politics'.

Beyond this general point, language is a key way we humans make and break our world, our institutions and our relationships through how we deal with social goods. Thus, discourse analysis can illuminate problems and controversies in the world. It can illuminate issues about the distribution of social goods, who gets helped and who gets harmed.

So, as an example, consider again sentences 1 and 2 and the variant in sentence 3, below. Note that it is odd – a bit funny – to say something like sentence 3:

(3) Hornworm growth sure exhibits a significant amount of variation.

Why is this odd? It mixes 'everyday language' ('sure') with specialist language. 'Sure' in sentence 1 is a way to express one's attitude and emotion about what one has observed about hornworms. The speaker is impressed and a bit surprised. Perhaps, the speaker is even showing enthusiasm for the hornworms he or she has raised. But the 'voice' of science – the 'voice' behind sentence 2 and most of sentence 3 – is not supposed to show attitude and emotion. It is supposed to be dispassionate, the voice of 'reason'. That is one of the 'rules' of the game of science.

Describing these 'rules' – explaining why sentence 3 is odd – is part of the job of any discourse analyst dealing with language like that in sentences 1–3. But then, we can also ask, in specific cases, is this claim to be 'dispassionate' being used for authentic scientific progress or as an evasion of one's own personal responsibility? (…)

In fact, we will see a case where such specialist language does, indeed, appear to be a way to hide and evade the ethical and emotional dilemmas of what was done in an experiment. Since this is part of the saying, doing, being going on in specific language in use, it is our responsibility as discourse analysts to study it, even though we are then having to make judgements with consequences in the world. In this sense, all discourse analysis is critical discourse analysis, since all language is political and all language is part of the way we build and sustain our world, cultures and institutions. So too then, all discourse analysis is 'practical' or 'applied', since it uncovers the workings – for good or ill – of this world building.

Jonathan Potter

Discourse and social psychology

Jonathan Potter (b. 1956) is an English social psychologist and professor of discourse analysis at Loughborough University, UK. He has established – together with Margaret Wetherell, Charles Antaki, Derek Edwards and, more recently, Elisabeth Stokoe and Alexa Hepburn – a school of Discourse Studies labelled 'discursive psychology'. Discursive psychology (also called the 'Loughborough School') draws on contributions to social psychology originally made by Henri Tajfel and elaborated by Michael Billig. Most importantly, discursive psychology rejects any cognitive theories (such as the theory of social representation by Serge Moscovici which has influenced Teun van Dijk and many other salient approaches to socio-cognition in the area of Discourse Studies). A most important publication which summarises discursive psychology is a book co-authored with Margaret Wetherell, *Discourse and Social Psychology* (1987). In sometimes heated debates with socio-cognitive discourse researchers, Potter and his collaborators maintain that traditional cognitive concepts, such as memory, attitude, stereotype, opinion, ideology and attribution, are not able to grasp authentic text and talk in context; all these concepts should, it is argued, be reformulated and re-theorised from a social-constructivist and discursive perspective. In contrast to socio-cognitive concepts, the concept of 'interpretive repertoires' is proposed to emphasise the interpretive and heteroglossic nature of interaction. After critically interrogating the role of attribution and attitudes (Edwards and Potter, 1992), Potter moved on to the analysis of spontaneous interactions while investigating police interrogations, help centres and other relevant institutional domains. More recently, discursive psychology has integrated ever more aspects of Conversational Analysis, so that the study of arguments, belief systems, opinions and ideologies has been backgrounded (but remained the focus of Billig, e.g. 1995) in contrast to detailed analyses of text and talk in interaction. The entry chosen for our Reader presents a summary of discursive psychology, juxtaposed with both quantitative and cognitive approaches to socio-psychology and discourse studies.

References

Billig, Michael. 1995. *Banal Nationalism*. London: Sage.
Edwards, Derek, and Jonathan Potter. 1992. *Discursive Psychology*. London: Sage.
Potter, Jonathan, and Margaret Wetherell. 1987. *Discourse and Social Psychology*. London: Sage.

Jonathan Potter. 2012. 'Re-reading Discourse and Social Psychology: Transforming Social Psychology.'
British Journal of Social Psychology 51(3): 436–455, selected 436–438, 442, 443–444, 446–447, 448–450.

In the early 1980s while the ideas that were formed into *Discourse and Social Psychology* (Potter and Wetherell, 1987) were being developed, social psychology in both the United Kingdom and North America was overwhelmingly based on experimental or questionnaire studies, most of them conducted on college students. At that time there were very few general texts on 'qualitative methods' in social science generally, and none in psychology. There was no use of open-ended interviews in psychology – although they were being used in ethnographic work in sociology and anthropology. There was no research using direct naturalistic records of interaction, although the use of indirect observational methods had been haltingly explored (Barker, 1968; Webb et al., 1966).

A so-called 'crisis in social psychology' had smouldered through the 1970s. In North America, the crisis focused on method and particularly the damaging role of 'demand characteristics', 'experimenter effects', the limited 'external validity' of laboratory experiments, and the difficulty of separating experimental findings from historical and cultural contexts (e.g. Elms, 1975; Gergen, 1973; McGuire, 1973). Self-styled 'European social psychology' supplemented these problems by highlighting the individualism of much social psychological research, its failure to adequately fit social psychological analysis to a broader social and political analysis, and its inadequate notions of causality (e.g. Harré and Secord, 1972; Israel and Tajfel, 1972; Schotter, 1975). The diagnosis and critique was in many ways brilliant and generated much debate. Yet it did not offer a fully realized research alternative to traditional approaches to social psychology. Rom Harré's (1979) 'ethogenic' perspective came closest to this, but did not build a sustained body of research studies. The success of *Discourse and Social Psychology* is at least partly due to its provision of a novel vision of how research might be done.

It was influenced by post-structuralist thinking (particularly the work of Roland Barthes and Michel Foucault). Such work had been earlier introduced into British psychology via the short-lived journal *Ideology and Consciousness* in the late 1970s and developed into a full perspective in the *Changing the Subject* (Henriques et al., 1984). The engagement of *Discourse and Social Psychology* with post-structuralism, however, came out of separate exploration which compared literary and social psychological constructions of human action (Potter et al., 1984). Post-structuralism offered tools for understanding the way language and meaning operated in social practices and, in particular, the complex constructive business done by ostensively straight descriptions, and it continues to be central in more ideological streams of discourse work (Wetherell, 1998).

At least as important as post-structuralism was an engagement with conversation analysis, ethnomethodology and linguistic philosophy (Coulter, 1979) and the sociology of scientific knowledge (itself stimulated by radical developments in philosophy of science derived from Popper, Kuhn and Feyerabend). Indeed, the version of discourse analysis drawn on in *Discourse and Social Psychology* did not come from linguistics (where there were already at least two analytic approaches called discourse analysis) but from Nigel Gilbert and Michael Mulkay's discourse analytic approach to the sociology of scientific knowledge (Gilbert and Mulkay, 1984; Mulkay et al., 1983). This introduced the notion of an 'interpretative repertoire' to describe the different kinds of accounts that scientists offered when they were justifying their own claims and explaining away the claims of competitors. A refined version of this became a central analytic tool in *Discourse and Social Psychology*.

Although *Discourse and Social Psychology* engaged with theory, metatheory and philosophy, it was distinctive in building its argument for a new way of doing social psychology on detailed, concrete analysis of actual discourse. As we will see, this distinctive, empirically driven, element in discourse analysis has sometimes been missed by critics working within social psychology who have focused on its constructionist or anti-foundationalist themes and have not appreciated how far this constructionism was married with careful empirical work on texts and talk (Potter, 1996). Some of the chapters worked with open-ended interviews, others primarily reworked analyses of real-life materials from everyday or institutional settings. Conversation analytic work was drawn heavily on for the analysis of mundane telephone calls, police interrogations and courtroom interaction – all records of interaction that would now be called 'naturalistic materials'. The *natural* is to mark the contrast from the 'got up' materials that have been at the centre of social psychology's development in North America and much of Europe – vignettes, experimental protocols, survey responses – while natural is qualified as *naturalistic* to highlight a sophisticated awareness of the potential for researcher involvement in such material (Potter, 2002).

Discourse and Social Psychology offered a complete approach to social psychological matters. It took the chapter headings of the textbooks of the time – attitudes, categories, and so on – and developed alternative analyses that often completely rebuilt the original notions. The aim of this paper is to offer something of an audit of the coherence and success of one major strand of discursive psychology after more than a quarter of a century. A full description of the different strands of this work is beyond the scope of this paper, let alone a full evaluation. Part of the problem here is that discourse work has been evolving with different emphases and as parts of different debates over this quarter century and the different critical responses have a range of specific targets. Inevitably, this audit of arguments and issues will engage in considerable simplification. (…)

Human action is contingent and voluntary. This need not be a philosophical point but reflects the normative organization of interaction which is a central and analytically tractable topic of discursive work and conversation analysis (Potter and Edwards, 2012; Schegloff, 2007). For example, requests are conventional and necessarily highly recognizable forms of action. If they cannot be recognized, they will not work as requests. They do not, however, *cause* what happens next in the way wind might cause a tree to bend. A request sets up at least two contrasting alternatives for the recipient – granting and rejecting. These options are systematically provided for in the design of the request and typically ordered such that acceptances are 'preferred', and therefore done differently, to declinations. Indeed, requests can be designed to display increasing levels of entitlement over the actions of another and to orient to different levels of contingency of the recipient being able to grant the request (Curl and Drew, 2008). This intricate social order is analysable in its detail and such analyses are repeatable and open to public scrutiny.

The general point here is that *statistical* relationships, even highly significant ones derived from experiments, need to be treated cautiously when considering what is implied by causality. Crucially, *contingent* relationships within action sequences are open to systematic analysis. Moreover, as Manstead notes when responding to the kinds of critical points raised in the 'crisis in social psychology', statistically significant effects may be very small. Discursive psychological work can identify clear and regular patterns, which can sometimes be in direct conflict with claims based on experimental work (see e.g. Edwards and Potter, 1999; Schmid and Fiedler, 1999). Ruling discourse work out on the basis of not studying 'causality' is surely based on a limited view of the processes that are amenable to scientific study and mixing together what is shown by a statistical experimental finding and the figuration of billiard balls and mechanical processes (Harré, 1989). (…)

Interviews

One of the features of *Discourse and Social Psychology* was its introduction of a new way of working with open-ended interviews. It suggested that interviews might be more effective if they were more engaged and even confrontative rather than trying to chase an impossible ideal of neutrality. Such engagement might bring into the open the varied interpretative resources (interpretative repertoires) drawn on by participants. Rather than simply interviewing participants about their lives or beliefs, the interview was intended to become an arena of ideological engagement where the different resources participants had available to manage ideological trouble could be identified and described. Such work with interviews is laborious, involving careful attention to the detail of constructions in the talk of both interviewer and interviewee. It emphasized that both parties would be drawing on ideologically live resources and the interviewees talk would need to be analysed in the context of analysis of the talk of the interviewer. The interview was conceived as an interactional laboratory for driving ideological resources out into the open and laying bare their organization rather than a pathway to the participants' past actions, experiences or opinions. This way of working with interviews was central to Wetherell, and Potter (1992) and they have been used in similar effective ways by, for example, Billig (1992) and Augoustinos, Tuffin, and Rapley (1999). For a cumulative body of work see Tileagă's (2005, 2009, 2011) important work on remembering, history and commemoration works with interviews and texts such as letters.

Since 1987, interviews (and sometimes focus groups) have become the default data generation method for a wide range of qualitative researchers from different perspectives in social psychology (e.g. ethnography, interpretative phenomenological analysis, narrative psychology, grounded theory and psychoanalysis). *Discourse and Social Psychology* undoubtedly played its part in this proliferation. Yet as Knorr Cetina's (1999) work showed, in other sciences there is a strong, careful reflexive attention to the operation of the machineries for data generation. This has been notably lacking with respect to interviews in social science generally and social psychology in particular. Open-ended interviews present many dangerous opportunities for conducting poorly analysed research backed by illustrative quotes shorn of their interactional context (Antaki et al., 2003; Silverman, 2011).

For some time, work in conversation analysis has focused on explicating the organization of questions and answers in a range of different institutional settings, including news interviews (e.g. Clayman and Heritage, 2002), court rooms (e.g. Atkinson and Drew, 1979), police interrogations (e.g. Stokoe and Edwards, 2010), psychological assessment interviews (Antaki and Rapley, 1996), and focus groups (Puchta and Potter, 2002), as well as in mundane settings such as everyday phone calls and family mealtimes (Heritage and Raymond, 2012; Stivers and Hayashi, 2010). This work highlights the extraordinary delicacy and complexity of questioning as a practice and the way it can embody preferences, manage neutralism, establish presuppositions and build a range of constraints that the recipient must manage (e.g. Raymond, 2003). On the one hand, this body of work highlights the bluntness of traditional notions of 'bias' and 'leading questions' in the social science methods literature. On the other, it highlights and describes the powerful role of the interviewer's questions in generating particular kinds of responses. The implications of these and other problems for qualitative work in psychology and the social sciences more broadly are profound and have been developed elsewhere (Edwards and Stokoe, 2004; Potter and Hepburn, 2005; Potter and Hepburn, 2005; Potter and Hepburn, 2007; Stokoe, 2011). They provide an important motive for discursive psychologists focusing on naturalistic materials. Ironically, although interviews were often lauded by 'qualitative researchers' as an advance over questionnaires, they are in many ways similar machineries guided by the agenda of the researcher (Attenborough and Stokoe, 2012). (...)

Experience, cognition, and the 'blank subjectivity' critique

One thing that distinguishes the conversation analytic influenced strand of discursive psychology from experimental work, and approaches based on qualitative interviews such as the 'free association narrative method' or 'interpretative phenomenological analysis' (Hollway and Jefferson, 2005; Smith and Osborn, 2008) is that it puts participants own orientations at the heart of its analysis. These are the live orientations that are practical parts of conduct unfolding in real time. This is a completely different order of phenomena to the *post-hoc* constructions and formulations that appear in qualitative interviews. Those are a major focus for discourse work on the organization of repertoires, commonplaces and constructions that are parts of actions – and they can be exploited when the research attends carefully to their role in practices in the interviews themselves (e.g. Condor, 2006; Tileagă, 2010).

The focus on orientations in real time in natural interaction makes 'psychological' matters inescapable; such matters are an essential resource for participants as they coordinate their actions, respond to expressions of liking and dislike, say, or as they manage incipient actions such as invitations or requests. The world of discourse is psychologically imbued in precisely the way real life is imbued. The organization of discourse with its lexical items, categories, grammatical organizations and plethora of different practices is highly normative. Moreover, it unfolds in real time with an extraordinary granularity in which delays of less than a fifth of a second, or minor changes in pitch contour, can mark a 'psychological state' (Drew, 2005; Heritage, 2005). The point, of course, as Wittgenstein argued so eloquently is that psychological business is necessarily hearable/visible, otherwise participants would not be able to coordinate with one another effectively (Coulter, 2008). The delicacy of this real time working of interaction is particularly difficult to capture experimentally (see Schegloff, 2004; Schegloff, 2006, on the insufficiency of cognitive models of dialogue), and it is a probably impossible challenge for qualitative interview-based approaches.

As conversation analysis has effectively demonstrated in a cumulative empirical programme for more than 50 years, turn organization supplies a key resource for understanding other people; indeed, Schegloff has suggested that it is a major resource for sustaining intersubjectivity and the practices of conversational repair can be seen as ways of (re)accomplishing intersubjectivity when it is under threat (Schegloff, 1992). More recently, classical psychological problems of shared knowledge – who knows what and how is knowledge shared – have been tackled in subtle ways (see papers in Stivers et al., 2011). Psychological matters are here studied in their home environment of live unconstrained interaction where the parties have a genuine and practical stake in outcomes (Edwards, 2006).

Far from blank subjectivity, then, the subjectivity that is live for participants is one that is voiced, expressed, sequentially organized. It is as rich as the lexical, intonational and sequential resources of interaction can allow. This is one of the reasons for emphasizing the virtues of both naturalistic materials and the careful transcription of interaction that can capture this linguistic theatre of the self (see Potter and Hepburn, 2005). As Billig (1999) argued, there is something problematic about those with a psychodynamic interest, for example, looking for hidden motives behind discourse and simultaneously failing to look carefully at what is actually there. Given participants treat prosody, delay, laughter and other features of delivery as crucial in their treatment of the psychological states of others, it is odd for social psychologists to argue that they do not need to take such things seriously in their materials (e.g. Hollway, 2005; Smith, 2005). Again, this emphasizes how vital it is for social psychologists to systematically study the machinery that generates their findings. If researchers interview people about their experience, then what is the status of this interview talk? Given that much 'cognitive' language is orientated to action, how will those actions be suppressed in favour of mere description when talking to a social researcher? These are generic issues that were highlighted in *Discourse and Social Psychology* in its discussion of a range of social psychological methods; but they are exaggerated with qualitative research interviews about 'experience' (Potter, 2012) (…)

A matrix of social psychological issues

In this brief final section, I will make some observations about the domain of social psychology. Some responses to *Discourse and Social Psychology* and the traditions of work that it generated suggested that it was interesting and yet more relevant in another discipline – linguistics or sociology, say, or even literary criticism. We can now see that, far from having an only oblique relation to social psychology, discourse work can claim to have made a profound contribution and has played a role in redefining the discipline. The work of Martha Augoustinos, Michael Billig, Margaret Wetherell, and others, on ideological matters and the way social organizations are legitimated and intergroup differences are disguised is now well established (see papers in Potter, 2007). Let me end by sketching the way more recent work offers a novel approach to core social psychological matters.

Key here is the way discourse work and, in particular, recent discursive psychology deals with direct records of actual people interacting with one another in real time, and its analysis situates that interaction within the social, physical and institutional contexts of what is going on as these things become live and relevant in the interaction. It would be hard to argue against this being a core, maybe even foundational, domain for a distinctively social psychology.

Take the traditional social psychological field of social influence. Typical social influence work considered the operation of variables such as credibility, status and information on the behaviour of individuals. Discourse work has taken a rather different path that has considered concrete situations where something that might be seen as influence takes place, that is, where individuals attempt to change the conduct of other individuals. Some form of influence is part of a range of practices that can be described using vernacular action descriptions such as requests, offers, admonishments, threats, complaints and advice. Studies of such practices have identified a range of often shared considerations that cut across the different practices.

Curl and Drew (2008) studied requests in environments such as after hours medical services or call centres that manage non-emergency calls to the police. Requests are actions where one party aims to modify the conduct of another. They noted that requests are build differently according (a) to the displayed entitlement of the request issuer to receive what the request demands and (b) to the contingencies the request recipient faces in delivering what is requested. Request forms thus become more presumptuous when the person requesting claims high entitlement and treats the recipient as likely to be able to comply with the request (low contingency). Thus 'I was wondering if...' prefaced requests display less entitlement than 'could you...' prefaced requests.

Craven and Potter (2010) extended this analysis to consider the nature of actions where one party directly directs the behaviour of another, using material from family mealtimes. A feature of these was that they did not use 'I was wondering if...' prefaces (which we might see in a call to an out of hours surgery where the caller is showing low entitlement to a home visit and orienting to the contingency of the doctor being able to perform such a visit). Neither did they use the kinds of constructions typical of requests that orient to the wants or abilities of the recipient – 'do you *want* to come to dinner', '*could* you come over on Saturday'. Rather, directives embodied *no* orientation to the recipients' desires or capacities: 'put that down', 'hold that with two hands'. There is also a subtle shift in the appropriate next action for a directive. While, for a request, the appropriate next action is acceptance, for a directive it is compliance.

Now contrast both requests and directives with advice. Here again one party is managing the behaviour of another. Heritage and Sefi (1992) noted that advice is normative – it is offering a course of action that *should* be followed. As a social institution advice builds a stance of disinterest, in contrast to requests which orient to the needs or requirements of the person who has issued the request. Advice is also epistemically asymmetric – the advice giver builds themselves as more knowledgeable than the advice recipient. This asymmetry can be worked with in various institutional situations.

For example, Butler, Potter, Danby, Emmison and Hepburn (2010) studied the way advice on a child support line was regularly delivered using interrogative grammar – 'have you thought about talking to a teacher?' Such constructions manage the asymmetry. The counsellor builds a picture of the caller's situation, but also provides a softened indication of appropriate action. This highlights a relevant and possibly appropriate action yet allows the child to follow the advice or not by fitting it to her or his particular circumstances. In contrast, Hepburn and Potter (2011) consider situations on a child protection helpline where advice is being resisted. Callers may use the detailed knowledge of their situation to resist the advice while the call takers can use generic social work knowledge or broader idioms and commonplaces – 'your child's health has got to come first', 'grown-ups have got to be grown up'.

What we see then is that these actions, all of which involve some kind of behaviour modification or social influence, orient to a set of core dimensions, notably entitlement, contingency, relative knowledge and the interests of the parties. All of these are live, oriented to, and relevant at different points as the practices unfold. The lexical and grammatical resources of a language, the different possibilities for delivery, and the physical affordances of the environment are used to build the specific action with specific implications for the recipient. Crucially, they are not factors that exert a simple causal influence; they are dimensions that participants orient to as they build their activities and respond to activities of others. Thus, this is a possible matrix for understanding core issues in a social psychology that is built up from observation of 'everyday lives, as they happen'. (…)

References

Antaki, C., M. Billig, D. Edwards, and J. Potter. 2003. 'Discourse analysis means doing analysis: A critique of six analytic shortcomings.' *Discourse Analysis Online* 1.

Antaki, C., and M. Rapley. 1996. ''Quality of life' talk: The liberal paradox of psychological testing.' *Discourse & Society* 7: 293–316. DOI: 10.1177/0957926596007003002

Atkinson, J. M., and P. Drew. 1979. *Order in Court: The Organization of Verbal Interaction in Juridical Settings*. London: Macmillan.

Attenborough, F., and E. Stokoe. 2012. 'Student life; student identity; student experience: Ethnomethodological methods for pedagogical matters.' *Psychology Learning & Teaching* 11, no. 1: 6–21. DOI: 10.2304/plat.2012.11.1.6

Augoustinos, M., K. Tuffin, and M. Rapley. 1999. 'Genocide or a failure to gel? Racism, history and nationalism in Australian talk.' *Discourse and Society* 10: 351–78. DOI: 10.1177/0957926599010003004

Barker, R. G. 1968. *Ecological Psychology: Concepts and Methods for Studying the Environment of Human Behavior*. Stanford: Stanford University Press.

Billig, M. 1999. *Freudian Repression: Conversation Creating the Unconscious*. Cambridge: Cambridge University Press.

Billig, M. 1992. *Talking of the Royal Family*. London: Routledge. DOI: 10.4324/9780203414910

Butler, C., J. Potter, S. Danby, M. Emmison, and A. Hepburn. 2010. 'Advice implicative interrogatives: Building 'client centred' support in a children's helpline.' *Social Psychology Quarterly* 73: 265–87. DOI: 10.1177/0190272510379838

Clayman, S., and J. C. Heritage. 2002. *The News Interview: Journalists and Public Figures on the Air*. Cambridge: Cambridge University Press. DOI: 10.1017/CBO9780511613623

Condor, S. 2006. 'Temporality and collectivity: Diversity, history and the rhetorical construction of national entitativity.' *British Journal of Social Psychology* 45: 657–82. DOI: 10.1348/014466605X82341

Coulter, J. 1979. *The Social Construction of Mind: Studies in Ethnomethodology and Linguistic Philosophy*. London: Macmillan.

Coulter, J. 2008. 'Twenty-five theses against cognitivism.' *Theory, Culture & Society* 25: 19–32. DOI: 10.1177/0263276407086789

Craven, A., and J. Potter. 2010. 'Directives: Contingency and Entitlement in Action.' *Discourse Studies* 12: 1–24. DOI: 10.1177/1461445610370126

Curl, T., and P. Drew. 2008. 'Contingency and Action: A Ccomparison of Two Forms of Requesting.' *Research on Language and Social Interaction* 41: 129–53. DOI: 10.1080/08351810802028613

Drew, P. 2005. 'Is confusion a state of mind?'. In *Conversation and Cognition*, edited by H. te Molder and J. Potter, 161–83. Cambridge: Cambridge University Press. DOI: 10.1017/CBO9780511489990.008

Edwards, D. 2006. 'Discourse, cognition and social practices.' *Discourse Studies* 8, no. 1: 41–49. DOI: 10.1177/1461445606059551

Edwards, D., and J. Potter. 1999. 'Language and causal attribution.' *Theory and Psychology* 9: 849–63. DOI: 10.1177/0959354399096006

Edwards, D., and E. Stokoe. 2004. 'Discursive psychology, focus group interviews, and participants' categories.' *British Journal of Developmental Psychology* 22: 499–507. DOI: 10.1348/0261510042378209

Elms, A. C. 1975. 'The crisis of confidence in social psychology.' *American Psychologist* 30: 967–76. DOI: 10.1037/0003-066X.30.10.967

Gergen, K. J. 1973. 'Social psychology as history.' *Journal of Personality and Social Psychology* 26: 309–20. DOI: 10.1037/h0034436

Gilbert, G. N., and M. Mulkay. 1984. *Opening Pandora's box: A Sociological Analysis of Scientists' Discourse*. Cambridge: Cambridge University Press.

Harré, R. 1989. 'Language games and the texts of identity.' In *Texts of Identity*, edited by J. Shotter and K. J. Gergen. London: Sage.

Harré, R. 1979. *Social being: A Theory for Social Psychology*. Oxford: Basil Blackwell.

Harré, R., and P. F. Secord. 1972. *The Explanation of Social Behaviour*. Oxford: Blackwell.

Henriques, J., W. Hollway, C. Urwin, C. Venn, and V. Walkerdine. 1984. *Changing the Subject: Psychology, Social Regulation and Subjectivity*. London: Methuen.

Hepburn, A., and J. Potter. 2011. 'Designing the recipient: Some practices that manage advice resistance in institutional settings.' *Social Psychology Quarterly* 74: 216–41. DOI: 10.1177/0190272511408055

Heritage, J. C. 2005. 'Cognition in discourse.' In *Conversation and Cognition*, edited by H. Te Molder and J. Potter, 184–202. Cambridge: Cambridge University Press. DOI: 10.1017/CBO9780511489990.009

Heritage, J. C., and S. Sefi. 1992. 'Dilemmas of advice: Aspects of the delivery and reception of advice in interactions between health visitors and first time mothers.' In *Talk at Work*, edited by P. Drew and J. C. Heritage, 359–419. Cambridge: Cambridge University Press.

Heritage, J., and G. Raymond. 2012. 'Navigating Epistemic Landscapes: Acquiescence, Agency and Resistance in Responses to Polar Question.' In *Questions: Formal, Functional and Interactional Perspectives*, edited by J. P. de Ruiter, 179–92. Cambridge: Cambridge University Press. DOI: 10.1017/CBO9781139045414.013

Hollway, W. 2005. 'Commentary.' *Qualitative Research in Psychology* 2: 312–14.

Hollway, W., and T. Jefferson. 2005. 'Panic and perjury: A psycho-social exploration of agency.' *British Journal of Social Psychology* 44: 1–18. DOI: 10.1348/014466604X23518

Israel, J., and H. Tajfel. 1972. *The Context of Social Psychology: A Critical Assessment*. London: Academic Press.

Knorr-Cetina, K. 1999. *Epistemic Cultures: How Scientists Make Knowledge*. Cambridge: Cambridge University Press.

McGuire, W. J. 1973. 'The Yin and Yang of progress in social psychology: Seven Koan.' *Journal of Personality and Social Psychology* 26: 446–57. DOI: 10.1037/h0034345

Mulkay, M., J. Potter, and S. Yearley. 1983. 'Why an analysis of scientists' discourse is needed.' In *Science observed: Perspectives in the social study of science*, edited by K. Knorr-Cetina and M. Mulkay, 171–203. London: Sage.

Potter, J. 2012. 'Discourse analysis and discursive psychology.' In *APA handbook of research methods in psychology: Vol. 2. Quantitative, Qualitative, Neuropsychological and Biological*, edited by H. Cooper, 111–30. Washington: American Psychological Association Press.

Potter, J. 2007. *Discourse and Psychology: Volume II. Discourse and Social Psychology*. London: Sage.

Potter, J. 1996. *Representing reality: Discourse, Rhetoric and Social Construction*. London: Sage.

Potter, J. 2002. 'Two kinds of natural.' *Discourse Studies* 4: 539–42. DOI: 10.1177/14614456020040040901

Potter, J., and D. Edwards. 2012. 'Conversation analysis and psychology.' In *The Handbook of Conversation Analysis*, edited by J. Sidnell and T. Stivers, 701–25. Oxford: Blackwell. DOI: 10.1002/9781118325001.ch35

Potter, J., and A. Hepburn. 2005. 'Action, interaction and interviews – Some responses to Hollway, Mischler and Smith.' *Qualitative Research in Psychology* 2: 319–25. DOI: 10.1191/1478088705qp045oa

Potter, J., and A. Hepburn. 2007. 'Life is out there: A comment on Griffin.' *Discourse & Society* 9: 277–83.

Potter, J., and A. Hepburn. 2005. 'Qualitative interviews in psychology: Problems and possibilities.' *Qualitative Research in Psychology* 2: 281–307. DOI: 10.1191/1478088705qp045oa

Potter, J., P. Stringer, and M. Wetherell. 1984. *Social Texts and Context: Literature and Social Psychology*. London: Routledge & Kegan Paul.

Potter, J., and M. Wetherell. 1987. *Discourse and Social Psychology: Beyond Attitudes and Behaviour*. London: Sage.

Puchta, C., and J. Potter. 2002. 'Manufacturing individual opinions: Market research focus groups and the discursive psychology of attitudes.' *British Journal of Social Psychology* 41: 345–63. DOI: 10.1348/014466602760344250

Raymond, G. 2003. 'Grammar and social organisation: Yea/no interrogatives and the structure of responding.' *American Sociological Review* 68: 939–67. DOI: 10.2307/1519752

Schegloff, E. A. 2006. 'On possibles.' *Discourse Studies* 8: 141–57. DOI: 10.1177/1461445606059563

Schegloff, E. A. 2004. 'Putting the interaction back into dialogue.' *Behavioural and Brain Sciences* 27: 207–08.

Schegloff, E. A. 1992. 'Repair after next turn: The last structurally provided defence of intersubjectivity in conversation.' *American Journal of Sociology* 98: 1295–345. DOI: 10.1086/229903

Schegloff, E. A. 2007. *Sequence Organization in Interaction: Volume 1: A Primer in Conversation Analysis*. Cambridge: Cambridge University Press. DOI: 10.1017/CBO9780511791208

Schmid, J., and K. Fiedler. 1999. 'A parsimonious theory can account for complex phenomena: A discursive analysis of Edwards and Potter's critique of nondiscursive language research.' *Theory and Psychology* 9, no. 6: 807–22. DOI: 10.1177/0959354399096005

Schotter, J. 1975. *Images of Man in Psychological Research*. London: Sage.

Silverman, D. 2011. *Interpreting Qualitative Data*. London: Sage.

Smith, J. A. 2005. 'Advocating pluralism.' *Qualitative Research in Psychology* 2: 309–12. DOI: 10.1191/1478088705qp046cm

Smith, J. A., and M. Osborn. 2008. 'Interpretative phenomenological analysis.' In *Qualitative psychology: A Practical Guide to Methods*, edited by J. A. Smith. London: Sage.

Stivers, T., and M. Hayashi. 2010. 'Transformative answers: One way to resist a questions's constraints.' *Language in Society* 39: 1–25. DOI: 10.1017/S0047404509990637

Stivers, T., L. Mondada, and J. Steensig. 2011. *The Morality of Knowledge in Conversation*. Cambridge: Cambridge University Press. DOI: 10.1017/CBO9780511921674

Stokoe, E. 2011. 'Simulated interaction and communication skills training: The 'Conversation Analytic Role-play Method.' In *Applied Conversation Analysis: Changing Institutional Practices*, edited by C. Antaki. Basingstoke: Palgrave Macmillan.

Stokoe, E., and D. Edwards. 2010. 'Asking ostensibly silly questions in police interrogations.' In *Why do you ask? The Function of Questions in Institutional Discourse*, edited by A. F. Freed and S. Ehrlich, 108–32. Oxford: Oxford University Press.

Tileagă, C. 2005. 'Accounting for extreme prejudice and legitimating blame in talk about the Romanies.' *Discourse & Society* 16: 603–24. DOI: 10.1177/0957926505054938

Tileagă, C. 2010. 'Cautious morality: Public accountbility, moral order and accounting for a conflict of interest.' *Discourse Studies* 12, no. 2: 223–39. DOI: 10.1177/1461445609356501

Tileagă, C. 2011. '(Re)writing biography: Memory, identity and textually-mediated reality in coming to terms with the past.' *Culture & Psychology* 17: 197–215. DOI: 10.1177/1354067X11398315

Tileagă, C. 2009. 'The social organization of representations of history: The textual accomplishment of coming to terms with the past.' *British Journal of Social Psychology* 48: 337–55. DOI: 10.1348/014466608X349487

Webb, E. J., D. T. Campbell, R. D. Schwartz, and L. Sechrest. 1966. *Unobtrusive Measures: Non-Reactive Research in the Social Sciences*. Chicago: RandMcNally.

Wetherell, M. 1998. 'Positioning and interpretative repertoires: Conversation analysis and post-structuralism in dialogue.' *Discourse & Society* 9: 387–412. DOI: 10.1177/0957926598009003005

Wetherell, M., and J. Potter. 1992. *Mapping the Language of Racism: Discourse and the Legitimation of Exploitation*. New York: Columbia University Press.

Section V

Sociopragmatics

Introduction

This section is dedicated to an approach to discourse that we call 'sociopragmatics'. In reality, such a label is not used by the authors of the texts who are presented here and there is no consensus in the area of discourse studies on what it refers to. For example, Paltridge claims that sociopragmatics is a basic notion of cross-cultural pragmatics; in his view, sociopragmatics is the study of 'specific conditions of language use; that is, the pragmatic performance of speech acts in specific social and cultural contexts' (2006:68). Leech (1983) divides the field of pragmatics into three areas: *general pragmatics*, focusing on the general conditions of language use, *pragmalinguistics*, focusing on the resources of a given language, and *sociopragmatics*, related to sociology, which focuses on the local conditions of linguistic communication. In his view, sociopragmatics can be considered as 'the sociological interface of pragmatics' (Leech, 1983:10). From this perspective, one can say that, by its nature, discourse analysis has a sociopragmatic dimension: most theorists consider discourse practices as social activities and draw on a pragmatic conception of language. This sociopragmatic trend overlaps with socially-oriented fields, such as sociolinguistics and Critical Discourse Analysis, which focus on the way situational contexts engender norms which speakers engage in or exploit for pragmatic purposes.

In this section, 'sociopragmatics' does not refer to a discipline or an area of pragmatics. Considering it as a sociologically-oriented specification of pragmatics, we give a narrower meaning to this term, which allows us to characterize a kind of approach to discourse that gives priority (1) to the resources and constraints of the linguistic system, (2) to institutional settings, in particular discourse genres. Indeed, implicitly or explicitly, discourse analysts whose research is sociopragmatically-oriented usually agree on the idea that the notion of genre plays a key role in their research. They refuse to reflect upon discourse practices without taking into account the linguistic properties of the texts (be them oral or written) that those practices make possible, or to reflect on texts without taking into account the communication settings they are part of. Therefore, such approaches differ from Conversation Analysis and from linguistic approaches that aim to describe the cohesion and coherence of texts; they also differ from sociological approaches that give priority to the institutional frame or the social situation of utterances, or psychology-oriented ones that pay little attention to the specific constraints of the linguistic system.

Sociopragmatic trends are well developed internationally, but it is no surprise that their leading authors have European origins. From its beginnings, European discourse analysis has been particularly interested in societal institutions, whereas in the U.S. discourse analysts have focused more on conversations.

This sociopragmatic conception of genre is very common in the area of discourse analysis, which by its nature attempts to articulate the constraints imposed by language and the constraints imposed by institutions. The main difficulty for scholars who claim that there is a specific 'order of discourse' (Foucault, 1981[1971]) lies in how to maintain a balance between sociological or psychological and linguistic aspects. In discourse analysis, the notion of genre is polysemous. There are many ways of classifying discourse practices, since the classification criteria may be quite diverse: in particular, linguistic criteria (the linguistic properties of texts), situational criteria (the circumstances in which speech events take place) and discursive criteria (criteria which combine linguistic, functional or situational features, e.g. what is known as the 'popularization' of science implies specific linguistic proceedings, specific didactic purposes, specific places of production, circulation and consumption of texts). From a sociopragmatic viewpoint, as a rule, the category of 'discourse genre' is defined by situational criteria. Discourse genres are thus considered to be sociohistorically constrained and changing communication devices to which metaphors such as 'contract', 'ritual' and 'game' can be easily applied.

The notion of genre originally comes from ancient Greece, in particular from the *Poetics* and *Rhetoric* of Aristotle. For more than 2,000 years, genres have been almost exclusively studied within the realm of literature and rhetoric; meanwhile the genres of everyday life have been largely unexplored. For some decades, particularly under the influence of the ethnography of communication and of Mikhail Bakhtin's explorations in genres (1986), the notion of discourse genre has been used for analyzing the manifold sorts of utterances produced in society: newspapers, talk shows on TV, transactions in shops, etc. They are characterized by criteria such as roles, goals, medium and text organization. Many of these descriptions have been influenced by the well-known 'S.P.E.A.K.I.N.G.' model formulated by D. Hymes (1972), the most prominent figure in the ethnography of communication: S ('Setting' and 'Scene'), P ('Participants'), E ('Ends'), A ('Act Sequence' = what happens first, second, etc.), K ('Key' tone, manner of the speech activity), I ('Instrumentalities' style, register), N ('Norms'), G ('Genre').

The favourite genres of sociopragmatic discourse analysis are institutional (political meetings, interviews, business negotiations, lectures, newspapers, etc.). These genres best correspond to a definition of discourse genre as a socially and historically constrained communication device: the roles played by the speakers are set a priori and, as a rule, remain stable during the process of communication. The participants enter a pre-established frame which, generally, they do not modify. Their parameters result from the stabilization of the speech constraints involved in specific social situations. But these genres have a wide range: at one end are ritualized genres, which leave speakers very little room for manoeuvre (juridical genres, for example); at the other end are genres which offer many possibilities for personal variation.

This conception of discourse genre cannot be used easily to study conversation, which is not closely related to institutions, roles or stable scripts. The text organization and content of ordinary conversations are usually rather fuzzy; their pragmatic frame, the relation between the participants, is constantly evolving during interaction. Thus, for Schegloff, conversation is that organisation of talk which is not subject to functionally specific or context-specific restrictions or specialised practices of conventionalised arrangements (1999: 407). One could say that *horizontal* and *local* constraints prevail in conversations: the participants are constantly negotiating their roles, whereas the constraints of institutional genres are predominantly *global* and *vertical*, that is to say, imposed by the 'place' of the participants. But, obviously, this distinction between conversation and institutional genres is not clear-cut: particularly in the case of ritualized conversations, verbal practices that have the properties of both regimes can be easily found. Moreover, both kinds of speech activity can be used in the same speech event.

The texts presented in this section come from various areas: the systemic functional model (Halliday, van Leeuwen), rhetoric and French enunciative pragmatics (Amossy), linguistic pragmatics and German functionalism (Ehlich). The texts by Swales and Charaudeau cannot be referred to as a specific current in linguistics; their viewpoint is typically sociopragmatic. While their research focuses on genres, they aim at articulating language and communication settings. But whereas Swales draws on sociology to work out the concept of discourse community, Charaudeau draws on social psychology to look into how speakers build strategies to achieve their goals.

Actually, one cannot say that the systemic-functional model of the British linguist M. A. K. Halliday belongs to discourse analysis. But it has been very influential, not only on discourse analysts from Great Britain but also on those from other English-speaking countries. The term *systemic* refers to a view of language as 'a network of systems' (for example mood, theme, agency etc.), which are interrelated sets of options for making meaning. Halliday rejects explicitly the claims about language from generative linguistics, which developed during the 1960s and 70s. His grammar does not only claim to be *systemic*, it wants to be *systemic functional*: for him, the study of language needs to be grounded in functional analysis, since language carries out certain functions, which are necessary for human beings. Like Halliday, K. Ehlich is not, strictly speaking, a discourse analyst: he is a linguist who brings to the fore the functions of language that are supposed to explain its structure. By drawing on these functions, he refuses to separate the analysis of the linguistic system from the social activities that the system makes possible.

References

Bakhtin, Mikhail. 1986. *Speech Genres and Other Late Essays*. Trans. by Vern W. McGee. Austin, Texas: University of Texas Press.

Foucault, Michel. 1981[1971]. 'The order of discourse'. In: *Untying the Text: A Poststructuralist Reader*, edited by R. Young, 48–78. Boston: Routledge and Kegan Paul.

Hymes, Dell Hathaway. 1972. 'Models of Interaction of Language and Social Life'. In *Directions in Sociolinguistics. The Ethnography of Communication*, edited by John J. Gumperz and Dell H. Hymes, 35–71. New York: Holt, Rinehart & Winston.

Leech, Geoffrey. 1983. *Principles of Pragmatics*. London: Longman.

Paltridge, Brian. 2006. *Discourse Analysis*. London, New York: Continuum.

Michael Alexander Kirkwood Halliday

Language as social semiotic

The British linguist M. A. K. Halliday (b. 1925, moved to Australia in 1976) is associated with the 'systemic-functional' model. Halliday focuses on the relationship between the linguistic system and the social structure within a theory of 'social semiotics'. The purpose of social semiotics is to study signifying practices in social and cultural contexts, to analyse human meaning-making as a social practice. In the 1970s, discourse analysis was still not identified as such. If Halliday in this text claims to be a 'sociolinguist' and the term 'discourse' does not yet play a key role, Halliday's work can be seen in many respects as a forerunner of discourse analysis. While he uses the vocabulary of structural linguistics ('text', 'code', 'semiotic', 'system') and terms that are specific to linguistics, he intertwines them with notions and questions from the social sciences. The best-known contribution of Halliday to discourse studies is his distinction between three functional components of language: 'ideational', 'interpersonal' and 'textual'. Grammar is organized according to these three 'metafunctions': (1) representing ideas about the world ('ideational'), (2) facilitating interpersonal and social interactions ('interpersonal'), (3) integrating these ideas and interactions into meaningful texts, which must be relevant to their context ('textual'). Any sentence is structured like a musical composition, with one strand of its meaning coming from each of the three semiotic areas or metafunctions. In this model the scope of the 'textual' metafunction is wider than in text linguistics: 'it expresses the relation of the language to its environment, including both the verbal environment and the nonverbal, situational environment'.

Michael Alexander Kirkwood Halliday. 1993[1975]. 'Language as Social Semiotic.'
In *Language and Literacy*, ed. by Janet Maybin, 23–43, selected 23–29.
Clevedon: Open University.

1. Introductory

Sociolinguistics sometimes appears to be a search for answers which have no questions. Let us therefore enumerate at this point some of the questions that do seem to need answering.

1. How do people decode the highly condensed utterances of everyday speech, and how do they use a social system for doing so?
2. How do people reveal the ideational and interpersonal environment within which what they are saying is to be interpreted? In other words, how do they construct the social contexts in which meaning takes place?
3. How do people relate the social context to the linguistic system? In other words, how do they deploy their meaning potential in actual semantic exchanges?
4. How and why do people of different social classes or other subcultural groups develop different dialectal varieties and different orientations towards meaning?
5. How far are children of different social groups exposed to different verbal patterns of primary socialization, and how does this determine their reactions to secondary socialization, especially in school?
6. How and why do children learn the functional-semantic system of the adult language?

How do children, through the ordinary everyday linguistic interactions of family and peer groups, come to learn the basic patterns of the culture: the social structure, the systems of knowledge and of values, and the diverse elements of the social semiotic?

2.0 Elements of sociosemiotic theory of language

There are certain general concepts which seem to be essential ingredients in a sociosemiotic theory of language. These are the text, the situation, the text variety or register, the code (in Bernstein's sense), the linguistic system (including the semantic system) and the social structure.

2.1 Text

Let us begin with the concept of *text*, the instances of linguistic interaction in which people actually engage: whatever is said, or written, in an operational context, as distinct from a citational context like that of words listed in a dictionary.

For some purposes it may suffice to conceive of a text as a kind of 'supersentence', a linguistic unit that is in principle greater in size than a sentence but of the same kind. It has long been clear, however, that discourse has its own structure that is not constituted out of sentences in combination and from a sociolinguistic perspective it is more useful to think of text as *encoded* in sentences, not as composed of them. (Hence what (Cicourel, 1969) refers to as omissions by the speaker are not so much omissions as encodings, which the hearer can decode because he shares the principles of realization that provide the key to the code.) In other words, a text is a semantic unit, it is the basic unit of the semantic process.

At the same time, text represents choice. A text is 'what is meant', selected from the total set of options that constitute what can be meant. In other words, text can be defined as actualized meaning potential.

Meaning potential, which is the paradigmatic range of semantic choice that is present in the system, and to which the members of a culture have access in their language, can be characterized in two ways, corresponding to Malinowski's distinction between the 'context of situation' and the 'context of culture' (1923, 1935). Interpreted in the context of culture it is the entire semantic system of the language. This is a fiction, something we cannot hope to describe. Interpreted in the context of situation, it is the particular semantic system, or set of subsystems, which is associated with a particular type of situation or social context. This too is a fiction but it is something that may be more easily describable (cf. 2.5 below). In sociolinguistic terms the meaning potential can be represented as the range of options that is characteristic of a specific situation type.

2.2   Situation

The situation is the environment in which the text comes to life. This is a well-established concept in linguistics, going back at least to Wegener (1885). It played a key part in Malinowski's ethnography of language, under the name of 'context of situation'; Malinowski's notions were further developed and made explicit by Firth (1957: 182), who maintained that the context or situation was not to be interpreted in concrete terms as a sort of audiovisual record of the surrounding 'props' but was, rather, an abstract representation of the environment in terms of certain general categories having relevance to the text. The context of situation may be totally remote from what is going on round and about during the act of speaking or of writing. It will be necessary to represent the situation in still more abstract terms if it is to have a place in a general sociolinguistic theory, and to conceive of it not as situation but as situation *type,* in the sense of what Bernstein refers to as a 'social context'. This is, essentially, a semiotic structure. It is a constellation of meanings deriving from the semiotic system that constitutes the culture.

If it is true that a hearer, given the right information, can make sensible guesses about what the speaker is going to mean – and this seems to be a necessary assumption, seeing that communication does take place – then this 'right information' is what we mean by the social context. It consists of those general properties of the situation which collectively function as the determinants of text, in that they specify the semantic configurations that the speaker will typically fashion in contexts of a given type.

However, such information relates not only 'downward' to the text but also 'upward' to the linguistic system and to the social system. The 'situation' is a theoretical sociolinguistic construct; it is for this reason that we interpret a particular situation type, or social context, as a semiotic structure. The semiotic structure of a situation type can be represented as a complex of three dimensions: the ongoing social activity, the role relationships involved, and the symbolic or rhetorical channel. We refer to these respectively as 'field', 'tenor' and 'mode' (following Halliday et al., 1964), as modified by Spencer, and Gregory (1964); and Gregory (1967)). The field is the social action in which the text is embedded; it includes the subject matter, as one special manifestation. The tenor is the set of role relationships among the relevant participants; it includes levels of formality as one particular instance. The mode is the channel or wavelength selected, which is essentially the function that is assigned to language in the total structure of the situation; it includes the medium (spoken or written), which is explained as a functional variable.

Field, tenor and mode are not kinds of language use, nor are they simply components of the speech setting. They are a conceptual framework for representing the social context as the semiotic environment in which people exchange meanings. Given an adequate specification of the semiotic properties of the context in terms of field, tenor and mode, we should be able to make sensible predictions about the semantic properties of texts associated with it. To do this, however, requires an intermediary level – some concept of text variety, or register.

2.3   Register

The term 'register' was first used in this sense, that of text variety, by Reid (1956); the concept was taken up and developed by Jean Ure (1974), and interpreted within Hill's (1958) 'institutional linguistic' framework by Halliday et al. (1964). The register is the semantic variety of which a text may be regarded as an instance.

Like other related concepts, such as 'speech variant' and '(sociolinguistic) code' (Ferguson, 1971: Chapters 1, 2; Gumperz, 1971: Part 1), register was originally conceived of in lexicogrammatical terms. Halliday et al. (1964) drew a primary distinction between two types of language variety: dialect, which they defined as variety according to the user, and register, which they defined as variety according to the use. The dialect is what a person speaks, determined by who he is; the register is what a person is speaking, determine by what he is doing at the time. This general distinction can be accepted, but, instead of characterizing a register largely by its lexicogrammatical properties, we shall suggest, as with text, a more abstract definition in semantic terms.

Table 2. Determination of semantic features by elements of semiotic structures of situation

	Situational	Semantic	
Field	manipulation of objects	process type and participant structure	Ideational
	assistance of adult	benefactive	
	movable objects and fixtures	type of relevant object	
	movability of objects & their relation to fixtures	type of location and movement	
	recall of similar events	past time	
	evaluation	modulation	
Tenor	interaction with parent	person	Interpersonal
	determination of course of action	mood and polarity	
	enunciation of intention	demand, 'I want to'	
	control of action	demand, 'I want you to'	
	sharing of experience	statement/question, monologue	
	seeking corroboration of experience	statement/question, dialogue	
Mode	dialogue	ellipsis (question–answer)	Textual
	reference to situation	exophoric reference	
	textual cohesion: objects	anaphoric reference	
	textual cohesion: processes	conjunction	
	furthering child's actions	theme (in conjunction with transitivity and mood; typically, parent or child in demands, child in two-participant statements, object in one-participant statements)	
	orientation to task	lexical collocation and repetition	
	spoken mode	information structure	

A register can be defined as the configuration of semantic resources that a member of the culture typically associates with a situation type. It is the meaning potential that is accessible in a given social context. Both the situation and the register associated with it can be described to varying degrees of specificity; but the existence of registers is a fact of everyday experience – speakers have no difficulty in recognizing the semantic options and combinations of options that are 'at risk' under particular environmental conditions. Since these options are realized in the form of grammar and vocabulary, the register is recognizable as a particular selection of words and structures. But it is defined in terms of meanings, it is not an aggregate of conventional forms of expression superposed on some underlying content by 'social factors' of one kind or another. It is the selection of meanings that constitutes the variety to which a text belongs.

2.4   Code

'Code' is used here in Bernstein's sense; it is the principle of semiotic organization governing the choice of meanings by a speaker and their interpretation by a hearer. The code controls the semantic style of the culture.

Codes are not varieties of language, as dialects and registers are. The codes are, so to speak, 'above' the linguistic system; they are types of social semiotic, or symbolic, orders of meaning generated by the social system (cf. Hasan, 1973). The code is actualized in language through the register, since it determines the semantic orientation of speakers in particular social contexts; Bernstein's use of 'variant' (as in 'elaborated variant') refers to those characteristics of a register which derive from the form of the code. When the semantic systems of the language are activated by the situational determinants of text – the field, tenor and mode – this process is regulated by the codes. Hence the codes transmit, or control the transmission of, the underlying patterns of a culture or subculture, acting through the socializing agencies of family, peer group and school. As a child comes to attend to and interpret meanings, in the context of situation and in the context of culture, at the same time he takes over the code. The culture is transmitted to him with the code acting as a filter, defining and making accessible the semiotic principles of his own subculture, so that as he learns the culture he also learns the grid, or subcultural angle on the social system. The child's linguistic experience reveals the culture to him through the code, and so transmits the code as part of the culture.

2.5   The linguistic system

Within the linguistic system, it is the *semantic system* that is of primary concern in a sociolinguistic context. The 'ideational', 'interpersonal' and 'textual' functional components of the semantic system are the modes of meaning that are present in every use of language in every social context. A text is a product of all three; it is a polyphonic composition in which different semantic melodies are interwoven, to be realized as integrated lexicogrammatical structures. Each functional component contributes a band of structure to the whole.

The ideational function represents the speaker's meaning potential as an observer. It is the content function of language, language as 'about something'. This is the component through which the language encodes the cultural experience, and the speaker encodes his own individual experience as a member of the culture. It expresses the phenomena of the environment: the things – creatures, objects, actions, events, qualities, states and relations – of the world and of our own consciousness, including the phenomenon of language itself, and also the 'metaphenomena', the things that are already encoded as facts and as reports. All these are part of the ideational meaning of language.

The interpersonal component represents the speaker's meaning potential as an intruder. It is the participatory function of language, language as doing something. This is the component through which the speaker intrudes himself into the context of situation, both expressing his own attitudes and judgements and seeking to influence the attitudes and behaviour of others. It expresses the role relationships associated with the situation, including those that are defined by language itself, which are relationships of questioner-respondent, informer-doubter and the like. These constitute the interpersonal meaning of language.

The textual component represents the speaker's text-forming potential; it is that which makes language relevant. This is the component which provides the texture, that which makes the difference between language that is suspended in *vacuo* and language that is operational in a context of situation. It expresses the relation of the language to its environment, including both the verbal environment – what has been said or written before – and the nonverbal, situational environment. Hence the textual component has an enabling function with respect to the other two; it is only in combination with textual meaning that ideational and interpersonal meanings are actualized.

These components are reflected in the lexicogrammatical system in the form of discrete networks of options. In the clause, for example, the ideational function is represented by transitivity, the interpersonal by mood and modality, and the textual by a set of systems that have been referred to collectively as 'theme'. Each of these three sets of options is characterized by strong internal but weak external constraints: for example, any choice made in transitivity has a significant effect on other choices within the transitivity systems, but has very little effect on choices within the mood or theme systems. Hence the functional organization of meaning in language is built into the core of the linguistic system, as the most general organizing principle of the lexicogrammatical stratum.

2.6   Social structure

Of the numerous ways in which the social structure is implicated in a sociolinguistic theory, there are three which stand out. In the first place, it defines and gives significance to the various types of social context in which meanings are exchanged. The different social groups and communication networks that determine what we have called the 'tenor' – the status and role relationships in the situation – are obviously products of the social structure; but so also in a more general sense are the types of social activity that constitute the 'field'. Even the 'mode', the rhetorical channel with its associated strategies, though more immediately reflected in linguistic patterns, has its origin in the social structure; it is the social structure that generates the semiotic tensions and the rhetorical styles and genres that express them (Barthes, 1970).

Secondly, through its embodiment in the types of role relationship within the family, the social structure determines the various familial patterns of communication; it regulates the meanings and meaning styles that are associated with given social contexts, including those contexts that are critical in the processes of cultural transmission. In this way the social structure determines, through the intermediary of language, the forms taken by the socialization of the child (see Bernstein, 1971; Bernstein, 1975).

Thirdly, and most problematically, the social structure enters through the effects of social hierarchy, in the form of caste or class. This is obviously a social hierarchy and also a symbolic expression of it, maintaining and reinforcing it in a variety of ways: for example, the association of dialect with register – the fact that certain registers conventionally call for certain dialectal modes – expresses the relation between social classes and the division of labour. In a more pervasive fashion, the social structure is present in the forms of semiotic interaction, and becomes apparent through incongruities and disturbances in the semantic system. Linguistics seems now to have largely abandoned its fear of impurity and come to grips with what is called 'fuzziness' in language; but this has been a logical rather than a sociological concept, a departure from an ideal regularity rather than an organic property of sociosemiotic systems. The 'fuzziness' of language is, in part, an expression of the dynamics and tensions of the social system. It is not only the text (what people mean) but also the semantic system (what they can mean) that embodies the ambiguity, antagonism, imperfection, inequality and change that characterize the social system and social structure. This is not often systematically explored in linguistics, though it is familiar enough to students of communication and of general semantics, and to the public at large. It could probably be fruitfully approached through an extension of Bernstein's theory of codes (cf. Douglas, 1972). The social structure is not just an ornamental background to linguistic interaction, as it has tended to be come in sociolinguistic discussions. It is an essential element in the evolution of semantic systems and semantic processes.

References

Barthes, R. 1970. 'L'ancienne rhétorique.' *Communications* 16. DOI: 10.3406/comm.1970.1236

Bernstein, B. 1971. *Class, Codes and Control 1: Theoretical Studies towards a Sociology of Language.* London: Routledge & Kegan Paul.

Bernstein, B. 1975. *Class, Codes and Control 3: Towards a Theory of Educational Transmissions.* London: Routledge & Kegan Paul. DOI: 10.4324/9780203011430

Cicourel, A. 1969. 'Generative semantics and the structure of social interaction.' Presented in the *International Days of Sociolinguistics* in Rome, September 15–17.

Douglas, M. 1972. 'Speech, class and Basil Bernstein [Radio Speech on BBC].' *The Listener* 2241.

Ferguson, C. A. 1971. *Language Structure and Language Use: Essays Selected and Introduced by Anwar S. Dil.* Stanford: Stanford University Press.

Firth, J. R. 1957. *Papers in Linguistics (1934–1951)*. London: Oxford University Press.

Gregory, M. 1967. 'Aspects of varieties differentiation.' *Journal of Linguistics* 3, 177–197.
DOI: 10.1017/S0022226700016601

Gumperz, J. 1971. *Language in Social Groups: Essays Selected and Introduced by Anwar S. Dil*. Stanford: Stanford University Press.

Halliday, M. A. K., A. McIntosh, and P. Strevens. 1964. *The Linguistic Sciences and Language Teaching*. London: Longman.

Hasan, R. 1973. 'Code, register and social dialect.' In *Class Codes and Control 2: Applied Studies towards a Sociology of Language*, edited by B. Bernstein. London: Routledge & Kegan Paul.

Hill, T. 1958. 'Institutional Linguistics.' *Orbis* 7, 441–455.

Malinowski, B. 1935. *Coral Gardens and their Magic*. London: Allen and Unwin.

Malinowski, B. 1923. 'The problem of meaning in primitive languages.' In *The Meaning of Meaning*, edited by C. K. Ogden and I. A. Richards, 451–510. London: Kegan Paul.

Reid, T. B.W. 1956. 'Linguistics, structuralism, philology.' *Archivum Linguisticum* 8, 28–37.

Spencer, J., and M. J. Gregory, et al. 1964. 'An approach to the study of style.' In *Linguistics and Style*, edited by Enkvist, *Language and Language Learning*, 57–105. London: Oxford University Press.

Ure, J., and J. Ellis. 1974. 'El registro en la lingüistica descriptiva y en la sociologia lingüistica.' In *La sociolingüistica actual: algunos de sus problemas, planteamientos y soluciones*, edited by Oscar Uribe-Villegas, 115–64. Mexico: Universidad Nacional Autonoma de Mexico.

Wegener, P. 1885. *Untersuchungen über die Grundfragen des Sprachlebens*. Halle.

Theo van Leeuwen

The representation of actors

Theo van Leeuwen (b. 1947) studied linguistics and communication theory; he also worked as a film and television producer, scriptwriter and director. He is one of the main developers of social semiotics (2005) and multimodality (Kress / van Leeuwen, 1996). The text presented here does not deal with multimodality. It attempts to answer questions which are formulated in the first paragraph: 'What are the ways in which social actors can be represented in English discourse? Which choices does the English language give us for referring to people?' This kind of interrogation is typical of the research conducted by people working within the frame of systemic-functional linguistics. Besides, this text is also oriented towards Critical Discourse Analysis: 'How are the relevant social actors represented in an instance of a particular kind of racist discourse – a discourse which represents immigration in a way that is founded on fear?' Many critical discourse analysts, drawing on Halliday's linguistics, study phenomena such as nominalization ('Paul arrived' → 'Paul's arrival') and transitivity (for example the difference between 'The police killed the man' and 'The man was killed': in the second sentence the agent or agency is hidden). In fact, van Leeuwen's conception of the representation of social actors does not remain within the domain of linguistics. He takes the stance of social semiotics, given that categories such as 'agent' or 'nomination' are not restricted to natural language: he does not only tackle the way these categories are shaped by language. His taxonomy distinguishes 'big' categories: 'exclusion', 'role allocation', 'genericization and specification', 'assimilation', 'association and dissociation', 'indetermination and differentiation', 'nomination and categorization', 'functionalization and identification', 'personalization and impersonalization' and 'overdetermination'. In this excerpt, only the first category ('exclusion') is outlined.

References

Kress, Gunther, and Theo Van Leeuwen. 1996. *Reading Images: The Grammar of Visual Design*. London: Routledge.
van Leeuwen, Theo. 2005. *Introducing Social Semiotics. An Introductory Textbook*. New York: Routledge.

Theo van Leeuwen. 1996. 'The Representation of Social Actors.'
In *Texts and Practices*: *Readings in Critical Discourse Analysis*,
ed. by Carmen Rosa Caldas-Coulthard, and Malcolm Coulthard, 32–70, selected 32–42.
London: Routledge.

1. Introduction

The question I shall attempt to answer in this chapter can be formulated simply: what are the ways in which social actors can be represented in English discourse? Which choices does the English language give us for referring to people? In addition I shall address another, more specific question: how are the relevant social actors represented in an instance of a particular kind of racist discourse – a discourse, which represents immigration in a way that is founded on fear – the fear of loss of livelihood and the fear of loss of cultural identity as a result of the 'influx' of immigrants who are perceived as 'other', 'different' and 'threatening'.

The first of these two questions is a grammatical one if, with Halliday, we take a grammar to be a 'meaning potential' ('what *can* be said') rather than a set of rules ('what *must* be said'). Yet, unlike many other linguistically oriented forms of Critical Discourse Analysis, I shall not start out from linguistic operations such as nominalisation and passive agent deletion, or from linguistic categories such as categories of transitivity, but instead seek to draw up a *sociosemantic* inventory of the ways in which social actors can be represented, and to establish the sociological and critical relevance of my categories before I turn to the question of how they are realised linguistically.

There are two reasons for doing so. The first stems from the lack of bi-uniqueness of language. Agency, for instance, as a *sociological* concept, is of major and classic importance in Critical Discourse Analysis: in which contexts are which social actors represented as 'agents' and which as 'patients'? But sociological agency is not always realised by linguistic agency, by the grammatical role of 'Agent'; it can also be realised in many other ways, for instance by possessive pronouns (as in 'our intake of migrants') or by a prepositional phrase with 'from', as in example 1.1, in which the grammatical Agent is sociologically 'patient':

(1.1)   People of Asian descent say they received a sudden cold-shoulder
        from neighbours and co-workers

There is no neat fit between sociological and linguistic categories, and if Critical Discourse Analysis, in investigating for instance the representation of agency, ties itself in too closely to specific linguistic operations or categories, many relevant instances of agency might be overlooked. One cannot, it seems, have it both ways with language.

Either theory and method are formally neat but semantically messy (as in the dictionary: one form, many meanings), or they are semantically neat but formally messy (as in the thesaurus: one concept, many possible realisations). Linguists tend towards preserving the unity of formal categories. I shall here attempt the opposite approach, hoping to provide a set of relevant categories for investigating the representation of social actors in discourse.

Halliday (1985: Chapter 10) has approached the problem of the lack of biuniqueness in another way, through his theory of grammatical metaphor: certain linguistic realisations are 'literal' or 'congruent', others 'metaphorical' or 'incongruent'. But in Halliday's account 'congruent' would seem to mean 'congruent with the grammatical system', rather than 'congruent with reality', the kind of congruence which, in the end, underlies most definitions of metaphor. For Halliday a clause like 'The report confirms...' would not be a metaphor, because it does not violate the criterion that verbal processes do not require a human 'Sayer' as their subject (cf. Halliday, 1985: 129). I would prefer to see 'The report confirms...' as just one of the ways in which we can refer to social actors in their role as 'Sayers', as metaphorical or unmetaphorical as any other way, but endowed with its own specific sociosemantic import and hence social distribution: it is likely to be found in contexts where the authority of utterances is bound up with the official status or role of 'Sayers' and/or the official status of genres. In the context of literature, on the other hand, it would be less likely to occur, because there the authority of utterances is bound up with the charismatic personality of the writer, so that we would expect 'Shakespeare says...' rather than 'The play says...', for instance. I would therefore prefer to ask: how can 'Sayers' be represented – impersonally or personally, individually or collectively, by reference to their person or their utterance, etc. – without privileging any of these choices as more 'literal' than others, and without thereby also privileging the context or contexts in which one or the other tends to occur as more normative than others.

The second reason is somewhat different, and follows from the assumption that meaning belongs to culture rather than to language and cannot be tied to any specific semiotic. Language can represent social actions impersonally, as in this headline:

(1.2)   Allied air activity over battlefield intensifies

but so can pictures – think of the difference between, on the one hand, 'personalised' pictures of bombardments, say in feature film sequences showing, in close up, the faces of the crew as they drop the bombs, as well as the faces of the villagers down below as they are about to be bombed, and, on the other hand, diagrams of the same event, for instance maps with large arrows pointing at the targets and schematic drawings representing the explosions.

There is no space here to explore this point in detail (cf. van Leeuwen, 1987, for the representation of social actors in music; Kress and van Leeuwen 1990, and van Leeuwen, 1993a, for parallels between language and images). Nevertheless, the categories I shall propose in this chapter should, in principle, be seen as pan-semiotic: a given culture (or a given context within a culture) has not only its own, specific array of ways of representing the social world, but also its own specific ways of mapping the different semiotics on to this array, of prescribing, with greater or lesser strictness, what can be realised verbally as well as visually, what only verbally, what only visually, and so on. And these arrangements will also be subject to historical change, sometimes even violent change, as in iconoclasms. The point is important for Critical Discourse Analysis, for, with the increasing use of visual representation in a wide range of contexts, it becomes more and more pressing to be able to ask the same critical questions with regard to both verbal and visual representations, indeed, with regard to representations in all the 'media' that form part of contemporary 'multimedia' texts.

Despite all this, this chapter still attempts to be grounded in linguistics. Each of the representational choices I shall propose will be tied to specific linguistic or rhetorical realisations. To return to my earlier examples, in the case of 'Shakespeare' the representational choice is that of 'nomination' and the realisation of the use of a proper name, while in the case of 'The report confirms…' the representational choice is that of 'utterance autonomisation' (…) and the realisation of the substitution of the utterance for its Sayer, hence a form of metonymical reference. The difference is that my primary focus is on sociological categories ('nomination', 'agency', etc.) rather than on linguistic categories ('nominalisation', 'passive agent deletion', etc.) and that the system network, the 'array of choices', I shall present later on will range over a variety of linguistic and rhetorical phenomena, and find its unity in the concept of 'social actor', rather than in a linguistic concept such as, for instance, 'the nominal group'. Finally, the chapter is part of a larger project (see van Leeuwen, 1993a, 1993b) in which I am attempting in addition to map how other elements of social practices (the social activities that constitute them, the times when and the locations where they occur, the dress and body grooming that go with them, etc.) are represented, and how representations add further elements to this, for instance the purposes and legitimations of the social practices, and the sentiments that accompany them. In short, the question addressed in this chapter is part of a larger question: how are social practices transformed into discourses about social practices – and this both in the sense of what means we have for doing so, and in the sense of how we actually do it in specific institutional contexts which have specific relations with the social practices of which they produce representations.

2. 'Our race odyssey'

Below I reproduce the first three sections of 'Our Race Odyssey', the text from which I shall draw most of my examples, and which I use to demonstrate how the categories I propose may be used in text analysis. It was published as the leading feature article in 'Spectrum', the Saturday supplement of the *Sydney Morning Herald*, a conservative broadsheet newspaper, on 12 May 1990.

The descriptive framework I shall present in the following sections was worked out with the aid of a much larger and generically diverse corpus of texts which included fictional narratives, comic strips, news stories, newspaper editorials, advertisements, textbooks and scholarly essays, all dealing, in some form or other, with the subject of schooling, and more specifically with the transition from home to school (van Leeuwen, 1993b). As one text can never provide instances of all the categories and modes of representation, I shall, throughout the chapter, also use examples from this corpus.[1]

1   2001: Our Race Odyssey.
2   This country will be vastly different next century if Australians feel they cannot voice legitimate fears about immigration without being branded racists, argues David Jenkins.
3   In Florence last month 80 young white thugs, many wearing costume masks and armed with iron bars, roamed the narrow cobbled streets attacking African street vendors.
4   In France, where non-European immigrants make up 6.5 per cent of the population, former president Valery Giscard d'Estaing proposed a total halt to immigration.
5   In Japan, a nation with a strong tradition of keeping foreigners at arm's length, similar concerns are being expressed about a mere trickle of Third World immigrants.
6   Japan's National Police Agency had to apologise recently for circulating an internal memo to police stations claiming that Pakistanis working in Japan 'have a unique body odour', carry infectious skin diseases and tell lies 'under the name of Allah' (…)
48 It is hardly surprising therefore that the immigration debate is building again.
49 Hardly surprising that there are calls for major cuts in the program.
50 Hardly surprising that a number of critics want to see our intake halved to 70,000 to 80,000, which would bring it into line with our postwar average.
51 Australia, these critics suggest, is being generous to a fault – and in danger of saddling itself with a lot of unwanted problems as a result.

---

1.   This text is too long to be reproduced in its entirety here, the excerpts that are selected preserve the main steps of the argument. (Note of the editors).

3. Exclusion

The 'Race Odyssey' text draws on a representation of the social practice of immigration itself, as institutionalised in Australia, as well as on the representation of other social practices, which serve to legitimise (or delegitimise) it: the practices of writing government-commissioned reports on immigration, or of conducting public opinion surveys about it, for instance. All these practices involve specific sets of social actors, but in a given representation, for instance that of the 'Race Odyssey' text, a feature article in a conservative middle-class newspaper, not all the social actors are included. Some are represented, for instance Prime Minister Bob Hawke, who 'presides over a near record intake of migrants', others are excluded, for instance the people who 'brand as racist' those who 'voice legitimate fears about immigration'. Representations include or exclude social actors to suit their interests and purposes in relation to the readers for whom they are intended. Some of the exclusions may be 'innocent', details which readers are assumed to know already, or which are deemed irrelevant to them, others tie in closely to the propaganda strategy of creating fear, and of setting up immigrants as enemies of 'our' interests.

Exclusion has rightly been an important aspect of Critical Discourse Analysis. To mention just one classic example, Tony Trew (1979: 97ff.) showed how, in *The Times* and the *Rhodesian Herald* (*anno* 1975), the police were excluded in accounts of the 'riots' during which they had opened fire and killed demonstrators, because it was in the interest of these papers and their readers to attempt to 'justify white rule in Africa', and this required

> a suppression of the fact that the white regimes apply violence and intimidation, and suppression of the nature of the exploitation this makes possible. It requires that the regimes and their agents be put constantly in the role of promoters of progress, law and order, concerned to eliminate social evil and conflict, but never responsible for it.
> (Trew, 1979: 106)

Some exclusions leave no traces in the representation, excluding both the social actors and their activities. Such radical exclusion can play a role in a critical comparison of different representations of the same social practice, but not in an analysis of a single text, for the simple reason that it leaves no traces behind. In my study of the representation of schooling (van Leeuwen, 1993b), for instance, I found that fathers were radically excluded in texts addressing teachers, but included in many children's stories, even if often only briefly, during the breakfast preceding the first school day, or as givers of satchels, pencil cases and other school necessities. Children's stories aimed at a mass market sometimes included school support staff, but excluded the headmistress, while more 'upmarket' children's stories included the headmistress but excluded people lower than teachers in the school hierarchy, in what is clearly a class-related pattern of inclusion and exclusion.

When the activities (e.g. the killing of demonstrators) are included, but some or all of the social actors involved in it (e.g. the police) are excluded, the exclusion does leave a trace. We can ask 'but who did the killing?' or 'but who was killed?', even though the text does not provide the answers. In this case a further distinction should perhaps be made, the distinction between *suppression* and *backgrounding*. In the case of suppression, there is no reference to the social actor(s) in question anywhere in the text. Thus we learn, in the 'Race Odyssey' text, that someone or some institution surveyed the opinions of the public, but we do not find out which individual or company or other institution did it, which takes away at least one possible avenue of contesting the results of the 'surveys'. In the case of backgrounding, the exclusion is less radical: the excluded social actors may not be mentioned in relation to a given activity, but they are mentioned elsewhere in the text, and we can infer with reasonable (though never total) certainty who they are. They are not so much excluded as de-emphasised, pushed into the background.

How is suppression realised? First there is, of course, the classic realisation through passive agent deletion. Example 3.1 tells us that 'concerns are being expressed', but not who expresses them:

(3.1)   In Japan similar concerns are being expressed about a mere trickle
of Third World immigrants

Suppression can also be realised through non-finite clauses which function as a grammatical participant. In example 3.2 the infinitival clause 'to maintain this policy' is embedded to function as the Carrier of an attributive clause, and this allows the social actor(s) responsible for the 'maintenance' of the policy to be excluded – and they *could* have been included, for instance, as 'for local education authorities'. The downranking of the process ('maintain') makes the fact that exclusion has taken place a little less accessible, the trace a little less clear:

(3.2)   To maintain this policy is hard

It is almost always possible to delete 'Beneficiaries', social actors who benefit from an activity. Example 3.3, for instance, does not include those to whom the 'National Police Agency' apologised (the Pakistanis who had been offended?):

(3.3)   Japan's National Police Agency had to apologise recently for circulating an
internal memo to police stations claiming that Pakistanis working in Japan
'have a unique body odour', carry infectious skin diseases and tell lies 'under
the name of Allah'

Nominalisations and process nouns similarly allow the exclusion of social actors. 'Support' and 'stopping', in example 3.4, function as nominals, although they refer to activities. The same applies to 'immigration'. Again the excluded social actors *could* have been included, for instance through postmodifying phrases with *by, of, from*, etc., but they haven't been:

(3.4)   The level of support for stopping immigration altogether was at a postwar high

Processes may also be realised as adjectives, as is the case with 'legitimate' in example 3.5. Who 'legitimises' the 'fear'? The writer? We cannot be sure. The fears simply *are* legitimate, according to this representation:

(3.5)   Australians feel they cannot voice legitimate fears about immigration

The activity in example 3.6 involves a human actor, the teacher who opens the door. But coding the activity in a middle voice (Halliday, 1985: 150–151) necessitates the exclusion of the agentive participant. The context may lead us to infer that the teacher was involved, but there can be no certainty – it might, for instance, have been the wind. The clause invites a reading in which the opening of the door, the intrusion of the teacher in the child's world of play, is given the force of a natural event.

(3.6)   The door of the playhouse opened and the teacher looked in

It is often difficult to know whether suppressed social actors are or are not supposed to be retrievable by the reader, or, indeed, the writer. Example 3.4, for instance, does not tell us who is involved in the act of 'stopping immigration'. Is this because readers are assumed to know already, so that more detailed reference would be overcommunicative, or is it to block access to detailed knowledge of a practice which, if represented in detail, might arouse compassion for those who are 'stopped'? The point is that the practice is here represented as something not to be further examined or contested.

Backgrounding can result from simple ellipses in non-finite clauses with *-ing* and *-ed* participles, in infinitival clauses with *to*, and in paratactic clauses. In all these cases the excluded social actor is included elsewhere in the same clause or clause complex. It can also be realised in the same way as suppression, but with respect to social actors who *are* included elsewhere in the text. The two realisations background social actors to different degrees, but both play a part in reducing the number of times specific social actors are explicitly referred to.

To discuss the pattern of inclusion and exclusion in the 'Race Odyssey' text, it is necessary to bring the various ways in which each category of social actor is represented under a common denominator. These common denominators do not, of course, form a more transparent or congruent way of referring to them. They merely serve as an anchor for the analysis, a kind of calibration. For the purposes of analysis, then, I shall call 'racists' those social actors who, actively or otherwise, oppose immigration and immigrants in countries other than Australia, and I shall refer to those who do the same in Australia as 'us'. Again, this is not to say that the latter are *not* racist, but merely to follow the distinction that underlies the way the author argues his case. I shall refer to the immigrants themselves as 'them', to the (Australian) Government as 'government', to the various experts involved by the writer as 'experts', to the writer himself as 'writer', and to his readers, who are sometimes addressed directly, as 'addressees'. Bruce Ruxton, the 'racist' Australians love to hate, is a category on his own ('our racist'), and finally there are a few minor characters who appear only once, the 'anti-racists' who 'brand as racist' the 'legitimate fears of Australians', 'Allah', 'European Governments' and (Japanese) 'police stations'. Table 3.1 displays the patterns of inclusion and exclusion.

Table 3.1 Inclusion and exclusion in the 'Race Odyssey' text

	Included %	Backgrounded %	Suppressed %
'racists' (N = 24)	67.25	20.25	12.5
'us' (N = 46)	72	24	4
'them' (N = 98)	61	38	1
'government' (N = 32)	73	18	9

Although the differences are not dramatic, it is clear that the most frequently included social actors are the Australian Government and 'us', Australians, who voice 'legitimate fears', while the most frequently backgrounded or suppressed social actors are, on the one hand, the immigrants, and on the other hand those in other countries who commit such racist acts as 'insulting' and 'denying entry to elegant restaurants', and, indeed, people in general, as they are 'naturally inclined to racism' and will 'display unpleasant characteristics when they feel threatened'. In short, those who do not take part in the 'debate' between the Australian people and its government which the writer stages for us in his argument form to some extent a backdrop to this debate.

I do not want to make great claims for treating texts statistically. On the contrary, it is important to realise that the frequencies may shift with the stages in the writer's argument. In the first section of the text, where the writer discusses racism in other countries, migrants are backgrounded in 17 per cent of cases. As soon as the writer moves to his discussion of Australian immigration policy, this increases to 36 per cent. In other words, the migrants close to home are backgrounded more often. In any case, the pattern of inclusion and exclusion must be integrated with the *way in which* they are represented. (...)

What, finally, remains most opaque in this text? First, the voice of the Opposition – those who 'brand as racist' Australians 'who voice legitimate fears' are fully suppressed. Second, many of the 'racists' in other countries: we are not told who exactly is responsible for 'insulting people of Asian descent' or 'denying them entry to elegant restaurants', for example. Third, the voice of legitimation, which 'legitimises fears', and which 'entitles' Hawke and 'us' to the view which, by virtue of their sheer prominence in the text, the writer obliquely favours. And finally, those who have to do the dirty work of actually 'stopping' ('halting', 'cutting', etc.) the immigrants.

References

Halliday, Michael Alexander Kirkwood. 1985. *An Introduction to Functional Grammar*. London: Edward Arnold.

Kress, Gunther, and Theo van Leeuwen. 1990. *Reading images*. Victoria: Deakin University Press.

Trew, Tony. 1979. 'Theory and ideology at work.' In *Language and Control*, ed. by Roger Fowler, Robert Hodge, Gunther Kress, and Tony Trew, 94–116. London: Routledge & Kegan Paul.

van Leeuwen, Theo. 1987. 'Music and ideology: notes towards a sociosemiotics of mass media culture.' *SASSC Working Papers* 2, 1–2, 19–45. Sydney Association for the Study of Society and Culture.

van Leeuwen, Theo. 1993a. 'Genre and field in Critical Discourse Analysis: a synopsis', *Discourse and Society* 4 (2): 193–225. DOI: 10.1177/0957926593004002004

van Leeuwen, Theo. 1993b. 'Language and representation: the recontextualization of participants, activities and reactions.' Unpublished PhD dissertation, University of Sydney.

Konrad Ehlich

Text and discourse

The pragmatic and functional theory of Halliday shares many assumptions with the theory of the German linguist Konrad Ehlich (b. 1942). But the functionalism of Ehlich refers more to the German tradition, in particular to the psychologist Karl Bühler (1879–1963). This short text by Ehlich aims to clarify the use of two terms: 'text' and 'discourse'. He begins by mentioning the concept of language found in the *Course of General Linguistics* (1974[1916]) of Ferdinand de Saussure, then in Chomsky's generative grammar and in text linguistics, which aims to go beyond the sentence. Then, a new problem emerges for him: in many contexts, the meanings of 'text', 'discourse' and 'conversation' are very similar. Ehlich proposes a way to overcome this obstacle: 'it would be worth searching for a unified concept of language that is able to give a basis for an integral analysis of the various areas of linguistic phenomena'. Ehlich's objectives are not far from Halliday's systemic-functional theory. But whereas Halliday wants to insert linguistics into social semiotics, Ehlich attempts to widen the scope of linguistics by sketching out a functional pragmatic framework, in which 'language and its various structures are analyzed as the result of action needs in human communication'. In many respects, K. Ehlich's conception of pragmatics perpetuates the European functionalist tradition: by considering the constraints imposed by human communication, the structure of language is accounted for.

References

Saussure, Ferdinand de. 1974[1916]. *Course in General Linguistics*. London: Fontana.

Konrad Ehlich. 1987. 'Text and Discourse: A plea for clarity in analysis and terminology.'
In *Proceedings of the 14th International Congress of Linguists*,
ed. by Werner Bahner, Joachim Schildt, and Dieter Viehweger, 2050–2052.
Berlin: Akademie Verlag.

'Text' and 'discourse' are current notions in present-day linguistic discussion. The two terms cover a wide range of meanings and connotations in linguistic and everyday scientific language. In this paper, my objective is to discuss the various theoretical contexts in which these terms have evolved and some of the notional implications in their use. Linguistics requires clarification of the two terms instead of only applying everyday commonsense terms in linguistic activity. The use of the terms in linguistics is dependent upon former linguistic theory formation. The reconstruction of the meaning of terms and of their connotations can be achieved by analyzing them as parts of, and as results of, main developments and issues in linguistic theory in our century.

The first stage of linguistics in our century was characterized by a close relationship to the notion of 'sign', as developed in Ferdinand de Saussure's and his followers' ideas about language. 'Signs' are the elements of a system Saussure (1916) called 'langue'. Strangely enough, the sentence, by and large, is not regarded as part of 'langue' but is attributed to the opposite part of 'langue', i.e. 'parole'. The idea of 'langue' makes use of two theoretical concepts, the idea of '*relation associative*' (associative relation), and of '*relation syntagmatique*' (syntagmatic relation). These two types of relation form the structural characteristics of language as a sign system.

Moving on to the 'Chomskyan revolution' (Chomsky, 1965) we realize the essential idea of '*langue*', the sign moved away from the focus of analysis with another concept taking its place, namely the 'sentence' – a concept or linguistic object that was not considered a proper object of linguistic analysis by Saussure. How could this major shift take place? I think we can find an answer along the following lines: The object 'sentence' which was only part of '*parole*' in Saussurian linguistics was re-analyzed in a theoretical manner. In doing this re-analysis, a new theoretical framework was established. It includes the notion of 'competence' as a leading theoretical idea which is used to account for the proper treatment of a proper linguistic object. 'Sign' is disregarded, and with it the idea of '*langue*'. (Of course, Chomsky tried to re-interpret the term 'langue' by using the term 'competence', but this does not work, because parts of competence have to be represented by the term 'langue' in Saussurian terminology.)

Looking at the inner structuring of the idea of 'sentence', again, I think there are two main notions, first the notion of 'structure' itself, and second the notion that sentences have clear-cut beginnings and ends. Linguistic phenomena beyond the notion of 'sentence', in the theoretical sense of the word, were disregarded as linguistic objects under the term 'performance'.

On the basis of the state of the art described so far, a new linguistic domain came into being. It has been called text linguistics. The theoretical operation and theoretical configuration which are its result are equivalent and analogous to that which is characteristic of the step from sign linguistics to sentence linguistics. There were two main forms of establishing this type of text linguistics.

The first one repeated the conceptualization of sentence linguistics by taking as its basic unit not a singular sentence but a combination of sentences. 'Text' is regarded as a macro-unit or as a unit beyond the sentence. The second form relied more on the internal structuring of sentence linguistics, transforming parts of previous theoretical notions into a text linguistic one by developing the ideas of 'coherence' and 'cohesion'. These terms – though being used in a very broad sense and sometimes even contradictorily – seem to be of great attractiveness. It is mainly the British tradition which constitutes this second form of text linguistics.

Unfortunately, in both forms of text linguistics, the terminological situation became very unclear from the beginning, because not only was the term 'text' used but also another term, namely 'discourse'. As early as 1952, Harris had used the term 'discourse' for units beyond the sentence in his tagmemic model. Some major research in text linguistics, by van Dijk, uses the term '*tekst*', the Dutch equivalent of 'text', in his Dutch publications, and the term 'discourse' in some of his English publications (van Dijk, 1978). On the other hand, also in the coherence-cohesion type of text linguistics, the term 'discourse' is used, especially in the English tradition, whereas others use the term 'text'. Part of the confusion in linguistics which seems to be characteristic of the present state of affairs in both discourse and text analysis obviously has to do with these terminological infelicity conditions; other misunderstandings are due to major uncertainties regarding the objects and methods of analysis themselves.

In the development which I have described so far, there remains an important part of linguistic phenomena which does not enter into the activity of linguistic analysis. It is the domain which Chomsky termed 'performance'. Here then, another expansion of linguistic analysis came into being. This expansion refers to those large areas of linguistic activity which were not considered proper objects of linguistic analysis. The most important theoretical contributions for the analysis of neglected areas have been achieved where the notion of orality has been taken seriously. It is mainly the field of conversation which has been analyzed in this respect. Since 'conversation analysis' has developed on different theoretical grounds, the term 'conversation' has not been treated in a proper relation to either 'discourse' or 'text'.

The situation characterized so far cannot result in clear-cut concepts or clear-cut terminology, because the theoretical development is not one of critical continuity but of contingent moves of the focus of attention from one area of phenomena to the other. Each of the various theoretical approaches, schools and ways of analysis take into account different aspects of language. In order to overcome the difficulties implied in this theoretical diffusion, which results in theoretical confusion, it would be worth searching for a unified concept of language that is able to offer a basis for an integral analysis of the various areas of linguistic phenomena. Sign, sentence, text, discourse, conversation – they are all part of linguistic activity. A linguistic theory that starts with linguistic activity is a pragmatic theory, 'pragmatic' in the action-theoretical sense. A pragmatic theory of language needs to be developed in such a way that language and its various structures are analyzed as the results of action needs in human communication. Such a type of pragmatics has 'function' as its main theoretical concept. Thus it can be called 'functional pragmatics'. Functional pragmatics starts with linguistic activity and theoretically reconstructs what the functions of various objects, such as sign, sentence, text, discourse and conversation, are in interlocutors' everyday linguistic activity.

References

Chomsky, Noam. 1965. *Aspects of the Theory of Syntax*. Cambridge, Mass.

Harris, Zellig S. 1952. 'Discourse Analysis.' *Language* 28 (1): 1–30. DOI: 10.2307/409987

Saussure, Ferdinand de. 1916. *Cours de linguistique générale*, ed. by Charles Bally, & Albert Sechehaye. Paris: Payot.

van Dijk, Teun A. 1978. *Studies in the Pragmatics of Discourse*. The Hague, Berlin: Mouton.

Patrick Charaudeau

Discourse strategies and the constraints of communication

Patrick Charaudeau (b. 1939) is a linguist and discourse analyst who aims to articulate language and social semiotics. His research focuses on the analysis of genres of discourse, which are considered as implicit 'communication contracts' that are established between the partners in discourse activity. Charaudeau has been developing his 'semio-communicative' approach since the 1970s (Charaudeau, 1983). His work focuses on the influence that speakers exert on each other through discourse, especially in media (newspapers, radio, TV, ads) and political discourses. The selected text focuses on the relationship between the strategies of the subject of discourse and the constraints imposed by the setting: the subject 'as a social being depends on the constraints that are delivered by the situation of communication, but as an individual, he/she attempts to give himself/herself existence through the use of strategies'. This viewpoint implies 'a theory of the language subject in keeping with the constraints of the situation of communication and with the strategies that this subject employs'. A distinction is made between three levels of constraints: *situational*, *discursive* and *formal*. The *situational constraints* refer to the identity of the partners and the places they occupy in the exchange, from the viewpoint of their aims and of the material setting of the discourse. According to situational constraints, *discursive constraints* allow the speaker to find out 'how to say it'. As for *formal constraints*, they are 'repetitive use-forms that, in becoming routine, are stabilized in manners of speaking', and which 'echo the situational constraint requirements through discursive constraints'. The *text* is constructed at this level. Then, special attention is paid to the notion of 'discursive strategy', which is defined in relation to the contract of communication.

References

Charaudeau, Patrick. 1983. *Langage et discours. Eléments de sémiolinguistique*. Paris: Hachette.

Patrick Charaudeau. 2002. 'A communicative conception of discourse.'
Discourse studies, 4 (3): 301–318, selected 301–302, 309–316.

The aim of this article is to demonstrate how the study of language centres around two important areas of study: 'communicational' and 'representational'. These two areas of study are inherent in several disciplines: *pragmatics*, in which all speech acts are endowed with illocutionary and perlocutionary force; *socio-ethnography,* in which the external conditions of language production have to be taken into account; and *psychology*, in which every speech act is derived from a perspective of influence. This position, which I term *semiocommunicative,* is dependent on several principles: 'alterity' (every speaker constructs and is constituted through the addressee); 'influence' (the speaker's objective is to allow the addressee entry into his or her discursive world); 'regulation' (by taking the Other and the circumstances of communication into account, the addressee is aiming to influence the Other); and 'relevance' (in order to understand each other, the speaker and addressee have to share the same representation of the world and of themselves – this has to be at an appropriate level and to be adjusted to the communicative situation). Our position thus presupposes a theory of discourse constrained by the communicative situation and the strategies employed by the speech participants. (…)

Constraints and discursive construction

The subject of discourse is both constrained and free, as this article demonstrates.

Situational constraints. The communicative situation is where constraints originate. These constraints determine what is at stake in the exchange. They come, as we have seen, both from the identity of the participants and from the place they occupy in the exchange, from the viewpoint of their aim, their content and the material circumstances in which the discourse is performed. Through linguistic exchanges, the discourse constructs itself. In order to arrive at shared comprehension, domains of communication are progressively built up (for example, a rally, a broadcast declaration, or an election programme are part of the political communication domain). These domains determine, through the features of their components, the conditions of production and recognition of communication acts. So the vast domain of social practice is structured in domains of communication that I call 'global situations of communication', which are the result of the 'particular' situations of communication related to them. Each communicative situation therefore includes the general conditions common to all these particular situations; in addition, each particular situation, in turn, also includes, at the level of its components, both the general data that the global situation supplies and the features that are appropriate to the particular situation. For example, the global situation of 'political communication' supplies the general features of 'incitement', the identities of the participants (e.g. political figure, member of the public, or opposition figure) and content (ideology). Every particular situation (rally, pamphlet, radio broadcast etc.) is made up of these components, including those emanating from material circumstances. So the discourses produced in each of these situations are different (a speech at a rally differs from one on television), whilst also having something in common (defending values, criticizing the opposition, establishing credibility). It is the same with the global situation of media communication whose general features are always apparent in the various channels for supplying information (press, radio and television).

Any communicative situation, global or specific, presents to its participants a certain number of conditions that define what is *at stake* in the communicative exchange: its purpose, the identity of its participants, its content domain and its material circumstances. While forming the hypothesis that without recognition of these conditions there will be no possibility of shared comprehension, I now introduce the concept of a 'communication contract'. It appears that a speaker and an addressee are bound by a reciprocal recognition contract that allows them to understand each other. This contract has the function of constraining the operating procedures of the production and interpretation of the communication act, while at the same time allowing the participants to co-construct the sense.

Considered from the point of view of discourse analysis, this concept allows us to group together the texts that take part in these situational conditions. Thus, data can be collected to support either the global contract of communication (e.g. advertising, media information or political texts), or particular situations (e.g. single advertisements as opposed to a poster campaign, political newspaper articles as opposed to radio broadcasts). Such a typology is, obviously, not the only principle behind ordering the texts; for example, in the case of political newspaper articles, it does not allow us to distinguish the differences between different types of newspapers or articles. I therefore propose to study in more detail what happens at the level of discursive construction.

Discursive construction. The discursive level is where, under the effect of the constraints of the situation, different and more or less codified 'manners of speaking' establish themselves. It is thus at the discursive level that the subject has to make choices which, without being absolutely constrained, are, nonetheless, not completely free. How can we distinguish situational, discursive and formal constraints?

Situational constraints are data external to what is said but, as already mentioned, they are communicational in that they determine: 'why something is said', 'who is addressing whom', 'about what' and 'under what circumstances'. These constraints thus generate instructions for 'how to say something'.

Discursive constraints are data internal to what is said and are dependent on situational constraints. If the link between external data and discursive construction is one of causality, it does not necessarily imply a correspondence between them. External data only determine the structure of the linguistic frame which orders them. Thus, data used to convey purpose determine a certain choice of descriptive, narrative or argumentative modes;[1] data concerning the identities of the participants determine a certain choice in the mode of utterance (allocutionary, elocutionary or delocutionary); data controlling content determine some modes of thematization, namely, how the themes and subthemes are to be organized; material circumstances data determine certain forms, namely, the organization of the material production (verbal and/or visual) of the communication act. Discursive constraints do not correspond to an obligation to use such-and-such a textual form, but to a whole range of possible discursive behaviours from which the communicating subject chooses those that are suitable to satisfy the external data conditions. For example, the aims of 'information' and 'incitement' which characterize a media contract[2] determine a frame for the treatment of discourse in which the media source has to: (a) give an account of the event in order to transform it into news (and turn it into a reported event) by using descriptive and narrative operating procedures, sometimes objectifying (in order to be credible), sometimes dramatizing (in order to keep the attention of its audience); (b) explain the event (analysis or commentary) by using argumentative operating procedures; and (c) produce a new event by using operating procedures which encourage interaction (debates, talk shows, interviews). The places assigned to the partners in this contract determine a frame for the treatment of utterances in which the media source must construct for itself the image of an uninvolved, distant and neutral speaker. It must also construct an image of the recipient who is supposed to be involved (in the name of citizenship), to be affected (in the name of human nature) and to be making attempts to understand (in the name of good will). The subject determines a rationalization of the thematic treatment around the events selected according to their potential 'realization', 'proximity' and 'social disorder'.[3]

The *formal constraints* are also internal to what is said, constituting its textual configuration. They use repetitive forms which, in becoming routine, are stabilized

---

1.   The *descriptive* mode refers to the state of people or things in the world; the *narrative* mode refers to human actions as well as actions with a specific purpose; the *argumentative* mode refers to reasoning that is itself broken down into an 'explicative' component, when the truth has already been established and certain phenomena have been explained, and into a 'demonstrative' component, when the truth has to be established or proven.

2.   I resume here the analysis outlined in the third part of Charaudeau (1997).

3.   For details of this description, see Charaudeau (1997).

ways of speaking. But – this is the original hypothesis – as these manners of speaking depend on the communicative situation, their 'routinization' shapes itself into discursive constraints that echo the situational constraint requirements. These play the role of mediator between the situational constraint data and textual configuration. All the components of the communicative situation condition the form, through discursive constraints, but the material circumstance component is perhaps the one that most directly influences the form, which is why this component creates 'material devices'. This starts with different oral or writing styles depending on whether the material device puts the participants in physical co-presence in an interlocutive situation, or in physical absence in a monolocutive situation; in the first case, the transmission channel is phonic, and in the second case, scriptural. In addition, if one is, for example, in a situation of interlocution, different roles will be assigned to the different partners in the exchange: those features that differentiate the elements of a speech and its enunciative attitudes, e.g. in an interview or debate (see Charaudeau, 1986, 1991). On the other hand, if one is in a monolocutive situation, without the physical co-presence of one's partner, the features of the material device will cause the presentation of a message to vary, depending on whether the communication is by letter, electronic mail or telegram. Taking account of these circumstances in my analysis of information discourse in the media has led me to devise this typology, first founded on the 'device as materiality of the production' (Charaudeau, 1986). This typology defines the radio as essentially a device of *contact*, the television as a device of *spectacle* and the press as a device of *legibility*; the different operating procedures of production are defined as various 'scenic devices' (interviews, reports, titles etc.). The organization of these forms obeys fewer rules than norms, with a more codified use, which are linguistically expressed in various ways. Therefore, if, owing to situational and discursive constraints, the qualities of the products being advertised must be demonstrated by using slogans (which should be as brief as possible), that does not stop the sentence construction of advertisements from being extremely variable. If the discourse of information in the press, owing to its situational and discursive constraints, must announce news using relatively short headlines, this does not stop these headlines – as demonstrated by comparing them – from appearing as diverse sentence constructions (which for the most part are not nominalized) depending on the type of newspaper and on the kind of news.

It is at this level that the *text* is constructed, which endows it with multiple properties. Since it is made up of a signifying materiality, it is characterized by general properties of oral, scriptural, mimo-gestural and iconic character, and their inherent conditions of morphological and syntactic construction. As the text is produced in a contractual situation, it depends for its significance on what characterizes this situation (purpose, identity, content and material circumstances); as it is based on a particular subject, the text discloses characterizations and specific features dependent on that choice of subject. So far, one could say that any text is both coded and has unique features. It is inscribed into a continuity that is limited by a closure, one that gives a text its structure, its internal coherence and the situational and discursive conditions that partly characterize it. At the same time, this continuity remains open, both because of its adherence to a situation that places it in relation to other similar texts and the unique circumstances conferred on it by the subject. Thus, one may say that the text is both autonomous and dependent.

This conception of language working at three levels of constraints offers a useful perspective for clarifying the often discussed topic of 'genres' of discourse: do they have to be defined and classified according to their formal recurrence or according to their conceptual devices?

Considering the variety of texts that can be grouped in the same range, definition by their formal recurrence always poses problems. If we look at an advertisement or a series of journalistic, scientific or political texts, it is difficult to find any exclusive recurrence (otherwise it would be impossible to make any differentiation) of a certain form of sentence construction, or a certain use of connectors or verb tenses. This seems natural if we consider that the constraints of the linguistic process result in the first place from a communicational device and that these constraints determine the others.

This is why I propose to define genres in 'situational' terms, from constraints that characterize this level, and then enumerate the possible variants through the description of discursive and formal constraints. Thus, contracts for global situations of communication, such as advertising, political, media or scientific contracts, correspond to big 'genres' that I call 'situational genres'. The variants of these contracts ('subcontracts' or 'subgenres') will be considered to be embedded in the big genre on which they depend. Let us take as an example, newspaper headlines: these are inscribed into a global situation of media 'communication' whose purpose is information that demands a discursive constraint of announcement of news; in this particular situation, the constraint of announcement appeals to a formal constraint of headlines. One also sees that it is possible to speak of genres at each of these different levels: the information genre determined by the media domain, the *announcement* subgenre determined by discursive constraints, and the *sub subgenre (sous sous-genre)* of titles determined by formal constraints.

Discursive strategies

The concept of strategy is bound to that of the subject who would be its organizer, even if s/he is unaware of it. It is hardly possible to develop here a theory of subjects and their strategies by reviewing those that prevail in the other social and human sciences.

Instead, I turn to what seems to constitute the conditions of a definition of this concept in the setting of the sciences of language. Four conditions determine the possibility of 'linguistic strategies':

1. It seems difficult to think about this concept without taking into account the complementary notion of 'constraints'. Subjects must have a fixed frame, ensuring the stability and predictability of their behaviour, in order to be able to ask themselves what is the margin of manoeuvre within which they can move. This represents to me the 'contract of communication' that sets constraints in relation to which linguistic subjects are confined in part, but only in part, and which leaves subjects a margin of manoeuvre in which they will be able to use strategies.

2. Any speech act is part of more general social behaviour that is defined by its goal. This represents the object of the quest toward which the subject is inclined; obtaining this object represents a final balanced state from which the subject benefits. To reach this goal, subjects must have the competence to utilize a certain number of types of behaviour, and to make some choices among those that are at their disposition in order to reach their goal. One could, perhaps, speak here of action strategies but not of linguistic strategies.

3. For this possibility, it is necessary that an obstacle exists, an uncertainty as to whether the goal is within reach, an uncertainty that can be bound either to a possible counteraction of the Other, to a possible superior performance of the Other, or to some material obstacle making it difficult for subjects to achieve their purpose. In any case, the realization of the goal depends on these Others that are opposing them.

4. From here an aim can be formed to resolve the problem posed by the existence of the obstacle. The aim therefore superimposes itself upon the goal. In order to behave correctly, one must conform to the usual norms and, at the same time, constantly be thinking of other procedures. This aim opens up a new field of activities which, this time, are strictly linguistic: this represents the dilemma for the subject of making some linguistic choices among a wide range of possibilities in order to influence the one on which resolution of the problem depends. This type of activity belongs to a conceptualization (and a plan) which consists of calculating in advance the advantages and drawbacks (risks) of every choice according to the obstacles and uncertainties that might arise.

Thus, for me, discursive strategies are defined in relation to the contract of communication. They consist for subjects first of all of an evaluation of the margin of manoeuvre available within the contract in order to negotiate between, and with, the situational, discursive and formal constraints. Subjects then have to choose, from among the modes of organization of the discourse and the modes of textual construction, in relation to the types of knowledge and beliefs, the operating procedures that will correspond best to the project of their own utterance, their aim of influencing the addressee (*visée d'influence*), vis-à-vis the addressee, and to what is at stake. In this negotiation between contract and strategies, one could say that the first is a matter of *choices* since behaviours can be anticipated, but the second cannot be planned in advance since they depend on the subject's will, and on his or her speech competence. However, these strategies are not necessarily so conscious. They can be non-conscious (this does not mean 'unconscious'), meaning that they may not always result from clear, rational planning on the part of the communicating subject.

Three stakes

The strategies are multiple, but they can be grouped into three categories, each of which corresponds to a type of stake (*enjeu*). These stakes are not mutually exclusive but are distinguished by the nature of their purpose. Here we can speak of stakes of *legitimation*, *credibility* and *captation*.

–   *Legitimation* is based on the necessity to create or reinforce the legitimacy of the speaker. It is about the operating procedure of claiming legitimacy, which explains the dynamic form of the word 'legitimization'. The speaker may have some doubts about the way in which he or she is perceived by the addressee/s as to his or her 'right to speak'. Speakers thus have to persuade their addressees that their grasp and manner of speech are appropriate for the position of authority that is conferred on them, either by their status ('institutional authority') or by their relation to it ('natural authority').

Since the strategy of legitimization consists especially of recalling or reinforcing a position of authority, it understandably comes with a 'justification' discourse. If the latter emerges without being requested, it can be called a 'self-justification' discourse. Subjects rarely give 'self-justification' discourses, as such, since confessing the need to recall their position of legitimacy could be counterproductive and may raise doubts in the minds of their addressees: 'If he or she justifies himself or herself, it is because he or she does not have enough authority to speak.' If the justification appears at the addressee's request, it might consist only of recalling the institutional position of the subject, a position that endows him or her with a certain knowledge (as expert, specialist or scientist) or a certain power (as a responsible person, able to take a decision or exercise a sanction). Use will be made of what is called in rhetoric an 'argument of authority'. Sometimes there may be no recourse of this sort, and the subject has to argue to explain his or her right to speak. In media communication, for example, this 'stake' of legitimization is expressed by a discourse of 'self-celebration' by the media source (especially in television) that submits evidence for the validity of its programmes, the veracity of its information or the relevance of its commentaries.

– *Credibility* is based on the need for the speaker to be believed, either in relation to the truth of the content of his or her discourse, or in relation to what he or she really thinks – in other words, his or her sincerity. The speaker has to defend an image of himself or herself (an 'ethos') that leads him or her strategically to answer the question: 'How can I be taken seriously?' To do that, he or she can adopt several discursive attitudes:

a. an attitude of *neutrality* which leads him or her to erase from his or her discourse all trace of judgement or personal assessment. This is the attitude of the witness that speaks on the nature of the report (*mode de constat*), reports on what he or she saw, heard, tried. Obviously, it is not necessary that one suspects the motives that induce a witness to speak, and one would not think that he or she (the witness) had been charged by someone to serve his or her cause. In this case, the testimonial discourse is a speech of truth 'in the raw' state that, by definition, cannot be doubted.

b. an attitude of *distancing* which drives the subject to adopt the specialist's cold and controlled attitude that reasons and analyses without passion, as an expert would, in order to explain the reasons for something, comment on the results of a survey or demonstrate a thesis.

c. an attitude of *commitment* which brings the subject, contrary to the case of neutrality, to opt (in a more or less conscious way) for a stand in the choice of arguments or choice of words,[4] or by an evaluative modalization brought to his or her discourse. This attitude is meant to construct the image of a subject 'speaking with conviction'. The truth, here, is confounded with the strength of conviction of the speaker, and this truth is supposed to influence the addressee.

In media communication, credibility is expressed by a discourse of authentication of the facts, mostly based on testimonies.

– *Captation* is based upon the subject's need to be sure that the partner in the communicative exchange accepts his or her project, in other words shares his or her ideas, his or her opinions and/or is 'impressed' or 'moved' (Charaudeau, 2000). The subject then has to answer the question of: 'How to act so that the other 'could be impressed' by what I say?' To do that, the subject can choose between several discursive attitudes among which are:

---

4. For example, Le Pen attacks his opponents by choosing the word *l'établissement* instead of *l'establishment*.

a. a *controversial* attitude, that brings him or her to question some of the values that a third party defends and to which the addressee could adhere in order to make him or her change his or her opinion. The question here is how to 'destroy an adversary' while not only questioning his or her ideas but also his or her person, so that the public audience that listens to him or her might share this implication.

b. an attitude of *dramatization*, in which the subject embellishes the facts with dramatic stories, multiple analogies, comparisons, metaphors etc. This way of speaking relies more on beliefs than on knowledge, because the question here is about putting over certain values or making certain that the speaker's emotions are shared.

For example, this occurs in media communication when dramatic events and other disasters are being described, for reasons that are, sometimes, presented as *human*. This allows us to designate a responsible person, or even a guilty one, against whom indignation or one's desire for vengeance[5] is to be directed; at other times, these reasons are presented as non-human – which allows us to construct a universe of events from which human beings are absent and in which they are powerless in the face of the dark strengths that overwhelm them.[6]

Conclusion

The fundamental question that is raised by discourse analysis is to know if one accepts as a theoretical proposition the fact that discourse (and not necessarily its analysis) results, as Maingueneau (1995) says, 'from the intermingling of a mode of enunciation and of a specific social place'. In fact, one could say, more precisely, that the 'social place' is made up of something similar to the 'communicative situation' and something that is a matter of the 'positioning' of the subject, and that these combine (in an explicit or implicit way) in the operating procedures of 'enunciation'.

The 'communicative situation' is where communicational conditioning takes place, in other words the set of psychosocial conditions that control the exchanges in which speech acts are produced. This conditioning is a matter of symbolic norms that

---

5. One can see this in cases of corruption where a villain, victims and a hero have to be identified, if possible.

6. For instance, according to the media, this applies to natural catastrophes. However, the way in which television treated 'snipers' in the Bosnian war (the images of people who were gunned down in the streets, and the pictures of windows behind which one could not see anything) is also an example of this strategy.

constitute the subject matter of evaluative discourses (whether explicit or implicit) on the well-founded nature of behaviour. It is in the setting of these situations that the subject operates according to micro-sociological regulations between constraints (contract) and strategies that consist of negotiating between the intra-discursive (the place of enunciation) and the extra discursive (the place of the situation). Thus the concepts of the 'situation of enunciation' and 'communication' will not be confused.

The concept of 'positioning' refers not only to doctrines, schools, theories etc. (Maingueneau and Cossutta, 1995). It is also a manifestation of the 'reflexive capacity' of the 'subject producers of sense in a determined historical conjuncture' (Branca-Rosoff et al., 1995); this capacity is relevant not only to language but to all social behaviour by way of discursive productions that determine the value of the more or less institutionalized ways in which behaviour is regulated. Thus, 'discursive spaces' are constructed, in which not only self-constituting texts and their derivatives circulate (Maingueneau and Cossutta, 1995), but also all sorts of discourses not necessarily institutionalized, but having a discursive homogeneity, and defined in opposition to other concurrent discourses. It is in this discursive space that the subjects construct their positioning.

Thus this article has shown how in a communicational conception of discourse, speech participants take part in a given situation according to the constraints that are imposed upon them and the margins for manoeuvre that are available to them.

References

Branca-Rosoff, Sonia, André Colinot, Jacques Guilhaumou, and Francine Mazière. 1995. 'Questions d'histoire et de sens.' *Langages* 117: 54–66. DOI: 10.3406/lgge.1995.1705

Charaudeau, Patrick. 1986. 'L'interview médiatique: qui raconte sa vie?' *Cahiers de sémiotique textuelle* 8–9: 129–137.

Charaudeau, Patrick. 1991. 'Contrats de communication et ritualisation des débats télévisés.' In *La Télévision: Les débats culturels. 'Apostrophe'*, ed. by Patrick Charaudeau, 11–35. Paris: Didier Erudition.

Charaudeau, Patrick. 1997. *Le Discours d'information médiatique*. Paris: Nathan-Ina.

Charaudeau, Patrick. 2000. 'Problématique discursive de l'émotion: A propos des effets de pathémisation à la télévision.' In *Les émotions dans les interactions*, ed. by Christian Plantin. Lyon: Presses Universitaires de Lyon.

Maingueneau, Dominique. 1995. 'Présentation.' *Langages* 117: 5–11.

Maingueneau, Dominique, and Frédéric Cossutta. 1995. 'L'analyse des discours constituants.' *Langages* 117: 112–25. DOI: 10.3406/lgge.1995.1709

Ruth Amossy

Argumentation and discourse analysis

Unlike other specialists in rhetorics, Ruth Amossy (b. 1946) believes that rhetoric must be integrated into the field of discourse analysis on condition that discourse analysis is deeply anchored in history. From this perspective, her position shares some properties with that of Wodak (see the section on 'Critical Approaches'). At the same time, Amossy's position is opposed to that of specialists in argumentation who ignore discourse as well as of those who defend a normative conception, i.e. those who think that there is a 'fair' or 'correct' way of arguing. One can find this normative point of view in various trends, particularly in the 'pragma-dialectic' of van Eemeren / Grootendorst (2004), which implies an idealized model of argumentation, or in the theory of 'fallacies' (i.e. errors in reasoning) developed by Hamblin (1970). In the first part of her text, she wonders whether argumentation is part of any discourse activity or is limited to certain kinds of discourse (in particular, politics, advertising, science etc.) in which one must defend one thesis against another. Unlike many specialists in rhetoric, she defends a broad conception of argumentation, 'which is understood as the attempt to change, reorientate, or reinforce, by the use of linguistic means, the addressee's view'. So, argumentation is 'intrinsic to discourse, according to a continuum which goes from explicit confrontation of theses to co-building a reply to a given question, and spontaneously expressing a personal point of view'. The second section of the text focuses on the relationship between the study of argumentation and discourse analysis. Amossy refuses to consider argumentation as a sequence of propositions, a kind of cognitive skeleton or pattern which is independent of the natural language that conveys it. Accordingly, an analysis of argumentation must take into account the linguistic characteristics of texts.

References

Eemeren, Frans van, and Rob Grootendorst. 2004. *A systematic theory of argumentation. The pragma-dialectical approach*. Cambridge: Cambridge University Press.
Hamblin, Charles Leonhard. 1970. *Fallacies*. London: Methuen.

Ruth Amossy. 2008. 'Argumentation et Analyse du Discours:
perspectives théoriques et découpages disciplinaires.'
Argumentation et Analyse du discours [online], 1, selected paragraphs 1–18,
http://aad.revues.org/200.

1. Argumentation as part of discursive functions

Given the fact that Discourse Analysis (DA) aims to describe how discourse works in situ, it cannot avoid its argumentative dimension. Certainly, not every given speech is intended to elicit the adherence of an audience to a thesis (Perelman, and Olbrechts-Tyteca, 1969 [1958]). As a matter of fact, many types of discourses do no have any argumentative goal – you find those in everyday speech as well as in literary texts – insofar as they do not have any intention to convince, nor win over, the addressee to a position that is clearly defined by planned strategies of persuasion. Yet, speech that does not aim at persuasion still strives to influence, by shaping the way people see and think. Benveniste noted that every discourse presupposes the presence of both a speaker (*locuteur*) and an addressee (*auditeur*), with the former's intention being to influence the latter (Benveniste, 1974: 241–242). Although most probably incomplete, this definition has the advantage of emphasizing that every verbal exchange is based on a game of mutual influences, as well as on the more or less conscious and confessed attempt to use speech in order to influence others. It stresses the illocutionary force of utterances, a perspective developed by pragmatics (*how to do things with words*), and interaction theories, for which speaking generally involves several participants that constantly influence one another: 'speaking is about exchanging, and about changing while exchanging' (Kerbrat-Orecchioni, 1990: 54–55).

According to Charaudeau, every speech act comes from a speaker who deals with his/her relationship to the other (principle of alterity) in order to influence (principle of influence), while also tackling a relationship in which the dialogue partner has his/her own agenda regarding influence (principle of regulation) (Charaudeau, 2005: 12).

Does this mean that speech is necessarily argumentative? The viewpoints on this topic vary widely. For classical rhetoric, that is to say the art of persuasion – and therefore the art of argumentation – only a few discourse genres fall into the domain of argumentation itself. Aristotle mentions judicial, deliberative and epideictic discourses as such, and although in Perelman's view the rhetoric domain is wider, and includes – as his examples show – philosophical discourse as well as literary discourse, he nevertheless restricts argumentation to the attempt to mobilize linguistic tools to elicit the adherence of the addressee. Current argumentation theories are in complete agreement with this restriction, since they clearly circumscribe discourses that aim to persuade the audience by the use of reasoning, i.e. logos, seen as speech and reason.

For example, according to Oléron, argumentation consists of the steps taken by an individual or a group of individuals to win an audience over to a given position by the use of presentations or assertions, i.e. arguments that aim to show how valid the position is (Oléron, 1987:4). In Breton's eyes, 'argumentation belongs to the type of human actions that aims at persuading. [...] [Its specificity is that] it implements reasoning in a communication situation' (Breton, 1996:3). Finally, for van Eemeren, the founding father of the *Amsterdam School*, and of the *pragma-dialectical* approach to the study of argumentation, argumentation is

> a verbal and social activity of reason aimed at increasing (or decreasing) the acceptability of a controversial standpoint for the listener or reader, by putting forward a constellation of propositions intended to justify (or refute) the standpoint before a rational judge. (Van Eemeren and Grootendorst, 1984:53)

However, we can also take into account, following the example of Grize, that

> ...argumentation does not see the speaker as a mere object to be manipulated, but rather as an alter ego with whom one's view is to be shared. Acting upon the speaker is about trying to change the various representations that are attributed to him, by giving prominence to some aspects of things, hiding others, and putting forward new ones. (Grize, 1990:41, *our own translation from French*)

We therefore reach a broader conception of argumentation, which is understood as the attempt to change, reorientate or reinforce, via linguistic means, the addressee's view. This is the definition I gave in *L'Argumentation dans le discours* (2010 [2000]), thus extending the one offered by Perelman's New Rhetoric to the attempt to make people support not only a thesis but also ways of thinking, seeing and feeling. Such an extension allows argumentation (synonymous with rhetoric, or the art of persuasion) to deal with the wide range of discourses, both private and public, that circulate in the modern world. It also allows argumentation to assert its place in language sciences, without the need to turn to psychology or social psychology, unlike what is claimed by Patrick Charaudeau (2008).

Even then, the divergence of opinions has to be clarified, since it is the very basis of argumentation. Indeed, such divergence only arises from dissension, or at least when another way of looking at things crops up. As Aristotle underlined, we do not argue about things that are obvious, i.e. about things which, in a given community, seem to make sense and to stand as the only possible answer to a particular question. This point is quite obvious in Michel Meyer's definition:

> Argumentation is about finding means to prompt a unique answer, as well as having the interlocutor support one's answer. As such, it is about doing away with the options of the interlocutor's original viewpoint, and therefore with the question that represents those options. (Meyer, 2005:15, *our own translation from French*)

However, we have to assert whether the other answers that can be prompted by this question have to be explained within a confrontational context or not. Christian Plantin expresses such a view and defines the 'typical argumentative situation as the development and confrontation of contradictory viewpoints in order to answer a same given question' (Plantin, 2005: 53). According to him, this 'active contrasting of discourses around the same issue' allows the 'avoidance of argument dilution in language', which could be, in his opinion, a real pitfall if one followed Grize's (or Vignaux's) views, for whom discourse and argumentation entail one another (*ibid.*). Like them, and unlike Plantin, I believe that discourse in real-life situations involves trying to influence and have people look at things in a certain way. There is no need to set out the opposite position or counter an argument in full, because speech always stands as a reply to something that has been said earlier, and as such, it attests, modifies or disproves it:

> Any utterance – the finished, written utterance not excepted – makes response to something and is calculated to be responded to in turn. It is but one link in a continuous chain of speech performances. Each monument carries on the work of its predecessors, polemicizing with them, expecting active, responsive understanding, and anticipating such understanding in return.   (Voloshinov, 1973: 72)

Thus, within this dialogical perspective, argumentation is a priori intrinsic to discourse, according to a continuum which goes from explicit confrontation of theses to co-building a reply to a given question, and spontaneously expressing a personal point of view. That is the reason why it falls to the analyst to describe the modes of argumentative speech in the same way as s/he describes other linguistic processes, and to do so in close connection with them.

Obviously, we must strive to avoid confusion: this is why it is important to distinguish the argumentative goal from the argumentative dimension. Indeed, although discourse – and this is intrinsic to its dialogic nature – acts on others in order to influence them, we have to differentiate between planned persuasion and the tendency for discourse to steer the way speakers look at things. In the first instance, discourse displays an argumentative aim – election campaign speeches and advertisements are obvious examples of this – and in the second instance, it simply has an argumentative dimension (Amossy, 2005, 2010a [2000]: 32–34). This is the case with papers that are meant to inform and to be objective, as well as with colloquial speech and fictional narratives.

When an argumentative aim is involved, at least one argumentative mode is chosen in speech. Such a speech structure optimizes persuasion. Among the different modes of argumentation available, we can mention the demonstrative mode, in which a thesis is presented by a speaker, within a self-monitored speech, or a dialogue, to an audience s/he wants to persuade, by using reasoned demonstration, such as articulated reasoning from proven facts. We can also mention argumentation-based negotiation, within which agents who hold divergent or even conflicting opinions strive to find a common solution to the issue that divides them, and to reach consensus through compromise. We can finally mention the polemical mode of argumentation, characterized by a violent confrontation of antagonistic theses: two agents, who totally disagree with one another, try to persuade either the opponent or a third party, by challenging the opposing thesis.

Things are different with the argumentative dimension of discourse, because the intention of convincing is not explicit. It appears in the wording of a speech whose avowed aim is other than argumentative, e.g. in media discourse, descriptions, narratives that aim at relating stories, reports found in travel or personal diaries, testimonials, colloquial conversations in which speakers exchange innocuous comments without trying to persuade one another of the validity of a particular viewpoint etc. Therefore, what is important to bring out and analyze is how speech influences the way the addressee looks at things.

In any case, argumentation is an integral part of the way discourse works, and as such it must be analyzed within the framework of discourse analysis. DA allows the study of argumentation as part of linguistic materiality, and within a concrete communication situation.

2. Argumentative analysis as part of DA

Treatises on argumentation inspired by Aristotle's rhetoric describe the main types of arguments and reasoning: syllogism, enthymeme and analogy. Some of them, e.g. Toulmin's pioneering book (1958), offer prototypes for an argument model.[1] Others set up a taxonomy of arguments by trying to group arguments together, within quite diverse classifications. And others, e.g. informal logic, strive to detect fallacies (paralogisms). Within all of these approaches[2] argumentation seems to be a series of logical propositions that have to be isolated from the natural language that both conveys and misrepresents them. However, as soon as patterns are reconstructed, thanks to a reasoning that sums up the concrete utterances as propositions in order to integrate them into an abstract argumentative string, language is generally seen as an obstacle. The researcher therefore strives to reduce it in order to extract the underlying reasoning behind it. He has to reveal the argumentation framework, the hidden 'skeleton' under the flesh of words.

---

1.   Grounds or data (D) are put forward in order to support a claim (C) that is legitimized by warrants (W), which are themselves certified by credentials or backing (B). Also, reservations (R) can be applied to the claim. For instance: unless there is evidence to the contrary (R), Harry was born in Bermuda (D), he is a British citizen (C), given the fact that people born in Bermuda will legally be British citizens (W).

2.   A panorama of these approaches is presented in Breton and Gauthier (2000).

Argumentation theory rooted in language sciences is opposed to this kind of approach. As Christian Plantin strongly states, 'natural language is not an obstacle but the necessary condition for argumentation' (1995:259; our translation). Looking at it as an integral part of discourse, and beyond a schematization that provides abstract reasoning, allows us to see how persuasion works efficiently in a given communication situation. Thus, beyond a series of logical propositions that sum up contents and the connections between them, we can take into account everything that is being worked out within the persuasion process. Argumentative speech does not take place within the abstract space of pure logic but within a communication situation where the speaker's viewpoint is brought forward by using natural language and its whole array of means, i.e. connectives, deictics, presuppositions, implicit stereotypical markers, ambiguity, polysemy, metaphor, repetition and rhythm. Argumentation is shaped and conveyed within the denseness of language, and is deployed through the use of language. One should not forget that argumentation is not about displaying self-sufficient reasoning but about two or more speakers virtually or actually communicating in order to try and influence one another.

Therefore, in addition to the condition of natural language, there is another intrinsic condition, that of the interaction within which a speaker takes into account the addressee s/he wants to influence, and for whom s/he mobilizes an array of linguistic means, and more or less planned discursive strategies. Argumentation stands within the framework of an enunciation system in which the speaker has to adapt to the addressee, or more precisely to the picture s/he has of that addressee (according to Perelman, the audience is always a construction of the speaker). Argumentation also supposes that a concrete enunciation situation is taken into account: who is speaking to whom, which power relation is involved, what the participants' statuses are, what the exact circumstances of the exchange are, and when and where it takes place. Moreover, speech necessarily takes place within the framework of a discourse genre that belongs to a given spatial setting, and has its own objectives, rules and constraints.

This approach, which pays attention to the axis of communication and interaction (actual or virtual) between the agents of the exchange, gives the argumentative analysis its social and institutional dimension. We then move from the realm of universals, which is implied by rhetoric focusing on logos as a-temporal reasoning, to the social realm, with its relativity, as well as its cultural and historical variations. This means that argumentative analysis endorses the vocation of DA, which consists of seeing 'discourse as the entwinement of text and social place', therefore its object 'is neither the textual organization, nor the communication situation, but what links them together through a specific enunciation system. Such a system falls both within the verbal and institutional provinces' (Maingueneau, in Charaudeau, and Maingueneau (eds.), 2002:43; see also Maingueneau and Angermüller, 2007).

The way argumentation is part not only of the materiality of the discursive system (word choice, semantic shifts, connectives, use of implicit elements etc.), but also of interdiscourse, has to be studied closely within this sociohistorical communication framework. What is of paramount importance is the way the text assimilates the other's words, thanks to the various possibilities speech offers, e.g. reported speech, direct speech, quotation and free indirect discourse. The relations of the text to the discourses that circulate prior to or around it are also significant, and this constitutive heterogeneity is actually at the root of argumentative speech, insofar as such speech has to react to the other's words, be it in order to correct, modify or refute them. It is therefore important to grasp the gist of whatever has been said or written in a given society on the topic under discussion. The fact that the speaker does not specifically refer to it does not mean that his/her speech does not draw from it: the viewpoint that is presented always has to be taken as part of a preexisting constellation of ideas. Finally, one must examine the textual organization that determines how arguments are displayed, as well as the way the speaker has adopted to sort out the elements of his/her discourse for the benefit of the audience.

It is also within this framework that *ethos* (the construction of an image of the self in discourse, cf. Amossy, 2010b) and *pathos* (the discursive construction of the emotional response the speaker intends to trigger in the audience, cf. Plantin, Doury, and Traverso, 2000) – two poles of classical rhetoric that have often been neglected by argumentation theories – have to be taken up. Persuasion consists of three discursive devices: *logos, ethos* and *pathos,* and it is the way they are intertwined that allows the speaker to form a strong and persuasive argument. Nowadays, it is not uncommon to hear the claim that *logos* – which means persuading by the use of reasoning, logical proof and rational argumentation – has lost momentum, and has been replaced in the public sphere by *ethos* – the speaker creates an ethos, meaning that s/he projects a favourable self-image with the intention of lending him/herself credibility, power and influence – and *pathos* – a speech appealing to the audience's emotions at the expense of rational thought. Whatever the possible drift of today's democracies might be, it seems that things are not that simple. *Logos, ethos* and *pathos,* the three classical components of Aristotle's rhetoric, are still necessary to persuasion, in varying amounts and combinations. It is for the researcher to spot them in texts, and to bring out the modes of combination they are subjected to in order to produce the desired effect.

To sum up, argumentative analysis

1. studies natural language argumentation within the materiality of discourse, and as an integral element of a global discursive functioning;
2. sets such argumentation within a specific enunciation situation whose elements (participants, place, time, circumstances etc.) should be known in full;
3. studies the way argumentation is part of interdiscourse by standing in relation to what has been told prior to, and at the time of, speech, through repetition, modification, refutation, negation etc.;

4. takes into account the way *logos* – the display of natural language arguments – is combined with *ethos* – the self-image projected by the orator in his/her discourse – and *pathos* – the emotional response s/he intends to create in the other and that s/he must build discursively.

References

Amossy, Ruth. 2005. The argumentative dimension of discourse. In *Practices of Argumentation*, ed. by Frans H. van Eemeren and Peter Houtlosser, 87–98. Amsterdam: John Benjamins Publishing Company.

Amossy, Ruth. 2010a [2000]. *L'Argumentation dans le discours*. Paris: Armand Colin.

Amossy, Ruth. 2010b. *La Présentation de soi*. Paris: PUF.

Benveniste, Émile. 1974. *Problèmes de linguistique générale, t. 2*. Paris: Gallimard.

Breton, Philippe. 1996. *L'Argumentation dans la communication*. Paris: La Découverte.

Breton, Philippe, and Gilles Gauthier. 2000. *Histoire des théories de l'argumentation*. Paris: La Découverte.

Charaudeau, Patrick. 2005. *Le discours politique. Les masques du pouvoir*. Paris: Vuibert.

Charaudeau, Patrick. 2008. 'L'argumentation dans une problématique d'influence.' Argumentation et Analyse du Discours [Online], 1 | 2008, online on 2 October 2008, accessed on 17 October 2011 at: http://aad.revues.org/193.

Charaudeau, Patrick, and Dominique Maingueneau (eds). 2002. *Dictionnaire d'analyse du discours*. Paris: Seuil.

Grize, Jean-Blaise. 1990. *Logique et langage*. Paris: Ophrys.

Kerbrat-Orecchioni, Catherine. 1990. *Les interactions verbales, t. I*. Paris: Armand Colin.

Maingueneau, Dominique, and Johannes Angermüller. 2007. 'Discourse Analysis in France. A Conversation.' *Forum Qualitative Sozialforschung / Forum: Qualitative Social Research*, 8 (2): 21, http://nbn-resolving.de/urn:nbn:de:0114-fqs0702218.

Meyer, Michel. 2005. *Qu'est-ce que l'argumentation?* Paris: Vrin.

Oléron, Pierre. 1987. *L'Argumentation*. Paris: PUF.

Perelman, Chaim, and Lucie Olbrechts-Tyteca. 1970 [1958]. *Traité de l'argumentation. La nouvelle rhétorique*. Bruxelles. Éditions de l'Université de Bruxelles.

Plantin, Christian. 1995. 'L'argument du paralogisme.' *Hermès* 15: 245–262, 'Argumentation et rhétorique I'.

Plantin, Christian. 2005. *L'Argumentation*. Paris: PUF.

Plantin, Christian, Marianne Doury, Véronique Traverso (eds). 2000. *Les émotions dans les interactions*. Arci: Presses Universitaires de Lyon.

Perelman, Chaim, and Lucie Olbrechts-Tyteca. 1969[1958]. *The New Rhetoric. A Treatise on Argumentation*. Notre Dame, London: University of Notre Dame Press.

Toulmin, Stephen E. 1958. *The Uses of Argument*. Cambridge: Cambridge University Press.

Van Eemeren, Frans H., and Rob Grootendorst. 1984. *Speech Acts in Argumentative Discussions*. Doordrecht: Foris. DOI: 10.1515/9783110846089

Voloshinov, Valentin N. 1973. *Marxism and the Philosophy of Language*. Trans. by L. Matejka and I. R. Titunik. Cambridge, Mass.: Harvard University Press.

John Swales

Genre and discourse community

John Swales (b. 1938 in the UK) is a linguist whose research on genre was based on his expertise in English for Academic Purposes (EAP). The selected text is taken from his best-known book, *Genre Analysis: English in Academic and Research Settings* (1990). Swales tackles the notion of genre as a researcher whose main purpose is to study discourse practices in academic settings. Indeed, for Swales, exemplars of a genre 'exhibit various patterns of similarity in terms of structure, style', but, contrary to other approaches, his definition of genre is not primarily based on the identification of typical linguistic characteristics: 'genres are communicative vehicles for the achievement of goals'. Another characteristic of his approach is that genres are associated with 'discourse communities'. Being a member of a community implies sharing the same genres. From this viewpoint, casual conversation is not considered by Swales as a genre but as a 'pre-genre'. Approaches such as these are typically sociopragmatic: texts are embedded in genres, which are embedded in institutions and communities.

John M. Swales. 1990. *Genre analysis: English in academic and research settings,*
selected 45–47, 52–60.
Cambridge: Cambridge University Press.

A working definition of genre

This section offers a characterization of genres that I believe to be appropriate for the
applied purposes that I have in mind. I shall proceed by making a series of short crite-
rial observations, which will be followed in each case by commentary. Sometimes the
commentaries are short and directly to the point; at other times they are more extensive
as they explore wider discoursal or procedural issues. I hope in this way – as the section
title indicates – to create a sufficiently adequate characterization for others to be able
to use, modify or reject as they think fit.

A genre is a class of communicative events

I will assume that a communicative event is one in which language (and/or paralan-
guage) plays both a significant and an indispensable role. Of course, there are a number of situations where it may be difficult to say whether verbal communication is
an integral part of the activity or not. Levinson neatly illustrates the possibilities for
speech contexts:

> On the one hand we have activities constituted entirely by talk (a telephone conversa-
> tion, a lecture for example), on the other activities where talk is non-occurring or if
> it does occur is incidental (a game of football for instance). Somewhere in between
> we have the placing of bets, or a Bingo session, or a visit to the grocer's. And there are
> sometimes rather special relations between what is said and what is done, as in a sports
> commentary, a slide show, a cookery demonstration, a conjurer's show, and the like.
>
> (Levinson, 1979: 368)

Activities in which talk is incidental, as in engaging in physical exercise, doing the
household chores, or driving, will not be considered as communicative events; nor will
activities that involve the eyes and ears in non-verbal ways such as looking at pictures
or listening to music.

Secondly, communicative events of a particular class will vary in their occurrence
from the extremely common (service encounters, news items in newspapers) to the
relatively rare (Papal Encyclicas, Presidential Press Conferences). By and large, classes
with few instances need to have prominence within the relevant culture to exist as a
genre class. If a communicative event of a particular kind only occurs once a year it
needs to be noteworthy for class formation: a TV advert using a talking dog will not
do. Finally, and to repeat an earlier claim, a communicative event is here conceived of

as comprising not only the discourse itself and its participants, but also the role of that discourse and the environment of its production and reception, including its historical and cultural associations.

The principal criterial feature that turns a collection of communicative events into a genre is some shared set of communicative purposes

Placing the primary determinant of genre-membership on shared purpose rather than on similarities of form or some other criterion is to take a position that accords with that of Miller (1984) or Martin (1985). The decision is based on the assumption that, except for a few interesting and exceptional cases, genres are communicative vehicles for the achievement of goals. At this juncture, it may be objected that *purpose* is a some-what less overt and demonstrable feature than, say, form and therefore serves less as a primary criterion. However, the fact that purposes of some genres may be hard to get at is itself of considerable heuristic value. Stressing the primacy of purpose may require the analyst to undertake a fair amount of independent and open-minded investigation, thus offering protection against a facile classification based on stylistic features and inherited beliefs, such as typifying research articles as simple reports of experiments.

In some cases, of course, identifying purpose may be relatively easy. *Recipes,* for example, would appear to be straightforward instructional texts designed to ensure that if a series of activities is carried out according to the prescriptions offered, a successful gastronomic outcome will be achieved. In others it may not be so easy. For instance, we might suppose that the examination and cross-examination of witnesses and par-ties carried out by lawyers under an adversarial system of justice are designed and structured to elicit 'the facts of the case'. However, independent investigation shows this not to be so (Atkinson and Drew, 1979; Danet et al., 1980). The elaborate sequences of closed 'yes–no' questions are designed to control how much the hostile or friendly wit-nesses are allowed to reveal of what, in fact, they do know. Or, to take another example, we might suppose that the purposes of party political speeches are to present party policies in as convincing a way as possible, to ridicule the policies and personalities of opposition parties, and to rally the faithful. However, especially in these days of mas-sive television coverage, party political speeches may now be being written, structured and delivered in order to generate the maximum amount of applause (Atkinson, 1984). And certainly there are signs in Britain that the 'applause factor' is becoming raised in consciousness, as it were, not only as a result of the interest in Atkinson's work, but also because of the recently established journalistic practice of measuring the length of ovations following major speeches at conventions.

The immediately preceding example suggests that it is not uncommon to find genres that have *sets* of communicative purposes. While news broadcasts are doubt-less designed to keep their audiences up to date with events in the world (including verbal events), they may also have purposes of moulding public opinion, organizing public behaviour (as in an emergency), or presenting the controllers and paymasters of broadcasting organization in a favorable light. When purposive elements come into conflict with each other, as in the early Environment Impact Statements studied by Miller (1984), the effectiveness of the genre as sociorhetorical action becomes questionable. In the academic context, a genre with high potential for conflicting purposes is that of the student written examination (Searle, 1969; Horowitz, 1986).

There remain, of course, some genres for which purpose is unsuited as a primary criterion. Poetic genres are an obvious example. Although there may be overt political, religious or patriotic tracts put out in the form of verse, the poetry that is taught, remembered known and loved is rarely of that kind and inevitably makes an appeal to the reader or listener so complex as to allow no easy or useful categorization of purpose. Poems, and other genres whose appeal may lie in the verbal pleasure they give, can thus be separately characterized by the fact that they defy ascription of communicative purpose. (…)

The rationale behind a genre establishes constraints on allowable contributions in terms of their content, positioning and form

Established members of discourse communities employ genres to realize communicatively the goals of their communities. The shared set of purposes of a genre are thus recognized – at some level of consciousness – by the established members of the parent discourse community; they may be only partly recognized by apprentice members; and they may be either recognized or unrecognized by non-members. Recognition of purposes provides the rationale, while the rationale gives rise to constraining conventions. The conventions, of course, are constantly evolving and indeed can be directly challenged, but they nonetheless continue to exert influence.

I will illustrate these observations by taking two simple examples: one from administrative correspondence and one from professional interviews. Correspondence, not yet administrative correspondence, itself does not constitute a genre as it does not represent a coherent set of shared purposes. Rather it represents, as a convenient label, a supra-generic assembly of discourse. Within administrative correspondence there are, however, a number of establishable genres. Two closely related ones are the individually-directed 'good news' and 'bad news' letter (Murphy and Hildebrandt, 1984). These genres are formal responses to applications, or sometimes complaints. Classic instances are responses to applications for jobs, scholarships or grants. At one level, it might be argued that both kinds of letter constitute a single genre of *responses to applications,* but a little reflection will show that, while the textual environment and the register may be the same, the rationale is sufficiently different to require a separate genre for each.

The rationale for the 'good news' letter is based firstly on the assumption that the information transmitted is welcome. It therefore is conveyed early and enthusiastically, while the rest of the letter is set out in such a way as to remove any remaining obstacles and engender a rapid and positive response. Part of the rationale behind a 'good news' letter is that *communications will continue*. In contrast, the 'bad news' letter is based on the assumption that the information is unwelcome. It therefore is conveyed after a 'buffer' has prepared the recipient for its receipt and couched in language that is regretful and non-judgmental. Part of the rationale of the 'bad news' letter is that it minimizes personal resentment so that no long-term disaffiliation from the institution occurs; another part is to signal that *communications have ended*. For that reason, in 'bad news' letters the negative decision is usually represented as having been taken by some impersonal body, such as a committee, over which the writer gives the impression of having little influence, the purpose being to insinuate that complaint, petition or recrimination will be of no avail. The rationale thus determines what Martin (1985) refers to as the schematic structure of the discourse and also constrains lexical and syntactic choice.

The second illustration is taken from medical consultations and is designed to highlight differences in rationale perception between established and non-established members of discourse communities. Apparently many medical doctors trained in Britain use the system called SOAP to structure their consultations (Jones, 1982):

1. S = Subjective (what the patient says is wrong; what the patient perceives as his or her symptoms)
2. O = Objective (results of tests; symptoms perceived by the doctor)
3. A = Analysis (of the symptoms so as to lead to a diagnosis)
4. P = Prescription (pharmaceutical and/or giving advice or treatment)

However, patients rarely have any conscious recognition that the doctor imposes order on the consultation by the use of a structuring system such as SOAP. Part of the reason may be that other things going on, such as greetings and leave takings and various types of utterance designed to settle and reassure patients and to effect transitions between stages (Candlin, Bruton and Leather, 1976; Frankel, 1984), could appear more salient to patients. Equally, there may be things apparently not going on: the doctor's carrying out of stages O and A may well be a largely silent and private matter.

Understanding of rationale is privileged knowledge, but is neither the whole story nor any guarantee of communicative success. Erickson and Schultz (1982) in their remarkable study of academic counselling sessions make the following observation:

> There is a similar sequential order of discourse topics across interviews – an order which manifests an underlying logic of gatekeeping decision making. But it is not the underlying logic, the interactional *deep structure*, that is essential, for much more is manifested in performance – in communicational *surface structure* – than an underlying abstract logic of gatekeeping. Distinctive packages of social meanings and social identities are also manifested communicatively in each interview.
>
> (Erickson and Schultz, 1982: 12)

The point to note here is that even when we grant that surface features and local decisions are highly contributory to the performance outcome, it is very much the case that for a participant to have a sense of the 'underlying logic' or rationale is facilitative in both reception and production.

A discourse community's nomenclature for genres is an important source of insight

As we have seen, knowledge of conventions of a genre (and their rationale) is likely to be much greater in those who routinely or professionally operate within that genre rather than in those who become involved in it only occasionally. In consequence, active discourse community members tend to have the greatest genre-specific expertise – as we often see in interactions between members of a profession and their client public. One consequence is that these active members give genre names to classes of communicative events that they recognize as providing recurring rhetorical action. These names may be increasingly adopted first by overlapping or close discourse communities and then by farther and broader communities. Particular attention therefore needs to be given to the genre nomenclatures created by those who are most familiar with and most professionally involved in those genres.

As far as academic genres are concerned, many, if not most, are terms that incorporate a pre-modifying nominal of purpose: introductory lecture, qualifying exam, survey article, review session, writing workshop. Others reverse the order by using a purposive head-noun: grant application, reprint request and course description. Still others indicate the occasion rather than communicative purpose, such as final examination, plenary lecture, festschrift, faculty meeting or graduation address. However, members of the discourse community typically recognize that particular occasional genres have particular roles to play within the academic environment and that, in consequence, the sets of purposes are, one the one hand, evident and, on the other, constrained.

In the previous section that dealt with linguistic contributions to genre analysis, it was argued that insider metalanguages should certainly be considered seriously, but also viewed with circumspection. Indeed, it was suggested that an appropriate approach for the analyst would be to establish genres based on investigations into actual communicative behavior, two aspects of which, among several, would be participants' naming procedures and elicited categorizations. There are a number of reasons for caution.

One reason is that the naming of communicative events that occur and recur in post-secondary educational settings – to restrict discussion to the main focus of this study – tend to be institutional labels rather than descriptive ones. I mean by this that the timetable or course handbook will identify group activity A in setting X as a *lecture,* and group activity B in setting Y as a *tutorial.* However, as every student in higher education knows one member of staff's 'tutorial' can be identical as a communicative event to another member of staff's 'lecture' and vice versa. Of course, instructors may modify their approach depending on whether they are *supposed* to be giving *lectures* or *tutorials,* but the fact that a communicative event is labeled by the institution as being an event of such-and-such a kind does not necessarily mean that it will be so.

Secondly, names tend to persevere against a background of substantial change in activity. *Lectures* may no longer be the monologic recitations they once were, but actively invite intercalated discussion and small-group tasks. *Tutorials* today may consist of student interaction with a computer program or a tape recorder and no longer involve a 'tutor' in the traditional sense of the term. We inherit genre categories that get passed down from one generation to another.

In direct contrast, genre-naming can equally be generative. While the coining and deliberate usage of new labels for event categories can at times create substance and structure out of an amorphous background, at others the names may reflect empty categories with no claim to genre status. A pertinent instance of these processes can be seen in the advance information for the Nineteenth International IATEFL Conference (*IATEFL Newsletters* no. 84, August 1984: 54). The section entitled 'Contributions' quotes at length from *The Working Party Report on Conferences,* April 1984.

> The range of ways in which presentations and workshops could operate might be broadened considerably. If contributors were offered a range of possible formats to choose from, there would be scope for many members who are currently inhibited by the formality of presentation. At the same time many presentations would continue in the well-tried formats of the past.

The *advance-information* then lists and glosses eleven possible suggestions:

1. Basic presentations
2. Haiku sessions
3. Resource rooms
4. Traditional talks/lectures
5. Experimental workshops
6. Creative workshops
7. The buzz-group lecture
8. Curran-style lecture
9. Screening panel lecture
10. The traditional debate
11. Specific interest groups

I think it reasonable to suppose that 11 different formats is decidedly more that the average conference-goer is familiar with, and I would guess that there are very few people in the English-teaching world who could confidently explain what is expected to happen in all 11. Certainly, I had not heard of haiku sessions ('People have one very good idea to present that can really be properly got across in 10 minutes or one minute') or screening panel lectures ('Before the lecture begins three to five people from the audience come to the front and spend five minutes discussing what they expect to and want to hear from the speaker and what they expect others will want to hear. This allows the speaker to pitch his talk right'). However, I now know what a haiku session or screening panel lecture might be like, even though I have never experienced either of them; and I dare say having read about such possibilities, my interest is raised and so my participation is encouraged. Thus it is that the naming and description of new sub-genres can have pre-emptive force. Oscar Wilde had an inimitable ability to stand the world on its head, and when he observed that 'life imitates art' rather than the commonly-held converse that 'art imitates life', he may have been closer to the truth than his witticism is generally given credit for. Certainly here we seem to have been discussing potential cases where 'conference life imitates format' rather than the converse. On the other hand, relatively few of these genre suggestions seem to have been realized. Documentation from subsequent conferences fails to make mention of the 'haiku' or the 'screening panel' formats, even if others such as 'resource rooms' and 'specific interest groups' have made some headway.

If there are genre names with no genres attached to them, so must there be genres without a name. I believe there is at least one of these that occurs quite commonly in my main professional discourse community and which I am sure many readers will recognize. This is a type of presentation given to colleagues and graduate students which is built around a number of episodes in which participants, often working in pairs or small groups, are asked to reach and then share conclusions on short texts distributed among them. The tasks might involve ranking texts in order of evolution or quality, re-assembling textual fragments into their original order, or using internal evidence to guess a text's provenance. While I have twice experienced the use of such informed guessing episodes in other disciplines (in geology and art history slide-supported presentations), interestingly in both these cases the presenter prefaced his remarks with the same phrase 'Now let's play a party game'. In my own discourse community, I believe that involving others in context-stripped and task-oriented text analysis is viewed as too central and too valuable an activity to be dismissed as 'playing a party game'. And as far as I am aware, presentations of this distinctive and relatively prevalent type have no name.

This section opened with the promise that it would produce an adequate characterization of genre. The working definition that follows may in fact not be fully adequate, but it has I believe benefited from the discussion of the term in allied fields and does represent some advance on my earlier formulations (e.g. Swales, 1981). Although there remain several loose ends, some to be discussed in the next two sections, my present understanding is summarized below.

A genre comprises a class of communicative events, the members of which share some set of communicative purposes. These purposes are recognized by the expert members of the parent discourse community, and thereby constitute the rationale for the genre. This rationale shapes the schematic structure of the discourse and influences and constrains choice of content and style. Communicative purpose is both a privileged criterion and one that operates to keep the scope of a genre as here conceived narrowly focused on comparable rhetorical action. In addition to purpose, exemplars of a genre exhibit various patterns of similarity in terms of structure, style, content and intended audience. If all high probability expectations are realized, the exemplar will be viewed as prototypical by the parent discourse community. The genre names inherited and produced by discourse communities and imported by others constitute valuable ethnographic communication, but typically need further validation.

Pre-genres

One of the basic assumptions underlying much of the preceding discussion is that human beings organize their communicative behaviour *partly* through repertoires of genres. Thus, it is not the case that all communicative events are instances of genres. In fact, there are at least two areas of verbal activity that I believe are best considered to lie outside genres: casual conversation or 'chat' and 'ordinary' narrative.

The nature and role of conversation will be considered first, and Levinson's opening position will serve perfectly well:

> Definition will emerge below, but for the present *conversation* may be taken to be that predominant kind of talk in which two or more participants freely alternate in speaking, which generally occurs *outside specific institutional settings like religious services, law courses, classroom and the like.*   (Levinson, 1983: 284, my emphasis)

The kind of talk has, of course, been massively studied and discussed, particularly since the advent of the tape recorder (e.g. Grice, 1975; Goffman, 1981; Levinson, 1983; Richards and Schmidt, 1983; Gardner, 1984); and Atkinson (1982) gives the ethnomethodological arguments for the centrality and significance of conversation. As he and many people have observed, 'ordinary' conversation is a fundamental kind of language use: for example Preston (1989: 225–226) comments: 'Since conversation in some sense is basic to all face-to-face interaction, it may seem to refer to such a ubiquitous level of speech performance that one would sense a difference between it and anything else one might wish to call a genre'.

Casual conversation presumably occurred early in the evolution of the human race, as it does in a child's acquisition of first language. It takes up, for most of us, a fair part of our days; indeed involvement in conversation can be quite hard to avoid. Further, our sense of the enveloping nature of conversation is brought home when we consider its absence. Therein, after all, lay many of the trials and tribulations of Robinson Crusoe. It is often said that the severity of placing a prisoner in 'solitary confinement' resides as much as anything in the denial of verbal interaction, and a 'vow of silence' is no light undertaking.

Additionally, there would appear to be attestable individual discrepancies between conversational and non-conversational skills. Probably all of us have known people who may be highly effective communicators in certain roles (as teachers, salespeople, joke-tellers, armchair critics and so on) yet who are adjudged to be lacking in the skills of ordinary conversation and thus are thought of as individuals who are 'difficult or uncomfortable to talk with'. Conversely, we probably know people who seem to have a remarkable facility to sustain casual conversation, but who are the first to announce, for instance, that they couldn't stand up and give a vote of thanks to save their lives. These observations all seem to point to the fact that general conversational ability and genre-specific verbal skills may be phenomena of a somewhat different kind.

If these observations have substance, it would seem that ordinary conversation is too persuasive and too fundamental to be usefully considered as a genre. Rather, it is a pre-generic 'form of life', a basis from which more specific types of interaction have presumably evolved or broken away. The interesting question for the genre analyst is not so much whether conversation is a genre; instead, the interest lies in exploring the kind of relationship that might exist between conversational patterns, procedures and 'rules' and those that can be discovered in (to give three examples) legal cross-examinations, medical consultations and classroom discourse. In those three cases, are the unfolding interactions best seen as mere extensions and modifications of common conversational practice and thus ultimately parasitic on such practice? Or, alternatively, would we gain a greater understanding of what is happening by considering them as existing independently in separate universes of discourse? Are *Unequal Encounters* (Candlin, 1981) such as normally occur between doctor and patient, lawyer and witness, teacher and pupil, of a different *kind* to the more equal and less goal-directed encounters that take place in casual conversation?

Another interesting aspect of the putative relationships between the pre-genre and genres occurs in situations where 'ordinary' face-to-face conversation is replaced by telecommunication. Schegloff (1979) has shown that telephone conversations actually open with the ringing of the telephone and that the person lifting the receiver and speaking is *responding* to a summons. He has also analyzed and described the limited range of procedures that Americans use to identify and recognize each other on the telephone (much less of a problem, of course, if you can see to whom you are about to talk). Owen (1981) has written interestingly on the use of 'well' and 'anyway' as signals given by British telephone speakers to indicate a wish to close a topic or a call. However, to establish that a particular kind of event has specific, situation-bound opening and closing procedures is not, in fact, to establish very much, because specificity may well be concentrated at initiation and termination (Richards and Schmidt, 1983: 132–133). For example, openings like 'Merry Christmas', 'Good morning, Sir', 'Oh, we are smart today', 'Come here often, do you?' reflect particular circumstances that are likely to be of rapidly diminishing importance as the conversation proceeds. Therefore, on present evidence, it would seem sensible to exclude personal telephone conversations from genre status and to consider them, despite their relatively short history, as part of the pre-genre.

In contrast, we can immediately recognize the unusual nature of radio-telephony. Robertson (1985, 1988), for example, outlines the purposes of plane-ground radio-telephony as to:

i.   prevent collisions in the air;
ii. prevent collisions between aircraft and between aircraft and obstructions on the manoeuvering area;
iii. expedite and maintain orderly flow of air-traffic;
iv. provide advice and information useful for the safe and efficient conduct of flights.

(Robertson, 1985: 295)

Given these aims it is not surprising that there have evolved especially rigid rules for *turn-taking* (Sacks, Schegloff, and Jefferson, 1974) and special conventions for clarifying both rhetorical function and identity. These conventions have to be learnt by native speakers as well as non-native speakers, as the following fragment illustrates:

Control: Sierra Fox 132, correction, Sierra Fox 123, what is your flight level?
Pilot: Flight level 150, Sierra Fox 123.
Control: Say again flight level, Sierra Fox.
Pilot: Flight level 150, Sierra Fox 123.

(Robertson, 1985: 303)

Radio-telephonic Air Traffic Control meets the criteria for genre status.

References

Atkinson, J. Maxwell, and Paul Drew. 1979. *Order in court: the organization of verbal behaviour in judicial settings*. London: Macmillan.

Atkinson, Max. 1982. 'Understanding formality: the categorization and production of formal interaction.' *British Journal of Sociology* 33: 86–117. DOI: 10.2307/589338

Atkinson, Max. 1984. *Our masters' voices*. London: Methuen.

Candlin, Christopher N. 1981. Discoursal Patterning and the Equalizing of Interpretive Opportunity. In *English for Cross-Cultural Communication*, ed. by Larry E. Smith, 166–199. London: Macmillan.

Candlin, Christopher. N., Clive J. Bruton, and Jonathan H. Leather. 1976. 'Doctors in casualty: specialist course design from a database.' *IRAL* 14: 245–272. DOI: 10.1515/iral.1976.14.3.245

Danet, Brenda, Kenneth B. Hoffman, Nicole C. Kermish, H. Jeffrey Rafn, and Deborah Stayman. 1980. 'An ethnography of questioning in the courtroom.' In *Language use and the uses of language*, ed. by Roger W. Shuy and Anna Shnukal, 222–234. Washington D. C.: Georgetown University Press.

Erickson, Frederick, and Jeffrey Schultz. 1982. *The counselor as gatekeeper*. New York: Academic Press.

Frankel, Richard. 1984. 'From sentence to sequence: understanding the medical encounter through microinteractional analysis.' *Discourse Processes* 7: 135–170. DOI: 10.1080/01638538409544587

Gardner, Roderick. 1984. 'Discourse Analysis: implications for language teaching, with particular reference to casual conversation.' *Language Teaching* 17: 102–117. DOI: 10.1017/S0261444800010545

Gilbert, Nigel, and Michael Mulkay. 1984. *Opening Pandora's box: a sociological analysis of scientists' discourse*. Cambridge: Cambridge University Press.

Goffman, Erving. 1981. *Forms of talk*. Oxford: Basil Blackwell.

Horowitz, Daniel M. 1986. 'What professors actually require: academic tasks for the ESL classroom.' *TESOL Quarterly* 20: 445–462. DOI: 10.2307/3586294

Jones, Priscilla. 1982. 'A stylistic analysis of minutes and its implications in preparing a business English course.' MSc Dissertation, The University of Aston, Birmingham, UK.

Levinson, Stephen C. 1979. 'Activity types and language.' *Linguistics* 17: 356–399.

Levinson, Stephen C. 1983. *Pragmatics*. Cambridge: Cambridge University Press.

MacDonald, Dwight. 1960. *Parodies*. London: Faber & Faber.

Martin, James R. 1985. 'Process and text: two aspects of human semiosis.' In *Systemic Perspectives on discourse*, ed. by James D. Benson, and William S. Greaves, Vol.1. Norwood: Ablex.

Miller, Carolyn R. 1984. 'Genre as social action.' *Quarterly Journal of Speech* 70: 151–167. DOI: 10.1080/00335638409383686

Murphy, Herta A., and Herbert W. Hildebrandt. 1984. *Effective business communications*. 4th edn. New York: McGraw-Hill.

Owen, Marion. 1981. 'Conversation units and the use of 'well''. In *Conversation and discourse*, ed. by Paul Werth, 99–116. London: Croom Helm.

Preston, Dennis R. 1989. *Sociolinguistics and second language acquisition*. Oxford: Basil Blackwell.

Richards, Jack C., and Richard W. Schmidt (eds.). 1983. *Language and communication*. Harlow, UK: Longman.

Robertson, Fiona. 1985. 'Teaching radiotelephony to pilots.' In *Pratique d'aujourd'hui et besoins de demain*, ed. by Michel Perrin, 295–314. Bordeaux: Université de Bordeaux.

Robertson, Fiona. 1988. *Airspeak: radiotelephony communication for pilots*. New York: Prentice-Hall.

Schegloff, Emanuel A. 1979. 'Identification and recognition in telephone conversation openings.' In *Everyday language: studies in ethnomethodology*, ed. by George Psathas, 23–78. New York: Irvington.

Searle, John R. 1969. *Speech acts: an essay in the philosophy of language*. Cambridge: Cambridge University Press. DOI: 10.1017/CBO9781139173438

Swales, John M. 1981. 'Definitions in science and law: a case for subject-specific ESP materials.' *Fachsprache* 81 (3): 106–112.

Section VI

Historical knowledge

Introduction

One should not forget the heritage of philological traditions, especially in Continental strands of Discourse Studies, which have placed much emphasis on the historical dimension of meaning production. Meanings are shaped by the historical and sociopolitical conditions in which texts are produced and received. Therefore, in order to investigate texts and discourses, discourse researchers have accounted for the historical knowledges informing the discursive practices of groups and communities.

History can intervene in the field of discourse analysis in various ways:

a. *Historiography as discourse*. History itself can be considered as discourse. Thus, discourse theorists have reflected on the way historiographical knowledge is produced and history is written. From this viewpoint, historians do not give neutral accounts of 'reality' but mobilize a range of discursive practices to represent historical time.
b. *Discourse analysis as a methodological toolkit for historians*. Discourse analysis can also provide historians with analytical tools to get a better understanding of texts from the past. Historians do not have to rely on their subjective interpretive capacities; they can use quantitative as well as qualitative methods to account for the production of historical knowledge.
c. *Historical discourse analyses*. Finally, discourse analysts can investigate discourses from a historical perspective. They can trace historical changes in discourse or account for discursive practices in their sociohistorical contexts.

a. Historiography as discourse

Since the 1970s, historians who have been influenced by structuralism or poststructuralism have propounded a 'linguistic' or 'discursive turn'; for them, history does not offer direct access to 'reality' but is a form of discourse which is subject to specific constraints, ruling out the possibility of truly 'scientific' history. In France, Roland Barthes (1915–1980) wrote about 'the discourse of history' (1981[1967]); for him, 'the only existence a fact has is a linguistic existence', and this linguistic existence is not a copy of *another* one situated in the 'reality', outside discourse. One can also cite Michel Foucault's discourse analytical explorations in his archaeological phase (1989[1969/1971]), when he mobilised linguistic theory to point to the historical contexts of knowledge production. Michel de Certeau (1925–1986, 1988[1974]) considers 'the writing of history' as the 'making of history' inside a specific community, emphasising the practice of writing, not what has been written (see the section on 'From Structuralism to Poststructuralism').

The 'linguistic turn' in history is usually associated with the American historian Hayden White (b. 1928, 1973), who was influenced by Barthes and Foucault's *The Order of Things* (2002[1966]). From a 'meta-historical' perspective, White radically criticized the positivist conception of history and analyzed the deep structure of the historical imagination of nineteenth-century Europe. He proposed a postmodern narrative conception of history; historians work out narrative structures which express ideologies; the underlying operations of the discourse of history correspond to four main tropes of rhetoric: metaphor, metonymy, synecdoche and irony. So, the discourse of truth that historians claim to produce should actually be regarded as a discourse of fiction (LaCapra, 1982; Jay, 1982).

b.   Discourse analysis as a methodological toolkit for historians

Historians have played an important role in the emergence and development of discourse analysis. Most historians, however, use discourse analysis as a toolkit of concepts and methods. This turn towards linguistic methods has been informed by the idea that interpretation is not the product of spontaneous understanding. Meaning production, they believe, is subject to certain constraints encoded in the formal-linguistic organization of textual material. Even though interpretation is bound to be subjective, it is assumed to follow certain rules. Interpretation does not have to be a black box, they argue; it can be accounted for rationally. In France, two historians close to the Pêcheux school, Robin (b. 1939) and Guilhaumou (b. 1948) in their groundbreaking work on discourses of the French Revolution, have made the case for both macro-oriented corpus analysis and a micro-analytical perspective of enunciative pragmatics (Guilhaumou et al., 1994; Guilhaumou, 2006). One might also mention the *Sociocritique* group (e.g. Angenot, 1989) whose aim was to place the production of literary works into their social, political and cultural contexts. In a similar vein, a group of Canadian sociologists have used methods of linguistic corpus analysis to account for the historical evolution of political discourse in Quebec (Bourque and Duchastel, 1988).

Drawing on a wealth of linguistic tools, the discourse-historical approach (DHA) provides a framework for looking at latent power dynamics, as it considers knowledge about historical, intertextual sources of social agents and the background of the social and political fields within which discursive events are embedded (see also the section on 'Critical Approaches, Reisigl and Wodak, 2009). The emphasis on contextuality, from speech act theory, conceptual history and the sociology of knowledge, has also informed studies of ideological vocabularies and imaginaries of values (Stråth and Wodak, 2009). History reveals how perceptions of specific events have changed over time due to conflicting narratives and accounts of a specific experience – a phenomenon which can be frequently observed in the discursive construction of national or transnational identities (Flowerdew, 2012; Heer et al., 2008[2003]; Wodak et al., 2009).

c.   Historical discourse analyses

We speak of 'historical discourse analysis' when discourse analysts study historical changes in meaning creation. Thus, Landwehr (2008:14) defines 'historical discourse analysis' as the 'empirical investigation of discourses with respect to their historical change over time'. As a 'genealogist' of discourse, Michel Foucault (1926–1984) made the historical nexus of power and knowledge the object of discourse analytical investigation (Foucault, 1980, see the section on 'From Structuralism to Poststructuralism'). For Foucault, genealogy means investigating historical documents in order to reveal the contingency of what *is* today (e.g. Foucault, 2007[1977/78]). Discourse analysis in this sense does not primarily aim to recover an overarching logic of History even though it requires painstaking precision in the analysis of historical documents. Nor does it try to revive a world buried under the debris of a culture vanished generations ago. To study discourse genealogically means tracing the vanishing lines of historical change. Influenced by the French epistemological tradition, Foucault's genealogy conceives of history as a series of ruptures rather than organic evolution. History is perceived from below, with a special focus on the micro-practices at the interstices of power and knowledge. Foucault's historical investigations stimulated the work of many historians and social scientists who study discourse as a stock of sociohistorical knowledge at a societal level.

In the United Kingdom, another strand of historical discourse analysis has been established in the encounter between intellectual history and the philosophy of language (e.g. Wittgenstein, Austin). Quentin Skinner (b. 1940), with his seminal work *The Foundations of Modern Political Thought* (1978), and others (e.g. Pocock, 1975) began to rewrite the history of Western political thought by reconstructing the precise contexts and meanings of words and ideas in the past (see historical studies of liberalism, e.g. Skinner, 1998; Freeden, 2005). Speech act theory has thus shifted the focus from the earlier approach in intellectual history towards a new focus on the intersection between rhetoric and action.

In Germany, too, historical investigations of discourses have had a long tradition. The study of social reality through language and discourse constitutes the core of the German conceptual history approach (*Begriffsgeschichte*) developed by Reinhart Koselleck (1923–2006, 1985). For conceptual history, language is an indicator of structural sociohistorical changes. Koselleck's point of departure is the continuing state of political crisis, by which he attempts to characterize 'modernity'. Social critique was made possible by the Enlightenment, which resulted in recurring states of crisis (Koselleck, 1988[1959]). While new concepts involve the anticipation of a possible future, different agents in the political arena use the same concepts, yet with varying meanings. Consequently, their interpretation is subject to controversy among political opponents who try to prevent each other from using the same words to say things that differ from one's own conception. How a concept is interpreted in the end is a contingent not a causative question.

Against the background of conceptual history, the German Düsseldorf School investigates the historical constitution of semantic fields. Thus, drawing on Koselleck's conceptual history as well as Foucauldian discourse theory, Busse (b. 1952) elaborated a discursive action model of historical semantics (1987). Here, semantic fields are analysed against the background of discursive action creating historical knowledge. In this context, Wengeler has shown (2003) how utterances are woven into argumentative patterns, content-related *topoi*, which can mobilise explicit as well as implicit knowledge.

The focus on the macro-societal organization of knowledge production is also shared by interpretive traditions in sociology. One can cite the social constructivism of Peter Berger (b. 1929) and Thomas Luckmann (b. 1927), who prolonged hermeneutic and phenomenological investigations of 'Meaning,' i.e. intersubjective meaning produced and shared by actors in everyday life. While social knowledge originates in the life worlds of actors, the question is how they are institutionalised on a macro-societal level. Even though in their *Social Construction of Reality* Berger/Luckmann (1966) do not speak of discourse, they have been widely acknowledged as the precursors of interpretive strands in discourse studies. Thus against the background of Foucault's historical explorations, Reiner Keller (2001) has elaborated a discourse research programme along the lines of Berger/Luckmann which conceives of discourse as knowledge shared by large social groups which can be reconstructed through hermeneutic analysis. These approaches rely heavily on interpretive methods, such as the documentary method, coding strategies and the analysis of interpretive schemes.

Four selections reflect this area of discourse analytical reflection at the crossroads of various disciplines. Two come from historians (Koselleck, Robin), but only Robin claims to practise discourse analysis. Another comes from a sociologist deeply interested in discourse practices (Luckmann), and the last one from two linguists (Busse/Teubert) whose research focuses on the historical dimension of semantics.

References

Angenot, Marc. 1989. *Mille huit cent quatre-vingt-neuf: un état du discours social*. Montréal / Longueuil.
Barthes, Roland. 1981[1967]. 'The Discourse of History.' *Comparative Criticism* 3: 7–20.
Berger, Peter L., and Thomas Luckmann. 1966. *The Social Construction of Reality: A Treatise in the Sociology of Knowledge*. Garden City, New York: Anchor Books.
Bourque, Gilles, and Jules Duchastel. 1988. *Restons traditionnels et progressifs. Pour une nouvelle analyse du discours politique. Le cas du régime Duplessis au Québec*. Montréal: Les Éditions du Boréal.
Busse, Dietrich. 1987. *Historische Semantik. Analyse eines Programms*. Stuttgart: Klett-Cotta.
Certeau, Michel de. 1988[1974]. *The Writing of History*. New York: Columbia University Press.
Flowerdew, John. 2012. *Critical Discourse Analysis and Historiography. The Case of Hong Kong's Evolving Political Identity*. Basingstoke: Palgrave.
Foucault, Michel. 1989[1969/1971]. *The Archaeology of Knowledge & The Discourse on Language*. London: Routledge.

Foucault, Michel. 2002[1966]. *The Order of Things. An Archeology of the Human Sciences*. London: Routledge.

Foucault, Michel. 1980. *Power/Knowledge: Selected Interviews and Other Writings 1972–1977*. Pantheon Books: New York, NY.

Foucault, Michel. 2007[1977/78]. *Security, Territory, Population. Lectures at the College de France*. Basingstoke: Palgrave, Macmillan. DOI: 10.1057/9780230245075

Freeden, Michael. 2005. *Liberal Languages: Ideological Imaginations and Twentieth-Century Progressive Thought*. Princeton: Princeton University Press.

Guilhaumou, Jacques. 2006. *Discours et événement. L'histoire langagière des concepts*. Besançon: Presses Universitaires de Franche-Comté.

Guilhaumou, Jacques, Denise Maldidier, and Régine Robin. 1994. *Discours et archive. Expérimentations en analyse du discours*. Liège: Mardaga.

Heer, Hannes, Walter Manoschek, Alexander Pollak, and Ruth Wodak, eds. 2008[2003]. *The Discursive Construction of History: Remembering the German Wehrmacht's War of Annihilation*. Basingstoke: Palgrave.

Jay, Martin. 1982. 'Should Intellectual History Take a Linguistic Turn? Reflections on the Habermas-Gadamer Debate.' In *Modern European Intellectual History. Reappraisals and New Perspectives*, edited by Dominick LaCapra and Steven L. Kaplan, 86–110. Ithaca, London: Cornell University Press.

Keller, Reiner. 2001. 'Wissenssoziologische Diskursanalyse.' In *Handbuch Sozialwissenschaftliche Diskursanalyse Bd. 1, Theorien und Methoden*, edited by Reiner Keller, Andreas Hirseland, Werner Schneider and Willy Viehöver, 113–44. Opladen: Westdeutscher Verlag. DOI: 10.1007/978-3-322-99906-1_5

Koselleck, Reinhart. 1988[1959]. *Critique and Crisis: Enlightenment and the Pathogenesis of Modern Society*. Oxford: Berg.

Koselleck, Reinhart. 1985. *Futures Past*. Cambridge, MA: MIT Press.

LaCapra, Dominick. 1982. 'Rethinking Intellectual History and Reading Texts.' In *Modern European Intellectual History. Reappraisals and New Perspectives*, edited by Dominick LaCapra and Steven L. Kaplan, 47–85. Ithaca, NY: Cornell University Press.

Landwehr, Achim. 2008. *Historische Diskursanalyse*. Frankfurt am Main: Campus.

Pocock, John, ed. 1975. *The Machiavellian Moment: Florentine Political Thought and the Atlantic Republican Tradition*. Princeton: Princeton University Press.

Reisigl, Martin, and Ruth Wodak. 2009. 'The discourse-historical approach (DHA).' In *Methods of Critical Discourse Analysis*, edited by Ruth Wodak and Michael Meyer, 87–121. London: Sage.

Skinner, Quentin. 1978. *The Foundations of Modern Political Thought*. Cambridge: Cambridge University Press.

Skinner, Quentin. 1998. *Liberty before Liberalism*. Cambridge: Cambridge University Press.

Stråth, Bo, and Ruth Wodak. 2009. 'Europe-Discourse-Politics-Media-History: Constructing Crises.' In *Europe in Crisis: The 'European Public Sphere' and National Media in the Post-War Period*, edited by Anna Triandafyllidou, Ruth Wodak and Michal Krzyżanowski, 15–33. Basingstoke: Palgrave.

Wengeler, Martin. 2003. *Topos und Diskurs. Begründung einer argumentationsanalytischen Methode und ihre Anwendung auf den Migrationsdiskurs (1960–1985)*. Tübingen: Niemeyer. DOI: 10.1515/9783110913187

White, Hayden. 1973. *Metahistory. The Historical Imagination in Nineteenth-Century Europe*. London: Johns Hopkins Press.

Wodak, Ruth, Rudolf de Cillia, Martin Reisigl and Karin Liebhart. 2009 [1999]. *The discursive construction of national identity*. Edinburgh: Edinburgh University Press.

Régine Robin

History and linguistics

Régine Robin (b. 1939) started her career as a professional historian, a specialist of French history of the 17th and 18th centuries. She was one of the early protagonists of the French school of discourse analysis before she moved to Canada, where she took up a post as a sociology professor at the University of Quebec in Montreal (UQAM) in 1982. In 1990 she co-founded the Centre for Discourse Analysis and Sociocriticism of Texts. In the early 1970s, she, like Michel Pêcheux, was deeply influenced by the Althusserian interpretation of Marx and attempted to account for the relationship between 'discursive practice' and 'ideological formation.' Her *History and Linguistics* [*Histoire et linguistique*] (1973) presents a number of analytical tools from linguistics and shows how they can be applied to historical examples. The text below is taken from the first chapter of this book. In a first step, Robin reflects on the term 'discourse', and in a second step she emphasizes the interest of 'discourse linguistics' which, for her, is closely connected with the enunciative-pragmatic approach (see the section on 'Enunciative Pragmatics'). In the third part of this excerpt, she presents a study that points out characteristic differences between speeches by French left-wing political leaders from the first half of the 20th century.

Reference

Robin, Régine. 1973. *Histoire et linguistique*. Paris: Colin.

Régine Robin. 1973. *Histoire et linguistique*, selected 21–26.
Paris: Armand Colin.

Let us say, in a first step, that a historian does not deal neither with a code nor with language; rather, he or she deals with both but as basic, raw material; his or her purpose, when s/he wants to be a historian of manifestations, of ideological effects, is not a system, a model of competence, or a language but precise facts of speech, on the understanding that this term must be made free of its philosophical connotations mentioned above, in short, discourses.

How can discourse be defined? At this point of our consideration, given that we have not discussed the concepts proper to a historian, in particular the concept of 'social formation' or its implications, we can only talk about a primary definition, vague on the terminological level, unsatisfactory on the theoretical level, about an approach to be reconstructed later.

L. Guespin wrote: 'Utterance and discourse are two words that tend to be organized into opposition. The utterance is a sequence of sentences emitted between two semantic blanks, two stoppings of communication; discourse is *the utterance considered from the perspective of the discourse mechanism that conditions it*. Thus, looking at the text from the perspective of its structuration in 'language' makes an utterance from it; a linguistic study of the conditions of production of this text will make a discourse from it.' (Guespin, 1971: 10). This indicates that contrary to the utterance, discourse is discourse only in relation to what conditions it, and thus must be considered in terms of process and not statically as an utterance, that discourse is discourse only when reported to its conditions of production. Here, there is an ambiguity because Guespin does not only consider the conditions of the production of text, but also the *linguistic* study of its conditions of production. If he means by this that the conditions of production (institutional framework, ideological apparatus in which it is taken, the representations that underlie it, the political conjuncture, the power relations, the desired strategic effects, etc.) are not only context, the 'circumstances' that would exercise in their own way simple constraints on discourse, but that these conditions characterize discourse, constitute it and, by constituting it, can be identified by linguistic analysis, we fully agree; if by this formula the author intends to show that discourse falls within only an internal analysis, in brief, that the linguistic space – even if it is the linguistics of discourse and not that of language – is sufficient to analyze discourse, we differ from him or her. We believe, with M. Pêcheux, that 'the linguistic phenomena of a dimension superior to the sentence can actually be conceived as functioning, but only if we immediately add that this functioning is not entirely linguistic in the current sense of that term and that we can define it only in reference to the mechanism of implementation of the protagonists and the object of discourse, the mechanism that we have called the conditions of production of discourse.' (Pêcheux, 1969:16). Therefore, at this point we can say that we consider discourse as a process in its relation to 'extra-linguistics', that is to say discourse *as a practice*. This is what M. Foucault introduces in *Archaeology of knowledge*. By practice he does not mean the free activity of a subject but the set of rules that surround and circumscribe the subject as soon as it takes part in discourse. Thus, discourse implies all the extra-linguistic relations that constitute it. Our persistence on this point risks causing many misinterpretations and therefore requires some clarifications. If we insist on the link between discourse and all material relations that structure it, we do not mean, like Marr in 1950s USSR, that we turn language into a superstructure. We wish to specify that discursive formations form an integral part of the instance of ideology, and so are fundamentally related to superstructures. Similarly, we do not intend to deny the linguistic level (meaning, as you may guess, the linguistics of discourse) by reducing the analysis of discourse to the sociology of discourse. Not at all. We are looking to establish in the field of history the discursive level as a new object of study, and at the same time, against a certain linguistic positivism, to postulate the impasses and shortcomings of an internal analysis from which we would like to deduct the interpretation of discourse, including its function, its efficiency, and its insertion process in social formation. This necessity to appeal to the 'extra-linguistic' for certain instances of social formation has recently been exposed with clarity by D. Slakta when he introduced the instance of ideology at the very level of linguistic competence: 'a discursive practice can be explained only in terms of double competence – (1) *specific competence*, the internalized system of specifically linguistic rules which are involved in the production and comprehension of always new sentences – the individual *I*, using those rules in a specific manner (performance) – (2) *ideological or general competence* that makes implicitly possible all the new actions and meanings' (Slakta, 1971:110). To introduce an ideology instance at the level of competence necessarily means to show that internal analysis does not exhaust the meaning of the discourse, to make a sign to the theory of social formations, and in the field of this theory to emphasize the place of the ideology instance and the impact of this instance at a discursive level. It means, therefore, however implicitly, to be oriented to *the problem of the link between discursive practices and non-discursive practices within a social formation*. The necessity to include ideology in the concept of discourse, so as not to reduce discourse to 'langue' in its ideological neutrality, was recognized and advocated by some Russian post-formalists, particularly Medvedev who, according to J. Kristeva, 'proposes to formulate the concept of language so that it could be both linguistic and ideological, and could at the same time combine meaning as it is posed by linguistics and ideology as it will be required by the theory taking history into account' (1970:25).

During the last ten years the *linguistics of discourse*[1] has developed, some elements of which fall within the so-called *enunciation,* as the attitude of the speaker to his own utterance, as the insertion of the subject within his own speech, as the positioning of the subject in relation to the system of representations and to the ideological framework that govern them and of which he is a support, as the act of producing discourse. Linguists, not without hesitation or reticence, accepted that these mechanisms fell within their field, because it trailed around them like the ever-suspected smell of mentalism. T. Todorov, presenting the state of questions concerning enunciation, noted: 'If we accept for now that enunciation is the individual act of language use, while the utterance is the result of this act, we can say that the purpose of current linguistics is utterance, not enunciation' (1970: 3). We can now understand the immense work that lies ahead in order to create the linguistics of discourse and beyond, the history of discursive formations. To give a few rough examples, we can point out what characterises the enunciation following the study by L. Courdesses (1971).

L. Courdesses shows that contrary to what happened in the context of structural linguistics, where the process of enunciation tended to disappear in the utterance, research within the transformational framework does not evade the problem of enunciation; on the contrary, it undertakes to theorize it. Four concepts allow the elucidation of the process of enunciation.

The concept of distance: it is the relative distance set by the subject between himself and the utterance. The speaking subject can fully assume his utterance. In this case there is an identification between the *I* as the subject of the utterance and the *I* as the subject of the enunciation. The distance can be maximized instead. We are then dealing with the standards of a didactic discourse. 'This is based on the idea that there is something common, universal – or almost universal – in the properties of discourse. The *I* then tends to become the formal *he* of the utterance' (Dubois, 1969: 104).

The concept of modalization: according to V. Weinreich it is defined as the mark that the subject continues to give to his utterance, that is to say, as the adherence that the subject gives to his discourse. Thus, we can distinguish between formalized modalizers as adverbs of opinion (maybe, probably, obviously, etc.), modalizing transformations as emphasis, the optional passive, the interdependencies of levels such as the use of colloquial, popular or literary language relations; modalizations of the attitude of the subject such as the accomplished / not accomplished verbal opposition forms; modalizations of types of utterances: various kinds of reported utterances from the 'I think that' to the performative (Dubois, 1969: 105).

---

1.   The precursors are Bally, Hjelmslev and the founders of the circle of Prague, especially Jakobson. In this area, as in many others, it is necessary to give a special place to E. Benveniste, a true pioneer in the field.

The concept of tension concerns the relationship between the speaking subject and the interlocutor. The system of tenses and aspects is the most proper to capture this type of enunciative mark because the verb appears as the true operator of the sentence. In addition, articles and determinatives play a key role at this level; and it is the same regarding the system of pronouns. However, according to L. Irigaray, the field of predilection of tension is manifested in the opposition *to have / to be* on the one hand, and auxiliaries such as *will, can, do, have to*, on the other. While in the first case we are dealing with the accomplished, postulating a state, the absence of tension, in the second one, on the contrary, there appears a tension, the subject takes over responsibility for the utterance in front of the interlocutor.

The concept of transparency or opacity considers the mark of enunciation from the perspective of the receiver. Maximum opacity appears in lyric poetry. The utterance is modalized in a specific, original way, and the subject of enunciation is then 'available to each reader, also transformed into the subject of enunciation, to assume an utterance the modalizations of which escape him' (Dubois, 1969: 106). Instead, if the utterance is a 'maxim' the reader adheres strongly to the texts because this utterance creates identification between the receiver and the subject of enunciation. Here, there is maximum transparency since the subject of enunciation is as if effaced. The *he* replaces the *I*. Thus, opacity and transparency are constitutive of the levels of ambiguity of the message according to the analysis by T. Todorov.

These basic concepts allow L. Courdesses to study two discourses voiced by Blum[2] and Thorez[3] in May 1936[4] from the perspective of enunciation. They are two completely different types of discourse from the perspective of the enunciative universe.

The system of personal references and substitute (see table) clearly demonstrates the differences. While the *I* is heavily used by Blum,[5] it is rare in Thorez where the subject of enunciation tends to be erased by maximum distance. On the contrary, while the use of the *we* by Blum creates tension in the group, in Thorez the *I* becomes the *we*. Here, we are within the framework of an essentially didactic discourse.

---

2. Leon Blum's speech was given at the Congress of the Socialist Party, 31 May 1936, Maurice Thorez's speech was held before the assembly of communists of Paris, 14 May. L. Courdesses admits that the conditions of production of the two discourses are roughly the same. This poses a problem because the situation of communication is not the same (…).

3. Maurice Thorez (1900–1964) was the leader of the French Communist Party (PCF) from 1930 until his death. [Trans. note]

4. Just after the victory of the Popular Front at the general election of 3 May 1936. [Trans. note]

5. Léon Blum (1872–1950) was a social democrat, Prime Minister of France during the Popular Front (1936), an alliance of left-wing movements, including the French Communist Party (PCF) and the French Section of the Workers' International (SFIO). Blum was a member of the SFIO. [Trans. note]

The enunciative verbs: 'I say', 'I believe', 'I mean', 'I think' etc. accentuate the difference. They are very frequent in Blum, constantly introducing the 'reflexive regard of the speaking subject on his own utterance' (Courdesses, 1971:25). Conversely, these verbs are rare in Thorez. In Blum these verbs are also associated with *shifters* of time (now, today, at present).

The system of adverbs is to be considered because it allows the modalization of the discourse. Here again the contrast between Blum and Thorez appears. Adverbs ending in -*ly* [*ment*] are very numerous in the discourse of Blum and they are almost absent from that of Thorez.

The system of transformations also modalizes the utterance.

- The negatives imply an inverse utterance, expressed or remaining implicit. They imply a certain mode of presence of the opposing utterance. While Blum frequently uses negative transformation, Thorez uses it less often and his negative transformations are essentially didactic.
- Most of the time, passives remove the agent of the action, the subject of the verb in the active form. While in Blum half the passives do not remove the agent, in Thorez the passives erase the agent and are followed by nominalizations, passive subordinates of purpose introduced by an injunctive verb, hence the didacticism of the analysis.
- The modalities express performatives (want, need, have to, must), they are distributed differently in the two discourses, corroborating the divisions identified by enunciative markers, as previously reported.

The system of verbs finally completes the locating of the two enunciative universes. The accomplished marks the state, the not-accomplished – on the contrary – the tension between the speaker and the receiver. In Blum, the not-accomplished dominate, creating the tension between the group and himself. In Thorez, the accomplished dominate, which reinforces the didacticism of the discourse.

L. Courdesses concludes her study by specifying the fundamental opposition of the two discourses. On the one hand, we have a traditional political discourse, the fact of asserting itself by the individuality wherein the subject assumes his utterance, establishes a tension between him and the group. From this point of view, such a discourse may bring to mind Jaurès.[6] On the other hand, we have a didactic discourse where enunciation is barely marked, where the tension is minimized.

This example, among others, concerning studying the process of enunciation, allows us to pave the way for the establishment of the linguistics of discourse relevant

---

6. Jean Jaurès (1859–1914) was, before L. Blum, the leader of the French Socialist Party, the French Section of the Workers' International (SFIO). Jaurès, who was an antimilitarist, was assassinated at the outbreak of World War I. (Trans. note)

Process	Utterance of Blum		Utterance of Thorez	
	Use and content	Value	Use and content	Value
I	76 times	Actualization minimum distance	11 times (12)	Subject of enunciation erased, maximum distance
WE	118 times (subject or object) = I + the participants of Congress (the notion always disambiguated by context)	Tension in the group between 'I' and 'we', play between exclusion and inclusion in group	- permanent = 80 times (90) - ambiguous notion = I + you (militants of the meeting) = I + you + communists = I + political office = the entire Party	The 'I' becomes the collective 'we' → transparency, didacticism, the will of total inclusion into the group
VOUS (second person plural)	54 times (subject or object) = the participants of the Congress	Opposition 'I' vs 'we' vs 'you' = tension, individualization of the leader and the participants	- very rare = 4 times (5)	- Minimum distance - No tension - Refusal of individualization
ON*	25 times = External political adversary (pejorative)	Reference to the external world	21 times (23) = All that is external to the Party, even the allies of the Popular Front	The will to define a closed group, meliorative with respect to the external world
IT	= Socialist Party overflowing entity: 'I' + 'us' + 'you' + 'they' (the Socialists who are not present)	Emotional personification of the Party		
Referent used with keywords *Party, people, France*	THE, THIS – almost exclusive OUR – only 4 times	Referential aspect	*the* = 9 times but marking a superlative or a meliorative *our* (Fr. *notre*) = 20 times with 'Party' (22); 12 times with 'People' (13) *our* (Fr. *nos*) = exclusive with 'militants'	The will of inclusion and uniqueness of the group
The proper nouns	Comrades cited with their first and last names + meliorative or emotional element	Individualized emotional relationships	- no names of comrades of the Party - mentioned names concerning personalities from outside the Party	Erasing all individuality

THE SUBSTITUTES

* On = the indefinite pronoun literally meaning 'one'; on can also mean 'we', 'they', 'someone', 'you' or 'people in general'. [Trans. note]
(Figures in brackets are the figures of Thorez corrected in relation to Blum)

to a historian in the first place. The linguistics of discourse which completely puts into question the distinction made by Saussure between language and speech, on condition that it distances itself from an individualistic model centered on the problematic aspect of the subject, can, as we shall see, relate to the theory of ideologies.

References

Courdesses, Lucile. 1971. 'Blum et Thorez en mai 1936 : analyses d'énoncés.' *Langue française* 9: 22–33. DOI: 10.3406/lfr.1971.5569

Dubois, Jacques. 1969. 'Énoncé et énonciation.' *Langages* 13: 100–10. DOI: 10.3406/lgge.1969.2511

Guespin, Louis. 1971. 'Problématique des travaux sur le discours politique.' *Langages* 23: 3–24. DOI: 10.3406/lgge.1971.2048

Kristeva, Julia. 1970. 'Idéologie du discours sur la littérature.' *La Nouvelle critique, special issue*, 39 bis: 122–27.

Pêcheux, Michel. 1969. *Analyse automatique du discours*. Paris: Dunod.

Slakta, Denis. 1971. 'Esquisse d'une théorie lexico-sémantique: pour une analyse d'un texte politique (cahiers de doléances).' *Langages* 23: 87–131.

Todorov, Tzvetan. 1970. 'Problèmes de l'énonciation.' *Langages* 17: 3–11. DOI: 10.3406/lgge.1970.2571

Reinhart Koselleck

Conceptual history

Reinhart Koselleck (1923–2006) was not a discourse analyst but a German historian whose main contribution was the development of the 'conceptual history' approach (*Begriffsgeschichte*). Between 1972 and 1997 he co-edited, with Brunner and Conze, an eight-volume encyclopaedia of almost 10,000 pages: *Basic Concepts in History: A Historical Dictionary of Political and Social Language in Germany* [*Geschichtliche Grundbegriffe. Historisches Lexikon zur politisch-sozialen Sprache in Deutschland*]. The contributions to these volumes study how the transformations occurring in German-speaking Europe from the Enlightenment to the Industrial Revolution were perceived, conceptualized and incorporated into discourse. Along with his colleagues, Koselleck believed that all historical reflection implies an understanding of historically contingent values and practices in their respective contexts. The focus of conceptual history is on the evolution of key concepts such as *citizen* [*Bürger*], *criticism* (*Kritik*), *party* (*Partei*) and *tolerance* (*Toleranz*) in early modern history. Koselleck was not influenced by discourse analysis in the way Robin refers to linguistics. Nor was he interested in epistemological or theoretical questions as much as representatives of the 'linguistic turn' like Hayden White or the poststructuralists. Yet, conceptual history can be considered a precursor of the work of many discourse analysts interested in the historical dimension of discourse (e.g. Busse/Teubert). The text below was published in 1994, more than twenty years after the beginning of the *Geschichtliche Grundbegriffe* project. Koselleck reflects on some of the theoretical and methodological problems he encountered: the context one needs to take into account to study a concept, the complexity of its meaning ('every concept has many layers in time'), the relation between semantics and pragmatics in language, the question of linguistic innovation and the sources that allow us to account for it.

References

Brunner, Otto, Conze, Werner and Reinhart Koselleck (eds). 1972–1997. *Historisches Lexikon zur politisch-sozialen Sprache in Deutschland*. Stuttgart: Klett-Cotta.

Reinhart Koselleck. 1994. 'Some Reflections on Temporal Structure of Conceptual Change.'
In *Main Trends in Cultural History. Ten Essays*, ed. by Willem Melching, and Wyger Velema,
7–16, selected 7–8, 10–16.
Amsterdam: Rodopi.

Before I start to address the complicated theoretical issue of the temporal structure
of conceptual changes, a word of warning is in order. My work in conceptual history has been closely associated with the huge research project of the *Geschichtliche
Grundbegriffe. Historisches Lexikon zur politisch-sozialen Sprache in Deutschland*.
Publication of that lexicon has been going on for two decades by now and, for me at
least, its theoretical and methodological presuppositions, first formulated some twenty-
five years ago, have grown into an intellectual straightjacket. While it was necessary
to maintain these presuppositions in relatively unchanged form in order to be able to
proceed with the collaborative project of the *Geschichtliche Grundbegriffe,* my own
thought on conceptual history has kept changing. It should therefore not surprise you
if the positions I shall be defending in this paper are somewhat different from the ones
that originally inspired the *Geschichtliche Grundbegriffe*. Indeed, it would be dreadful
and depressing if years of reflection had not led to significant change in my approach
to conceptual history.

Let me first make a brief remark about the position of concepts within the larger
linguistic framework. It has been said, not altogether without foundation, that it is very
hard, maybe even impossible, to write the history of single, isolated concepts. What is
needed, it is claimed by some critics, is a larger context: a whole text, or even a series of
texts. Without such an enlarged context, so the argument goes, it is impossible to reconstruct the meaning and the changes of meaning of individual concepts. I am disinclined
to deny the truth of such criticisms on a theoretical level. It is sufficient, it seems to me,
to answer them on a practical level. Once you start considering the contexts within
which the meaning of individual concepts may be analyzed, there is no end to it. You
start with the paragraph within which the concept is mentioned. From the paragraph,
you proceed to the whole book. From the book, you move to the entire social and political debate of the historical period in question, for all concepts are related to other
contemporary concepts, for instance to their *Gegenbegriffe,* in a variety of ways. But it
is not sufficient to limit yourself to learned language, since obviously the conventions
of ordinary speech are also relevant to your investigation. You end up, in other words,
by studying all aspects of a certain language at a given point in time. Since it is impossible to do all these things at the same time, what the individual researcher in the end
decides to do simply depends on his own interests and on the kinds of questions he
wishes to ask. Research, in a way, is like looking through the lens of a camera. You can
focus on one concept, on one text, on a series of texts, or on the whole language. All

these choices are equally legitimate, but to a certain extent they are mutually exclusive. Much depends on personal preferences and practical considerations. (…)

Let us now turn to the main theme of the present paper and, by way of example, look at the long term changes in the meaning of one concept. We shall take as our example an expression which has been translated into all European languages and which has been and is of fundamental importance in European history. Aristotle's *koinonia politike,* a concept I have already had occasion to mention before, has been translated as *societas civilis* by the Roman political theorists and jurists. Both concepts refer to full citizens only and leave the slaves, by no means a negligible part of the population, totally out of consideration. Yet despite this fact, the theory of *koinonia politike* and *societas civilis* contains a great many elements still considered relevant in modern discussions about the good society. Aristotle's reflections on the relatively even distribution of riches among all citizens as one of the necessary preconditions of a healthy and stable polity still find many admirers today. The old theory, in other words, still has some life in it. It is also abundantly clear, however, that when *societas civilis* was translated into civil society or *société civile,* the original meaning was fundamentally changed. During the early modern period the expression was applied to a society of orders and estates. Aristotelian and Ciceronian arguments were adapted to societies characterized by a sharply hierarchical formal mode of political organization.

After the Enlightenment and the French Revolution, with the rise of theories of equal freedom and justice for all, the meaning of civil society once more drastically changed. What we see in ancient, in early modern, and in modern history, is one and the same expression with a great many different meanings attached to it. This raises the very important question of the layers of time contained in a concept. Every concept, so it would seem, has many layers in time. Today, for instance, you may use the expression civil society with some remnants of its Aristotelian meaning still present and still understandable. Many other meanings of the term as used in antiquity, in the Middle Ages, or in the early modern period, however, will have disappeared. The concept, in other words, has various time layers, its meanings have different *durées*.

The all-important fact that each concept has a complicated temporal structure suggests a way around the problem posed by the uniqueness of each individual use of a certain concept. As we have seen, it can be claimed that it is impossible to write the history of a specific and concrete concept. It is not possible to doubt, however, that a concept, regardless of its original application, accumulates a variety of meanings over time and that the history of these temporal layers of meaning can be written. This can be done by following Aristotle's *koinonia politike* up to modern civil society. It can also be done, to give another example, with *res publica,* the common weal, or the common good. In this conceptual area, Ciceronian notions long reigned supreme. At the beginning of the eighteenth century, however, the new term of republicanism was coined.

The point of this new term was to indicate the existence of a gap between the existing political state of affairs and the ideal of a perfect republic, to be realized at some future point in time. The concept of republicanism no longer just described reality, but contained an important element of expectation. It clearly pointed to the future.

Indeed, it can be maintained that all modern '-isms' are characterized by a certain tension between experience and expectation. These '-isms' are, so to speak, concepts of movement. The slow and gradual dissolution of the society of orders and estates in Europe was accompanied by the emergence of liberalism, socialism, and communism. These key words stood for alternative ways in which to organize society in the future, with an emphasis on either legal or social equality. The concepts were invented before any reality corresponded to them. Thus, the term liberalism was coined around 1810. Socialism in its modern meaning – the word itself was older – was developed during the twenties and the thirties of the nineteenth century. The same was true for communism. Communism might, from our present point of view, be the most remarkable of these three concepts, for nobody has ever unambiguously claimed that it existed. The example of the former Soviet Union is illuminating in this respect. There the orthodox Marxists contended that they were living in a socialist society and that they were permanently on their way to a more perfect communist future. Communism, in other words, functioned as a concept of pure expectation, with hardly any relationship to existing reality. It should be clear by now that the meaning of concepts can contain past experience, present reality, and expectations for the future. All key words in the language of politics have a layered temporal structure and transcend the so-called reality of the present. It is extremely fascinating and instructive to try and write the history of concepts by laying bare the elements of the past, of the present, and of the future which they contain.

The next question we have to address is that of the relation between pragmatics and semantics in language. It can of course be said that all words spoken or written in a particular situation at a given point in time are unique, as unique as Ferdinand de Saussure's *parole*. Semantics, however, are not unique, but repeatable. Indeed, it is very important to emphasize this in any discussion of the temporal structure of concepts. Even when I try to explain something to you that is clearly unique, a minimum of consensus about the meaning of the words I use is necessary for you to understand me. A pre-existing semantics, in other words, is needed for me to be able to convey a unique message or speech-act to you. Just as economic life knows its *longue durée*, so does language. Repetition constitutes the *longue durée* of language. Semantics can be defined as the possibility of repetition. Semantics, however, are not universal, but closely linked to a particular language. This is what makes translation such a fascinating phenomenon. This, too, is what makes the comparative study of the history of certain key concepts in different languages so worthwhile an activity. In Bielefeld we are at the moment engaged in researching and writing the comparative history of *citoyen* and *Bürger*. I shall not discuss the results of that project here, but it has made it very clear that the nineteenth-century debate about citizenship was semantically preprogrammed in a completely different way in France and Germany. Semantics, one might say, have a way of organizing and steering thought. Every unique speech-act is dependent upon a repeatable semantics. This fundamental fact constitutes a temporal structure in every concept we use.

The peculiar German term *Bildung* may serve further to illustrate some of the problems we are discussing here. At first sight, the meaning of *Bildung* would seem to be fairly close to that of culture. On closer inspection, however, this similarity turns out to be deceptive. *Bildung* has a great many temporal layers of meaning, all of them German. It has medieval, early modern, and modern connotations and is has grown into a central concept in German self-understanding. One of the many meanings of *Bildung* is religiosity. Being *gebildet* means being religious. The religiosity we are speaking about here is not of the confessional type, but of a secular nature. This type of secular religiosity was first recognized as an essential part of *Bildung* around 1770, but the religious meaning of *Bildung* has its roots in the German Middle Ages. The religious element is the first difference in meaning with culture. A second difference between the English and French concept of culture on the one hand and German *Bildung* on the other, is constituted by the fact that culture has more to do with education, whereas *Bildung* primarily refers to self-cultivation. Civilization, too, would be an inadequate translation of *Bildung*. Civilization is always, in some way, related to civil society. In the history of the concept of civilization in the English and French languages the tradition of the *civis* remains a living presence. Indeed, it even takes on a new significance during the eighteenth century. *Bildung*, on the other hand, is a concept in which the internal autonomy of the individual is all-important. The political and social elements in its meaning are negligible. *Bildung* and civilization may overlap in meaning, but they are certainly not identical.

There are, of course, good reasons for the difficulties arising in the attempt to translate German words. In many European languages there is a long tradition of Greek original concepts being translated into Latin, and Latin concepts subsequently and very gradually being translated into Italian, Spanish, or French. There is no clear and firm line of demarcation. Even with the rise of the various vernacular languages, Latin remained the language of philosophers, theologians, and other scholars until deep into the eighteenth century. There was a certain degree of harmony between these languages and Latin, there was no need to emphasize the differences. In the Germanic and Slavonic languages, as is easily understandable, the relationship with Latin was much more strained, As a result, many social and political concepts were consciously invented instead of gradually translated.

So far, I have emphasized that concepts have complicated temporal structures and that [it] is possible to discern a number of distinct temporal layers of meaning each time a concept is used. I have, in other words, emphasized the element of semantic continuity. But obviously there is also linguistic innovation, a subject to which we now turn. How does linguistic innovation take place? Does is it occur suddenly or is it a slow process? It is clearly impossible to answer these questions in the abstract. Let us therefore look at an example from German history. *Bund* is an extremely important concept in the German language. It is obviously not a translation of Latin terms such as *confederatio, unio, liga*. The term was first coined in the later Middle Ages. Initially it was used as a verb, not as a noun. In the German sources we come across expressions such as *wir verstricken uns* and *wir verbinden uns*. It was after these self-imposed obligations had given rise to stable institutions that it became possible to use *Bund* as a noun. Once *Bund* existed as a noun, it turned out to be feasible to formulate a coherent theory about this phenomenon. During the Reformation Luther came to use the term *Bund* for *berith* from the Old Testament. As a result, the term acquired a strong theological connotation and was subsequently avoided in purely political discourse. What is today referred to as the *Schmalkaldischer Bund* in fact never called itself by that name. *Bund,* with all its theological implications, long remained a purely religious concept, meaning a union initiated by God.

Indeed, Luther's theological interpretation of the word survived into the nineteenth century, where we find Marx and Engels still aware of it. In 1847, they were asked to write a catechism for the *Bund der Kommunisten*. Highly conscious of the historical connotations of these concepts, they decided to make a drastic move. Instead of writing a catechism of the *Bund der Kommunisten,* they authored the famous 'Manifesto of the Communist Party'. This was a deliberate act of linguistic innovation and one that was to have lasting consequences. Today, I might add, the theological implications of the term *Bund* have completely disappeared. The concept: of a *Bundesrepublik* has no theological significance whatsoever. It would be easy to give many more examples of linguistic innovations here. Let me just very briefly draw your attention to two interesting cases. The terms *Geschichte* and *Staat* in German have a history of slow and gradual development, followed by a sudden and swift transformation of meaning. In German, both concepts gained their modern meaning in the short time span between 1770 and 1800. The situation in France offers an interesting contrast, for in the French language the word state was already used in its modern meaning as early as the seventeenth century.

Let us now turn from the problem of linguistic innovation to that of the wide variety of sources that can be used in reconstructing the history of concepts. We have seen how concepts may be said to have temporal structures. The same thing can be said about sources. It is of course true that to some extent the meaning of sources depends on the kinds of questions a researcher chooses to ask and on the methodology he chooses to apply. Sources, however, also have an independent time-structure of their own. One can, so to speak, put them on a scale that ranges from uniqueness to repeatability. Using such a scale as our criterion, it is possible to distinguish three basic types in the source material we utilize.

First of all, there are sources characterized by their uniqueness. Newspapers are a good example: they are intended to have a very short life span. People read them because they want to inform themselves about today's or yesterday's news, about the direct *histoire événementielle*. Nobody wants to read a newspaper that is several weeks or months old, except maybe historians or sociologists. Newspapers, in short, are *ad hoc* texts, written for immediate use, with a very low content in theoretical or repeatable subject matter. The same is true for letters. The letter-writer generally intends to convey unique information. He does not as a rule write with the purpose of being constantly reread. There are, of course, exceptions. Rainer Maria Rilke, for instance, wrote his letters on high quality *Büttenpapier,* because he was aware of the fact that they would be published at some later date. My point, however, is that there is a type of sources – newspapers, letters, memoranda, speeches – that is produced for instant consumption and immediate use, a type of sources that consists of one single temporal layer.

Lexica and dictionaries constitute a second type of sources. We are dealing here with a more interesting variety of source, because it contains several temporal layers. A lexicon, an encyclopedia, or even a handbook is always normative. It does not simply claim to provide information, it claims to provide correct information. The fascinating thing about this type of source is that in most cases it offers you a slowly developing series. Each new lexicon both copies older ones and makes some significant changes. In this way, it becomes possible to observe the gradual surfacing of new layers of meaning. One can, for instance, follow the word 'Estate' in different lexica from the seventeenth century on and see how on the one hand it keeps its old meaning of *Zustand* or *Stand,* while on the other hand it acquires new meanings in the course of the development of the modern state apparatus and its legal organization. The comparison of lexica offers the researcher an opportunity empirically to establish the repeatability of semantics. Lexica, in other words, are indispensable tools in any attempt to establish the pace of conceptual change.

A third and final type of source is that of the so-called classic texts. Unlike lexica, these texts are never adapted to changing circumstances. In so far as they are adapted at all, it is with the purpose of establishing greater authenticity, never with the purpose of updating their meaning. The message contained in these classic texts has a claim to permanent truth, to endless repeat ability. It should be clear from all this, to sum up, that there are basically three types of texts or sources, each with a different temporal structure. There are unique texts, intended to be used once and to be permanently discarded thereafter; there are slowly changing texts, texts that are gradually adapted to changing realities; finally, there are texts with a claim to permanent and timeless value and truth in their original and unchanging form. Much more could be said about all topics I have touched upon, but I hope and trust that I have now offered you sufficient material for a fruitful exchange of opinions about the complicated and many layered temporal structure of both concepts and sources.

Dietrich Busse and Wolfgang Teubert

Using corpora for historical semantics

Known for their seminal contribution to discourse linguistics, Dietrich Busse (b. 1952) and Wolfgang Teubert (b. 1946) come from different backgrounds. As a representative of the Düsseldorf School of historical semantics, Busse has made the case for discourse analysis since the 1980s. In his *Historical Semantics* (1987), Busse theorises discourse as semantic knowledge embedded in a historical context of action. More recently, he has turned to cognitive theories that account for the nexus of knowledge, language and society. Teubert is a corpus analyst from Mannheim, Germany, who went to the UK in the early 1990s to take up the chair formerly held by John Sinclair at Birmingham. A theorist of the uses of corpuses in discourse analysis, he conceives of discourse as a macro-societal conception system of meaning production (2010). While discourse is defined as a space of meaning production in which written texts circulate, it is typical of many discourse analysts from Germany to focus more on the semantic content of discourses. In the selected passage, Busse and Teubert sketch out a programme of 'linguistic discourse analysis' which investigates virtual text corpora. Their project for 'a language-oriented history of words and concepts that works with genuine linguistic methods' can be seen as a way of embedding the project of conceptual history in linguistics.

References

Busse, Dietrich. 1987. *Historische Semantik. Analyse eines Programms*. Stuttgart: Klett-Cotta.
Teubert, Wolfgang. 2010. *Meaning, Discourse and Society*. Cambridge: Cambridge University Press. DOI: 10.1017/CBO9780511770852

Dietrich Busse and Wolfgang Teubert. 1994. 'Ist Diskurs ein sprachwissenschaftliches
Objekt? Zur Methodenfrage der historischen Semantik'
(Is discourse a linguistic object? Methodological questions of historical semantics)
Begriffsgeschichte und Diskursgeschichte, ed. by Dietrich Busse, Fritz Hermanns, and
Wolfgang Teubert, 10–28, selected 10–19. Translated by Chris Newton and Johannes
Angermuller.
Opladen: Westdeutscher Verlag.

1. Current situation

After twenty years of discourse analysis research in France and more than fifteen years
after the recognition and discussion of this research orientation in Germany, it seems
that discourse analysis and the term 'discourse' still have not reached German language
studies (not, in any case, in the sense that the term is predominantly used outside
linguistic speech analysis or 'discourse analysis' in the English sense, and outside the
Habermasian discourse empire). Where lies the explanation for this striking belated-
ness, this non-reaction to a meanwhile internationally recognised scholarly movement?
As acknowledged by Jacques Guilhaumou (1979: 7f.), among others, discourse analysis
in France had essentially two branches: a systematic linguistic branch which goes back
to the distributional analysis in the vein of Harris (this branch can admittedly be traced
back to a controversial misunderstanding of Harris' term 'discourse', which is only
meant to refer to trans-sequential, 'trans-phrasal' linguistic structures); and an ideological, critical branch beginning with Althusser and having gained influence through
Michel Foucault[1] (the work of Pêcheux (1975) has received little attention in Germany).
It would not be unreasonable then, to assume that the widespread rejection of discourse
analysis and indeed the word 'discourse' in German linguistics can be traced back to
the fact that, in Germany, it is primarily the Foucauldian version that has been referred
to, particularly in response to the euphoric reception to, and the almost ideological
enthusiasm for, so called 'post-structuralism', which from the beginning was markedly
rejected in Germany and, for example, still has not infiltrated the fields of academic
philosophy and scholarship. Indicative of the contestedness of this academic stream
is perhaps the title of an influential discussion volume 'The New Irrationality', which
indiscriminately subsumes, from Glucksmann through Levy, and to Foucault, anything
attributed to the 'new French philosophy' (Manthey, 1978). Thus one could say that
in Germany the discourse around discourse analysis by those who do not practise it
is, to some extent, even today, characterised by a discourse about irrationality. What

---

1.   Theoretically extrapolated and substantiated above all in Foucault (1972[1969]), as an example
of an exemplary analysis Foucault (2002[1966]).

was overlooked here, however, was the presence (or at least former presence) of a discourse analysis in France that was based on linguistics and academically established, and not directly inspired by Foucault, and which had to grapple with nowhere near the same resistance as it did in Germany. All this meant that, in Germanistic linguistics, *Diskursanalyse* is mostly understood as 'discourse analysis' in the Anglo-Saxon sense of dialogue and conversation analysis. Moreover, in Germany, the term *Diskurs* has come to take on strong philosophical associations through Habermas, a movement also incompatible with French discourse analysis.

One could further assume that the glaring discrepancy between the acceptance and spread of discourse analysis in Romance and Anglo-Saxon (see Macdonell, 1986) communities and the resistance to the term in German linguistics relates to the wide acceptance of the word *discours* or 'discourse' in French and English, something which has not happened to the same extent in German. Clearly, discourse analysis transcends the narrow boundaries that modern, post-Saussurean linguistics had applied to itself. Given that, in French linguistics, discourse analysis has been equated with the investigation of utterances, illocutions, presuppositions and speech acts (Guilhaumou and Maldidier, 1979: 10), it is somewhat surprising that the above themes which all lie on the boundary of traditional *langue* linguistics have been taken up as part of the development of pragmatics in the canon of German linguistics, while at the same time discourse analysis, and even the term 'discourse', has been avoided. Thus there are German studies practitioners and even important pioneers of linguistic pragmatics who flatly deny the existence of the phenomenon 'discourse'. The reasons given for this, however, are not particularly sustainable. In response to a statement such as 'I know what texts are: I can investigate texts; they are a meaningful object of linguistics but what discourses are is wholly unclear; they are not definable', it should be pointed out that it is barely twenty years since the attempt to establish the category 'text' as a linguistic object encountered the same resistance as discourse analysis does today.

Some of the arguments then put forward as to why texts should not be considered as linguistic objects (in the narrow terminology of the then influential system linguistics) are uncannily similar to those used today against the term discourse. Then too, the argument was that text relations (coherence structures) were not genuine linguistic objects, just as today it is doubted whether there are semantic relations that are fundamental to the semantics of a word, sentence or text which cannot be accounted for by the traditional investigation of aspects of meaning (semes; the meaning relations of structuralism). One can summarise many of the objections to the term 'discourse' (and indeed previous objections to the term 'text') into one point. What has been explicitly or implicitly disputed is any extension of linguistics in which semantics, i.e. the analysis of meaning of individual units, transcends the boundaries of word and sentence. Hence the boundaries of traditional linguistics are primarily those that are supposed to seal it off from the semantic analysis of speech units on the level of utterances. Among the various reasons for this is that a study of language exclusively within the paradigm of system linguistics still regards the goal of linguistics solely as the formulation of language laws and principles. One sees here the effects of eliminating the diachronic perspective, the insights of which (following Saussure's plausible justification and in contrast to the Neogrammarians of the nineteenth century) cannot be precisely accounted for through laws. However, many linguists also eliminated the perspective that the study of language could be *philology*, referring as it does to the analysis of concrete texts and their constituent parts, a perspective long rejected or ridiculed in modern linguistics, but one which (albeit not exclusively) explores content rather than simply laws, forms and structures. If a large body of modern linguistics delimits itself from the unsystematic nature of diachronic research and from the content focus of philology, one may explain but not necessarily accept that linguistics in the German-speaking countries still has to integrate discourse analysis into its thematic canon. Hence for us, a renewed acceptance of the diachronic perspective as well as a widening of interest in a semantics which does not stop at word or sentence boundaries represents a return of linguistics to its roots, unashamedly a return which does not fall short of the progress made by system linguistics but rather builds upon it: in other words, on its basis, completing the extension of linguistics from *langue* to *parole*, which indeed Saussure himself aspired to.

2.   Basic principles of a linguistic discourse analysis

In the following, we put forward the basic principles of a linguistic discourse analysis and how, in our view, it could lead to a fruitful, yet uncanonised research perspective and methodology of discourse semantics.[2] We understand a potential discourse semantics (the term itself allows only for a diachronic semantics, i.e. a semantics of discourse) as an extension of the possibilities of a language-oriented history of words and concepts that works with genuine linguistic methods. Specifically, this constitutes an extension with regard to objectives and initial questions, an extension of the subjects and objects of research and finally, thereby, an extension of the methods of diachronic semantics. At this point a timely observation: the word *extension* should clarify (and we emphasise this in light of past misunderstandings) that a discourse semantics is not something wholly unlike a history of word meanings or concepts: it builds upon such methods.

---

2.   We are at the same time aware that many of the aspects formulated here have been more exhaustively formulated in the praxis of non-Foucauldian discourse analysis; a full reception of this research and its methodological as well as theoretical findings (often relatively inaccessible) is still lacking in Germany; their very existence in Germany is – due to a fixation on Foucault – barely known.

Fundamental here, however, is that the chosen texts and corpora are investigated with different interests and from different viewpoints. Such a difference in the type of questions and perspectives (among otherwise similar corpora and investigation methods) is not altogether as insignificant and unworthy of attention as once claimed, rather it is predicated on the possible results that can be achieved with the kind of semantic analysis pursued (this is actually a philosophical truism and it is still astounding how often the very autonomy of semantic analysis is questioned, simply because it *also* but not *only* employs the available methods of word semantics and the history of concepts).

2.1 Discourse and corpus

Now a few observations on the term *discourse* itself. By discourses we understand, in a practical research sense, virtual text corpora whose composition is determined in the widest sense by contextual (or semantic) criteria. Discourses are any texts which:

- deal with an entity chosen as an object of investigation, theme, knowledge-complex or concept and exhibit semantic relations and/or the shared context of a statement, communicative act, function or purpose;
- come within the perimeters arising from the research programme with respect to period of time, point in time, geographical area, societal cross-section, field of communication, text type or other parameters;
- either refer back to each other through explicit or implicit (textual or context semantic) references or build intertextual coherence.

Concrete text corpora (and by concrete we mean being the basis of a discourse-semantic investigation) are components of the given discourse. Their selection involves practical considerations such as the availability of sources, as well as context-oriented relevance criteria; of prime importance remains the approach of the researcher, which determines the concrete text corpus and thereby the object of investigation. The phrase 'historians' debate' (the 'historians' dispute' (*Historikerstreit*) of 1986 in Germany over the comparison and possible equation of National Socialism and Stalinism) can serve as an example. All contributions to this dispute constitute, together, the discourse. A concrete corpus on the historians' debate would thus contain a selection of the texts in which, implicitly or explicitly, a position is taken – agreement, disagreement or some other position – or in which elements of this dispute determine, wholly or partly, the semantic aspect of words, sentences or sentence relations. In establishing the corpus, it is helpful to avoid, for instance, redundancies and consciously include texts, the structure and progression of which have been significantly influenced. This also means, however, that the building of the corpus cannot be independent from premeditated first glances and a testing of the suitability of individual texts – a process following necessarily from the perspective provided by the aims of the study.

Corpus questions are a well-known problem in linguistics, particularly in lexicography where, as in discourse analysis, questions arise as to the representativeness of a gathered corpus and as to the criteria for the inclusion of certain items and the exclusion of others. While in standard lexicography representativeness is a statistical problem (it depends, for example, on whether the chosen corpus represents the standard language as accurately as possible), in discourse analysis it is primarily a problem of (semantic) content: a corpus can only be representative with respect to an aspect of its content which is inevitably chosen in advance as the basis for investigation. In lexicography, the selection of corpus texts is external to the research goal, while in discourse analysis the corpus and object of investigation are inextricably linked: the corpus itself constitutes the object of investigation, and with that the obtainable findings. It is not simply a medium or database for research objectives, objectives which in themselves are alien to the object of research. In history and other disciplines, this is known as 'the open corpus', a group of texts forming the basis of a discourse analysis investigation also builds an open corpus in this sense. The linguistic definition of discourses as corpora suggests itself, but is not interchangeable. We have the impression that in French discussions on discourse analysis, the term is used in a way that is, at best, ambiguous. On the one hand, the term is used to refer to individual examples of texts, corresponding thus to standard French vernacular. On the other hand, it can also refer to those content relations between utterances (or complexes of utterances) through different examples of texts, which above all, for Foucault, were the rationale for his 'discursive mechanisms/structures' and the like (on Foucault's concept of discourse see the discussion in Busse, 1987:222ff.).

Clearly this ambiguity has ensued in part from the fact that, in France, Michel Pêcheux spoke of 'interdiscursive relations' while Foucault spoke of 'discursive structures' (Pêcheux, 1983:35). Discourse in the Foucauldian sense is not first and foremost a text corpus, but rather relations of utterances or elements of utterances (in the sense of the French énoncé) through a large number of texts (Foucault, 1972[1969]:120). This perspective indeed led Pêcheux, too, to speak of 'interdiscursive' rather than just 'discursive' structures. The term discourse, above all in Pêcheux's sense of 'inter-discourse' has a certain proximity to 'intertextuality',[3] a term long recognised but not pursued in Germany. At the same time, however, the term has a certain connotation in the direction of the speaking subject (or author of the text). Whether one speaks of 'intertextual' or 'interdiscursive' relations is nevertheless unimportant in the case of Pêcheux. For the term discourse in the Foucauldian sense, this seems not to apply in the same way.

---

3. See Zimmerman (1978:187). De Beaugrande/Dressler (1981:188) write that *they* introduced this term; according to Zimmermann (1978:102) the term had nevertheless already been used (at least) by J. L. Houdebine (1968:280).

What can be sustained, however, is that any attempt to put the term discourse into a linguistically concrete form will refer back to the problem of corpus composition. Every constitution of a(n) (inter)discursive materiality (Pêcheux) assumes simultaneously the constitution of a corpus. Thus a single discourse as object of investigation, with all attempts at objectivity, cannot be conceived of without the constitutive act of the researcher compiling the corpus. Essential therefore, as to whether and how discourse can become an object of linguistic research, is the question of the unity and/or definability of the object under investigation, that is, of the individual, concrete discourse as research object.

2.2   The unity of discourse

The unity of a discourse (with regard to semantic relations, themes, objects, knowledge complexes, functional and/or purpose) will be determined by the objectives of research, and the interests and perspectives of the researcher. Discursive relations are – in the widest sense of the word – *semantic* relations, or at least their detection and delineation involve semantic analysis. Discursive relations can only be pinpointed when a criterion for the building of the corpus is established. Regardless of what type of criterion this may be, it presupposes recognition of the context of the given texts. Corpus building, i.e. the constitution of a discursive unity as a prospective object of linguistic investigation, is thus based on acts of interpretation. Discursive relations (like intertextual relations of any kind) cannot, as semantic relations, be available independently from their interpretations. With the compilation of the discourse intended as an object of research, the researcher is constantly confronted with the act of interpretation. Presumably it is precisely this dependence on interpretation in selecting the object of investigation that has given many linguists the impression that discourse does not exist at all, or else that it is too elusive and enigmatic to qualify as an object of serious linguistic investigation. Against this, it must be objected that the dependence on the interpretation involved in creating an object of research for discourse analysis is not in principle any different from the creation of research objects in semantics more generally. Lexicography, too, for instance, cultivates the constitution of the object's 'lexical meaning' out of practical and scientific interests; there too, the concrete object, the individual word meaning, is dependent on interpretation and ultimately the result of a constitutive act (albeit one often oriented towards everyday understandings). The only distinction is that, in lexicography, the science simply brings pre-scientific acts of interpretation (what 'the word X' or 'the meaning Y' is) onto a scientific level. On the level of discourse however, a unifying everyday understanding of the object does not take place in the same way. Everyday expressions identified as discourse, such as 'the historians' debate' or 'the new debate about the (German) nation', nevertheless show that there is a certain awareness of discursive unities in everyday knowledge.

Along with the constitution of the unity of a concrete corpus chosen as object of investigation there needs to be a reconstruction of the discourse's semantic coherence which gave rise to the reason for its very choice. It must be made plausible through the demonstration of content-related and structural features common to the texts it contains. In this sense the discourse is indeed, like the concrete corpus itself, always the simultaneous result of both scientific interpretation and relations yielded from the empirical material (much like other objects of linguistic research). This aspect needs to be highlighted: if discourse analysis were, in fact, a random construction of intertextual relations, regardless of their type, as the goal of linguistic analysis, then the objection of arbitrariness would be justified. Discourse analyses must therefore start by justifying their choices of subject matter (the constituted discourse, i.e. also the constituted corpus as well as the hypothesis about intertextual relations within the corpus that forms the basis of its composition) through the results of their analyses. This demonstrates the semantic, or rather the philological, character of discourse analysis. Just as a critical-theoretical interpretation of a literary work, along with its inherent hypothesis, only substantiates itself through its findings, a discourse analysis, and the justification for its constitutive and interpretive decisions, cannot be objectified in advance. It is only when the findings (the presented relations, structures, groupings of utterances, connections between statements etc.) appear plausible through the presented corpus material and its discourse semantic analysis, and only when it yields the observed and/or established materiality of a thesis which (as far as it is possible with semantic statements) is materially objective, that the existence of the given discourse as a meaningful object of investigation is fully established. Discourse analysis, then, always demands credit for work yet to be completed. Those who start from a position of doubting the existence of discursive relations, and with that the possibility and necessity of discourse analysis itself, will not be convinced of its value, nor allow themselves to be confronted with the findings and justifications of discourse analytical research.

Here, we would like to invoke Michel Pêcheux, who characterised discourse analysis in terms of criteria for composition and therefore the unity of the corpus as 'reading, the structure of which changes itself depending on this very act of reading' (Pêcheux, 1983: 54). This is nothing more than the metaphorical description of what philology and history call an 'open corpus'. Seen in this way, a feature of a concrete discourse analysis must be that the appropriateness of the choice of the corpus that underlies the research is examined and, where necessary, amended. It operates here in essence no differently from philology or lexicography. Every (hermeneutic) text interpretation, every lexicographical definition of a meaning produces (willingly or not) a hypothesis, the justification of which must be examined, confirmed or amended through gathering of further exemplars. The view of discourse analysis as a kind of corrective reading driving the corpus composition shows here a structural parallel with the single-text oriented hermeneutic approach, and with the lexicographical approach, which must also proceed from the interpretation of word meanings.

Discourse analysis, however, does not focus its interest on 'a better understanding' of an individual text, nor with 'what the author really meant', rather, it is a reading which seeks to uncover the implicit preconditions of the possibilities of what is said in the text as a result of interdiscursive (intertextual, semantic, epistemological, thematic, intellectual) relations. In other words, a reading that pursues the 'pre-constructed', and pursues that within the text or corpus which 'originates in a socio-historical elsewhere' (Pêcheux).

2.3   Objects of investigation for discourse analysis

Our linguistic interest in discourse analysis springs from the intention to locate, document and trace the relations and manifestations of alternative viewpoints, imaginations, language/thought paradigms and epistemological conditions and key elements which determine the theme and/or object of research. For linguistic praxis, the question centres on the chosen target of analyses. A fruitful object of analysis is the way words are used in their given contexts. This way of proceeding allows not only for the tracing of conceptual equivalence (or part equivalence) between words in different texts of the corpus (e.g. when alternative accounts appear in lexically comparable surroundings) but this access to words also allows for the identification of meanings shifts (when the same word increasingly occurs in other contexts). A history of discourse without a history of words (and their meanings) or at least without semantic reference to individual lexemes and their usage is neither conceivable nor meaningful: a word history, rather, is always part of a more comprehensive history of discourse. As an alternative to discourse analysis (also seen from epistemological interests and goals), the history of concepts is, as before, often chosen, and in its own right legitimate.

Discourse analysis should not, however, be equated to the history of concepts.[4] The distinction is determined not so much by individual empirical procedures, but rather by the question of which criteria are used for the determination of a text corpus, and how the discourse is selected as the object of investigation. Guilhaumou, and Maldidier (Guilhaumou and Maldidier, 1979: 13) point out that early French discourse analysis primarily investigated the distribution of individual concepts; this tendency,

---

4.   The question of whether the history of concepts can be regarded as a part of the history of discourse or juxtaposed against this as a competing methodology is of little concern here. Hermanns (1994) subsumes the history of concepts within the history of discourse. We ourselves assume that the history of discourse employs and must employ such methods, as they are applied in the new methodologically reflective history of concepts (Koselleck, 1979). At the same time, the history of discourse is not restricted to only these concepts (and above all, in so far as they semantically transcend word level and text level).

as well as the findings arrived at by the history of concepts in Germany (see Brunner et al., 1972ff.), reflect a strong motive in diachronic semantics for word unit-oriented analyses. For example, if one selects a particular lexeme as an object of investigation, the composition of a corpus is automatic and all (and only those) texts in which the individual lexeme appears are included in such a corpus. Discourse analysis, on the other hand, seeks to investigate semantic and epistemological relations not only expressed through a cluster of lexemes but which also transcend lexical units. Whether there is conceptual equivalence between two words, or semantic equivalence between two sentences does not necessarily manifest itself either in the text or in the given situation, but must be established and made plausible. This holds also for the question of whether the supposition is justified that a new lexical environment around a particular word constitutes a meaning shift. (…)

References

Beaugrande, Robert Alain de, and Wolfgang Ulrich Dressler. 1981. *Einführung in die Textlinguistik.* Tübingen. DOI: 10.1515/9783111349305

Brunner, Otto, Werner Conze, and Reinhart Koselleck, eds. 1972ff. *Geschichtliche Grundbegriffe: Historisches Lexikon zur politisch-sozialen Sprache in Deutschland.* Stuttgart.

Busse, D. 1987. *Historische Semantik.* Stuttgart.

Foucault, Michel. 1972[1969]. *The Archaeology of Knowledge & the Discourse on Language.* New York: Pantheon.

Foucault, Michel. 2002[1966]. *The Order of Things. An Archeology of the Human Sciences.* London: Routledge.

Guilhaumou, Jacques, and Denise Maldidier. 1979. 'Courte critique pour une longue histoire. L'analyse du discours ou les (mal)leurres de l'analogie.' *Dialectiques* 26: 7–23.

Hermanns, Fritz. 1994. 'Sprachgeschichte als Mentalitätsgeschichte. Überlegungen zu Sinn und Form und Gegenstand historischer Semantik.' In *Sprachgeschichte des Neuhochdeutschen. Gegenstände – Methoden – Theorien*, edited by Andreas Garth, Klaus J. Mattheier and Oskar Reichmann, 69–101. Tübingen: Niemeyer.

Houdebine, Jean-Louis. 1968. 'Première approche à la notion du texte.' In Tel Quel. Paris.

Koselleck, Reinhart. 1979. 'Begriffsgeschichte und Sozialgeschichte.' In *Historische Semantik und Begriffsgeschichte*, edited by Reinhart Koselleck, 19–36. Stuttgart: Klett.

Macdonell, Diane. 1986. *Theories of Discourse. An Introduction.* Oxford, New York: Basil Blackwell.

Manthey, Jürgen. 1978. *Der neue Irrationalismus.* Reinbek.

Pêcheux, M. 1975. *Les Vérités de La Palice.* Paris: Maspéro.

Pêcheux, M. 1983. 'Über die Rolle des Gedächtnisses als interdiskursives Material. Ein Forschungsprojekt im Rahmen der Diskursanalyse und Archivlektüre.' In *Das Subjekt des Diskurses. Beiträge zur sprachlichen Bildung von Subjektivität*, edited by M. Geier and Woetzel H. Argument-Sonderband, 50–58. Berlin.

Zimmermann, Klaus. 1978. *Erkundungen zur Texttypologie.* Tübingen.

Thomas Luckmann

Communicative genres

Thomas Luckmann (b. 1927) is an American-Austrian sociologist who mainly taught in
Germany. He is known for a social constructivist strand in the sociology of knowledge
which began with his *The Social Construction of Reality* (1966), co-authored with Peter
Berger (b. 1929), another Austrian-born American sociologist. For both, the question
is how actors produce shared stocks of knowledge in their life worlds which is then
established on a societal level. Luckmann is especially interested in language, which he
perceives as the medium through which social knowledge is shared among actors and
which changes over time. He is one of the major proponents of qualitative strategies in
social research. In the selected passage, Luckmann reveals his theory of communicative
genres as institutionalised patterns which help the actors come to terms with problems
of social action. His conception of communicative genres is tightly connected with a
historical perspective, as one can see by considering the notion of 'communicative
budget'. With this concept he points out that different societies have markedly different
inventories of communicative genres.

Thomas Luckmann. 1985. 'Grundformen der gesellschaftlichen Vermittlung des Wissens: Kommunikative Gattungen.' ('Basic forms of the social mediation of knowledge: communicative genres')
In *Kultur und Gesellschaft*, ed. by Friedhelm Neidhardt, M. Rainer Lepsius, and Johannes Weiss, 191–211, selected 200–211. Translated and adapted by Chris Newton and Johannes Angermuller.
Opladen: Westdeutscher Verlag.

Patterns for the solution of communicative problems of social action

The processes via which social realities are 'originally' constructed are no doubt mostly (but not always, and not necessarily) communicative processes. While all *reconstruc-tions* of social realities involve communicative action, reconstructions in the form of 'simple' descriptions of experiences, actions and observations, and in the form of interpretive accounts of social life on 'higher levels', take up a large slice of daily existence. Furthermore, they are of particular importance for coping with daily life, since as reality-fixing formulations they operate either overtly or covertly, as accounts of reality. This fundamentally normative character of reconstructive communicative processes bestows on them a particular importance for the mediation of knowledge orienting social action, below the level of explicit practical recipes, in the form of instructions and prohibitions, recipes, maxims and catechisms.

In every society there is of course a wide range of communicative processes and, naturally, not all of them fulfil reconstructive functions. If we set aside functions for the moment and consider communicative processes generally, then a formal distinction becomes apparent. Some processes may indeed be communicative in the widest sense without being actions. On the other hand, there are some social actions which are specifically communicative forms of action and some which are not. In what follows, we are not interested in communicative processes in general, nor in social actions, but rather in the specifically communicative forms of action which, when viewed formally, reveal an additional, distinctive feature. Some communicative actions are spontaneously constructed, case by case as it were, by the participants, and follow their own logics, whereas in others participants will conform to pre-constructed patterns in a typical way and carry out actions by adhering closely to this pattern. Let us examine this distinction in a little more detail.

In 'spontaneous' communicative actions, the participants construct their messages step by step. To a certain extent, they pursue a conscious communicative purpose. Under certain conditions, they may even draft a communicative plan. In so doing, they select more or less 'autonomously' from the linguistic (and more generally communicative) resources available to them in their subjective stock of knowledge. They build sentences, more or less habitually and more or less consciously, by selecting words and phrases from the semantic inventory of their language. By forming a sequence of words and phrases, participants adhere, in a generally predictable way, to the syntactic rules (along with the phonology and semantics of the 'code' as part of their native [or non-native] tongue) that they have acquired with or without the corresponding grammatical 'theory'. This selection occurs step by step, in accordance with a more or less overt plan for the participants' communicative purposes, in light of the given conditions of the situation and with more or less 'automatic' anticipation of the addressees' typically ex-pected interpretations. Depending on circumstances, skill and education, participants can then insert stylistic resources and rhetorical figures and comply with the prevailing rules of communicative etiquette, or (un)consciously break them. Throughout all this, the participants proceed with their communicative steps in a (changing) combination of an established routine and a strategic project – they do *not* however follow the course of a communicative act according to an overall preconstructed pattern.

Yet there are indeed, in all societies, communicative actions in which participants do in fact, during the process of conception, orientate themselves towards an overall pattern as *the* means that serves their ends. This pattern largely determines the selec-tion of different elements from the communicative 'code' and thus the progress of the action is, in terms of the elements determined by the pattern, relatively predictable. If such patterns are available and part of the social stock of knowledge, and if they are typically recognizable in concrete communicative actions, then we should speak of communicative genres.

Clearly this opposition of 'spontaneous' and 'genre pattern' is an exaggeration of what can be inferred from the empirical data available. Even setting aside 'pre-coding' in language and other sign systems, no communicative process is completely 'spon-taneous', just as none is wholly determined by a generic pattern. Thus idiosyncrasies (linguistic and gestural), and stereotypes and phrases, are also used without adherence to genre-like rules. Moreover, communicative etiquette (…) demands a fixed order of communicative steps determined by the deployment of prescribed communicative means. Hence, for example, even in forms of address, greetings and farewells, in thank-ing and apologising etc., we cannot speak of genre-like formations, at least not in a general sense. These so-called ritualizations of communicative actions are, however, in many ways more genre-like, even when relatively developed obligatory constructions of communicative elements build upon simpler components, such as the making and building upon personal contacts.

Naturally, the different communicative genres, quite apart from their various spe-cial functions, are not similar in a formal sense. It need hardly be emphasized that the stock of available communicative genres varies from culture to culture and that function-like genres can differ markedly from culture to culture and epoch to epoch in the sense of which layers and elements of communicative actions seem to become most strongly embedded in them. Depending on the society, epoch, situation and basic communicative purpose, participants are sometimes left free to act relatively 'spontaneously', yet at other times they are not. Under specific conditions the participants may only be able to act by adhering closely to a preconstructed pattern. Thus, in one society, a declaration of love must be delivered in song, and in another society through an intermediary. In certain societies, and in some groups, one must be able to conduct verbal duels, in others tell jokes. In our society, one is not obliged to gossip, for example, but if one does, then one submits to the specific genre norms which can be sanctioned with silence or a slap.

If one speaks of unfulfilled expectations of sanctions after breaking norms, the sociologist begins to think of social institutions. Communicative genres can indeed be understood in an analogy with the social in a way that comes close to sociology – so long as one crucial difference is not overlooked: social institutions are more or less effective and binding 'solutions' to the 'problems' of social life, while communicative genres are more or less effective and binding solutions to *communicative* problems. Under the concrete circumstances of daily life, they are nevertheless closely linked, since whenever there is hunger, eating, sex, love, power, justice, life and death, so will there be communicative action. However, hunger will not be satisfied by words. What is essential is that something be done, even if there is talking before and afterwards. In human life every action is, in a certain sense, a 'speech', and every speech is an 'action'. Sometimes, however, speech is an action without the metaphorical extension of word meanings (in the sense of Austin: things are being done with words), such as when communicative actions are constitutive parts of the solutions to underlying social problems: a wedding ceremony or a court's verdict. Generally, however, communicative genres are not institutions of actions, rather they are prescribed generic models of speech (and, in general, communication).

'Communicative genres' is, in any case, a second-order concept, a scientific term which nevertheless has a bearing on first-order concepts, such as those in everyday understanding. This does not of course mean that participants who rely on genre-like norms must have a fully formed genre *theory*. Even without being able to cite the rules we follow when telling jokes, we 'know' how, when, to whom and which jokes can be told. This knowledge, along with its often wholly everyday conceptualizations, suffices as an initial empirical basis for the systematic application of the analytical concept. Suffice to say that theories of communicative genres, explicitly formulated to a greater or lesser extent, are nevertheless virtually universal components of the social stock of knowledge, since in their communicative actions, members of a society orientate themselves to this pre-theoretical and theoretical knowledge, thus constantly producing concrete exemplars of communicative genres for each other. These are then, to use a different terminology, 'real cultural objects'.

The structure of communicative genres

Communicative genres have a common base function, namely to 'solve' specific communicative problems in the general context of social action and they all have the same 'material' basis – the various sign systems (communicative 'codes') that are available in the social knowledge store and which are, additionally in some oral genres, at least partly systematized though not fully symbolized forms of expression. It is here that we find marked similarities in the structure of communicative genres. These similarities, which arise from the relationship between base function and 'material' basis, can perhaps best be described as the internal structure (*Binnenstruktur*) of communicative genres.

Communicative action is – whatever other features it may have – social action. It is intimately linked then to the rules for social action which prevail in a given social order, and to the structure of social institutions and social stratification. The ranks of structure which ensue from the relationship between communicative actions and the social structure can be described as the 'external structure' of communicative genres.

What is common in the internal structure of the various communicative genres is that, in contrast to 'spontaneous' actions, preconstructed patterns are available to the participants. These preconstructions are components of the social stock of knowledge and consist of preselections from the communicative 'codes'. They can involve the full range of a code's ranks, from phonology and prosody to semantics and syntax; they can involve base elements of the code or single-rank arrangements of elements, obtain narrowly in linguistic ('textual') aspects, or determine connections between the linguistic, gestural, mimetic, kinesic, etc. Thus the internal structure of a genre consists of preconstructed patterns of extremely varied elements, which in turn are determined by various connections: words and phrases, general registers, formalities and formal chunks, rhetorical figures and tropes, stylistic techniques such as metre, rhyme, lists, oppositions, etc. plus melody, specific rules of dialogue, such as turn-taking, repair strategies and alternations of topic.

The external structure of communicative genres is also, on the whole, determined by a higher order of connections than is the case in 'spontaneous' actions. It consists essentially of preconstructed definitions of the communicative milieu, communicative situations and the type and role of the reciprocal relationship of the participants. These definitions are of course never completely independent of the prevailing definitions of the social milieu, social situations and social actors but, nevertheless, need not be identical to them. The two types of definition (in which age, gender, status, etc. normally play a role) come closest when a communicative genre is closely linked to a social institution. There are, however, in some genres, also *relatively* independent definitions, e.g. the actor as narrator, singer, etc.

Together, these two structural levels account for the general pattern of the genre-specific communicative action and determine the degree of obligation. They are thus 'coercive' on the one hand and 'permissive' on the other; in this sense they are fully analogous with social institutions and wholly independent of any partial overlap between them.

The identification of these rather abstract commonalities represents only a first, though in the current environment not wholly redundant, step. Clearly, there must be applications of more accurate and generalisable studies of communicative genres, the basis of which should enable the systematic appraisal of the general 'field' of communicative genres in a particular society in a particular epoch. A subsequent ensuing analysis of what is socioculturally embedded, of the social conditions and consequences of a society's typical, and above all, communicative procedures which are equipped with genre patterns will enable gaining important insights into the communicative dimension of the construction and the maintenance and alteration of social order.

Quite apart from such implications of the sociology of science or cultural theory, a first examination of the structural commonalities will focus subsequent attention on the particularities of the various communicative genres, all the more so since these differ not only in the special functions that are built upon base functions (i.e. the solving of certain types of communicative problems: narrating, ordering, appealing, praying, etc.), but also in the structural features that are governed by these functions (i.e. in the type of 'preselection' and/or in the level of connection in the composition of elements in general patterns). And one need only examine the genres which are important for the distribution of action-oriented knowledge (i.e. major reconstructed patterns, such as conversational narratives, interviews, and gossip) and non-reconstructed – didactic, devotional, etc. – forms, such as sermons, or smaller-scale 'moralising' forms such as sayings, and parables (…) The relationship between the external and internal structures of communicative genres and their historical shifts can perhaps still be examined via a few short observations about genres that have reconstructive functions. It appears that certain social milieus are signified by particular manifestations of reconstructive genres and a recognizable 'narrative culture'. In our society, for example, doctors and carers in a psychiatric clinic distinguish themselves very clearly through the form and manner of their speech. The analysis of reconstructive genres in the context of their meaning for the distribution of action-oriented knowledge (general as well as specific) and related social functions is still in its infancy, although there have been some notable studies, such as Dingwall's analysis of 'atrocity stories' regarding the maintenance of professional expectations and the definition of professional rules for English 'health visitors'.

In the field of historical shifts between the oral and the written, there is a large number of notable studies, both detailed and general. Yet the relationship between the oral and the written in reconstructive genres remains an important area of research. For the formal organisation of modern societies (and not only for them) one characteristic seems to be that oral reconstructions of events or circumstances will be transcribed and thus fixed in a written version – court witness statements are recorded according to a protocol, descriptions of illness are entered into medical records. In everyday knowledge, we believe we know what occurs overall; yet, a systematic analysis of the rules governing the transformation from the written to the spoken is still lacking.

Afterword on the communicative 'budget' of a society

The entire 'field' of communicative genres (because of the existence of a systematic diachronic and synchronic context, one can indeed speak of a 'field') builds, along with the typical 'spontaneous' actions in a society, a whole. This 'whole' can be described as the 'communicative budget' (*kommunikativer Haushalt*) of a society. While this 'whole' is only identified with great difficulty (as is the case with other types of 'budget'), its core concern, the 'field' of communicative genres is, at least to a reasonable extent, analyzable. And since communicative genres represent prevailing 'solutions' to the communicative problems of a society, their analysis would be useful even for an appraisal of the communicative 'budget', as well as for accountable explanations of the relevance system within a society. What is generally (and specifically communicatively) important or problematic in one society in one epoch is not necessarily what is important or problematic in another society or epoch. Despite the fundamental commonalities of human life across cultures and epochs, it is hardly surprising that different societies have markedly different inventories of communicative genres: compare hunter-gatherer societies with the old 'high' cultures, or the Germans of Luther's time with the citizens of modern Germany. Communicative genres of one epoch may unfold in a loosely regulated form or disappear altogether (the shift from oral culture to mass literacy can be seen as a major factor), and vice versa.

The term 'communicative budget' is, in contrast to communicative genres, a purely analytical term which does not correspond to a pure 'real cultural object'. Its functionality can only reveal itself in a so-called typological overview of wholly variant communicative events. This approach should be abandoned if it proves to be unfruitful since the relationship with everyday realities (first-order constructs) is only accessible through multiple mediation strategies and, above all, through the concepts and theories of communicative genres.

Section VII

Critical approaches

Introduction

People have always lived together but not always in ways they have chosen or would consider acceptable. Thus, while a society can exist in many forms, (some of) its members will always challenge the way it is structured and organized, and not take everything as given or for granted – this is what is implied by the concept of 'critique'. Relations of inequality and domination, for instance, are typically considered illegitimate as long as they are at odds with hegemonic norms and values (such as freedom and equality in modern liberal and democratic societies). Societies, in other words, do not only define what is but also what should or should not be.

Various traditions in social and political theory emphasize the critical potential of society. While in ancient philosophy and mediaeval theology critical ideas were typically considered as emanating from divine and other transcendent instances, critical theories have since increasingly insisted on their immanent character: not only is the social and political order a product of human beings, but the norms and values which allow citizens to criticize certain aspects of social life are person-made, too.

Among the critical projects that have inspired discourse research are:

- Emancipatory theories of the Enlightenment (e.g. by Locke, Rousseau, Kant), which point to the universal capacity of humans (i.e. their critical reason) to question the status quo (e.g. traditional powers, laws or religious institutions such as the Catholic Church);
- Socio-historical theories of power and inequality (from Marx to Adorno, from Beauvoir to Bourdieu, from Weber to Arendt), which reveal the range of social forces influencing the actors in society. Here the critical aim is to reveal the contradictions that may emerge between what actors intend to do (e.g. to act with a sense of fair play in the market) and the unintentional social effects of their actions (e.g. reproducing a class structure);
- Critical-constructivist theories, influenced by the 'linguistic turn' (e.g. Habermas, Foucault, Butler), which show how the social order can be 'naturalized' and also criticized through communicative practices. Here, the aim is to deconstruct essentializing claims (e.g. the underlying 'biological' nature of humans) by revealing their inherent aporias.

While discourse research can refer to some or all of these strands at the same time, some currents in Critical Discourse Analysis – or, as recently labelled (see van Dijk's contribution), Critical Discourse Studies – tend to rely more on emancipatory models that draw on Critical Theory and the Frankfurt School, while other schools as well as sociolinguistic ethnographic approaches integrating analyses of power and ideology point to the unintended/latent effects of social and linguistic practices; yet others (such as poststructuralist discourse theories) prefer more constructivist epistemologies.

Discourse studies deal with critical questions from various angles. They can make the criticism of certain aspects of social life an object of either (a) theoretical or (b) empirical investigation. Or (c), it can take the position of a critical subject itself and criticize certain aspects of social life and remain self-reflective during the research process. These aims can also be pursued simultaneously. The seminal work of Habermas is a case where theoretical, empirical and reflexive approaches have been combined.

Theoretically, Jürgen Habermas is known as a proponent of the communicative/linguistic turn in Critical Theory (1985[1981]). In the wake of the Frankfurt School, Habermas proposes a theory of communicative action which points to the critical potential inherent in any speech act. For Habermas, discourse participants claim universal norms such as equality and freedom whenever they engage in communicative action. Whereas Adorno/Horkheimer (1972[1944]) theorize the loss of true authentic criticism in late capitalism, Habermas is more optimistic and points out that any normative claim can be challenged in a free deliberative exchange to counter the best rational argument. Yet Habermas has also dealt with the problem of social critique empirically. In his early work (1991[1962]), he traces the historical emergence of a critical bourgeois public sphere through a network of debating clubs, public salons and publication outlets from the 18th century onwards. Last but not least, Habermas has also acted and continues to act as a powerful public intellectual defending the welfare state and taking a liberal stance in debates on the 'postnational constellation' (Habermas, 2001[1998]). His role as a public intellectual notwithstanding, Habermas' main challenge and focus are theoretical and epistemological: Given his theoretical interests, one might define Habermas as a critical discourse theorist who explores theoretical possibilities ('How is critique possible?'), rather than a critical discourse analyst who studies social problems ('How can a social problem be accounted for critically?').

Even though Habermas is known for his scathing attacks on the French poststructuralists (such as Foucault, whom in 1981 he denounced as a 'young conservative'), many French discourse theorists share the same critical sensitivity over power in discourse. Indeed, one could refer to the Marxist background of discourse theorists such as Althusser, who renewed the Marxist critique of ideology by drawing on Lacanian psychoanalysis (Althusser, 1969). In line with other poststructuralist theories, discourse analysis should therefore aim to decentre the sovereign, autonomous and unified (i.e. 'speaking') subject (Pêcheux, 1982[1975]). In contrast to Foucault who outlined a genealogical critique of the entrepreneurial subject as a dominant form in the contemporary regime of (neo-)liberal governmentality (Foucault, 2007[1977/78]), Butler pleaded for deconstructing binary heterosexual identities and biological 'matter' through critical strategies of ironic subversion (Butler, 1990).

While discourse theorists such as Habermas and the poststructuralists have put the question of criticism on the agenda of the epistemological and intellectual debate, more empirical approaches in the social sciences focus on how the various actors actually voice or are enabled to voice their critical stance (or not) as they deal with power relations. Interactionists and ethnomethodologists are sceptical about power-oriented perspectives on discourse which transcend actors' perspectives. For these actor-oriented approaches, actors are endowed with a critical reflexive capacity which allows them to deal creatively with rules, norms and constraints. Therefore, some critical social scientists have pushed for letting the actors speak and taking their concerns seriously (Boltanski, 2011). This is also what ethnographers of power such as Blommaert (2005), Duchêne and Heller (Duchêne and Heller, 2012) have reminded us of in their sociolinguistic work on language ideologies (see Unger et al., 2014; Flowerdew, 2014). The point here is to observe how discourse participants negotiate certain linguistic norms and the social value that is attributed to them in text and talk. However, some critics of these approaches maintain that it is not possible to attribute all social behaviour to power relations (see Wodak et al. (2012) for an overview).

Even though there is no clear-cut distinction between empirical and critical approaches such as those categorized as Critical Discourse Analysis/Studies (CDA/CDS), a primary concern of all approaches under the umbrella of CDA/CDS is to reveal how complex social problems are linguistically represented and to suggest ways of challenging them, deconstructing them, understanding them and opening up possibilities of overcoming them. As the many entries in this *Reader* testify, there is no clear-cut distinction between theoretical, empirical and critical approaches. However, in contrast to many other strands in discourse studies, CDA/CDS can be defined as a problem-oriented interdisciplinary research field which mobilizes a variety of theoretical models and research methods. Major trends in CDA/CDS, which started in Europe (in the UK and on the continent) in the late 1980s, encompass: Norman Fairclough's *Dialectical-Relational Approach* which is situated in the Marxian tradition as well as in the Cultural Political Economy; the *Socio-Cognitive Approach*, originating from Teun van Dijk, in the tradition of French socio-psychology and theories of social representation (Serge Moscovici); *Socio-Semiotics* and *Visual Grammar,* established by Theo van Leeuwen and Gunter Kress, which led to the systematic analysis of visual communication by elaborating Systemic-Functional Linguistics; so-called *Dispositif Analysis* proposed by Siegfried Jäger, which draws heavily on Foucault; and the *Discourse-Historical Approach* proposed by Ruth Wodak which integrates theories from history, sociology and the political sciences with linguistic analysis, in the tradition of Critical Theory (see Wodak and Meyer, 2009; Hart and Cap, 2014 for an overview of these trends). In the meantime, these trends have been much elaborated, challenged, changed and reformulated; many new approaches have been developed. What unites all approaches in CDA/CDS is a shared interest in the semiotic dimensions of social problems and social change.

CDA/CDS does not study a linguistic unit *per se* but rather social phenomena which are necessarily complex and thus require a multi/inter/trans-disciplinary and multi-methodical approach. The objects under investigation do not have to be related to what is widely perceived as problematic or negative; this is a frequent misunderstanding of the aims and goals of CDS and of the term 'critical', since any social phenomenon can lend itself to critical investigation, to being challenged and not taken for granted. CDA/CDS is thus characterized by not taking anything at face value, taking an interest in de-mystifying ideologies and power relations through the systematic investigation of semiotic data (written, spoken or visual). CDA/CDS researchers attempt to make their own positions and interests explicit while keeping some distance from the data and their analysis, retaining their respective scientific methodologies and remaining self-reflective about their own research process (see Hart and Cap, 2014).

CDA/CDS sees discourse – language use in speech and writing – as a form of 'social practice'. Describing discourse as social practice implies a dialectical relationship between a particular discursive event and the situation(s), institution(s) and social structure(s) which frame it. The discursive event is shaped by them, but also shapes them. That is, discourse is socially constitutive as well as socially conditioned – it constitutes situations, objects of knowledge, and the social identities of and relationships between people and groups of people. It is constitutive both in the sense that it helps to sustain and reproduce the social status quo, and in the sense that it contributes to transforming it. Since discourse is so socially consequential, it gives rise to important issues of power. Discursive practices may have major ideological effects – that is, they can help produce and reproduce unequal power relations between, for instance, social classes, women and men, and ethnic/cultural majorities and minorities through the ways in which they represent things and position people (Fairclough and Wodak, 1997).

'Being critical' in CDA/CDS includes being self-reflective and self-critical. In this sense, 'critical' does not only mean to criticize others; it also means to criticize the 'critical' itself. Critical analysis itself is a practice that may contribute to social change (Fairclough, 1992). Reisigl and Wodak (2001: 32ff.) distinguish between 'text-immanent critique', 'socio-diagnostic critique' and 'prospective (retrospective) critique'. While text-immanent critique is inherently oriented towards careful retroductable text analysis, socio-diagnostic critique is based on integrating the socio-political and structural context into the analysis and interpretation of textual meanings. Prospective critique builds on these two levels in order to identify areas of social concern that can be addressed by direct social engagement in relation to practitioners and wider audiences.

Furthermore, CDA/CDS is primarily interested in the latent type of everyday beliefs, frequently appearing disguised as conceptual metaphors and analogies (Lakoff and Johnson, 1980). Dominant ideologies may appear 'neutral', with assumptions that stay largely unchallenged. When people in a society think alike about certain matters, or even forget that there are alternatives to the status quo, one arrives at the Gramscian concept of *hegemony* (Gramsci, 1978[1921–1926]) and becomes interested in questions of power. Some researchers draw more on a Habermasian notion of 'discourse', 'critique' and 'power' (such as the discourse-historical approach), others' work stands in the tradition of Foucault, such as the theory proposed by Jäger (2007[1993]), or Fairclough, who also draws heavily on post-Marxian approaches such as the Cultural Political Economy (2010). The *Dialectical-Relational Approach* (DRA) from Norman Fairclough focuses upon social conflict in the Marxian tradition and tries to detect its linguistic manifestations in discourses, in particular elements of dominance, difference and resistance. According to DRA, every social practice has a semiotic element (Chouliaraki and Fairclough, 1999). Teun Van Dijk argues that whereas (critical and other) Discourse Studies have extensively considered the structures of text and talk, they have only paid lip service to the necessity of developing the complex relations between text and context. Therefore, he argues for a socio-cognitive approach which points out how cognition mediates between text and context (van Dijk, 2008). Ruth Wodak proposed the discourse-historical approach (DHA) which also integrates new methodologies for CDA/CDS: the use of ethnography, focus groups and narrative interviews, combined with more traditional data sets such as newspapers and political speeches. Research in this area necessarily considers a historical dimension (Reisigl and Wodak, 2009). Apart from rhetoric and pragmatics, the DHA also applies concepts from argumentation theory, notably the pragma-dialectics of the Amsterdam School (van Eemeren, 2004) in its analysis

The section consists of five contributions, starting with Habermas's philosophical interrogations of critique and discourse. The other four contributions confront certain social problems such as the othering of immigrants in Belgium (Blommaert/Verschueren) or anti-Semitism in Austria (Wodak). Van Dijk elaborates his sociocognitive approach to discourse while Fairclough points to the need for a critical agenda in education.

References

Adorno, Theodor W., and Max Horkheimer. 1972[1944]. *Dialectic of Enlightenment*. New York: Herder & Herder.

Althusser, Louis. 1969. *For Marx*. Harmondsworth: The Penguin Press.

Blommaert, Jan. 2005. *Discourse. A Critical Introduction*. Cambridge: Cambridge University Press. DOI: 10.1017/CBO9780511610295

Boltanski, Luc. 2011. *On Critique. A Sociology of Emancipation*. Cambridge: Polity.

Butler, Judith. 1990. *Gender Trouble. Feminism and the Subversion of Identity*. Routledge: London, New York.

Chouliaraki, Lilie and Norman Fairclough. 1999. *Discourse in Late Modernity. Rethinking Critical Discourse Analysis*. Edinburgh: Edinburgh University Press.

Duchêne, Alexandre, and Monica Heller, eds. 2012. *Language in Late Capitalism: Pride and Profit.* London: Routledge.

Fairclough, Norman. 1992. *Discourse and Social Change.* Cambridge, Oxford: Polity Press.

Fairclough, Norman. 2010. 'Discourse, change and hegemony.' In *Critical Discourse Analysis: The Critical Study of Language*, edited by Norman Fairclough, 126–45. Harlow: Longman.

Fairclough, Norman, and Ruth Wodak. 1997. 'Critical discourse analysis.' In *Discourse as Social Interaction*, edited by Teun A. van Dijk, 258–84. London: Sage.

Flowerdew, John, ed. 2014. *Discourse and Context.* Bloomsbury: London.

Foucault, Michel. 2007[1977/78]. *Security, Territory, Population. Lectures at the College de France.* Basingstoke: Palgrave, Macmillan. DOI: 10.1057/9780230245075

Gramsci, Antonio. 1978[1921–1926]. *Selections from the Political Writings.* London: Lawrence and Wishart.

Habermas, Jürgen. 1981. 'Modernity versus Postmodernity.' *New German Critique* 228: 3–14. DOI: 10.2307/487859

Habermas, Jürgen. 2001[1998]. *The Postnational Constellation.* Cambridge: MIT Press.

Habermas, Jürgen. 1991[1962]. *The Structural Transformation of the Public Sphere. An Inquiry Into a Category of Bourgeois Society.* Cambridge, Mass.: MIT Press.

Habermas, Jürgen. 1985[1981]. *The Theory of Communicative Action.* Boston: Beacon Press.

Hart, Chris, and Pjotr Cap (eds.). 2014. *New Approaches to Critical Discourse Studies.* London: Bloomsbury Publishers.

Jäger, Siegfried. 2007[1993]. *Kritische Diskursanalyse. Eine Einführung.* Münster: Unrast.

Lakoff, George, and Mark Johnson. 1980. *Metaphors We Live By.* Chicago: University of Chicago Press.

Pêcheux, Michel. 1982[1975]. *Language, semantics and ideology. Stating the obvious.* London: Macmillan.

Reisigl, Martin, and Ruth Wodak. 2001. *Discourse and Discrimination. Rhetorics of Racism and Antisemitism.* London, et al.: Routledge.

Reisigl, Martin, and Ruth Wodak. 2009. 'The discourse-historical approach (DHA).' In *Methods of Critical Discourse Analysis*, edited by Ruth Wodak and Michael Meyer, 87–121. London: Sage.

Unger, Johann W., Michał Krzyżanowski, and Ruth Wodak, eds. 2014. *Multilingual Encounters in Europe's Institutional Spaces.* London: Bloomsbury.

van Dijk, Teun A. 2008. *Discourse and Context. A Sociocognitive Approach.* Cambridge: Cambridge University Press. DOI: 10.1017/CBO9780511481499

van Eemeren, Frans. 2004. *A Systematic Theory of Argumentation: The Pragma-Dialectical Approach.* Cambridge: Cambridge University Press.

Wodak, Ruth, and Meyer, Michael. 2009. 'Critical Discourse Analysis: history, agenda, theory' In *Methods of Critical Discourse Analysis*, edited by Ruth Wodak and Michael Meyer, 1–33. London: Sage.

Wodak, Ruth, Michal Krzyżanowski, and Bernhard Forchtner. 2012. 'The interplay of language ideologies and contextual cues in multilingual interactions: Language choice and code-switching in European Union institutions.' *Language in Society* 41, no. 2: 157–86. DOI: 10.1017/S0047404512000036

Jürgen Habermas

A normative conception of discourse

Jürgen Habermas (b. 1929) can certainly be considered one of the leading philosophers of our time. In 1964, he took over Horkheimer's chair in philosophy and sociology at Frankfurt, which he occupied until his retirement in 1993. In line with the Frankfurt School of Critical Theory, he addresses classical questions in social philosophy: What are the principles guiding critical thinking? How can we distinguish between what is socially acceptable and what is not? How is criticism possible in a society with huge inequalities and a plurality of values? More than many preceding generations of Critical Theorists, Habermas refers to theoretical debates from the Anglo-American world, notably from the universe of discourse pragmatics, including analytical philosophy, speech-act theory and interactionism. As a result, he presents a more liberal version of Critical Theory, which places high hopes on the positive social effects of common, rational and deliberative exchange among citizens in the public sphere. For Habermas, there are inherent principles in discourse which we cannot *not* apply when we engage in communicative action with others. In order to make certain normative claims and criticize those of others, the discourse participants need to respect the principles of equality and universality: e.g. if I claim the right to speak, then it is difficult to deny the right of others to speak. If Habermas believes that the discourse participants always need to maintain the ideals of the free speech situation, then he implies that discourse normally takes places among free discourse participants. But as he makes clear in the selected passages, he insists on the difference between 'real' discourse, that is discourse biased by relations of power and domination, and the counterfactual, utopian character of the ideal speech situation, which creates critical potentials as it always accompanies 'real' discourse.

Jürgen Habermas. 2001. 'Reflections on the Linguistic Foundation of Sociology:
The Christian Gauss Lecture, Princeton University, February-March 1971.'
In *On the Pragmatics of Social Interaction. Preliminary Studies in the Theory
of Communicative Action*, 1–105, selected 100–105.
Cambridge: Polity/Oxford: Blackwell.

(…) In conclusion, I want to elucidate the meaning of normative validity, which is a fundamental concept of the communicative theory of society. The naive validity of norms of action involves a very far-reaching claim. This claim is the source of the counterfactual power that allows prevailing norms to sustain, without violence, their immunity to violation. Let me take as my starting point a phenomenon of which every subject capable of action has an intuitive awareness. If we encounter another as a subject and not as an opponent, let alone as an object that we can manipulate, we (inevitably) take her to be accountable for her actions. We can only interact with her or, as I would put it, encounter her at the level of intersubjectivity, if we presuppose that under appropriate questioning she could account for her actions. Insofar as we *want* to relate to her as we do to a subject, we *must* proceed on the basis that the other *could* tell us why, in a given situation, she behaved as she did and not otherwise. Thus we perform an idealization, and one that affects us as well, since we see the other subject through the same eyes through which we look at ourselves. We suppose that the other, were we to ask her, can give us reasons for her actions, just as we believe that we can account for our own actions if asked by another subject. This intuitive knowledge which, in the course of action, conceals from itself the status of a supposition (or anticipation), can be broken down into two counterfactual expectations: (a) We expect that actors intentionally obey the norms that they follow. Thus we are incapable of imputing unconscious motives to the other in the course of an interaction. As soon as we make such an imputation we leave the level of intersubjectivity and treat the other as an object *about* which we can communicate with third parties but *with* whom communication has broken down. In addition, this *expectation of intentionality* includes the assumption that all nonverbal expressions can, if necessary, be transformed into linguistic utterances. (b) We expect that acting subjects obey only those norms that they consider justified. Thus we are incapable, in the course of interaction, of expecting the other to obey a norm that she would not also recognize as legitimate (if she is obeying it intentionally). Even if a subject is obviously only bowing to an empirically imposed constraint, we impute to her general principles, according to which she would justify this behaviour, too. This *expectation of legitimacy* also includes the assumption that the only norms (or general principles) that are considered justified in the eyes of acting subjects are those that they are convinced would stand up, if necessary, under unrestricted and uncoercive discourse.

These two counterfactual expectations, contained in the idealization of reciprocally imputed accountability, which is inevitable for actors, refer to a mutual understanding that is, in principle, attainable in practical discourse. The meaning of the claim to validity for norms of action resides therefore in the promise that the norm-governed behaviour of subjects, which is in fact habitual, can be understood as the responsible action of accountable subjects. We presuppose that subjects can say what norm they are obeying – *and why* they accept this norm as justified. In so doing, we also suppose that subjects to whom we can discursively demonstrate that they do not meet the two above conditions would abandon the norm in question and change their behaviour. We know that, as a rule, institutionalized actions do not correspond to this *model of pure communicative action,* although we cannot help but always act counterfactually as though this model were realized. On this inevitable fiction rests the humanity of social intercourse among people who are still human, i.e. those who have not yet become completely alienated from themselves in their self- objectifications.

However, the status of the unavoidable anticipation of an ideal speech situation (in discourse) and of a model of pure communicative action (in interaction) remains unclear. I want to conclude by cautioning against two obvious misunderstandings. The conditions under which arguments actually occur are clearly not the same as those of the ideal speech situation – at least not often or usually. Nevertheless, it is part of the structure of possible speech that, in performing speech acts (and actions), we act counterfactually as though the ideal speech situation (or the model of pure communicative action) were not merely fictitious but real – this is precisely what we call a presupposition. Thus the normative foundation of linguistic communication is both anticipation and yet, as an anticipated basis, operative. The formal anticipation of idealized conversation (perhaps as a form of life to be realized in the future?) guarantees the 'ultimate' underlying counterfactual mutual agreement, which does not first have to be created, but which must, a priori, connect potential speaker-hearers. Moreover, reaching a mutual understanding regarding this agreement must not be required if communication is to be possible. Thus the concept of the ideal speech situation is not merely a regulative principle in the Kantian sense. For in our first act of linguistic communication we must in fact always, already, be making this presupposition. On the other hand, the concept of the ideal speech situation is not an existing concept in the Hegelian sense. For there is no historical society that corresponds to the form of life that we anticipate in relation to the concept of the ideal speech situation. The ideal situation might best be compared to a transcendental illusion [*Schein*], were it not, at the same time, a constitutive condition of possible speech instead of an impermissible projection (as in the non-empirical employment of categories of understanding). For every possible communication, the anticipation of the ideal speech situation has the significance of a constitutive illusion that is, at the same time, the prefiguration [*Vorschein*] of a form of life. Of course, we cannot know, a priori, whether that prefiguration is a mere delusion – no matter how unavoidable are the presuppositions that give rise to it – or whether the empirical conditions of an even approximate realization of this supposed form of life can be attained in practice. From this viewpoint, the fundamental norms of possible speech that are inherent in universal pragmatics contain a practical hypothesis. This hypothesis, which must first be developed and justified in a theory of communicative competence, is the point of departure for a critical theory of society.

Jan Blommaert and Jef Verschueren

A pragmatics of the cultural other

Jef Verschueren (b. 1952) teaches linguistics at the University of Antwerp (Belgium). For him, linguistic pragmatics must take into account the cognitive, social and cultural dimensions of language. He therefore defends a broad notion of pragmatics covering a wide range of meaning-making practices (Verschueren, 1999; Verschueren et al., 1996). In his research he refers to pragmatics when dealing with social problems, intercultural and international communication, language and ideology. Jan Blommaert (b. 1961) is a Belgian sociolinguist and linguistic anthropologist at Tilburg University (Netherlands) with a background in African Studies. Since 2002 his research has focused on new socio-cultural inequalities emerging from globalisation. For him, traditional sociolinguistics cannot take into account 'super-diverse' sociolinguistic realities, which result from in-creased mobility and new technologies. Blommaert emphasizes the historical dimension in a similar way to the discourse-historical approach. He proposes the term 'entextualisa-tion' for the multi-layeredness of discourse, defined in a similar way as 'recontextualisa-tion' (see Blommaert, 2005). Both entextualisation and recontextualisation imply tracing meanings over time, intertextually and interdiscursively. In their controversial book, *Debating Diversity* (1998), they address social and political issues in Belgian society: the debate(s) about immigration, racism and nationalism. They turn the very debate about these issues into a problem: 'a major part of the problem consists precisely in viewing diversity as a problem'. In the excerpt selected below, they present their theoretical and methodological background. In the first section, they emphasise the importance of the analysis of language as an entrypoint into ideology and mention a wide range of rel-evant phenomena that must be considered. In the second section, they deal with some epistemological implications of their research, emphasizing three topics: the role of the investigator in the process under investigation, the interaction in the analysis between micro- and macro-levels, and interdisciplinarity.

References

Blommaert, Jan. 2005. *Discourse. A Critical Introduction*. Cambridge: Cambridge University Press. DOI: 10.1017/CBO9780511610295

Verschueren, Jef. 1999. *Understanding Pragmatics*. London, et al.: Arnold.

Verschueren, Jef, Jan-Ola Östman, Jan Blommaert, and Chris Bulcaen, eds. 1996. *Handbook of Prag-matics*. Amsterdam, Philadelphia: John Benjamins Publishing Company.

Jan Blommaert and Jef Verschueren. 1998. *Debating Diversity: Analysing the Discourse of Tolerance*, selected pp. 32–38. London: Routledge.

Language and the pragmatics of ideology research

In this book we use language, the central medium of discourse, as a way into ideology. Such an enterprise is necessarily interpretative. This interpretative effort bears on a genuinely communicative phenomenon: the debate about diversity or about immigrants and immigration is quite literally a debate. An eminently suitable theoretical background for such an undertaking is provided by linguistic *pragmatics,* to be defined as a general functional perspective on (any aspect of) language, i.e. as an approach to language which takes into account the full complexity of its cognitive, social and cultural (i.e. 'meaningful') functioning in the lives of human beings.[1] Pragmatics provides us with the tools for tracing the construction of meaning in discourse. And ideological processes, to the extent that discourse or language is their medium, are fundamentally processes of meaning construction.

Linguistic pragmatics assumes that cognitive images and conceptual habits are reflected in the behaviour of language users, their forms of communication and their rhetorical habits. All forms of communication are accompanied by more or less hidden meaning systems which determine the interpretation of what is said. One of the basic premises of a pragmatic approach is that every utterance relies on a world of implicit background assumptions, supposedly shared or presented as shared, which combines with what is explicitly said in the construct ion of meaning. In other words, it is impossible to find utterances which express their full meaning fully explicitly.[2] Let us briefly summarize some of the methodological requirements for a scientifically tenable scrutiny of such double-track meaning processes.

Given the nature of the enterprise (i.e. the reconstruction of an ideology which, as suggested, and contrary to common practice in mainstream sociology, cannot simply be carried out on the basis of what is said literally), the major concern is to separate clearly interpretation from speculation.[3] After all, just as it is impossible to say explic-

---

1. In the linguistic literature, many divergent views are to be found of what 'pragmatics' is supposed to stand for. We opt for the widest possible interpretation, involving a necessary interdisciplinary perspective on language in use. See Verschueren et al. (1995).

2. This premiss is shared by researchers involved in the analysis of ideology in discourse (e.g. Robert Hodge and Gunther Gress, 1993), even if they would not label their research 'pragmatic'.

3. 'Speculation' is basically the same as what Eco (1990, 1992) would call 'overinterpretation'. The only difference is that the product of speculation (interpretation which goes beyond the limits set

itly everything one means, it is impossible to 'mean' (not to be confused with 'intend') everything that is possibly implied by what one says. The task is less impossible than it might seem, thanks to a significant degree of conventionality involved in the use of 'carriers' of implicit meaning, and thanks to the observability of how pieces of potential meaning actually get used or fail to get used.

Every pragmatics textbook contains numerous types of examples of conventional presupposition- and implication-carrying constructions such as 'I regret that … ' or 'I'm sorry that … ', typically presupposing that what follows is both factual and known to the interlocutors. Thus 'I am sorry that I didn't come to your party yesterday' pre-supposes minimally that the speaker was not at the party and that she/he assumes that the hearer noticed her/his absence. This presupposition can be elaborated strategically by adding other ingredients. 'I am sorry that I couldn't come to your party' adds an excuse to the fact which is presupposed, viz. the speaker's inability to come. Because this excuse is not brought up as a separate assertion but is simply embedded in the factive structure, it also presents itself as factually valid and becomes less susceptible to questioning or criticism. For someone with a trained eye, such intricacies of implicit meaning are quite clear.

As to the scientific study of how meaning potential is actualized in discourse, the latest pragmatic literature draws special attention to empirically observable traces of the dynamic negotiation of meaning, not only at the explicit but also at the implicit level. Thus Charles Goodwin (1994) shows, for instance, how lawyers succeed in de-fining Rodney King, lying face down and surrounded by four police officers, as being 'in control of the situation' while being beaten, just by framing the event in terms of categories that are normally descriptive of responsible police behaviour. Detailed analy-ses such as Goodwin's make the actual meaningful *functioning* of linguistic choices visible. This is possible because words and linguistic structures are observable beacons referring to wider contexts and at the same time creating contexts as largely implicit meaning complexes which serve as frames of reference for interpretation. The beacons are there, open to the eye, and we are learning more and more about the ways in which they signal the less visible but equally functional aspects of meaning.

In practical terms, a few of the more relevant phenomena that we looked at sys-tematically are the following:

1. *Wording patterns and strategies.* Words and structures are not meaningful in their own right. Meaning derives from the grammatical and lexical choices which lan-guage users make from the range of possible choices, in relation to subject matter and context. For instance, if farmer demonstrations in Brussels, no matter how

---

by and adopted methodology) may be 'true', whereas the term 'overinterpretation' already suggests a deviation from the truth.

much damage they do to the city, are systematically referred to as 'farmer *demonstrations*', while 'migrant *riots*' is used consistently when describing a group of migrant youngsters protesting police brutality in the streets of Brussels and breaking a window here and there, this pattern of word choice is meaningful. Though the two types of events have many common characteristics (the dissatisfaction of a social group, the public voicing of protest, the lack of respect for public and private property), the first one is clearly placed – and kept – in a frame of legitimate social action, while the second is condemned by the very act of labelling it.

2. *'Local' carriers of implicit information,* i.e. the types of implication- and presupposition-carrying constructions already referred to. For instance, when a group of well-intentioned social scientists organizes a symposium under the title 'Towards a liveable multicultural municipality', this seemingly innocent form of expression carries interesting implications. The combination of the process marker 'towards' with an explicit description of the end product of the process, 'liveable', implies a denial of the liveability of multicultural municipalities as they are now, or as they would remain without special measures.

3. *Global meaning constructs.* The way in which (explicit and implicit) meanings are combined, for instance into patterns of argumentation, is just as important as the meaning of individual utterances or their sum. Coherence and recursivity create meaning networks, in which social patterns of signification are embedded. Many examples will emerge from the data. One of the quite general or global patterns we detect, for instance, is what we will refer to as a process of systematic problematization, as in certain types of documents which invariably begin with phrases such as 'No one can deny that the presence of foreigners in our country causes problems'. Note the presupposed status of the fact that 'foreigners cause problems'. Another example is the abnormalization to which foreigners are subject (…). Yet another one is the recurrent reference to 'poor socio-economic circumstances' as a staple argument to explain racist incidents. All of these will be fully documented and their functioning will be discussed at length.

4. *Interaction patterns* The debate on diversity is a real 'debate' in the sense that it involves many types of direct and indirect interaction between different points of view. Consider, for instance, a televised debate between a member of the extreme right Vlaams Blok and a member of what we have called the 'tolerant majority': the member of the extreme right says: 'It must be possible to revise naturalization procedures that have been completed since 1974', to which the member of the tolerant majority responds: 'Also for those who have *adapted* themselves?' What is interesting about the example is that the response seems to accept the premise that under certain circumstances denaturalization should be possible; the only contribution is that a condition is formulated under which this should *not* be possible.

These are just a few of the levels of analysis at which the search for implicit meaning proves to be particularly fruitful. The totality of presuppositions and implied meanings constitutes the general world view which a language user assumes to be or handles as if shared with others in the same community. Methods of pragmatic analysis, when efforts are concentrated in areas such as the ones listed above, allow one systematically to uncover ideologies in terms of common frames of reference.

A common frame of reference includes what is felt to be 'normal' within the group, i.e. a set of assumptions about acceptable or appropriate social behavior which is un-problematic, natural, etc. This explains why frames of reference are hardly visible to members of the group and are not normally questioned. Forms of communication grounded in assumptions which deviate from the common frame of reference tend to be experienced as 'marked', 'shocking' or as simply incomprehensible; alternatively, they are 'explained' as expressions of maladjustment; at any rate, they are noticed. For a newspaper such a lack of fit with the expected patterns of ideas and attitudes can lead to a drop in sales figures; for a political party, a loss in votes may result. When scientific research is aimed at uncovering unconsciously adopted frames of reference, it inevitably becomes a critique and usually it meets with a wave of criticism and denials. It is always a painful experience to uncover what is taken for granted, because it forces one to question and sometimes revise one's own opinions.

To uncover the ideas of a group about their own identities, those of others and their reciprocal relations, one must indeed analyse 'normal' (i.e. unquestionable) forms of expressions. 'Automatic' expressions of ideas contain the highest degree of information, not so much about the communicated thoughts, but certainly about ways of thinking (see, e.g., Jacob Mey, 1985; Donal Carbaugh, 1989). It is precisely in apparently non-strategic uses that implicit, normal strategies are brought in. Concepts, when experi-enced as 'normal', do not require an explicit definition. Paradoxically, this makes them all the more susceptible to conscious forms of manipulation, but even in the absence of any manipulatory intent, they can still give rise to forms of communication which are misleading. The avoidance of definitions (cf. Obermeier, 1986 and Blommaert, 1989 on notions like 'peace' and 'human rights') entails an enormous strategic potential, because almost any referent can be assigned to a term in an *ad hoc* fashion. One result of this 'flexibility' is that terms may acquire a contextual meaning which deviates con-siderably from the meaning which language users would take for granted, without the deviation being noticed. The abundant use of undefined and underdefined concepts is characteristic for the discourse which we have examined.

In the foregoing, we have already repeatedly talked about patterns of recurrence, or about consistency. Together with the issue of 'normalcy', this leads us to the topic of *coherence*. While distinguishing between interpretation and speculation was no doubt the most elementary recommendation to keep in mind, establishing coherence is an important methodological goal – where 'coherence' is used both in the sense of conceptual connectedness and patterns of recurrence or of absence. This is not meant to suggest that the ideological world of meaning under investigation would itself have to be coherent in a strict sense. Ideologies may be, and usually are, full of internal contradictions. But in order for empirical claims to be possible, even such contradictions have to emerge coherently from the investigated data.[4]

Establishing coherence or 'normality' can only be done reliably if there is enough variability in the types of data, if a representative amount of data is studied, and if the data are selected on the basis of criteria warranted by the specific research goal. This is why four quite distinct discourse types were investigated. This is also why the materials we used consist literally of hundreds of documents, with a time depth of roughly seven years. Robert Hodge and Gunther Kress (1993: 210) may be right when they say that large data samples are not always necessary to *demonstrate* the mere *existence* of widely shared background meanings. However, when it comes to *assessing* the *distribution* of ideological patterns, the fact of their being widespread, a significant body of data is a requirement.

Finally, since interference with one's own ideology is to be expected, the research requires a phase of counterscreening during which meaning constructions incompatible with the tentative research conclusions are systematically searched for, in spite of the fact that it would be a mistake to think that all bias can (or should) be eliminated.

Wider perspectives

This study is only one building block for a pragmatic programme of research into problems of intercultural communication. It shares, in its own particular way, a number of crucial problems with other types of investigations in the same general area.

First, there is the role of the investigator in the communicative process under investigation. In the field of intercultural communication there is no real theoretical difference between talking with the other and talking about the other. Linguistic analysis, as a way of talking about the other, is an instance of intercultural communication itself, subject to all the influences, conditions and rules that govern intercultural interactions in general. Therefore the linguist can never be a detached bystander. He

---

4. The demand for 'coherence' implies that the end product of our research can never be a full description of the ideological work that goes on. It is not possible to 'make sense', scientifically, of each and every ingredient of the manifestation of an ideology. Human beings, as complex organisms, are simply not mechanical or consistent enough. The same is true, by extension, of human societies. The main challenge for the researcher is to push the limitations of an approach as far as possible, and to know where to cut off.

or she exerts direct control over the interaction, and 'constructs' it as an object on the basis of available assumptions. This activity is never culture-free; neither is it free from social influences (see Boon, 1982 and Fabian, 1983 for stimulating discussions; other parallels can be found in Foucault, 1969). The emphasis we placed on a counterscreening phase of the research process should not be misread as a denial of such basic constraints. The main question is whether pragmatics can offer a scientifically justifiable framework while being in line with its own implicit ideological assumptions based on the inescapable involvement of the researcher. Our answer to this question is affirmative, though clearly dependent on strict adherence to the principles of our methodological starting point. The answer is also related to two other major problems in the study of intercultural communication.

Second, coming to terms with the integration of micro- and macro-influences on communication in an intercultural context proves to be particularly tricky. Most of the analyses are situated on a micro-level (the level of what is directly inferable from textual properties), while most of the conclusions are supposed to have a wider societal and cultural bearing. The problem is not, as the traditional social scientist might be tempted to suggest, one of representative sampling. It is not a quantitative, but a qualitative one: the interdependence of individual cognition and socially constructed meaning is what we have to come to grips with. Again, approaching the issue from a practical research point of view, the related problem of unwarranted inferences from idiosyncratic data can only be avoided by following a methodology which pays due attention to the coherence of the emerging picture. Further, it should be kept in mind that the wider societal and cultural implications of our work on the level of group relations (the macro object of investigation) are not even approached in terms of micro-processes constitutive of those relations as such, but micro-processes of textual communication between majority members (minority members being at best indirectly addressed) about majority-minority relations.

Third, the problem of utilizing the full potential of the interdisciplinarity which necessarily characterizes pragmatics is also extremely acute. As will be clear from the foregoing discussion of the complexities of the research topic, for a study such as this one it is imperative to take into account data of a historical, ethnographic, socio-scientific and socio-psychological nature, going far beyond linguistic communication proper. But at the same time the purpose is to show that a clear focus on communication, from the point of view of linguistic pragmatics, contributes something to the discussion which the other disciplines cannot substitute. Every social conflict is always a communicative conflict, on which linguistic analysis can shed some new light.

In other words, although our approach is linguistic, it is clear that some of our concerns are shared with anthropology, social psychology, historiography and sociology. Some of our positions have been borrowed from critical theory. This kind of interdisciplinary set-up is simply characteristic for any valid linguistic pragmatic approach to real-life data. In this specific case, the migrant debate is not a unified object of research: there are linguistic dimensions to it, but at the same time it is clearly caught up in historical and contemporary social structures and processes, interwoven with power relationships and attitudes. As we pointed out at the beginning of this chapter, the migrant debate is largely a subjective phenomenon, in which group relations occupy a central position. These group relations constitute the non-objective – but often objectified – part of the debate. As is usually the case with group identities, 'the Belgians' and 'the migrants' are products of the mind, classic examples of what Anderson (1983) calls 'imagined communities' which are subject to all the problems that surround ethnic boundaries (cf. Barth, 1982). It is the subjective construction of so-called objectively given, 'natural' groups, and of the relations which hold between these, which will be one of the main preoccupations of this study. This field of subjectivity is virtually absent in Belgian scientific research about the migrant problem – except for some research about image formation. As a result of this, a lot of research (including work in training and education) is based on very vague notions about the identities of those involved. What is more – as will become clear from our research – as a result of this lack of attention to the subjective constructions which inform verbal and non-verbal actions, a lot of the pro migrant rhetoric is not really very different from that directed against the migrants. Underneath both kinds of rhetoric are the same basic notions about group identities, the problems they pose and the solutions which are possible, and also the same key analytical concepts like 'culture', 'integration', etc. We hope, therefore, to contribute to the development of a more precise understanding of what, at the moment, is seen as one of the most urgent social and political problems, not only in Belgium, but on a wide international scale. Elsewhere, the actors may be very different, as are the facts of history and social structure, but many of the underlying ideological processes are similar.

An ulterior motive for the writing of this book is to show the importance of linguistic pragmatics for dealing with current social problems. Minority politics, and the socio-scientific study of the issues involved, is usually approached in terms of quantifiable aspects of employment, housing, education, etc. The role of face-to-face communication in the implementation of any policy decision is usually ignored.[5] Even less attention is paid to the conceptual underpinnings of the related political debate. The qualitative basis of any type of discourse on or with the others in our society seems to be a phenomenon which is largely taken for granted (again, 'normal') and unquestioned (or even unquestionable). Yet it is precisely at the qualitative level that socio-scientific research seems to suffer from the three problem areas which have just been outlined.

---

5.   See J. J. Gumperz, T. Jupp and C. Roberts (1979), J. J. Gumperz (1982) and C. Robers and P. Sayers (1987) for evidence that the implementation of policy decisions, however, carefully designed and whatever the amount of goodwill on the part of the participants, may go wrong.

The pragmatic analysis which we will put forward is aimed at integrating the methodological insights derived from a critical consideration of these research problems into a strongly developed descriptive and interpretative framework, a reliable research apparatus for capturing otherwise intangible phenomena. Thus a pragmatic analysis should help us to disclose, and thereby to question, what is usually taken for granted.

References

Anderson, Benedict. 1983. *Imagined Communities: Reflections on the Origin and Spread of Nationalism*. London: Verso.

Barth, Fredrik (ed.). 1982. *Ethnic Groups and Boundaries: The Social Organization of Culture Differences*. Oslo: Universitetforlaget.

Blommaert, Jan. Kiswahili politieke stijl, unpublished Ph. Dissertation, University of Ghent.

Boon, James. 1982. *Other Tribes, Other Scribes: Symbolic Anthropology in the Comparative Study of Cultures, Histories, Religions and Texts*. Cambridge: Cambridge University Press.

Carbaugh, Donal. 1989. *Talking American: Cultural Discourses on Donahue*. Norwood, NJ: Ablex.

Eco, Umberto. 1990. *The Limits of Interpretation*, Bloomington: Indiana University Press.

Eco, Umberto. 1992. *Interpretation and Overinterpretation*. Bloomington: Indiana University Press.
DOI: 10.1017/CBO9780511627408

Fabian, Johannes. 1983. *Time and the Other: How Anthropology Makes its Objects*. New-York: Columbia University Press.

Foucault, Michel. 1969. *L'Archéologie du savoir*. Paris: Gallimard.

Goodwin, Charles. 1994. 'Professional Vision,' *American Anthropologist* 96, 3: 606–33.
DOI: 10.1525/aa.1994.96.3.02a00100

Gumperz, John Joseph. 1982. *Discourse strategies*. Cambridge: Cambridge University Press.
DOI: 10.1017/CBO9780511611834

Gumperz, John Joseph, Tom Jupp, and Celia Roberts. 1979. *Crosstalk*. Southall: The National Centre for Industrial Language Training.

Hodge, Robert, and Gunther Kress. 1993. *Language as Ideology*. London: Routledge.

Mey, Jacob. 1985. *Whose language? A Study in Linguistic Pragmatics*. Amsterdam, Philadelphia: John Benjamins. DOI: 10.1075/pbcs.3

Obermeier, Klaus K. 1986. 'Human rights: An international linguistic hyperbole,' in *Languages in the International Perspective*, edited by Nancy Schweda-Nicholson, 105–14. Norwood, NJ: Ablex.

Roberts, Celia, and Pete Sayers. 1987. 'Keeping the Gate,' in *Analysing Intercultural Communication*, edited by Karlfried Knapp, Werner Enninger and Annelie Knapp-Poothoff, 111–35. Berlin: Mouton de Gruyter.

Verschueren, Jef, Jan–Ola Östman and Jan Blommaert (eds). 1995. *Handbook of Pragmatics: Manual*. Amsterdam, Philadelphia: John Benjamins.

Norman Fairclough

A critical agenda for education

Norman Fairclough (b. 1941) is an English linguist. His *Dialectical-Relational Approach* (DRA) focuses on social conflict in the Marxian tradition and tries to detect its linguistic manifestations in discourses, in particular elements of dominance, difference and resistance. According to the DRA, every social practice has a semiotic element. Productive activity, social relations, social identities, cultural values, consciousness and *semiosis* are dialectically related elements of social practice. Fairclough understands Critical Discourse Analysis (CDA) as the analysis of the relationships between semiosis (including language) and other elements of social practices. These semiotic aspects of social practice are responsible for the constitution of genres and styles. The semiotic aspect of social order is called the 'order of discourse'. His approach to CDA oscillates between a focus on structure and a focus on action. CDA should, by all means, pursue emancipatory objectives and focus on problems (or 'social wrongs') confronting what can be referred to as the 'losers' within particular forms of social life. DRA draws upon Systemic Functional Linguistics (Halliday, 1985), which analyzes language as shaped (even in its grammar) by the social functions it has come to serve. In the text below he summarises his main ideas on the semiotic aspects of social structures, social practices and social events and the consequences for questions of learning.

References

Halliday, Michael A. K. 1985. *Introduction to Functional Grammar*. London: Edward Arnold.

Norman Fairclough. 2004. 'Semiotic aspects of social transformation and learning.'
In *An Introduction to Critical Discourse Analysis in Education*, ed. by R. Rogers, 225–235.
Lawrence Erlbaum.

Semiotic aspects of social transformation and learning

This paper has the character of a theoretical reflection on semiotic aspects of social transformation and learning (…). Its particular focus will be one gap in my work in Critical Discourse Analysis which a number of contributors have pointed out: it has not addressed questions of learning. So my objective will be to incorporate a view of learning into the version of Critical Discourse Analysis which has been developing in my more recent work (Chouliaraki, and Fairclough, 1999; Fairclough, 2000a; Fairclough, 2001; Fairclough, 2003; Fairclough, Jessop and Sayer, 2004; Chiapello, and Fairclough, 2002). I shall approach the question of learning indirectly, in terms of the more general and in a sense more fundamental question of the 'performativity' of texts or, in critical realist terms (Fairclough, Jessop, and Sayer, 2004), their causal effects on non-semiotic elements of the material, social and mental worlds, and the conditions of possibility for the performativity of texts. I shall use the term 'semiosis' rather than 'discourse' to refer in a general way to language and other semiotic modes such as visual image, and the term 'text' for semiotic elements of social events, be they written or spoken, or combine different semiotic modes as in the case of television texts.

Semiotic aspects of social structures, social practices and social events

Let me begin with the question of social ontology. I shall assume that both (abstract) social structures and (concrete) social events are real parts of the social world which have to be analysed separately as well as in terms of their relation to each other – a position of 'analytical dualism' (Archer, 1995, 2000; Fairclough, Jessop, and Sayer, 2004).

Social structures are very abstract entities. One can think of a social structure (such as an economic structure, a social class or kinship system, or a language) as defining a potential, a set of possibilities. However, the relationship between what is structurally possible and what actually happens, between structures and events, is a very complex one. Events are not in any simple or direct way the effects of abstract social structures. Their relationship is mediated – there are intermediate organisational entities between structures and events. Let us call these 'social practices'. Examples would be practices of teaching and practices of management in educational institutions. Social practices can be thought of as ways of controlling the selection of certain structural possibilities and the exclusion of others, and the retention of these selections over time, in particular areas of social life. Social practices are networked together in particular and shifting ways – for instance, there has recently been a shift in the way in which practices of teaching and research are networked together with practices of management in institutions of higher education, a 'managerialisation' (or more generally 'marketisation', Fairclough, 1993) of higher education.

Semiosis is an element of the social at all levels. Schematically:

Social structures: languages
Social practices: orders of discourse
Social events: texts

Languages can be regarded as amongst the abstract social structures I have just been referring to. A language defines a certain potential, certain possibilities, and excludes others – certain ways of combining linguistic elements are possible, others are not (e.g. 'the book' is possible as a phrase in English, 'book the' is not). But texts as elements of social events are not simply the effects of the potentials defined by languages. We need to recognise intermediate organisational entities of a specifically linguistic sort, the linguistic elements of networks of social practices. I shall call these 'orders of discourse' (see Fairclough, 1992; Chouliaraki, and Fairclough, 1999). An order of discourse is a network of social practices in its language aspect. The elements of orders of discourse are not things like nouns and sentences (elements of linguistic structures), but discourses, genres and styles (I shall differentiate them shortly). These elements, and particular combinations or articulations of these elements, select certain possibilities defined by languages and exclude others – they control linguistic variability for particular areas of social life. So orders of discourse can be seen as the social organisation and control of linguistic variation.

There is a further point to make: as we move from abstract structures towards concrete events, it becomes increasingly difficult to separate language from other social elements. In the terminology of Althusser, language becomes increasingly 'overdetermined' by other social elements. So at the level of abstract structures, we can talk more or less exclusively about language – more or less, because 'functional' theories of language see even the grammars of languages as socially shaped (Halliday, 1978). The way I have defined orders of discourse makes it clear that at this intermediate level we are dealing with a much greater 'overdetermination' of language by other social elements – orders of discourse are the *social* organisation and control of linguistic variation, and their elements (discourses, genres, styles) are correspondingly not purely linguistic categories but categories which cut across the division between language and 'non-language', semiosis and the non-semiotic. When we come to texts as elements of social events, the 'overdetermination' of language by other social elements becomes massive: texts are not just effects of linguistic structures and orders of discourse, they are also effects of other social structures, and of social practices in all their aspects, so that it becomes very difficult to separate out the factors shaping texts.

Semiosis as an element of social practices: genres, discourses and styles

Social events and, at a more abstract level, social practices can be seen as articulations of different types of social elements. They articulate semiosis (hence language) together with other non-semiotic social elements. We might see any social practice as an articulation of the following elements:

Action and interaction
Social relations
Persons (with beliefs, attitudes, histories etc.)
The Material World
Semiosis

So, for instance, classroom teaching articulates together particular ways of using language (on the part of both teachers and learners) with particular forms of action and interaction, the social relations and persons of the classroom, the structuring and use of the classroom as a physical space.

We can say that semiosis figures in three main ways in social practices. It figures as:

Genres (ways of acting)
Discourses (ways of representing)
Styles (ways of being)

One way of acting and interacting is through speaking or writing, so semiosis figures first as 'part of the action'. We can distinguish different *genres* as different ways of (inter)acting discoursally – interviewing is a genre, for example. Secondly, semiosis figures in the representations which are always a part of social practices – representations of the material world, of other social practices, reflexive self-representations of the practice in question. Representation is clearly a semiotic matter, and we can distinguish different *discourses*, which may represent the same area of the world from different perspectives or positions. An example of a discourse in the latter sense would be the political discourse of New Labour, as opposed to the political discourse of 'old' Labour, or the political discourse of 'Thatcherism' (Fairclough, 2000b). Thirdly and finally, semiosis figures alongside bodily behaviour in constituting particular ways of being, particular social or personal identities. I shall call the semiotic aspect of this a *style*. An example would be the style of a particular type of manager – the way a particular type of manager uses language as a resource for self-identifying. Genres, discourses and styles are realised in features of textual meaning and form, and we can distinguish three main aspects of textual meanings and their formal realisations (similar to the 'macro-functions' distinguished by Halliday, 1994) corresponding to them: actional, representational and identificational meanings. These meanings are always simultaneously in play in texts and parts of texts.

Social effects of texts and on texts

I have begun above to discuss the causal effects of social structures and social practices on texts. We can see texts as shaped by two sets of causal powers, and by the tension between them: on the one hand social structures and social practices, and on the other hand the agency of people involved in the events they are a part of. Texts are the situated interactional accomplishments of social agents whose agency is, however, enabled and constrained by social structures and social practices. Neither a broadly interactional perspective nor a broadly structural perspective (the latter now including social practices) on texts can be dispensed with, but neither is sufficient without the other.

We also have to recognise both that texts are involved in processes of meaning-making, and that texts have causal effects (i.e. they bring about changes) which are mediated by meaning-making. Most immediately, texts can bring about changes in our knowledge, our beliefs, our attitudes, values, experience, and so forth. We learn from our involvement with and in texts, and texturing (the process of making texts as a facet of social action and interaction) is integral to learning. But texts also have causal effects of a less immediate sort – one might for instance argue that prolonged experience of advertising and other commercial texts contributes to shaping people's identities as 'consumers', or their gender identities. Texts can also have a range of other social, political and material effects – texts can start wars, for instance, or contribute to changes in economic processes and structures, or in the shape of cities. In sum, texts have causal effects upon, and contribute to changes in, persons (beliefs, attitudes etc.), actions, social relations, and the material world.

But we need to be clear what sort of causality this is. It is not a simple mechanical causality – we cannot for instance claim that particular features of texts automatically bring about particular changes in people's knowledge or behaviour or particular social or political or material effects. Nor is causality the same as regularity: there may be no regular cause-effect pattern associated with a particular type of text or particular features of texts, but that does not mean that there are no causal effects.[1]

---

1. The reduction of causality to regularity is only one view of causality – what is often referred to as Humean causality, the view of causality associated with the philosopher David Hume (Sayer, 2000; Fairclough, Jessop, and Sayer, 2003).

Texts can have causal effects without them necessarily being regular effects, because many other factors in the context determine whether particular texts as parts of particular events actually have such effects, and can lead to a particular text having a variety of effects.

Contemporary social science has been widely influenced by 'social constructivism' – the claim that the (social) world is socially constructed. Many theories of social constructivism emphasise the role of texts (language, discourse, semiosis) in the construction of the social world. These theories tend to be idealist rather than realist. A realist would argue that although aspects of the social world such as social institutions are ultimately socially constructed, once constructed they are realities which affect and limit the textual (or 'discursive') construction of the social. We need to distinguish 'construction' from 'construal', which social constructivists often do not: we may textually construe (represent, imagine etc.) the social world in particular ways, but whether our representations or construals have the effect of changing its construction depends upon various contextual factors – including the way social reality already is, who is construing it, and so forth. So we can accept a moderate version of the claim that the social world is textually constructed, but not an extreme version (Sayer, 2000).

One of the causal effects of texts which has been of major concern for critical discourse analysis is ideological effects – the effects of texts in inculcating and sustaining ideologies. I see ideologies as primarily representations of aspects of the world which can be shown to contribute to establishing and maintaining relations of power, domination and exploitation. 'Primarily', because such representations can be so to speak enacted in ways of interacting socially, and inculcated in ways of being, in people's identities (see below). Let us take an example: the pervasive claim that in the new 'global' economy, countries must be highly competitive to survive (something like this is presupposed in this extract from a speech by Tony Blair to the Confederation of British Industry:

> Competition on quality can't be done by Government alone. The whole nation must put its shoulder to the wheel.

One could see such claims (and the neo-liberal discourse they are associated with) as enacted in for instance new more 'business-like' ways of administering organisations like universities, and inculcated in new managerial styles. We can only arrive at a judgement about whether such claims are ideological by looking at the causal effects they have in particular areas of social life, for instance factories or universities, asking whether they contribute to sustaining power relations (e.g. by making employees more amenable to the demands of managers).

Dialectical relations

The relations between elements of a social event or a social practice, including the relation between semiosis and non-semiotic elements, are dialectical relations. We can say that elements are different, cannot be reduced to another, require separate sorts of analysis, yet are not discrete. In Harvey's terms (1996), each element 'internalizes' other elements. What I said above about 'overdetermination' can be seen in terms of the internalization of non-semiotic elements in semiotic elements (texts, orders of discourse). And what I said about the causal effects of texts can be seen in terms of the internalization of semiotic elements in non-semiotic elements.

We can see claims about the socially constructive effects of semiosis, including the 'moderate' social constructivism I advocated above, as presupposing the dialectical internalization of semiosis in the non-semiotic – presupposing for instance that discourses can be materialized (internalized within the material world) in the design of urban spaces. We can also see claims about how people learn in the course of communicative interaction (such as the claims in the papers of this volume) as presupposing the dialectical internalization of semiosis in the non-semiotic. What people learn in and through text and talk, in and through the process of texturing as we might put it (making text and talk within making meaning), is not merely (new) ways of texturing, but also new ways of acting, relating, being and intervening in the material world which are not purely semiotic in character. A theory of individual or organizational learning needs to address the questions of retention, of the capacity to recontextualize what is learnt, to enact it, inculcate it and materialize it.

Dialectical relations obtain intra-semiotically as well as between semiotic and non-semiotic elements. For instance, processes of organizational learning often begin (and especially so in what has been conceived of as the contemporary 'information society' or the 'knowledge society') with the recontextualization within organizations of discourses from outside – an obvious example these days is the discourse of 'new public management' (Salskov-Iversen et al., 2000). But such discourses may (the modality is important in view of the moderate version of social constructivism I have advocated above) be enacted as new ways of acting and interacting, inculcated as new ways of being, as well as materialized in for instance new buildings and plant. Enactment is both semiotic and non-semiotic: the discourse of new public management may be enacted as new management procedures, which semiotically include new genres, for instance new ways of conducting meetings within an organization. Inculcation is also both semiotic and non-semiotic: the discourse of new public management may be inculcated in new managers, new types of 'leader', which is partly a matter of new styles (hence partly semiotic), but also partly a matter of new forms of embodiment. Bodily dispositions are themselves open to semioticization (as indeed are buildings), but that does not mean they have a purely semiotic character – it is, precisely, a facet of the dialectical internalization of the semiotic in the non-semiotic. What this example (and the case study by Salskov-Iversen et al.) also points to is the dialectic between colonization and appropriation in processes of social transformation and learning: recontextualizing the new discourse is both opening an organization (and its individual members) up to a process of colonization (and to ideological effects) and, insofar as the new discourse is transformed in locally specific ways by being worked into a distinctive relation with other (existing) discourses, a process of appropriation.

Let us come back to the modality of the claim that discourses *may* be enacted, inculcated and materialized. There are social conditions of possibility for social transformation and learning which are in part semiotic conditions of possibility (Fairclough, Jessop, and Sayer, 2004). In the example of 'new public management' discourse, for instance, the semiotic conditions of possibility for the recontextualization and dialectical enactment, inculcation and materialization of the discourse within particular organizations refer to the order of discourse: the configuration of discourses, genres and styles which is 'in place' not only within a particular organization but in the social field within which it is located, but also relations between the orders of discourse of different fields. To cut through the complexities involved here, we can say broadly that the openness of an organization to transformations 'led' by a new discourse, and the openness of the organization and its members to learning, depends upon on the extent to which there is a discourse or configuration of discourses in place within the organization and the field for which the dialectic of enactment, inculcation and materialization is fully 'carried through', and the capacity for autonomy with respect to other fields (not, of course, a purely semiotic matter).

Emergence and learning

The critical discourse analysis of texts includes both 'interdiscursive analysis' of the genres, discourses and styles drawn upon and how different genres, discourses and styles are articulated together ('textured' together), and analysis of how such 'mixes' of genres, discourses and styles are realized in the meanings and forms of texts (which entails linguistic analysis, and other forms of semiotic analysis such as analysis of visual images or 'body language'). (…) In the critical realist frame I have been drawing upon, one can see this as the basis for semiotic 'emergence', the making of new meanings. But as Lewis, and Ketter indicate, the possibilities for emergence depend upon the relative dialogicality of text and talk, the orientation to difference. We can schematically differentiate five orientations to difference, with the proviso that this is not a typology of texts; individual texts and talk may combine them in various ways (Fairclough, 2003):

a.   an openness to, acceptance of, recognition of difference; an exploration of differ-
     ence, as in 'dialogue' in the richest sense of the term;
b.   an accentuation of difference, conflict, polemic, a struggle over meaning, norms,
     power;
c.   an attempt to resolve or overcome difference;
d.   a bracketing of difference, a focus on commonality, solidarity;
e.   consensus, a normalisation and acceptance of differences of power which brackets
     or suppresses differences of meaning and over norms.

Scenario (e) in particular is inimical to emergence. Dialogicality and orientation to
difference depend upon the sort of broadly structural conditions I pointed to in the
previous section – conditions to do with social practices, fields, and relations between
fields, which have a partly semiotic character (in terms of orders of discourse). But as
I suggested earlier, the 'causal powers' which shape texts are the powers of agency as
well as of structure – whatever the state of the field and the relations between fields,
we can ask about both latitudes for agency, and their differential uptake by different
agents, including agents involved in the sort of critical educational research reflected
in the papers of this volume.

A relatively high degree of dialogicality and orientation to difference can be seen as
favouring the emergence of meaning through interdiscursive hybridity, though to talk
about learning there needs to be some evidence of continuity and development (...)
and retention (which one might see as requiring evidence of transfer, recontextualization, from one context to others). Learning can be seen as a form of social transformation in itself, but as a necessary but not sufficient condition of social transformation
on a broader scale. Learning through text and talk can be interpreted as part of what I
referred to above as the semiotic conditions for social transformation.

Critical research, learning and social transformation

In assessing the possibilities for and limitations of critical educational research motivated by emancipatory (e.g. anti-racist) agendas for learning and social transformation, one needs to consider both factors of a broadly structural character and factors
to do with agency. With respect to the former, educational research can be seen as
part of a network of social practices which constitutes an apparatus of governance (in
part semiotically constituted as an order of discourse – Fairclough (2003), a network
which includes practices of classroom teaching, educational management, educational
research, and (national, state, local etc.) government and policymaking (Bernstein,
1990). The nature and workings of the apparatus are internally as well as externally
contested – critical educational researchers are for instance often seeking to create

more open and equal relations between academic research and classroom teaching. One issue they must consider is what I referred to earlier as the social conditions of possibility for social transformation and learning, which include latitudes for agency within educational research itself. These issues can be partly addressed from a semiotic perspective in terms of latitudes for agents in social research to develop, recontextualize and seek to enact and inculcate new discourses. But there are also considerations (touched upon in this volume) to do with forms of agency in recontextualizing contexts, e.g. questions of the dialogicality of interactions between educational researchers and teachers. Once again, neither a structural nor an interactional perspective can be dispensed, but neither is sufficient without the other.

References

Archer, Margaret. 1995. *Realist Social Theory; the Morphogenetic Approach*. Cambridge: Cambridge University Press. DOI: 10.1017/CBO9780511557675

Archer, Margaret. 2000. *Being Human: the Problem of Agency*. Cambridge: Cambridge University Press. DOI: 10.1017/CBO9780511488733

Bernstein, Basil. 1990. *The Structuring of Pedagogic Discourse*. Routledge. DOI: 10.4324/9780203011263

Chiapello, Eve, and Fairclough, Norman. 2002. 'Understanding the new management ideology. A transdisciplinary contribution from Critical Discourse Analysis and the New Sociology of Capitalism.' *Discourse and Society* 13 (2): 185–208. DOI: 10.1177/0957926502013002406

Chouliaraki, Lilie, and Norman Fairclough. 1999. *Discourse in Late Modernity*. Edinburgh: Edinburgh University Press.

Fairclough, Norman. 1992. *Discourse and Social Change*. Polity Press.

Fairclough, Norman. 1993. 'Critical discourse analysis and the marketisation of public discourse: the universities.' *Discourse & Society* 4: 133–168 DOI: 10.1177/0957926593004002002

Fairclough, Norman. 2000a. 'Discourse, social theory and social research: the case of welfare reform.' *Journal of Sociolinguistics* 4 (2): 163–195. DOI: 10.1111/1467–9481.00110

Fairclough, Norman. 2000b. *New Labour, New Language?* Routledge.

Fairclough, Norman. 2001. 'The dialectics of discourse.' *Textus* 14: 231–242.

Fairclough, Norman. 2003. *Analysing Discourse: Textual Analysis for Social Research*. London: Routledge.

Fairclough, Norman, Bob Jessop, and Andrew Sayer. 2004. 'Critical realism and semiosis.' In *Realism, discourse and deconstruction*, ed. by Jonathan Joseph, John Michael Roberts, 23–42. London: Routledge.

Halliday, Michael Alexander Kirkwood. 1978. *Language as Social Semiotic: The Social Interpretation of Language and Meaning*. London: Edward Arnold.

Halliday, Michael Alexander Kirkwood. 1994. *Introduction to Functional Grammar*. Edward Arnold.

Harvey, David. 1996. *Justice, Nature and the Geography of Difference*. Blackwell.

Salskov-Iversen, Dorte, Hans Krause Hansen, and Sven Bislev. 2000. 'Governmentality, globalization and local practice: transformations of a hegemonic discourse.' *Alternatives*, 25: 183–222.

Sayer, Andrew. 2000. *Realism and the Social Sciences*. Sage.

Teun A. van Dijk

Discourse, cognition, society

Teun van Dijk (b. 1943) is a Dutch scholar. Until 2004 he was Professor of Discourse Studies at the University of Amsterdam; in 1999 he moved to Barcelona. He had started as a scholar of French literature and developed narrative theory from a more formal, generative approach. Later, he also became involved in text linguistics and logic, before he finally turned to CDA/CDS and the study of racism, influenced by social psychology and cognition studies in the tradition of Moscovici. He argues that whereas (critical and other) Discourse Studies have paid great attention in the last few decades to the structures of text and talk, they have only paid lip service to the necessity of developing the relations between text and context (e.g. Panagl and Wodak, 2004). He maintains that no such direct influence exists, because social structures and discourse structures cannot be related directly and require the mediation of a socio-cognitive interface, in the sense that it is not objective social situations but subjective definitions and perceptions of the relevant properties of communicative situations that influence text and talk. These definitions are then made explicit in terms of *mental models* (see van Dijk, 2008, 2009). Thus, van Dijk emphasizes that language use and discourse always presuppose intervening mental and context models, goals and general social representations (knowledge, attitudes, ideologies, norms, values) of language users. In the selected pages below, van Dijk presents his conception of 'Critical Discourse Studies' as a problem-oriented field based on an 'ethical assessment'. Characterising his own orientation as a 'sociocognitive' approach, he shows how the shared knowledge (or *endoxon*) of specific epistemic communities is shaped by hegemonic interests and power relations. Thus, cognitive models mediate between social structure and group as well as individual knowledge, perceptions, attitudes and activities.

References

Panagl, Oswald, and Ruth Wodak, eds. 2004. *Text und Kontext*. München: Konigshausen.
van Dijk, Teun A. 2008. *Discourse and Context. A Sociocognitive Approach*. Cambridge: Cambridge University Press. DOI: 10.1017/CBO9780511481499
van Dijk, Teun A. 2009. *Society and Discourse. How Social Contexts Influence Text and Talk*. Cambridge: Cambridge University Press. DOI: 10.1017/CBO9780511575273

Teun A. van Dijk. 2009. 'Critical Discourse Studies: A Sociocognitive Approach.'
In *Methods for Critical Discourse Analysis*, ed. by Ruth Wodak, and Michael Meyer, 62–86,
selected 62–67, 75–80.
London: Sage.

Terminology and definitions

Although critical approaches to discourse are commonly known as Critical Discourse
Analysis (CDA), I prefer to speak of Critical Discourse Studies (CDS). This more general term suggests that such a critical approach not only involves critical *analysis*, but
also critical *theory*, as well as critical *applications*. The designation CDS may also avoid
the widespread misconception that a critical approach is a *method* of discourse analysis.

For the same reason, I favour the term Discourse Studies (DS), rather than
Discourse Analysis, to designate a multidisciplinary field of scholarly activities that
are obviously not limited to the *analysis* of text and talk. Moreover, as a *discipline*, DS
has many types and methods of analysis: it is not 'a' method among others within the
humanities and the social sciences.

CDS is not a method, but rather a critical perspective, position or attitude within
the discipline of multidisciplinary Discourse Studies. Critical research makes use of
a large number of methods, both from Discourse Studies itself, as well as from the
humanities, psychology and the social sciences.

The critical approach of CDS characterizes scholars rather than their methods:
CDS scholars are sociopolitically committed to social equality and justice. They also
show this in their scientific research, for instance by the formulation of specific goals,
the selection and construction of theories, the use and development of methods of
analysis and especially in the application of such research in the study of important
social problems and political issues.

CDS scholars are typically interested in the way discourse (re)produces social
domination, that is, the *power abuse* of one group over others, and how dominated
groups may discursively *resist* such abuse.

CDS is not just any social or political research, as is the case in all the social and
political sciences, but is premised on the fact that some forms of text and talk may be
unjust. One of the tasks of CDS is to formulate the norms that define such 'discursive
injustice'. CDS aims to expose and help to combat such injustice. It is *problem oriented*
rather than discipline or theory oriented. Such a research policy presupposes an *ethical* assessment, implying that discourse as social interaction may be *illegitimate* according to some fundamental *norms*, for instance those of international human and
social rights. At the same time, critical analysis should be aware of the fact that such
norms and rights change historically, and that some definitions of 'international' may

well mean 'Western'. As a criterion, we thus call any discourse unjust if it violates the internationally recognized human rights of people and contributes to social inequality. Typical examples are discourses that ultimately (re)produce inequalities of gender, race or class.

What are Critical Discourse Studies (CDS)?

Although it is virtually impossible to briefly and adequately define a type of scholarly investigation, critical studies of discourse typically have the following properties:

- They aim to analyse, and thus to contribute to, the understanding and the solution of serious social problems, especially those that are caused or exacerbated by public text and talk, such as various forms of social power abuse (domination) and their resulting social inequality. Finally, socially committed research should be carried out in close collaboration and solidarity with those who need it most, such as various dominated groups in society. This also means, not least for students, that CDS research, and especially its practical applications, should be accessible and avoid an esoteric style. In that and many other senses, CDS researchers are profoundly aware of the role of scholarly activities in society.
- This analysis is conducted within a normative perspective, defined in terms of international human rights, that allows a critical assessment of abusive discursive practices as well as guidelines for practical intervention and resistance against illegitimate domination.
- The analysis specifically takes into account the interests, the expertise and the resistance of those groups that are the victims of discursive injustice and its consequences.

The discourse-cognition-society triangle

It is within this framework that I propose to formulate and illustrate some of the principles I try to observe when doing CDS. Given my multidisciplinary orientation, the overall label I sometimes use for my approach is that of 'sociocognitive' discourse analysis. Although I dislike labels (because they are reductionist and because I have many times changed my area and perspective of research), I have few quarrels with this one, especially since it emphasizes that – unlike many of my colleagues in CDS and various interactionist approaches – I value the fundamental importance of the study of *cognition* (and not only that of society) in the critical analysis of discourse, communication and interaction.

This means, among other things, that I am also interested in the study of mental representations and the processes of language users when they produce and comprehend discourse and participate in verbal interaction, as well as in the knowledge, ideologies and other beliefs shared by social groups. At the same time, such an approach examines the ways in which such cognitive phenomena are related to the structures of discourse, verbal interaction, communicative events and situations, as well as societal structures, such as those of domination and social inequality, as mentioned above.

What is 'cognition'?

As is the case for other fundamental notions, 'cognition' is a notion that is jointly defined by all the disciplines currently integrated under the label 'cognitive science', such as psychology, linguistics, philosophy and logic as well as the brain sciences. Some typical cognitive notions used here are, for instance:

- *Mind*, defined, for example, as a central function of the human brain.
- *Cognition* as the set of functions of the mind, such as thought, perception and representation.
- *Memory*: Short Term (Working) Memory (STM) and Long Term Memory (LTM).
- *Episodic* (personal, autobiographic) *Memory* (EM) and *Semantic* (sociocultural, shared) *Memory* – as part of LTM.
- *Semantic Mental Models* (represented in EM) as the subjective representations of the events and situations observed, participated in or referred to by discourse.
- *Goals* as mental models of the situations to be realized by action.
- Pragmatic *Context Models*: specific mental models of subjective representations (definitions) of the relevant properties of communicative situations, controlling discourse processing and adapting discourse to the social environment so that it is situationally appropriate.
- *Knowledge* and its organization: shared, sociocultural *beliefs* that are certified by the (knowledge) criteria or standards of a (knowledge) community.
- *Ideology* as the shared, fundamental and axiomatic beliefs of specific social groups (socialism, neoliberalism, feminism, (anti)racism, pacifism, etc.).
- *Attitudes* as the socially shared, ideologically based opinions (normative beliefs) about specific social issues having given rise to debate or struggle (abortion, divorce, euthanasia, immigration, etc.).
- *Cognitive processes* such as the production and comprehension of discourse/interaction on the basis of specific mental models, controlled by context models, and based on knowledge and ideologies.

The label of the 'sociocognitive' approach does not mean that I think that CDS should be *limited* to the social and cognitive study of discourse, or to some combination of these dimensions. It only means that (at present) I am personally most interested in the fascinating sociocognitive interface of discourse, that is, the relations between mind, discursive interaction and society. For instance, in my work on racism (van Dijk, 1984), and in my research on ideology (van Dijk, 1998) and context (van Dijk, 2008), I have shown that these are *both* mental *and* social phenomena. It goes without saying, however, that the complex, 'real-world' problems CDS deals with also need a historical, cultural, socioeconomic, philosophical, logical or neurological approach, among others, depending on what one wants to know (see, for instance, the various approaches represented in van Dijk, 1997, van Dijk, 2007).

Given the verbal-symbolic nature of discourse, explicit CDS of course also needs a solid 'linguistic' basis, where 'linguistic' is understood in a broad sense. Whatever cognitive and social dimensions of discourse CDS deals with, it always needs to account for at least some of the detailed structures, strategies and functions of *text* or *talk*. These may include grammatical, pragmatic, interactional, stylistic, rhetorical, semiotic, narrative, argumentative or similar forms and meanings of the verbal, paraverbal and multimodal structures of communicative events.

Having emphasized the necessity of a broad, diverse, multidisciplinary and problem oriented CDS, I thus limit my own endeavours to the domain defined by the discourse-cognition-society triangle.

In a more or less informal way, we may view the combined cognitive and social dimensions of the triangle as defining the relevant (local and global) *context* of discourse. Indeed, the sociopolitical and problem oriented objectives of CDS especially need sophisticated theorization of the intricate relationships between text and context. We shall see that adequate discourse analysis at the same time requires detailed cognitive and social analysis, and vice versa, and that it is only the *integration* of these accounts that may reach descriptive, explanatory and especially critical adequacy in the study of social problems.

It should be emphasized that context, as I define it, is not simply some kind of social environment, situation or structure – such as the social 'variables' of gender, age or 'race' in classical sociolinguistics. Rather, a context is a subjective mental representation, a dynamic online model, of the participants about the for-them-now relative properties of the communicative situation. I call such a representation a *context model* (van Dijk, 2008). It is this mental 'definition of the situation' that controls the adequate adaptation of discourse production and comprehension to their social environment. This is just one of the ways in which cognition, society and discourse are deeply and mutually integrated in interaction.

Within the theoretical framework of the discourse-cognition-society triangle, context models mediate between discourse structures and social structures at all levels of analysis. This means that 'society' is understood here as a complex configuration of situational structures at the local level (participants and their identities, roles and relationships engaging in spatiotemporally and institutionally situated, goal direction interaction), on the one hand, and societal structures (organizations, groups, classes, etc. and their properties and – e.g. power – relations), on the other hand. This side of the triangle also includes the cultural and historical dimensions of interaction and social structure, that is, their cultural variation as well as their historical specificity and change. It is also at this side of the triangle that we locate the consequences of discursive injustice, for instance in the form of social inequality.

Finally, it should be stressed that the use of the triangle is merely an analytical metaphor representing the major dimensions of critical analysis. It should *not* be interpreted as suggesting that cognition and discourse are *outside* society. On the contrary, human beings as language users and as members of groups and communities, as well as their mental representations and discourses, are obviously an inherent part of society. It is also within social structure that language users interpret, represent, reproduce or change social structures such as social inequality and injustice.

What is 'discourse'?

Discourse analysts are often asked to define the concept of 'discourse'. Such a definition would have to consist of the whole discipline of discourse studies, in the same way as linguistics provides the many dimensions of the definition of 'language'. In my view, it hardly makes sense to define fundamental notions such as 'discourse', 'language', 'cognition', 'interaction', 'power' or 'society'. To understand these notions, we need whole theories or disciplines of the objects or phenomena we are dealing with. Thus, discourse is a multidimensional social phenomenon. It is at the same time a linguistic (verbal, grammatical) object (meaningful sequences or words or sentences), an action (such as an assertion or a threat), a form of social interaction (like a conversation), a social practice (such as a lecture), a mental representation (a meaning, a mental model, an opinion, knowledge), an interactional or communicative event or activity (like a parliamentary debate), a cultural product (like a telenovela) or even an economic commodity that is being sold and bought (like a novel). In other words, a more or less complete 'definition' of the notion of discourse would involve many dimensions and consists of many other fundamental notions that need definition, that is, theory, such as meaning, interaction and cognition. (…)

Discourse semantics: event models

Crucial to any theory of discourse is its semantics, which provides a theory of discourse meaning and interpretation. Traditionally, a linguistic semantics is formulated in terms of abstract meanings: concepts, propositions and their mutual relations. Thus, local coherence of discourse is defined as constraints on relations between propositions, on the one hand, and on the relations between the referents ('facts' of some mental model) of such propositions, on the other hand. For instance, a sequence of propositions may be said to be coherent if the facts (states of affairs, events, actions, etc.) referred to by these propositions are related, for instance by relations of causality or more generally by relations of conditionality (such as enabling). We may call this *referential* or *extensional* coherence. On the other hand, coherence may also be established by intentional (meaning) relations among the propositions themselves, for instance when a proposition Q is a Generalization, Specification, Example, Illustration, etc. of a previous proposition P. Since Q is defined here in terms of its function relative to P, we may call this *functional* coherence.

As suggested, such an account is rather abstract, and appears to have little empirical relevance: this is not the way language users go about producing and understanding meaningful discourse. Instead of an abstract theory of meaning, therefore, we may define meaning and interpretation in cognitive terms, that is, in terms of mental operations and representations.

Such an approach also solves a major problem of the more formal account, namely the nature of reference: notions that define referential coherence, such as referents, facts and causal relations between facts, are not defined in linguistic (grammatical) semantics. A cognitive approach to discourse meaning not only may solve that problem, but at the same time accounts for the subjectivity of coherence: discourses are not coherent in the abstract, but are coherent for language users, and according to their intentions, interpretations or understandings.

Thus, discourses are not so much coherent because their propositions refer to related 'objective' facts in some possible world, but rather to the episodes (events and situations) as interpreted, defined and (seen to be) related by language users. We have seen above that such subjective interpretations are represented in episodic memory as *mental models* of events and situations. We may now simply say that a discourse is coherent if language users are able to construct a mental model for it. We may call these models *event models* in order to account for the fact that they subjectively represent the events the discourse refers to. Whereas context models, as discussed above, are pragmatic, event models are *semantic*.

Since context models are a specific kind of event model (namely a model of communicative events), event models have more or less the same structure organized by a *schema* with *categories* such as Setting, Participants and Actions/Events – and their respective subcategories and properties.

Thus, in the analysis of our example, we have repeatedly seen how at all levels of the petition text, structures are geared not only to the adequate expression of the mental model of the (authors in the) Center for the Moral Defense of Capitalism, but also to the persuasive construction of a preferred model among the addressees. That is, this intended model features the macro-opinion that the US Government through its antitrust laws in general, and its case against Microsoft in particular, violates the basic principles of the freedom of the market. That is, the current mental model of the Microsoft case is a fairly direct instantiation of more general attitudes about antitrust legislation and their basic ideologies about the freedom of enterprise. The polarization between Us and Them, or between Business and Government, and its respective Good and Bad qualities, is thus a specification of more general opinions about ingroups and outgroups as we know them from the study of ideology (van Dijk, 1998). In other words, the authors of the text not only try to adequately express their own model of the events, but formulate the text in such a way that the intended model be accepted by the readers. This is what persuasion is all about, and it may be obvious that without an account of mental model structures, such a verbal act and its concomitant verbal structures cannot be adequately described, let alone explained.

The notion of a mental model also explains another fundamental property of discourse meaning: its *incompleteness*. Semantically speaking, a discourse is like the tip of an iceberg: only some of the propositions needed to understand a discourse are actually expressed; most other propositions remain *implicit*, and must be inferred from the *explicit* propositions (given a body of world knowledge, to which we shall come back below). It is the model that provides these 'missing propositions'. Implicit or implied propositions of discourse are thus simply defined as those propositions that are part of the mental model for that discourse, but not present in its semantic representation. That is, for pragmatic reasons as defined by the context model of a discourse (including the beliefs attributed to the recipient by the speaker), only part of the propositions of a model need to be expressed – for instance, because the speaker believes that such information is irrelevant, because the recipient already knows these propositions, or because it may be inferred from other propositions. Hence, mental models at the same time provide an excellent definition of presuppositions, namely as those propositions of event models that are implied but not asserted by the discourse.

Besides discourse coherence and implications, the notion of event models provides a framework for many other, hitherto problematic, aspects of discourse and discourse processing, briefly summarized as follows:

- Event models are a crucial cognitive aspect of the *constructionist* way people view, understand, interpret and recall 'reality'. In other words, our personal *experiences*, as represented in episodic memory, consist of mental constructs: models.
- Event models are not only the result of discourse comprehension, but are also the basis of discourse *production*. Event models may be part of our planning of discourse ('what we want to say'). Thus, stories are contextually appropriate (relevant, interesting) formulations of underlying event models, for instance of personal experiences as stored in episodic memory.
- Event models are *subjective* (personal interpretations of events), but have a *social* basis, because they instantiate socially shared knowledge and possibly also group ideologies (see below). That is, context models explain how discourse may be ideologically 'biased', namely when based on event models that instantiate ideological propositions.
- Event models account for the fact that different language users, members of different communities and of different social (e.g. ideological) groups, may have *different interpretations* of events, and at the same time, different interpretations of the same discourse. This implies that the *influence* of discourse on the minds of recipients may also be different.

Social cognition

CDS is not primarily interested in the subjective meanings or experiences of individual language users. Power, power abuse, dominance and their reproduction typically involve collectivities, such as groups, social movements, organizations and institutions.

Therefore, besides the fundamental interface of personal mental models that account for *specific* discourses, a cognitive approach also needs to account for *social cognition*, that is, the beliefs or *social representations* they share with others of their group or community. Knowledge, attitudes, values, norms and ideologies are different types of social representations.

These social representations also play a role in the construction of personal models, as we have seen in some detail in our brief analytical remarks about the Petition text. That is, socially shared knowledge and opinions may be 'instantiated' in such models. In other words, models are also the interface of the individual and the social, and explain how group beliefs may affect personal beliefs and thus be expressed in discourse. Ethnic or gender prejudice, which are typically defined for social groups, thus also appear as an (instantiated) property of individual discourses. And conversely, if the personal mental model of social events of an influential person is shared by others of a group or community, mental models may be generalized and abstracted from to form social representations such as knowledge, attitudes and ideologies. This is of course precisely the aim of the Petition text.

It is one of the aims of CDS research to analyse specific discourses in this broader, social framework, for instance by trying to infer (sometimes quite indirectly) which shared social representations are being expressed or presupposed by discourse. Thus, critical discourse studies of racism, sexism or classism need to relate properties of discourse with these underlying, socially shared, representations, which group members use as a resource to talk about (members) of other groups. *Outgroup derogation* and *ingroup celebration* are the social-psychological strategies typically defining this kind of chauvinist discourse.

Ideology

Dominance, defined as power abuse, is often based on, and legitimated by, ideologies, that is, by the fundamental social beliefs that organize and control the social representations of groups and their members. Many forms of CDS research require such an ideological analysis, especially because ideologies are typically expressed and reproduced by discourse.

It is important to stress here that the cognitive framework sketched above suggests that *there is no direct link between discourse and ideology*. The basic beliefs of an ideology (for instance, about the equality of women and men in a feminist ideology) organize specific attitudes, that is, the socially shared opinions of a group (for instance, about abortion, sexual harassment or equal pay), which in turn may influence specific event models (about specific participants and actions), which finally may be related to discourse under the final control of context models. In other words, to 'read off' ideologies from discourse is not always possible, precisely because ideologies need to be very general and fairly abstract. Although we still ignore what the general structure of ideologies are (van Dijk, 1998), it may be assumed that they are organized by a *general schema* consisting of the basic categories that organize the self and other representations of a group and its members, such as:

-   membership devices (how does it belong to us?)
-   typical acts (what do we do?)
-   aims (why do we do it?)
-   relations with other (opponent) groups
-   resources, including access to public discourse.

Note that many of the features that were traditionally examined in the (critical or other) analysis of discourse are here accounted for in more explicit, separate theories of cognition. That is, meaningfulness, interpretation and understanding of text and context are described here in terms of specific mental representations, such as event models, context models and social representations. We are thus able not only to abstractly *describe* text and talk, but also to *explain* how real language users go about producing and understanding discourse, how their personal and socially shared beliefs affect discourse production and how these are in turn affected by discourse. No critical account of discourse is theoretically complete without such a cognitive interface.

Social situations

We shall be relatively brief about the third main component of our CDS approach: society. For obvious reasons, the social dimensions of CDS usually receive more attention from CDS researchers than its cognitive aspects, as is also shown in the other chapters in this book. Note though that our sociocognitive theory explains how social structures may affect (and be affected by) discourse structures via a theory of social cognition.

An account of the role of social structures in CDS requires an analysis of both micro (local) and macro (global) structures of society, that is, of individual social actors and their situated interactions, on the one hand, and of social groups, movements, organizations and institutions, as well as their relations, such as power and dominance, on the other hand.

Note that the micro-macro distinction is only analytic. In real life, social members may experience and interpret such structures at the same time: by 'locally' responding to a question from a student, which may be part of the somewhat more comprehensive social activity of giving a class, I at the same time may teach a course and reproduce the organization of this university as well as higher education – at increasingly 'higher', macro and abstract levels of analysis and (diminishing degrees of) awareness.

Unlike, for instance, therapists, CDS scholars are less interested in the account of specific discourses, interactions and situations – such as, indeed, the example analysed in this chapter. Rather, they focus on the more general ways specific discourses may be *instances* of more general discourse properties and how such discourse may contribute to social inequality, for instance by the formation of biased models and ultimately by the formation or confirmation of ideologies.

Micro vs. macro

As is the case for micro-sociologists, discourse analysts deal primarily with text and talk, and hence with a typical 'micro' dimension of society. Indeed, it is generally assumed that society and its structures – as well as its structures of inequality – are 'locally' produced by its members. Yet, I additionally assume that *such local production in interaction is possible only if members have shared social representations such as knowledge and ideologies.* In that sense, 'local' social interaction is again 'enabled' by a macro dimension such as the social cognitions of collectivities. But then again, such a macro dimension is itself constructed cognitively by the mental representations of groups of individual social actors. We thus see how for CDS, the micro and macro dimensions of society, and their analysis, are multiply integrated, as is also embodied in the slogan that CDS is mainly interested in the *discursive* reproduction of the *social structure* of inequality. One of the reasons CDS research (critically) analyses specific discourses is the methodologically important fact that these are more directly analysable than abstract structures, and that abstract structures can only be inferred (as language users do) by studying special cases. Although the macrosocial dimensions of society (such as social inequality) will usually be the main reasons and aims of CDS, we can only observe and analyse such abstract structures in terms of how they are expressed or enacted locally in social practices in general, and in discourses in particular, that is, in specific situations.

As part of an analysis of social situations, let me briefly say a few words about two central categories of social situations: *action* and *actors.* (…)

References

van Dijk, Teun A. 2008. *Discourse and Context. A Sociocognitive Approach.* Cambridge: Cambridge University Press. DOI: 10.1017/CBO9780511481499

van Dijk, Teun A, ed. 1997. *Discourse as Structure and Process. Discourse Studies: A Multidisciplinary Introduction.* 2 vols. London: Sage.

van Dijk, Teun A, ed. 2007. *Discourse Studies.* 5 vols. London: Sage.

van Dijk, Teun A. 1998. *Ideology. A Multi-Disciplinary Approach.* London: Sage.

van Dijk, Teun A. 1984. *Prejudice in Discourse.* Amsterdam: Benjamins. DOI: 10.1075/pb.v.3

Ruth Wodak

The discourse of exclusion

Xenophobia, racism and anti-Semitism

Ruth Wodak (b. 1950) is an Austrian discourse analyst; for 30 years she taught Applied Linguistics at the University of Vienna, Austria, and then, from 2004 onwards, discourse studies at Lancaster University, UK. Starting out in Slavic Studies and History, she moved on to formal linguistics, text linguistics and sociolinguistics. Her first research consisted of organisational studies (courtrooms, hospitals, schools etc.). She worked on therapeutic discourse (1986) and gender studies, on mothers and daughters (Wodak, and Schulz, 1986). Since the late 1980s, she has focused more on research into identity politics and the study of racist and anti-Semitic prejudiced talk and texts, and the politics of the past. In the course of these studies, she established the discourse-historical approach (DHA), which puts much emphasis on the interdisciplinary analysis of multi-layered contexts and historical development/intertextuality and the recontextualisation of all forms of semiosis. More recently, Wodak has focused on European identity politics (multilingualism, the re/emergence of radical right-wing populist parties and the European Parliament (2011). Wodak is also concerned with the possible practical relevance of critical research and has been involved in the formulation of anti-discriminatory guidelines (related to gender and also ethnicity) for the media and public sphere in Austria. The entry selected for this volume relates to her extensive research on Austrian populist right-wing rhetoric and its anti-Semitic undertones.

References

Wodak, Ruth. 2011. *The Discourse of Politics in Action: Politics as Usual*. Second revised edition. Basingstoke: Palgrave DOI: 10.1057/9780230316539

Wodak, Ruth. 1986. *Language Behavior in Therapy Groups*. L. A.: Univ of California Press

Wodak Ruth, and Schulz, Muriel. 1986. *The Language of Love and Guilt*. Amsterdam: Benjamins.

Ruth Wodak. 2007. 'Pragmatics and Critical Discourse Analysis.
A cross-disciplinary Analysis.'
Pragmatics and Cognition, 15 (1): 203–225, selected 203–207, 215–218.

Introduction: Stating the problem

This paper addresses some important dimensions of recent pragmatic theories and methodologies which can be fruitfully applied in contemporary CDA research on racism, xenophobia and anti-Semitism; I will illustrate this application and cross-disciplinary fertilisation through a brief case study on recent Austrian political discourse.

Pragmatic devices such as insinuations/allusions, wordplay, presuppositions and implicatures will be analysed in their multiple functions in political rhetoric where they frequently and intentionally serve to convey anti-Semitic prejudices in post-war Austria.[1] I will investigate some propaganda slogans and rhetoric in the regional election campaign in Vienna 2001.

In this campaign, Dr. Jörg Haider, then leader of the Austrian Freedom Party (FPÖ), employed a coded discourse which many considered to include anti-Semitic and racist meanings and connotations. However, because of the implicit, coded character of these prejudiced utterances, Haider was able at first successfully to deny having had such intentions; thus, he negated the indirect and implied meanings and – instead – emphasized the literal meanings of the respective linguistic units. Such discursive strategies are, of course, not new in the Austrian (or other national) context(s); they have a discursive history since the end of the Second World War, due to the consensual taboo on explicit anti-Semitic prejudice in the public sphere.

Hence, an in-depth critical discourse analysis which deconstructs inferred and indirect linguistic devices as well as explicit prejudiced utterances has to turn to theories in pragmatics and to the 'pragmatic toolbox' to be able systematically to detect and analyse anti-Semitic traces, the hidden and coded meanings which often appear as conversational cues in the text.

Due to space restrictions, I will have to neglect recent research in cognitive linguistics into anti-Semitic language behaviour: I can only very briefly point to the functions of conceptual metaphors (Chilton, 2005; Musloff, 2006). This research analyses very explicit anti-Semitic writing in Hitler's *Mein Kampf* and deconstructs the conceptual metaphors contained in Hitler's anti-Semitic ideology. Moreover, Chilton (2005)

---

1. An extensive analysis of the whole election campaign is published elsewhere (Wodak, and Reisigl, 2002). See also Wodak et al., 1990; Mitten, 1992, 1997, 2000; Reisigl, and Wodak, 2001; Wodak, and Reisigl, 2002; Wodak, 2004a; Martin, and Wodak, 2003; Benke, and Wodak, 2003a, 2003b; Heer et al., 2003.

emphasizes that his cognitive approach, which is based on much work by neuro-linguists and cognitive linguists, will prove that a CDA approach becomes obsolete.

However, such a purely cognitive approach is not able to explain the emotional and affective components of anti-Semitic rhetoric nor the wide range and contextual factors necessary for its mass-psychological impact at a specific time in a specific context (Why are some people are affected and others not? Why do some people believe in anti-Semitic/racist ideologies at certain times? Why do these ideologies trigger specific actions which have led, for example, to the extermination of millions?). Moreover, the cognitive approach does not (and cannot) consider indirect or latent anti-Semitic meanings and connotations.

This paper proposes a different argument: precisely because of the indirectness and context-dependency of the anti-Semitic post-war rhetoric in Austria, an integrative interdisciplinary theory as well as methodology is needed, combining pragmatics, CDA, socio-cognition, history, socio-psychology, political science and so forth.

In the following, I will focus, in detail, on three utterances by Jörg Haider during the election campaign in 2001:[2]

(1) (…) Mr. Häupl has an election strategist: he's called Greenberg (loud laughter in the hall). He had him flown in from the East Coast. My friends, you have a choice: you can vote for spin-doctor Greenberg from the East Coast, or for the heart of Vienna!

(2) (…) We don't need any proclamations from the East Coast. Now we've had enough. Now we're concerned with another part of our history, reparations for those driven from their homes.

(3) (…) Mr. Muzicant: What I don't understand is how someone called Ariel can have so much dirty linen … I don't understand that at all, but I mean … he will certainly comment this tomorrow, won't he? … but I am not frightened by these questions.
(Haider on 28 February, Ash Wednesday Speech, transl. RW)

To be able to understand, analyse and explain these latently anti-Semitic utterances, it is necessary to propose the following theoretical claims:

– In order to capture the multidimensional nature of racism/anti-Semitism, the concept of syncretic racism/anti-Semitism lends itself; it encompasses everyday racism, xeno-racism and other concepts of exclusion (such as racialisation, otherism, discrimination, etc.). By syncretic anti-Semitism I mean the construction of

---

2. Within argumentation theory, topoi or loci can be described as parts of argumentation which belong to the obligatory, either explicit or inferable premises. They are the content-related warrants or 'conclusion rules' which connect the argument or arguments with the conclusion, the claim. As such, they justify the transition from the argument or arguments to the conclusion (Kienpointner, 1992: 194).

'differences' which serve ideological, political and/or practical discrimination at all levels of society. Old and new stereotypes form a mixed bag of exclusionary practices; they are used whenever they are seen to be politically expedient – such as in gaining votes. It is a 'racism without races' in which the discourse of exclusion has become de-referentialized, i.e. removed from any direct relation with a specific constructed racial subject (Jews, Blacks, Roma), and has become a 'floating discourse' (almost an 'empty signifier' in the view of Ernesto Laclau, and Chantal Mouffe, 1985) in which anti-Semitic/racist/xenophobic attitudes are combined with specific negative stereotypes.

– The discursive construction of 'us' and 'them' is the foundation of prejudiced, anti-Semitic and racist perceptions and discourses. This discursive construction starts with the labelling of social actors, proceeds to the generalization of negative attributions and then elaborates arguments to justify the exclusion of many and inclusion of some. The discursive realizations can be more or less intensified or mitigated, more or less implicit or explicit, due to historical conventions, public levels of tolerance, political correctness, and the specific context and public sphere.

– Hence, the concepts of 'text, discourse, context and co-text' have to be clarified and theorized in an interdisciplinary framework combining and integrating CDA and pragmatics. Although pragmatics has always clearly seen itself as complementary to semantics, as Paul Chilton has clearly illustrated in his book *Analysing Political Discourse* (2004), and research in pragmatics has attempted to distinguish important features of the immediate context (speakers, hearers, settings, expectations, intentions, etc.), these and other relevant dimensions have frequently been left vague or sometimes simply to the researcher's subjective intuition (see Reisigl, 2004). On the other hand, much research in CDA has neglected the subtle and intricate analysis of latent meanings and has left the interpretation of implicit, presupposed and inferred meanings to the intuition of the researcher and/or readership.

– Moreover, an integrative pragmatic and discourse-analytic approach has to be further complemented with a range of other linguistic theoretical concepts as well as with theories from neighbouring disciplines. Such a theoretical framework should not only exist as an 'abstract umbrella or general framework', unrelated to explicit and concrete analysis; it should rather be able to choose and justify the relevant categories for analysis itself (see van Dijk, 2003; Wodak, 2000a, b).

The linguistic analysis of pragmatic devices in a particular setting – in our example political discourse expressing anti-Semitic prejudice (speeches and media) – would thus have to draw on a range of analytical tools selected for that specific purpose. In the concrete case I am addressing here, I suggest the following procedures and stages for analysis:

- Historical analysis of anti-Semitism and its verbal expressions (i.e. 'coded language');
- Socio-cognitive analysis of collective memories and frames guiding the acquisition of specific knowledge to be able to understand the 'coded language';
- Socio-political analysis of the election campaign, the ongoing debates and the political parties taking part; these three dimensions form the broader context;
- Genre theory; the functions of political speeches (persuasive strategies, positive self-presentation / negative other-presentation, populist rhetoric, etc.);
- The setting, speakers, etc. of the concrete utterances; this is the more narrow context;
- The co-text of each utterance;
- Finally, the verbal expressions have to be analysed with regard to linguistic pragmatic/grammatical approaches (presuppositions, insinuations, implicatures, etc. as relevant characteristics of the specific 'coded anti-Semitism').

Such devices are embedded in discursive macro-strategies of positive self and negative other presentation; these strategies employ various other linguistic features, rhetorical tropes and argumentation/legitimization patterns. In our case, moreover, we have to contextualize this election campaign into other discourses on foreigners, Jews, minorities and marginalized groups in Austria and Europe, in order to be able to grasp the interdiscursivity, intertextuality and recontextualization of certain topoi[3] and arguments throughout many genres and public spheres.[4]

In sum, my aim throughout this paper is to illustrate the wide and systematic range of methodological instruments needed to achieve an explicit, retroductable and valid linguistic analysis. At this point, it is also important to emphasize that – even though my primary research focus as a (critical) discourse analyst is directed towards the investigation of a 'social problem', such as racism or anti-Semitism – this epistemological perspective does not imply that a detailed linguistic analysis and linguistic theorizing would be of lesser importance. Quite the contrary: the schools in the CDA framework all define explaining/understanding 'social problems' as their main research goal; but at the same time, all the different schools in CDA tend to embrace very precise linguistic analysis.[5]

---

3. See Reisigl, and Wodak (2001), Wodak (2001) for precise definitions of these terms, which are central to CDA.

4. See Wodak, and Meyer (2001); Fairclough (2003); Blommaert (2005); Wodak (2004b, 2006, 2008); see Reisigl, and Wodak (2001: Chapter 2) for details of the discourse-historical approach (DHA) employed in this paper.

5. 'Context models and event models are mental representations in episodic memory … in which people store their knowledge and opinions about episodes they experience or read/hear about … Context models control the 'pragmatic' part of discourse and event models the 'semantic part''

In the following, I will first present some very brief historical/political information (the broader context) regarding my case study; secondly, the most important linguistic concepts and the discourse-historical approach (DHA) in CDA applied for this analysis have to be elaborated. Finally, a detailed analysis of the aforementioned examples of the election campaign and Jörg Haider's speeches illustrates the integrative theoretical framework of pragmatics and CDA. (…)

4.1 The immediate co-text of the incriminated utterance on 28 February 2001 in Ried: The 'textual chain of abuse'

Below, I list some of the macro topics Jörg Haider addressed in the Ried speech:

- The topics of the BSE crisis and EU agricultural policy – these topics illustrate the EU-sceptical position of the FPÖ. In this context he characterized the then Austrian EU commissioner Franz Fischler as a political Rübezahl[14] suffering from an outburst of rage over European agricultural policy.
- The topic of the introduction and stability of the euro – thus repeating EU scepticism by linking this to unemployment and rising living costs.
- The topic of the presumed high salaries of SPÖ politicians, thus hinting at and alluding to the corruption and privileges of politicians. In this context he refers on one occasion to the leader of the SPÖ, Alfred Gusenbauer, as Gruselbauer.[15]
- The topic of the 'EU-14 sanctions against Austria', which had caused a huge shift to the right in 2000 when the right-wing government had overcome the centre-left grand coalition. The sanctions of fourteen EU member states immediately after the takeover of the new government had proved counterproductive: they triggered a chauvinistic discourse of 'Austria against the EU' which swept all oppositional voices aside and allowed the labelling of opposition politicians as 'traitors' and 'non-patriotic' (see Möhring, 2001).

(van Dijk, 2001:112). 'We can characterize a [metaphor] 'scenario' as a set of assumptions made by competent members of a discourse community about 'typical' aspects of a source situation, e.g. its participants and their roles, the 'dramatic' storylines and outcomes, and conventional evaluations of whether they count as successful or unsuccessful, permissible or illegitimate, etc. These source-based assumptions are mapped onto the respective target concepts' (Musloff, 2006:28). 'These highly specific source scenarios … are ubiquitous and constitute an essential feature of metaphor use in public discourse registers. Scenarios appear to dominate public discourse not just in terms of overall frequency but also in that they help to shape the course of public debates and conceptualizations in the respective discourse communities' (ibid.:28).

14. Rübezahl is the name of a German giant destroying turnips, in German folklore.

15. This play on words implies a 'mess-maker'.

– Dr. Ariel Muzicant is attacked by Dr. Jörg Haider in the course of discussing the 'EU-sanctions', which the speaker claims had their origin in Austria, and thus presupposes that Muzicant might have been part of a 'conspiracy' which started or at least supported these sanctions. Then, Haider stated explicitly that the 'Austrian socialists' and 'the left' had asked their 'friends abroad' for the sanctions and that Dr. Ariel Muzicant had contributed to this process.

If one compares the wordplays with the names of Fischler, Gusenbauer and Muzicant, significant pragmatic differences immediately become apparent. In the first two cases, irony is used and only small changes in the names are suggested or comparisons hinted at, none of which derogate the person viciously. In the case of Muzicant, the wordplay alludes to seemingly inherent negative characteristics of the 'Jew'.

After his verbal attack, in which Dr. Jörg Haider accuses Dr. Ariel Muzicant of being a Jew hostile to Austria, and with a lot of 'dirty linen' (i.e. being criminal), Haider, governor of Carinthia, in the remainder of his speech, moved on to abusing other political opponents from Austria, France and Germany. Thus, the abuse of Dr. Ariel Muzicant in Haider's speech in Ried fits into a series of abusive remarks, some of which Dr. Jörg Haider made before or later. If one looks at this series of insults one is struck by the fact that Dr. Ariel Muzicant is the only non-politician (in the narrower sense of professional politician) among those selected and subjected to verbal attack. So, whereas Dr. Jörg Haider attacks political opponents inside and outside Austria, he insults Dr. Ariel Muzicant personally and in his function as president of the Jewish community in Austria.

4.2 Detailed linguistic-pragmatic analysis

The linking of compensation/restitution of war victims and Holocaust survivors in relation to the criminalization of Muzicant began at the New Year meeting on 22 January 2001 (Examples 1, 2). In what was expressed there it was said of Muzicant that he had himself piled up debts and that the restitution would partly serve his own interest (that of paying off debt).

At this point, we can zoom in to the pragmatic analysis proper. These first utterances imply many existential presuppositions. The properties of the presupposed content (see above) are extensively exploited in our particular case. Below, I list some interesting existential presuppositions at work in Haider's utterances.

First, the utterance presupposes that Muzicant has actually made criminal moves, because he seemingly exploits the interests of Holocaust survivors for himself and his business. Secondly and simultaneously, a chain of anti-Semitic insinuations and associations are triggered by this presupposition: 'Jews are rich, are all businessmen, etc.' At the same time the topic of restitution is, in general terms, rhetorically devalued as a not very important 'problem' (euphemism). This first macro topic is pursued at the beginning of the election campaign, when there is an onslaught on the 'East Coast' (a synecdoche, see below), and the apparent influence of the 'East Coast' (this topos is related to the Mayor of Vienna, Dr. Michael Häupl and to the Social-democratic Party [SPÖ], as well as to the restitution negotiations); such an argumentation is a good example of implicature directly connected with the network of presuppositions. The specific implicature related to these insinuations is, on the one hand, that the Jews are treated better than the Sudeten Germans, and that this, on the other hand, is unfair.

Further, use of the insinuation 'East Coast' goes back at least as far as the 'Waldheim Affair' (1986), when 'the Jewish Lobbies in New York' were alluded to through this synecdoche (Wodak et al., 1990; Wodak, 2004a). The latent meaning implies that the Socialist Party seems to be dependent on these 'powerful Jews', thus the traditional stereotype of the 'world conspiracy' as topos is presupposed. Moreover, in this speech, the extermination of the Jews and the matter of restitution are explicitly set against the Sudeten Germans expelled after 1945 (discursive strategy of equation; topos: 'we are all victims').[16]

The criminalization of Muzicant is then pursued in the form of an allusion and wordplay ('dirty linen') which, however, loses its vagueness and is clarified in the following quotations (see Example 3). The play on Muzicant's name ('Ariel'), which is also the name of a detergent, was laughed at during the speech. The speech was tape-recorded and thus also available for multimodal analysis and analysis of the intonation structure.

The ambiguity here is twofold: on the one hand, the criminality of Muzicant (and the Jews) is represented; on the other hand, the ancient anti-Semitic stereotype of 'dirty Jews' is alluded to. The intentionality of this utterance can be illustrated through the spontaneous reaction of the audience as well as the shared prejudicial frame of the audience. The following utterance by Haider manifests very clearly that he knew precisely what he was doing: he wanted to provoke Muzicant – and he succeeded. Through this abusive wordplay, with the function of an indirect challenge or invitation to a debate (fight), Haider started an interaction with Muzicant who responded the next day and took Haider to court. Historically, such wordplays with Jewish surnames allude to Nazi times when Goebbels used this device while abusing prominent lawyers in Berlin in the 1930s.

Hence, this first argumentative pattern can be adequately analysed with the help of pragmatic concepts, namely through detecting presuppositions, wordplay, implicatures and allusions (many in the form of rhetorical tropes). In this concrete case, the

---

16. The Sudeten Germans were expelled from the then Czechoslovakia because the Beneš government sought revenge for the collaboration of many Sudeten Germans with the Nazis before and during the occupation in the Second World War.

argumentative pattern serves to present Dr. Ariel Muzicant as a criminal, in order to focus sharply on his role in the restitution negotiations. Ultimately, however, what also seems important for Haider is to devalue the restitution claims of Jewish victims of the Holocaust per se and to equate the Holocaust to the expulsion of the Sudeten Germans.

The second discursive macro strategy concerns the sub-division of Austrian citizens, i.e. the discursive construction of social groups through membership categorization devices (MCD) into: those with a 'true Viennese heart' ('us'); those who allow themselves to be influenced by the 'East Coast' (i.e. the apparently powerful Jewish lobbies in New York ('them')).

In an article in *Profil* in 2 April 2001 (in a liberal progressive weekly), Peter Sichrovsky, then general secretary of the FPÖ, during an interview, even offers this interpretation of the allusion used explicitly and thereby contradicts Haider's later justification of 16 March 2001, i.e. that 'East Coast' is a 'purely geographical description', a literal semantic meaning as opposed to the alluded and shared synecdoche.

This categorization concerns, on the one hand, the electoral debate in Vienna; Stanley Greenberg, the adviser to the mayor of Vienna, is presented as, among other things, a Jew who is now working for the Social-democratic Party (SPÖ) as a 'spin-doctor'. The singular characterization of a person in his quality as a 'Jew' serves exclusively to arouse anti-Semitic attitudes, because this attribution was – of course – totally unimportant for Greenberg's work. Jews are thus juxtaposed to and contrasted with 'real' Austrians. The topos of the 'real Austrian' is also not new. This topos had already been used in the 1970s when Bruno Kreisky, later Chancellor of Austria, a social democrat of Jewish origin, campaigned against the People's Party (ÖVP). The use of 'real Austrians' appeared again in the national election campaign in 1999 (during which Haider presented himself as a 'real Austrian') and alluded to the belief that Jews or other Austrians of other ethnic origin are not to be considered as being 'on the same level', even if they have Austrian citizenship. The Austrianness (or citizenship) of Austrian Jews is thereby implicitly denied. There are of course many more examples of pragmatic and grammatical/rhetorical devices in the whole textual chain which have to be left aside here due to space restrictions. (…)

References

Benke, G., and Wodak, R. 2003a. 'The discursive construction of individual memories. How Austrian 'Wehrmacht' soldiers remember WWII'. In *Re/reading the past. Critical and functional perspectives on time and value*, ed. by J. R. Martin, and R. Wodak, 115–138. Amsterdam: Benjamins.

Benke, G., and Wodak, R. 2003b. 'Remembering and forgetting: The discursive construction of generational memories.' In *At War with Words*, ed. by M. N. Dedaic and D. N. Nelson, 215–243. Berlin: Mouton de Gruyter.

Blommaert, J. 2005. *Discourse*. Cambridge: Cambridge University Press.
DOI: 10.1017/CBO9780511610295

Chilton, P. A. 2004. *Analysing Political Discourse*. London: Routledge.

Chilton, P. A. 2005. 'Missing links in mainstream CDA: Modules, blends and the critical instinct'. In *A New Agenda in Critical Discourse Analysis*, eds. by R. Wodak and P. Chilton, 19–52. Amsterdam: Benjamins. DOI: 10.1075/dapsac.13

Dijk, T. A. van. 2001. 'Critical Discourse Analysis'. In *Handbook of Discourse Analysis*, ed. by D. Tannen, D. Schiffrin, and H. Hamilton, 352–371. Oxford: Blackwell.

Dijk, T. A. van. 2003. 'The Discourse-Knowledge Interface'. In *Critical Discourse Analysis. Theory and Interdisciplinarity*, eds. by G. Weiss, and R. Wodak, 85–109. Basingstoke: Palgrave Macmillan.

Fairclough, N. 2003. *Analysing Discourse*. London: Routledge.

Heer, H., Manoschek, W., Pollak, A., and Wodak, R. (eds.). 2003. *'Wie Geschichte gemacht wird'. Erinnerungen an Wehrmacht und Zweiten Weltkrieg*. Vienna: Czernin.

Kienpointner, M. 1992. *Alltagslogik. Struktur und Funktion von Argumentationsmustern*. Stuttgart-Bad-Cannstatt: Frommann-Holzboog.

Laclau, E., and Mouffe, Ch. 1985. *Hegemony and socialist strategy towards a radical democratic politics*. London: Verso.

Martin, J., and Wodak, R. (eds.). 2003. *Re/reading the Past*. Amsterdam: Benjamins.
DOI: 10.1075/dapsac.8

Mitten, R. 1992. *The Politics of Antisemitic Prejudice. The Waldheim Phenomenon in Austria*. Boulder, CO: Westview Press.

Mitten, R. 1997. 'Das antisemitische Vermächtnis: Zur Geschichte antisemitischer Vorurteile in Österreich'. In *Zur 'Judenfrage' im Nachkriegsösterreich. Die Last der Vergangenheit und die Aktualisierung der Erinnerung*, ed by R. Mitten, 77–165. Vienna: Project Report, Ministry of Science and Education.

Mitten, R. 2000. 'Guilt and Responsibility in Germany and Austria'. *Paper presented at the conference 'Dilemmas of East Central Europe: Nationalism, Totalitarianism, and the Search for Identity. A Symposium Honouring István Déak'*. Columbia University, March 24–25.

Möhring, R. (ed.). 2001. *Österreich allein zuhause. Politik, Medien und Justiz nach der politischen Wende*. Frankfurt and Main: IKO-Verlag für interkulturelle Kommunikation.

Musolff, A. 2006. 'Metaphor scenarios in public discourse'. *Metaphor and Symbol*, 21 (1): 28–38.
DOI: 10.1207/s15327868ms2101_2

Reisigl, M. 2004. "Wie man eine Nation herbeiredet'. Eine diskursanalytische Untersuchung zur sprachlichen Konstruktion der österreichischen Nation und Identität in politischen Fest- und Gedenkreden'. Unpublished PhD thesis, University of Vienna.

Reisigl, M., and Wodak, R. 2001. *Discourse and Discrimination*. London: Routledge.

Wodak, R. 2000a. 'La sociolingüística necesita una teoría social? Nuevas perspectivas en el análisis crítico del discurso'. *Discurso y Sociedad*, 2 (3): 123–147.

Wodak, R. 2000b. 'Recontextualization and the transformation of meanings: A critical discourse analysis of decision making in EU-meetings about employment policies'. In *Discourse and Social Life*, eds. S. Sarangi and M. Coulthard, 185–206. Harlow: Pearson Education.

Wodak, R. 2001. 'The discourse-historical approach'. In *Methods of Critical Discourse Analysis*, eds. R. Wodak, and M. Meyer, 63–95. London: Sage. DOI: 10.4135/9780857028020.n4

Wodak, R. 2004a. 'Discourses of Silence: Anti-Semitic Discourse in Postwar Austria'. In *Discourse and Silencing*, ed. by L. Thiesmeyer, 179–209. Amsterdam: Benjamins.

Wodak, R. 2004b. 'Critical discourse analysis.' In *Qualitative Research Practice*, eds. C. Seale, G. Gobo, J. F. Gubrium, and D. Silverman, 197–213. London: Sage.

Wodak, R. 2006. 'Mediation between discourse and society: assessing cognitive approaches in CDA.' *Discourse Studies* 8: 179–190. DOI: 10.1177/1461445606059566

Wodak, R. 2008. 'The Contribution of critical linguistics to the analysis of discriminatory practices and stereotypes in the language of politics.' In *Handbook of Applied Linguistics*, Vol. 4, eds. R. Wodak and V. Koller. Berlin: De Gruyter.

Wodak, R. and Reisigl, M. 2002. "'…wenn einer Ariel heisst…' Ein linguistisches Gutachten zur politischen Funktionalisierung antisemitischer Ressentiments in Österreich.' In *Dreck am Stecken. Politik der Ausgrenzung*, eds. by Pelinka and Wodak, 134–172. Vienna: Czernin.

Wodak, R., Pelikan, J., Nowak, P., Gruber, H., de Cillia, R., and Mitten, R. 1990. '*Wir sind alle unschuldige Täter!' Diskurshistorische Studien zum Nachkriegsantisemitismus*. Frankfurt and Main: Suhrkamp.

Index